GULAG MEMORIES

Gulag Memories

The Rediscovery and Commemoration of Russia's Repressive Past

Zuzanna Bogumił

Translated by Philip Palmer

berghahn
NEW YORK • OXFORD
www.berghahnbooks.com

First published in 2018 by
Berghahn Books
www.berghahnbooks.com

English-language edition
© 2018, 2022 Berghahn Books
First paperback edition published in 2022

Polish-language edition
© 2012 Universitas
Originally published by Universitas as *Pamięć Gulagu* in 2012

All rights reserved. Except for the quotation of short passages
for the purposes of criticism and review, no part of this book
may be reproduced in any form or by any means, electronic or
mechanical, including photocopying, recording, or any information
storage and retrieval system now known or to be invented,
without written permission of the publisher.

The translation of this publication is funded by the Ministry of Science and Higher Education of
the Republic of Poland as part of the National Programme for the Development of Humanities,
in the years 2016–2018. This publication reflects the views only of the author, and the Ministry
cannot be held responsible for any use which may be made of the information contained herein.

NARODOWY PROGRAM
ROZWOJU HUMANISTYKI

Library of Congress Cataloging-in-Publication Data

Names: Bogumił, Zuzanna, author.
Title: Gulag Memories: The Rediscovery and Commemoration of Russia's Repressive Past /
  Zuzanna Bogumił; translated by Philip Palmer.
Other titles: Pamięć Gulagu. English.
Description: English-language edition. | New York: Berghahn Books, 2018. | "Polish-
  language edition, © 2012 Universitas." | Includes bibliographical references and index.
Identifiers: LCCN 2018023353 (print) | LCCN 2018025354 (ebook) |
  ISBN 9781785339288 (Ebook) | ISBN 9781785339271 (hardback: alk. paper)
Subjects: LCSH: Concentration camps—Soviet Union. | Political prisoners—Soviet Union. |
  Memorialization—Russia (Federation)
Classification: LCC HV8964.S65 (ebook) | LCC HV8964.S65 B6413 2018 (print) |
  DDC 365/.4509470904—dc23
LC record available at https://lccn.loc.gov/2018023353

British Library Cataloguing in Publication Data

A catalogue record for this book is available from the British Library

ISBN 978-1-78533-927-1 hardback
ISBN 978-1-80073-437-1 paperback
ISBN 978-1-78533-928-8 ebook

Contents

List of Illustrations	vi
Acknowledgements	vii
Introduction	1
Methodology	15
Chapter 1. The Solovetsky Islands	23
Chapter 2. The Komi Republic	95
Chapter 3. Perm Krai	141
Chapter 4. Kolyma	165
Conclusion	187
Bibliography	205
Index	230

Illustrations

Map 0.1. Map depicting the sites where I completed field research between 2006 and 2008 — 16

Figure 1.1. The Solovetsky Prisoners Memorial — 27

Figure 1.2. The exhibition titled *The Solovetsky Special Purpose Camp 1923–1939* — 37

Figure 1.3. The Solovetsky stone on St Petersburg's Troitskaya Square — 49

Figure 1.4. Sandarmokh Cemetery — 57

Figure 1.5. Icon of the New Martyrs and Confessors of Russia — 71

Figure 1.6. The Solovetsky cross at Butovo, near Moscow — 79

Figure 2.1. History exhibition at the Vorkuta Interregional Local History Museum — 109

Figure 2.2. The Pioneers of the North Memorial — 113

Figure 2.3. The Victims of Political Repressions Memorial erected in 1988 — 117

Figure 2.4. The Victims of Political Repressions Chapel — 121

Figure 2.5. The Yur-Shor Cemetery, Vorkuta — 131

Figure 2.6. The Memorial Cemetery, Abez — 133

Figure 2.7. The Makarikha Cemetery, Kotlas — 135

Figure 3.1. The Victims of Political Repressions Memorial — 145

Figure 3.2. The Perm-36 Museum, Kuchino village, Chusovskoy region — 149

Figure 3.3. The *Gulag, History, Work, Life* exhibition — 151

Figure 3.4. The screening room known as the Soviet Club — 152

Figure 4.1. The Mask of Sorrow Memorial Complex — 171

Figure 4.2. Sergey Golunov's memorial to the victims of political repressions — 178

Figure 4.3. The *Kolyma. Sevvostlag. Years and Fates. 1932–1956* exhibition — 184

Acknowledgements

This book is a supplemented and updated English version of *Pamięć Gulagu,* a book originally published in Polish in 2012 by the academic publishing house Universitas. The Polish edition was based on my research conducted in Russia between 2006 and 2008 and sponsored by the Polish Ministry of Science and Higher Education. I would like to express my particular gratitude to the people who helped me organize and conduct that research. Without their support and assistance, I would not have been able to collect the material upon which this publication is based.

Particularly deserving of my gratitude are the members of the St Petersburg chapter of Memorial, especially Irina Flige, Tatyana Kosinova and Tatyana Morgacheva. Without their willingness to assist me with the design of the programme I used for my field research and pass on useful contact details and practical tips about travelling around the Russian Federation, I would not have been able to complete this field research. I would also like to express my special gratitude to the former Consul General of the Republic of Poland in St Petersburg, Jarosław Drozd, for providing me with assistance and support. Also deserving of my heartfelt gratitude are all the people who helped me organize my stay in various places, provided valuable information and helped me find materials and organize meetings with the people I had conversations with. I have reserved my special gratitude for Olga Bochkareva from the Solovetsky Islands, Tatyana Afanasyeva from Pechora, Evgeniya Zelenskaya from Ukhta, Nikolay Baranov and Evgeniya Kulygina from Inta, Viktor Troshin from Vorkuta, Viktor Lozhkin from Abez, Mikhail Rogachev and Nadezhda Bushmanova from Syktyvkar, Anatoly Smilingis from Kortkeros, Irina Dubrovina from Kotlas, Ivan Panikarov from Yagodnoye, Anna Plashevich and Sergey Yefimov of Magadan, Anna Pastukhova of Yekaterinburg and Aleksandr Kalikh, Viktor Shmyrov and Robert Latypov from Perm.

I would also like to express my gratitude to the incumbent directors of the museums at which I collected materials for their consent and assistance: Mikhail Lopatkin, Director of the Solovetsky Museum-Reserve, Tatyana Afanasyeva, Head of the Pokayanie Kedrovy Shor Museum, Evgeniya Kulygina, Director of the Inta Local History Museum, Galina Trukhina, Director of the Vorkuta Interregional Local History Museum, Valentina Strekalova, Director of the Syktyvkar National Museum of the Komi Republic, Sergey Bekarevich, Director of the Magadan Regional Local History Museum, Ivan Panikarov, Director of the Victims of Political Repressions Museum in Yagodnoye and Viktor Shmyrov from the Perm-36 Museum. I would also like to express my gratitude to all the people I conversed with as well as the people whose names I have not mentioned despite the help they provided during my research.

In 2016, I received a grant from the Ministry of Science and Higher Education (No. 0164A/NPRH4/H3a/83/2016) to update and translate a book into English. At this point, I began working with Philip Palmer, who completed the translation of this book. Without his invaluable comments and hard work on the translation, this book would never have been published. I would also like to offer my heartfelt gratitude to Liliya Khudzik, who translated and checked the Russian transliterations. While working on the book, I received substantial support from the Maria Grzegorzewska University, in particular the University's Chancellor, Prof. Stefan Kwiatkowski, the Deputy Vice-Chancellor, Prof. Jarosław Rola, the Dean of the Department of Applied Social Sciences, Prof. Irena Jelonkiewicz-Sterianos, the Director of the Institute of Philosophy and Sociology, at which I work, Danuta Duch-Krzystoszek, and my immediate superior, Prof. Anna Firkowska-Mankiewicz. I am also especially grateful to Krzysztof Kozina from the research department, who assisted me by administering the grant.

The Gulag memory situation is continuously changing in the regions I have analysed in this book, so I needed to undertake additional research and introduce changes into the text to ensure that its content was up to date. In July 2017, I co-organized The Archipelago of Shared Memory in the Solovetsky Islands, a summer school for young people from Poland and Russia financed by the Centre for Polish-Russian Dialogue and Understanding. Ten years previously, I had viewed the design for a new exhibition on the history of the Solovetsky camp. While organizing the summer school, I had an opportunity to view the actual exhibition. I also participated in an excursion to Sekirnaya Hill and talked about the museum's development and the changing situation on the Islands with Oleg Volkov, deputy to the Solovetsky Museum's incumbent director and Anna Yakovleva, Head of the Department of History. While updating the chapter on the Solovetsky Islands, I also analysed issues of *Solovetski Vestnik,* a newspaper published by the museum.

At the summer school, I met Darya Khlevnyuk, a young researcher, who had just returned from an international summer school for young history scholars organized within the framework of the annual Petersburg Dialogue forum. She told me about how the memory situation was changing in Magadan. I am immensely grateful to her for our discussions on Gulag museums. However, the majority of the information I acquired about the current situation in the regions that I am analysing in this book was gained from analysing articles in newspapers and materials available online.

Finally, I would like to offer my heartfelt gratitude to family members and friends who supported me while I wrote this book. In particular, I would like to thank Tatyana Voronina and Małgorzata Głowacka-Grajper, memory researchers who have also become my friends, for the many hours we spent talking together about memory and Russia, their valuable comments and their observations and support. First and foremost, however, I would like to express my gratitude to my husband, Dariusz

Bogumił. For years, he has supported my research, frequently assisting with its organization and sometimes accompanying me in the field and documenting my work photographically. At such times, we discuss what we have seen in depth. When I was preparing the Polish, and then the English, version of the manuscript, he read my drafts, offering valuable critical comments as the work progressed. These conversations we shared, which sometimes turned into friendly disputes, were of invaluable assistance when the time came to determine the shape the book was finally to take.

Some passages from the book have been published in different versions as part of academic articles. Some passages from the chapter on the Solovetsky Islands appeared in the following articles: 'Kresty i kamni: Solovetskiye simvoly v konstruirovanii pamyati o Gulage', *Neprikosnovenny Zapas* 3(71) 2010: 1–19; 'Wyspy Sołowieckie jako "rosyjska Golgota" — o prawosławnym języku mówienia o represjach sowieckich', in A. Zielińska (ed.), *Konstrukcje i dekonstrukcje tożsamości* Vol. 1/ *Wokół religii i jej języka.* (Warsaw 2011): pp. 307–18; 'The Solovetski Islands and Butovo as Two "Russian Golgothas": New Martyrdom as a Means to Understand Russian Repression', in F. Fischer von Weikersthal and K. Thaidigsmann (eds), *(Hi-)Stories of the Gulag: Fiction and Reality.* (Heidelberg 2016): pp. 133–54. Passages from the book also appeared in the following articles: 'Konflikty pamięci? — o interpretacjach historii GUŁagu', *Kultura i Społeczeństwo* (4) 2010: 23–40; 'Cmentarze GUŁagu — teksty zapomnianej kultury w tłumaczeniu współczesnym', in A.S. Czyż and B. Gotowski (eds), *Sztuka cmentarzy w XIX i XX wieku.* (Warsaw 2010); 'Pamięć drugiej wojny światowej w rosyjskich regionach: na przykładzie na przykładzie muzeów regionalnych Republiki Komi', Kultura i Społeczeństwo (3) 2014: 47–65; 'Stone, Cross and Mask: Searching for Language of Commemoration of the Gulag in the Russian Federation', *Polish Sociological Review* 177(1) 2012: 71–90; articles co-written with Dominique Moran and Elly Harrowell. 2015. "Sacred or Secular? 'Memorial', the Russian Orthodox Church, and the Contested Commemoration of Soviet Repressions", *Europe-Asia Studies* 67(9) 2015: 1416–44.

Introduction

In April 2007, during the 'Sites of Memory' seminar organized by the Krzyżowa Foundation,[1] I had an opportunity to view a documentary created by Georg Restle and Andreas Maus titled *Volunteers in Stalin's Gulag: Young Germans Restore a Russian Corrective Labour Camp.*[2] The film relates the story of a group of young German people who spend the summer working on the reconstruction of the wooden fencing surrounding the Perm-36 camp, the only open-air museum in the Russian Federation composed of Gulag buildings. The documentary shows how arduous the work is, yet the motivation to complete it remains strong. The young Germans are aware of the crimes the Third Reich committed during the Second World War, yet believe, at the same time, that the manner in which modern Germans have taken responsibility for the sins of their forebears by creating sites memorializing their forebears' victims is the correct method for working through the past. They realize that this process has only just begun in Russia, so they treat this kind of physical labour as a kind of mission – a way of demonstrating that such actions are important and necessary.

At one point, the young people discover that a former Perm-36 camp guard called Ivan Kukushkin is working at the museum. This discovery provokes general consternation. The young Germans refuse to work beside the ex-guard, who appears in their eyes to be a Russian SS functionary. The following day, Sergey Kovalev, a former dissident and Perm-36 prisoner commanding respect and authority, comes to meet the young people. The young people confide to him how outraged they feel at the existing situation. But instead of agreeing with them, Kovalev flies into a rage, making it very clear that Ivan Kukushkin is a decent person, and the Germans have no right to judge him. The young people were certainly not expecting such a reaction. The conversation breaks off and everyone silently retires without reaching any common consensus. The following day, the young people bid a tepid farewell to Kovalev, who returns to Moscow. They continue working on the fence's reconstruction, even though they no longer see any sense in what they are doing.

I decided to begin my reflections on Gulag memory by evoking the contents of this documentary to underline that this book deals with issues that may seem at first sight to be obvious but are in fact anything but that. I attempt in this book to establish why actors involved in Gulag memory have constructed their own memory in one way rather than another. My goal was to understand the 'assumptions made by people when they organise their worlds in the ways that they do' (Macdonald 2013: 2). I tried to establish why images over the past have assumed one particular form to the exclusion of others. I also examine what this form expresses and consider – inspired by Barbara Szacka, a pioneer of memory research in Poland – what social function it performs (Szacka 2003). Consequently, I am interested in the process whereby memory of the Gulag is formed, and, in particular, how it was formed during one specific period, the end of the eighties, when it assumed a particularly intensive form operating on many levels.

In this book, I therefore refrain from reflecting on the extent to which what has been remembered accords with what actually happened. In any case, this would be an extremely challenging task for a number of reasons.

Firstly, historians have failed to reach any consensus over the years as to the scale of the repressions, their social meaning and the manner in which they should be investigated. A prime example of this is the lively debate that flared up at the end of the nineties between Robert Conquest, John Keep and Stephen Wheatcroft in the journal *Europe-Asia Studies* (Conquest 1997, 1999; Keep 1999; Wheatcroft 1999, 2000; cf. Ellman 2002). The first history publications to comprehensively describe the functioning of the Gulag system on the basis of archival documents did not appear until the beginning of the twenty-first century (Ivanova 2000; Ivanova 2006; Khlevnyuk 2004). It was also the time of publication of the first collections of archival documents (Artizov, Kosakovsky and Naumov 2004; Artizov, Sigachev, Khlopov 2002; Artizov, Sigachev, Shevchuk 2003; Edelman, Zavadskaya, Lavinskaya 1999; Shostakovsky 2001). Even today, scholars are yet to reach a consensus on whether the Gulag was performing a genocidal role (Naimark 2010; Supady 2001) or whether it was merely a poorly functioning penal system whose primary aim was the re-education of society (Barnes 2011).

Secondly, the particularity of Gulag memory primarily resides in the fact that it is shaped by the literature and memoirs of witnesses (Etkind 2013; Sherbakova 2015). The work that played the largest role in this process is Aleksandr Solzhenitsyn's *The Gulag Archipelago* (see Brunet 1981: 216; Reeves 2015: 184). From the moment of its publication, this book became the source that was primarily responsible for shaping comprehension of the Gulag, even though the author himself wrote that it was not a work of history, but rather an attempt at 'literary enquiry' based on witnesses' memoirs that had reached him second or third hand. A very good example of *The Gulag Archipelago* (1974) being used to describe history is Anne Applebaum's book *Gulag: A History* (2003), in which the author treats archival documents and passages from Solzhenitsyn's work or Varlam Shalamov's short stories (1994) and Eugenia Ginzburg's *Into the Whirlwind* (2002 [1967]) as equally valid historical sources.

In publications relating to the repressions and Gulag memory, there is clearly a preponderance of works based on ex-prisoners' testimonies that describe how the system of repression functioned by showing the traumatic experiences of the people who passed through it. Although these are primarily based on memoirs (Figes 2007; Hellbeck 2006; Jones 2008; Owsiany 2000; Toker 2000), some make use of oral histories (Gheith and Jolluck 2011; Skultans 1998). Another group of publications is composed of detailed case studies demonstrating the social consequences of the repressions and their influence on the lives and deaths of selected social groups (Adler 2002; Kuntsman 2009; Viola 2007; Werth 2007). There are some works presenting the origins of the Gulag (Jakobson 1993) or describing the specific nature of inmates' lives at a particular camp (Gullotta 2018), but there is an increasing prevalence of works devoted to transformations in social perception of the Soviet past (Fitzpatrick 2005; Koposov 2011; Malinova 2015; Paperno 2009; Yurchak 2006), including transformations in the meanings of selected elements of the system of repression (Fedor 2011). Other works demonstrate the social consequences of the mass experiencing of terror (Etkind 2013; Figes 2014; Gessat-Anstett 2007; Merridale 2000; Ulturgasheva 2015), analyse what was left after the Gulag (Anstett and Jurgenson 2009; Chuykina 2015; Ulturgasheva 2012; Von Weikersthal and Thaidigsmann 2016) and explain what it entailed (Anstett 2011; Barnes 2011).

This book contributes to the area of study dedicated to transformations in perception of the Gulag in post-Soviet society and the traces it has left in the cultural landscape. Like many researchers, I believe that certain meaningful statements did in fact appear as early as Khrushchev's Thaw, when the prisoner rehabilitation process began (Adler 1993, 2012: 327–38; Cohen 2011; Dobson 2006, 2009; Elie 2010; Etkind 2013; Sherbakova 1998: 235–45; Smith 1996). However, it is not until the end of the eighties that we can meaningfully speak of the creation of a new discursive situation, and, above all, about attempts being undertaken to create what Young (1993) would term the 'texture of Gulag memory'. Consequently, it is the late eighties period that I have chosen to investigate in this book, a time when the first monuments, museums, exhibitions, commemorative events and memory rituals that are the primary focus of my analysis first appeared. I am interested in how these first memory projects came into being, why the actors engaged in this process favoured some forms of commemoration over others and what meanings they were ascribing to them.

As I was conducting research at sites that had physically contained Soviet labour camps, or *lagers*, during various historical periods, Maurice Halbwachs's work *Legendary Topography of the Gospel in the Holy Land* (1941; published in English in 1992) proved to be of assistance when it came to establishing the process whereby Gulag memory is formed. The conclusions drawn by Halbwachs's work seem to be particularly important for this book, so I would like to briefly outline them here. Halbwachs's critical analysis of various kinds of written sources such as pilgrimage and travel memoirs, but also academic works devoted to the Holy Land, leads him to argue that Jerusalem's space began to be transformed by Christians in accordance with their religious perceptions long after the occurrence of events of crucial importance for Christianity. Consequently, sacred places do not so much commemorate facts supported by historical testimonies as the beliefs that formed around them, most of which relate to the supernatural deeds of Christ around which Christian dogmas were created. Halbwachs demonstrates that the meanings conferred on Christianity's holy sites are derived from the past, especially from Jewish memories that continue to be associated with these sites, even though any material repositories of these memories have long since been removed (Halbwachs 1941: 184; cf. Bulle 2006; Sakaranaho 2011; Truc 2012). In other words, the current appearance of these sites has arisen from the adaption of this past heritage, while current beliefs are a material trace of ancient ones. What is more, the manner in which these sites are perceived is powerfully influenced by the actions of the groups of believers who become involved in the commemoration process (Halbwachs 1941: 205). Halbwachs's work offers important insights into the process whereby Gulag memory formed on the grounds of former camps, because it not only shows that commemorative processes often start to take shape many years after the historical events they commemorate actually took place, but also that there is no historical evidence that these sites are chosen because they are authentic. In the case of the Holy Land, sites of memory were simply places that were important for Jews, and in the case of Gulag memory, as will later become clear from such examples as the memorials to the first pioneers in Komi Republic, sites of memory were often associated with the Soviet heritage. Moreover, Halbwachs's conclusion that when the memory of some event is starting to be constructed, it is in fact memory actors and the commemorative actions they undertake that exert a crucial influence on the shape this memory eventually assumes, explains why I have concentrated so much in this book on memory actors and their projects.

Halbwachs makes it extremely clear that memory not only operates within a socially created framework but is also determined culturally and spatially: 'It would be very difficult to describe the event if one did not imagine the place' (quotation after Truc 2012: 148). However, as Jan Assmann – the German scholar of memory – points out, Halbwachs does not explain the workings of the process whereby communicative memory is transformed into cultural memory (Assmann 1995: 128), and hence how memory orally transmitted between members of a community is transformed into memory that is both constitutive of this community's identity and defines its attitude towards the past (Assmann 2008). This German Egyptologist has therefore chosen to focus his research on connective structure – that is, structures that bind society in the here and now and over time. They unite people, creating a symbolic world of meanings that enable the manner in which society constructs self-representations to be understood (Assmann 2008; J. Assmann 2011). Jan Assmann's concept of cultural memory explains the process whereby meanings are transmitted and national identities created. As Assmann points out, the connectivity principle repeatedly causes actions to assume the form of certain patterns that are common components of a given culture (Assmann 2008). However, this scholar does not explain how the formation of meanings (or the conferral of a specific meaning) occurs or what place (if any) is occupied in cultural memory by the memory of marginalized groups and memory forcibly supplanted into oblivion, which can even threaten a given group's identity. Another German researcher, Aleida Assmann, partially addresses these issues. She is not interested in the memory of marginalized groups, but by analysing transformations in German social memory, she shows how memory of self-committed crimes against

Others can become a component of a group's memory (Assmann 2011a). However, the Gulag memory formation process cannot be understood without examining the actions of marginalized groups attempting to divorce themselves from the prevailing official narrative and recast their experience of the past as a new national narrative.

Foucault's conception of how discourses are shaped helped me to comprehend why some actions, rather than others, were undertaken by memory actors during the carnival of memory and thus to explain why Gulag memory began to be inscribed in the cultural landscape in one way rather than another. This conception shows how human communities are imbedded within semantic networks that possess their own internal structure (Geertz 1973).

Another useful Foucauldian concept is that of counter-history, which can be understood as a history of those who 'came out of the shadows' (Foucault 2003a: 70) – that is, those whose memory is not preserved in institutional information repositories. This is undoubtedly the kind of situation we are dealing with in the case of Gulag memory. Foucault writes that counter-history is a history of the Others, by which he means those thrust to the margins, the defeated – represented by women and sexual minorities, but also prisoners of the Gulag. This is not a history of continuity, possessing its own genealogy, but rather a history of intersection points, of rupture. Rather than extolling the irreproachable glory of the overlord, it focuses on the misfortunes of his ancestors – their disappointed aspirations, exile and slavery. As the history of the oppressed is not recorded in chronicles from the moment it starts to take shape, it draws from eschatological or mythical motifs that help to shape a discourse for it. This explains why Foucault also refers to counter-history as 'a biblical-style historical discourse' (Foucault 1972: 73). It is worth noting that Chakrabarty, when investigating 'histories from below', reflects on how the history of repressed groups can be described and how stories can be created about groups or classes that have left no sources behind. This scholar notes that quite often researchers, while attempting to respond to these questions, acknowledge the influence of supernatural forces on historical events (Chakrabarty 2000: 97–113).

The counter-history concept would appear to be useful for explaining how Gulag memory is comprehended, because it shows that the Soviet 'sovereign power' discourse is a manifestation of the: 'revolutionary discourse of social struggles – the very discourse that derived so many of its elements from the old discourse of the race struggle – and articulating it with the management and the policing that ensure the hygiene of an orderly society' (Foucault 1972: 83). Foucault explained as follows:

> It is undoubtedly true that the Soviets, while having modified the regime of ownership and the state's role in the control of production, for the rest have simply transferred the techniques of administration and power implemented in Capitalist Europe of the 19th century. The types of morality, forms of aesthetics, disciplinary methods, everything that was effectively working in bourgeois society already around 1850 has moved en bloc into

the Soviet regime ... Just as the Soviets have used Taylorism and other methods of management experimented in the West, they have adopted our disciplinary techniques, adding to our arsenal another arm – party discipline. (after Plamper 2002: 262)

In other words, the French philosopher was arguing that Soviet discourse, rather than being – as the Soviet authorities asserted – a history of repressed marginalized groups emerging from the shadows, was merely a mutation of the old discourse of power. Clearly, the most pressing task for the new counter-histories finding their voice in the late eighties was to demonstrate that the Soviet discourse was only a falsehood, an illusion. Only then would their alternative interpretations of the past have any chance of forcing their way through to public consciousness.

Another of Foucault's theoretical insights that could aid comprehension of how Gulag memory functions is his assertion that no freshly appearing statement is completely new. It will also draw on a reservoir of previous statements that are already circulating in a specific culture, mutating and transforming themselves. Foucault refers to this place as the Archive (Foucault 1972; cf. Kharkhordin 1999). He does not investigate which rules govern a given statement, preferring instead to ask 'how is that one particular statement appeared rather than another?' (Foucault 1972: 27). He also emphasizes that seeking the origins of any discourse would be a fruitless task, as this would force scholars to continuously withdraw into the past to create the appearance in the discourse of constancy and continuity. As Foucault writes: 'Discourse must not be referred to the distant presence of the origin, but treated as and when it occurs' (Foucault 1972: 25). He recommends that an arbitrary moment should be regarded as the beginning of any scholarly analysis and the first task for any scholar should be to investigate various discursive formations. This is exactly what Foucault did in *The Birth of the Clinic*. At the same time, he stressed that the period from the late eighteenth and early nineteenth century was exceptionally fertile for the appearance of new statements in various spheres of social life and these began to comprise a new medical discourse (2003b [1973]). There was such a period for Gulag memory too, in the late eighties, a time when many new discursive statements relating to the Gulag came into existence.

This was undoubtedly an important time of transformation for conceptions of the past (Davies 1997; Smith 2002). The political and social political changes that took place during this period were so sudden and unpredictable (Kotkin 2001) that they bore the hallmarks of cultural rupture and intersection. This begs the question of whether this was, to cite Lotman, a period of cultural 'explosion' involving the complete and unconditional destruction of the old and the apocalyptic birth of a new order (Lotman 2009: 172–74). It appears that this was not in fact the case. I have decided to utilize the term 'carnival of memory', first used by Mikhail Bakhtin in *Rabelais and His World* (1984), to explain what occurred during this period. I selected this term to emphasize that the attitude towards Gulag memory suddenly reversed during this period. Previously, the history of the Gulag had been a taboo topic. Suddenly, this wall of silence was breached. Before this point, witnesses had kept silent, so it would have been difficult to find information on the Gulag, but now this suddenly began to appear in newspapers and on television, and witnesses began to speak. Some scholars perceive this period as a time of rediscovered memory. It could also be perceived as a distinctive kind of living memory (Traba 2003: 181). However, the term 'carnival' appears to be more apt to me.

A carnival is a time when a previously existing world is 'stood on its head', transforming into a world with reversed values (Bakhtin 1984). As the Russian scholar writes, the carnival was an officially approved time for 'catching one's breath' from the restrictions imposed on society, a moment of liberation from the prevailing system of governance, a period when norms and prohibitions were suspended. It is bound by laws of its own that are inflected by a carnivalesque sense of liberation, reversing the norms prevailing during official time. It is precisely here that I see a resemblance to the Gulag carnival of memory that proceeded in opposition to the existing order.

It is worth stressing that the reality that set in during the last phase of the USSR's existence was being perceived similarly throughout Central and Eastern Europe. As Padraic Kenney writes:

> A carnival . . . breaks down borders of all kinds. It forces a suspension of the usual rules in society, issuing a challenge to the existing order and reversing social and political hierarchies. And indeed, social movements in Central Europe in the second half of the 1980s appeared to disregard the fear that held so many others back, and to act almost with impunity. It didn't matter to them if the police detained participants in a demonstration, because that was part of the game, too . . . These new movements, instead, paid a great deal of attention to one another . . . This interaction is a central feature of the carnival story . . . These social movements also broke the rules of politics . . . Discarding the old politics, they broke free of the usual opposition sites: shop floor, church hall, national monument, underground text. In this revolution, opposition could take place anywhere, on almost any grounds. (Kenney 2003: 5)

The fundamental difference between the Gulag carnival and that of the Middle Ages is that it did not become a cyclical phenomenon. The period of social awakening that began to transform the system of governance was followed by the political, economic and ideological crisis of the nineties (Magun 2008: 62–88). Many people would subsequently compare this time to the Russian Revolution, treating it as a genuine social tragedy (Service 2003; Shtuden 1999: 197). It could be said that this was another era of 'cultural trauma', a concept Sztompka (2004) uses to describe periods in which traumatic changes on a macro level are translated into the world experienced by individuals on a day-to-day basis (Sztompka 2004).

This renewed need to focus on day-to-day life brought the carnival of Gulag memory to an end. Nevertheless, this period left a lasting impression on the manner in which Gulag memory subsequently functioned. This influence had two dimensions.

First, the reconstruction of the past that was completed at the time shaped that memory. As Halbwachs emphasizes, memory is shaped by language: 'We express our memories in words before we evoke them, so speech and the whole system of social conventions that are bound up with it enable us to recreate our past on every occasion [we so wish]' (Halbwachs 1969: 407). For Gulag memory, which long existed beyond the realms of social discourse, the carnival of memory created the space for shaping conventions that were to facilitate the comprehension of spoken memories and written memoirs. The Gulag memory frameworks shaped during this period continue to influence the manner in which this event is perceived today.

Secondly, the facts, sites and public figures that were the focus of discussions and press articles co-created what is currently understood as Gulag memory. In other words, they have assumed the status of symbolic markers. Memory often accumulates around objects and sites (Assmann 2011b; Doss 2008; Grider 2005; Truc 2012; Yates 1966; Young 1993) that are permeated by symbolic associations with past events, enabling collective memory to be preserved (Assmann 2011b; Grider 2005; Kapralski 2010; Misztal 2007: 385; Saryusz-Wolska 2011). During this period, statements became a social phenomenon, objects became historical proof, and rediscovered cemeteries became cultural heritage, so the need arose to situate all of these within the cultural landscape and protect them. It was felt that there was a particularly urgent need to create sites of memory that would protect Gulag memory and memory markers that would express it.

I allude in my work to the meaning of 'site of memory' proposed by Pierre Nora (1984–92, 1989; cf. Ricoeur 2004), even though my understanding of sites of memory and memory markers more closely resembles the definitions proposed by Robin Wagner-Pacifici or Jeffrey Olick. Unlike Pierre Nora, who perceives sites of memory as static space where the past flickers and endures (1989), these two authors perceive memory and sites of memory as a process undergoing dynamic change. Wagner-Pacifici writes:

> the memorial, the speech, and the museum are only provisionally congealed moments of the events themselves. While events do have both inchoative and terminative aspects, I would argue that they can never be determined to have ended once and for all. So, for example, I would argue that the 9/11 Memorial and Museum are part of the event of 9/11, one of its myriad shapes or forms. (Wagner-Pacifici 2016: 23)

Olick also views memory as a dynamic process, adding that it is a moment or act of remembering, a 'medium of our existence in time', which should be evaluated in terms of its authenticity rather than its accuracy (Olick 2014: 28).

Without a doubt, during the carnival of memory, Gulag memory became, for most memory actors, a medium of their existence in time. As they understood the meaning of this past differently from each other, they began shaping it in different ways and sought different forms to commemorate it. Their objective was not, however, to perform acts of commemoration for their own sake. They sought, instead, to create stable sites that would become permanent repositories of the past – sites where the communities of which they were members would store their 'souvenirs' and regard them as an inalienable part of their personalities (Nora 1989; cf. Szpociński 2003: 21, 2008). The distinguishing feature of these sites was not so much that memory of the repressions endured in them after their original *milieux de mémoire* (Nora's realms of memory) had been lost, but rather that these sites had to be (re)discovered, (re)created and revived, because there was no such memory left in them. There was a need to shape this memory and inscribe it into authentic historical sites – like the grounds of former camps and cemeteries – and other sites of memory such as museums, monuments, archives, Days of Remembrance and the Memorial Society, which was founded at this time to both protect and form memory of the repressions (Adler 1993; White 1995). My research mainly focused on sites of memory that had been created on the grounds of former Soviet lagers or other areas strongly linked semantically with this history. My main areas of interest were therefore memory markers, monuments, cemeteries and museums that were meant to convey the history of the Gulag. Below I briefly explain the manner of understanding these sites of memory that I have adopted in this book.

Memory markers (e.g. crosses, commemorative plaques) and *monuments* are physical structures that are created to commemorate a particular event or person(s) (Etkind 2004a, 2004b; Williams 2007: 8; Young 1993: 4). By virtue of their form, they both express and co-shape collective memory (Koselleck 1997; Winter 2005). Monuments are *signa temporis* that reflect the social, political, state, national or universal values of the era in which they were erected (Grzesiuk-Olszewska 1995: 11–12; Doss 2008; Margry and Sánchez-Carretero 2011; Winter 2005). They form a kind of narrative matrix, termed the 'texture of memory' by Young (1993: 1–15), which expresses the physical and metaphysical value of given texts, and their temporal and real dimension (Young 1993: XII). As Young stresses, the investigation of monuments involves the discovery of the meanings concealed within them and the interrogation of the processes that influence how they are understood. It is also important to establish their local context, because it is this that determines how a given work is defined (Young 1993: VIII).

In my view, *museums* are sites of memory that tend to construct history rather than commemorate it (Macdonald 1996, 1998; Williams 2007). Inspired by Macdonald's research (1996: 1–18), I have adopted her assumption that museums actively participate in the construction of a vision of the modern world. On the one hand, they are symbols by means of which society expresses itself and on the other they offer society an interpretation of reality – by proposing diverse classifications that prescribe a particular order of things. It is therefore fair to claim that they are not only an inherent part of a given time and space, but also help to express a specific temporal and spatial order. Rather than simply existing within a given cultural context, they also help to form it (Bogumił, Moran and Harrowell 2015; Dias 1998; Kreamer 1992). When analysing history exhibitions, I aimed to determine which discourses influenced the shape of the narratives these exhibitions were presenting (Bogumił, Moran and Harrowell 2015; Hooper-Greenhill 1992). I also reflected on how individual exhibitions incorporated signs and symbols, either rooted in Russian culture or comparatively new, into their narratives. While doing this, I examined to what extent these exhibitions were making use of the meanings of these signs and symbols and to what extent they were transforming them by granting them new meanings. I regarded these transformations as being of prime importance, because as Lotman emphasizes, symbols are some of the most stable elements of cultural continuity. They fulfil an important role in the functioning of cultural memory, as they are capable of transmitting texts, narrative structures and other semiotic formations from one level of culture to another, in effect protecting culture from disintegration. They may also undergo transformation themselves, but this process is very slow, and in the case of primary symbols almost impossible (Lotman 1990: 103). Given the fact that the USSR produced many new symbols, many of which formed the nucleus of Soviet culture, I was intrigued by how new history exhibitions dealt with old symbols and told the story of the Gulag.

By contrast, I treat *former camp cemeteries* as closed texts of culture, because they no longer fulfil their original function (Kolbuszewski 1981: 29–36; 1995: 17–37). As Jacek Kolbuszewski writes, a cemetery's spatial layout, monuments and epitaphs express, in their role as markers, the consciousness of a specific community, its culture and system of values (Kolbuszewski 1985: 53). According to this viewpoint, camp cemeteries and the graves and memory markers they contain should be perceived as space organized according to the principles of the camp system's method of burying the dead. As Gulag history and culture were taboo topics for a long time, searching for prisoner burial sites became a priority and comprehending their space became a task of fundamental importance (Merridale 2003; Paperno 2001). This explains why memory actors undertook various kinds of commemorative tasks that would confer new meanings on the cemeteries by translating the Gulag 'transcript' into a language of symbols and meanings understandable to those alive today. My main aim was to establish the cultural meanings of these translations as well as the role performed by the symbols being used today and the memory markers erected in these cemeteries' grounds.

Memory markers, monuments, cemeteries and museums also interest me because all of them represent what may be termed unconventional histories (Domańska 2006) – that is, interpretations of history that allude to languages of description that are non-verbal. In fact, memory markers and monuments employ the language of art and search for an image equipped to present the inexpressible nature of the

Gulag reality and what it was like to experience this (Jedlińska 2001). Furthermore, cemeteries are a space for establishing meanings, a forum of negotiation between the past and present. Their contemporary space expresses what given local communities have understood from the history concealed within the cemetery and what they wish to preserve. By contrast, museums would appear to be texts operating on many levels that employ both verbal and non-verbal methods to construct a coherent historical narrative. I was therefore interested in how camp history is materialized in the ruins and relics that have out-survived it (Kranz 2002: 40) and what meanings and functions are being conferred on these sites today by virtue of the commemorative activities that are being undertaken there.

The notion of sites of memory is so broad in scope that it can even incorporate Days of Remembrance – that is, the ceremonies marking the history of the repressions that are organized every year on a particular date (30 October across the Russian Federation or 5 August in Sandarmokh). However, I have chosen in this book to refer to these holidays as *memory rituals* rather than sites of memory, because I wish to emphasize their performative aspect. When conceived as sites of memory, Days of Remembrance mainly comprise a date containing information about a historical event that took place on a given day. However, the symbolism of these dates is not my main area of interest. Inspired by Handelman (1990), who wrote that the essence of a ritual is expressed in the manner of its organization, I primarily focus on how Gulag memory is expressed through the choice of site and the commemorative actions that are undertaken there. Handelman also emphasizes that the manner in which a ritual is performed determines the meaning it, and the event to which it is dedicated, will gain within a given community. The term 'memory ritual' therefore more fully captures the meaning of the Days of Remembrance as well as more accurately explaining the set of specific symbolic activities performed to achieve their organizers' desired goal.

I refer to the people, institutions or organizations involved in the memorialization process as *memory actors*. I use the term *memory projects,* after Irwin-Zarecka, to refer to the aims and functions memory actors ascribe to the images of the past they create. In practice, these are planned and thought-through actions whose aim, often hidden, is to preserve certain elements of history for the future (Irwin-Zarecka 1994: 8, 133). I therefore understand the notion of memory project to first and foremost incorporate the set of ideas (or assumptions) ascribed by their authors to the commemorative actions they undertake. I employ this term as a synonym of memory marker, monument or museum when I wish to emphasize the objectives memory actors have attributed to a project they are implementing.

Memory projects often operate on many levels, so I use the term *memory infrastructure* to collectively refer to monuments, memory markers or museums that are the outcome of activities undertaken for specific projects and share a common aim. This term has not been reserved to exclusively describe the outcomes of actions undertaken by a single memory actor, although I do often use it in this way. As Irwin-

Zarecka points out, memory infrastructures are various kinds of space, object and text that facilitate contact with the past (Irwin-Zarecka 1994: 13). Consequently, I also use this term in this book to describe memory markers situated at a specific site that collectively delineate and shape a Gulag memory framework for that space.

However, the problem with memory, as Kontopodis (2009: 6) writes, is that: 'There is no past, no present and no future as such; the relation between the past, the present and the future is always made from some point of view and must be expressed or enacted for the past, the present or the future to emerge. There are multiple ways of performing pasts, presents and futures by way of interrelating them'. Memory of the Gulag and the transformation it is undergoing are a prime example of this. When I was travelling through Russia from 2006 to 2008, many years had already passed from the period I am calling the carnival of memory, a time when memory of the repressions was being publicly discussed, the first Days of Remembrance for Victims of the Repressions took place, the first memorials were erected, the first exhibitions devoted to Gulag history were opened and the memoirs of ex-prisoners were published. Nevertheless, the same memory actors who had actively participated in the events of the late eighties and early nineties were still engaged in work commemorating the victims of the repressions. It appeared that the situation of memory in Russia was stable and static. However, this turned out to be a false assumption. Over the last ten years, this situation has transformed again. In 2015, when an official state policy on the remembrance of political repressions was introduced, the generation of postmemory (by which I mean the second and third generations born after the Gulag but affected by a repressive past because it was transmitted to them through memoirs and pictures; see Hirsch 2008) became increasingly vocal, and new actors, such as the pro-Kremlin Sut Vremeni (Essence of Time) entered the arena.

This book describes the period preceding the strong revival in memory of the repressions that is currently so evident. I show how, in this liminal period, memory of the repressions was shaped – at a time when the state no longer made memory of the repressions a taboo topic, but had not yet become actively involved in shaping it – by people for whom this memory was important. Since a broader interpretative framework was yet to develop, they were forced to show their creativity and often took local history and the local experience of the repressions as a reference point. Both my detailed description of how the first monuments and exhibitions dedicated to the Soviet repressions came into being and my conversations, quoted in this book, with the people who created these projects demonstrate the symbolic value and social impact of memory markers, which many people today believe to be ill-equipped to preserve the memory of the repressions (Etkind 2004b, 2013; Sherbakova 2015: 119). This book also enables the reader to better comprehend the meanings of today's projects and memorialization activities. Many of the described institutions, such as the Local History Museums in Inta, Pechora and Magadan or the Ivan Panikarov Museum in Yagodnoye in the Kolyma region, developed their memory projects over a number of years based on their own concepts and the way the repression was expressed in their localities. Today, these institutions have become part of the Association of Museums of Memory created by the GULAG History Museum in Moscow and actively participate in the shaping of Gulag memory within the framework of the state policy on commemorating the political repressions.

To avoid misunderstandings, I should explain the terminology used in this publication. The terms 'memory of the Soviet repressions' and 'Gulag memory' are used interchangeably in this book in full awareness that these terms may be interpreted variously and are not strictly synonymous. Initially, my main focus of interest was the manner in which memory is shaped at authentic historical sites and in the grounds of former Soviet lagers. However, once I started conducting research and speaking with people, it turned out that, as Anne Applebaum wrote: '"Gulag" has come to mean the Soviet repressive system itself . . . the destruction of families, the years spent in exile, the early and unnecessary deaths' (2003). When I was conducting my research from 2006 to 2008, the term 'Gulag' had become very popular and memory actors used it readily during our conversations, even if I was asking a question about the repressions. Maybe this can be explained by the fact that this period followed the recent publication of Anna Applebaum's bestselling book *Gulag: A History* (2003; Russian edition 2006) and Tomasz Kizny's photograph album *Gulag* (2003; Russian edition 2007), both of which were widely discussed within the milieu of people involved in memorializing the repressions. I therefore decided to use both terms synonymously in this book, according to the meaning both words conveyed to memory actors of the time. I also hoped that if these terms were used interchangeably, my book would more authentically render the atmosphere of the period of working through the repressions that it describes.

Finally, the transliteration into English of Russian names, terms, places and textual sources, such as books and articles, was completed using Nevill Forbes's system of transliteration. Forbes's system was originally described in his classic primer *Russian Grammar* (1916: 12–13). It is not as phonetically precise as the Library of Congress system, but is often recommended to anglophone students of Russian and frequently used by experienced Russian–English translators due to its comparative legibility and accessibility to non-specialists. In a few cases, alternatives that do not conform to Forbes's system have come into general use or been adopted by convention. Such exceptions include anglicized versions (for example, Joseph, not Iosif; Stalin, and Felix, not Feliks, Dzerzhinsky) and specific preferences (for example, one Russian organization prefers to transliterate its name as Pokayanie, rather than Pokayaniye). The Christian names of Russian authors have been rendered according to the way their names are spelt in the titles of their publications, for example, Alexander Etkind and Eugenia Ginzburg, rather than Aleksand(e)r and Yevgeniya, respectively. This on occasion has led to an unavoidable lack of consistency between the spellings of Christian names shared by different people. The same applies to surnames, so Shcherbakova has been transliterated as Sherbakova.

Notes

1. On 12 November 1989, the incumbent Polish prime minister, Tadeusz Mazowiecki and German chancellor, Helmut Kohl, participated in a Holy Mass in Krzyżowa that constituted an important stage in the reconciliation process between the two nations. In 1990, the Krzyżowa Foundation for European Understanding was created to commemorate both this event and the Germans based at Krzyżowa (Germ. *Kreisau*), who resisted the Nazis during the Second World War. The Foundation organizes youth meetings, history seminars and conferences.
2. *Freiwillig in Stalins Gulag: Junge Deutsche restaurieren ein russisches Straflager.* A documentary film directed by Georg Restle and Andreas Maus, Köln: WDR (between 1998 and 2006).

Methodology

A sociological approach to memory and, in particular, the theoretical texts I mentioned earlier devoted to this field served as a starting point when I began my research. The actual manner in which I collected and systematized the material may be characterized as being typical of qualitative field research (Babbie 2007). The distinguishing feature of this kind of research is not so much that it is carried out in a particular space, but rather that it attempts to reconstruct the social worlds of selected groups and human communities (Głowacka-Grajper 2016: 69–77; Lutyński 2004: 12). Apart from this, I also utilized ethnographic techniques that require the researcher to collect any available data that could throw light on the issues under investigation (Hammersley and Atkinson 2007). This book is mainly based on empirical material collected during field research I conducted in the Russian Federation from 2006 to 2008,[1] but has been supplemented by materials and analyses collected and completed during two further field research projects in Russia.[2]

I conducted a pilot study in 2006 in the Solovetsky Islands, Sandarmokh and St Petersburg.[3] Subsequently, from the end of July to mid-September 2007, I completed the first stage of a study funded by a research grant, first in Sandarmokh, and then in the Solovetsky Islands and the Komi Republic (Vorkuta, Inta, Abez, Ukhta, Pechora and Syktyvkar). I also stopped for a few days in Kotlas (the Arkhangelsk Region) and Moscow. In autumn 2007, I visited Kotlas a second time to participate in the Polish Culture Days and the 30 October Days of Remembrance.[4] In 2008, I was engaged in field research in Magadan, Yagodnoye and Debin in Kolyma and also in Perm and at the Perm-36 Museum, where I participated in a youth camp organized by the Memorial Society's Perm youth chapter. I also went to Yekaterinburg for two days. I broke up my return to Poland by spending a few days in Moscow, where I visited, among other sites, the cemetery at Butovo (Map 0.1).

As I took part for the first time, in 2006, in the Days of Remembrance in Sandarmokh and the Solovetsky Islands, and travelled the following year through the Komi Republic, I began to think that my research was twenty years too late. What I was finding in the field appeared to be little more than the remnants of the great carnival of memory that had taken place during the final phase of the USSR's history. I found myself wondering whether I was fully equipped to understand the stones and crosses that surrounded me. After all, I had neither participated in nor felt the atmosphere of the First Days of Remembrance in the Solovetsky Islands. Nor had I been involved in the unveiling of the monument to Victims of Stalinism in Vorkuta or the

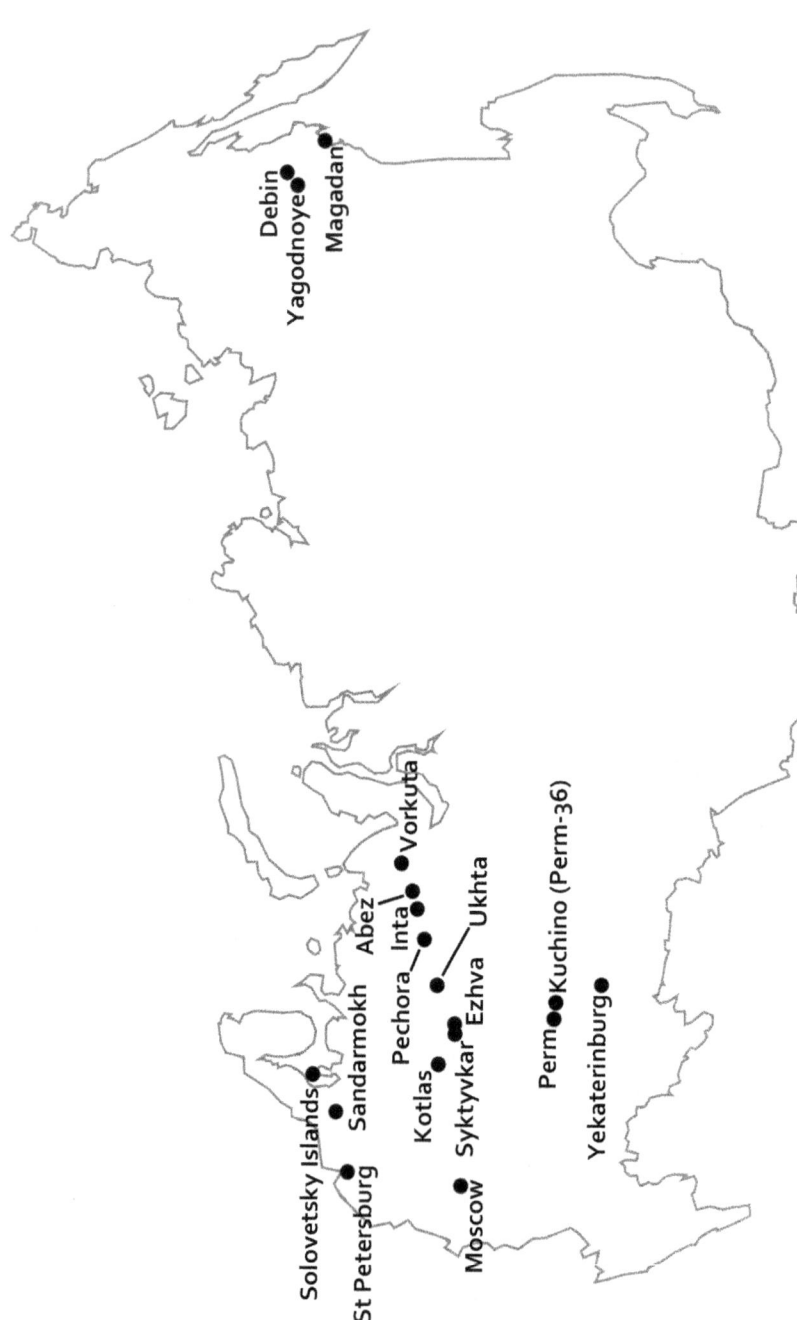

Map 0.1. Map depicting the sites where I completed field research between 2006 and 2008. Created by Universitas Publishing.

march past the MVD headquarters in Syktyvkar. Furthermore, my access to these experiences turned out to be extremely limited. Witnesses had very selective memories of these events (they had much more to say about their emotions and the atmosphere than facts and figures). More often than not, it was difficult to make contact with these people (some had moved away, and others had gone on holiday). Materials such as information in newspapers or photographs turned out to be fragmentary or almost non-existent. While the carnival of memory was taking place, no one thought to archive such materials. Everyone was focused on the here and now.

However, the more I visited these sites, the more aware I became that the very fact that I had neither participated in these events nor allowed myself to be carried away by their atmosphere would quite possibly enable me to evade any problems caused by being too heavily involved in them. Maintaining such an emotional distance from the investigated phenomenon would enable me to better comprehend what was left after the carnival and recognize genuine contemporary modes of storing and transmitting Gulag memory.

Since I was most intrigued by the meanings and functions ascribed to memory projects by memory actors and local communities, the empirical material I collected in the course of my research is very diverse. I intended to collect as much as possible in the belief that this would enable me to, first, notice existing semantic structures and then help me to interpret these and establish their social bases and importances. My main concern was to avoid – if I may quote Clifford Geertz – labelling as data what was actually nothing more than my own constructions 'of other people's constructions of what they and their compatriots are up to' (Geertz 1973: 9). The material was thus meant to help me uncover existing semantic webs woven by memory actors and local communities to explain to themselves, in their own way, what they understood by the Gulag. I wanted to create a 'thick description', by which I mean a detailed analysis of the symbolic dimension of social activity (Geertz 1973: 3–30).

The bulk of the materials I collected in the course of my research consist of interviews, or rather conversations, I conducted with memory actors, people visiting sites of memory or *platskart* passengers I encountered while travelling through the Russian Federation. I prefer the term 'conversation' to 'interview' because an interview involves asking questions and waiting for answers, but a conversation is more conducive to listening. I tried to be open to what the people I started conversations with wanted to tell me, a procedure described by Tokarska-Bakir (1995; cf. Bogumił, Wawrzyniak et al. 2015: 16–17). I had no intention of identifying with the Other. Dialogue was my only aim. I therefore formulated questions, and helped my interlocutors to respond to them. As the Polish researcher Katarzyna Kaniowska stresses:

> the manner of experiencing the subject with whom we are conducting the dialogue requires understanding that will take place on two planes, as it were, at the same time. The dialogue is not only about comprehending You. The things that are the object of the dialogue and (or) its outcome are

also important. Understanding in this sense is interpreting a text, a work of art, someone's views or behaviour, but not the intentions, subjective attitudes and judgements they conceal. (1999: 34)

I recorded[5] most of the thirty-five conversations I conducted, but the contents of some were noted down immediately afterwards (if the person did not agree to being recorded or circumstances did not allow it). However, the thoughts and reflections that arose during conversations with train passengers found their way into my field notes (on the importance of field notes see Emerson and Fretz 2011).

Articles appearing in the local press became another important source. I was intrigued by the language they used and how they described and presented the Days of Remembrance and unveiling of monuments. I made use of publications or journalistic reports covering public debates. I focused on the arguments being used in discussions on the forms assumed by monuments. The local press also helped me to establish dates, names and orders of events that had become confused in my interlocutors' memories or forgotten. I primarily used press cuttings that had been collated and stored in the archives of museums or those of the Memorial Society. Most of these institutions collect and classify press articles, so I was able to obtain folders containing materials on various topics; for example, the Memorial Society's activities, Days of Remembrance or monuments. These catalogues in themselves became a valuable source indicative of local methods of categorizing events. However, one negative aspect of these collections is the lack of information in some cuttings in the newspaper they were taken from and the day particular texts were published. I have therefore created a separate section in the bibliography for these newspapers, which provides all the information on these sources that was available.

Other written sources I refer to in my book are Internet articles and informational sites. These are frequently referred to when I am describing the ongoing commemorative activity of the memory actors I investigate in the book. The problem is that these resources are very ephemeral, disappearing after some time to make way for new news. This explains why some of the web pages I refer to in the book are no longer active. I have therefore left in the original links to these summarized sources to make it clear that I am referring to them.

Museum archives also became an important resource for my research. These contain detailed scripts for guided tours as well as *tematiko-ekspozitsionnyye plany vystavok*; namely, plans in which curators explain their conceptions for individual exhibitions, elaborating the aims, form and assumptions behind each one. In addition to providing me with this valuable information, these materials also helped me to compile a complete list of Gulag-themed temporary exhibitions organized by specific museums.

The book comprises four studies devoted, respectively, to the Solovetsky Islands (also known as Solovki), the Komi Republic, the Perm region and Kolyma. All these studies are similar in structure. I begin with very brief information about the Gulag history of each region and then explain how the carnival of memory manifested itself at particular sites. Finally, I describe the contemporary language used for commemorating Gulag history at these sites. My intention was not to create a catalogue of sites of memory, because these already exist. Information about monuments and memory markers located in the territory of the Soviet Union can be found on the Sakharov Centre's website. The Memorial Society in Moscow's website contains information about mass burial sites and monuments to victims of political repressions, and the St Petersburg chapter of Memorial manages the Virtual Gulag project, a website containing information about and photographs of museums telling the history of the Gulag. The St Petersburg chapter of Memorial also manages the Gulag Necropolis project, which describes cemeteries and mass burial sites. Finally, on the Last Address project's website, the last places of residence of persons repressed by the Soviet authorities can be viewed. In the West, a German organization, the Federal Foundation for the Reappraisal of the SED Dictatorship, collects information from all over the world on sites commemorating victims of communism (see, for example, Kaminsky, Gleinig and Heidenreich 2007).

Therefore, the aim of my research, rather than being the creation of a catalogue of sites of memory, was to describe and interpret the most distinctive components of the memory infrastructure of each region. Each study reveals issues and meanings that vary significantly with regard to the impact Gulag history has had on the contemporary appearance of individual sites, the manner in which the carnival of memory manifested itself, comprehensions of the memorialization process and the number of competing memory actors.

Some of these differences have also arisen from certain research assumptions. As I delved deeper into the meanings of contemporary memory of Gulag history, my findings magnified my initial impression that many of the publications on topics associated with the sites I was investigating, particularly the publications that discussed their contemporary reality and activities, had greatly distorted their image. This made it more difficult for me to comprehend the meanings that local communities ascribed to these sites. This distortion is clear in an article published in the Polish newspaper *Gazeta Wyborcza,* which was titled 'They Are Rebuilding the Gulag for Tourists' (Bielecki 2005). In this article, the author described how the Mayor of Vorkuta, Igor Shpektor, was planning, against the wishes of the city's inhabitants, to reconstruct the local forced labour camp, so that foreign tourists could come there, live in barracks, eat camp soup and experience the attractions of a 'camp amusement park'. The article unreservedly condemned Shpektor, presenting him as someone who was completely ignorant of Gulag history. The author of the piece, Tomasz Bielecki, both failed to mention that this was only one of a number of ideas that surfaced in Vorkuta at the time to save the city from bankruptcy and also that such a project was never implemented. He also did not inform the reader that Shpektor supported efforts to turn Vorkuta into a 'City-Memorial of international importance' by creating an enormous Gulag memory complex composed of monuments and architectural constructions created by artists from various countries (I write about this in a later part of the book). There is also no information about the Mayor participating every year in the 30 October Days of Remembrance ceremonies and encouraging people to display candles in their windows to commemorate the victims of repressions. Finally, the article fails to mention that municipal funds were allocated very year to the provision of transport for people wishing to take part in the remembrance ceremonies held at the Yur-Shor Cemetery for those executed by firing squad at Mine No. 29. When Shpektor came to power, he reconstructed the social infrastructure that had been destroyed during the crisis of the nineties. In particular, he effectively combated drug addiction among young people and a wave of violent street crime by opening sports centres and supporting extra-curricular programmes for children and young people. In fact, he was greatly respected by local inhabitants. But the author of this article is not alone. Similar omissions have been made by many others representing the situation in the Russian Federation. Naturally, if such information were more widely available, it would enable Igor Shpektor's actions and the form assumed by Gulag memory in Russia to be better understood.

This book's structure arose from an attempt to deal with the classic problem facing every field researcher, aptly characterized by Clifford Geertz as 'Being There, Writing Here'. My primary aim was to describe the world of another culture in a language understandable to the world of research institutions and universities where this book will be read and evaluated (Geertz 1988). I therefore set myself the task of creating a description that would explain, as effectively as possible, the investigated reality to a reader coming from another culture and environment. However, the primary inspiration behind the shape my book finally assumed was Boris Uspensky's observation that the distinguishing feature of Russian culture is that it is both similar and dissimilar to other cultures. He develops this observation as follows: 'Consequently, Russian culture can be described using the same terms – according to the same model – as is the case with any other culture, but certain distinctive features of Russian culture will then be unavoidably ignored and remain outside the researcher's field of vision' (2002: 97–98). It is these distinctive features of Russian culture that are most important for my analysis.

In the first study, which examines the Solovetsky Islands, I focus on providing a detailed description that enables the context accompanying the beginnings of the formation of a commemorative language to be better understood. In the other studies, despite the fact that I also describe the carnival of memory period, I do not present it with such precision. However, whenever the collected material reveals a new motif, I try to outline this in more detail. Each study may therefore be seen as one further step towards a deeper understanding of the investigated material. This also explains why if some process has manifested itself in similar fashion in a preceding study, rather than re-explaining this process in detail, I focus on analysing new dimensions of Gulag memory that become apparent as I investigate one site after another. The studies should therefore be read in the order in which they have been presented, because the earlier studies enable the later studies to be fully comprehended.

In the first part, devoted to the Solovetsky Islands, the main accent falls on a description of the three memory actors that are active there: the Solovetsky Museum, Memorial Society and Orthodox Church. I highlight similarities and differences between the memory projects they create and analyse the meanings they conceal. In the case of the museum's memory project, I place the main emphasis on revealing the sources this project utilizes. In the descriptions that follow of the Memorial and Orthodox memory projects, I attempt to outline the infrastructures they create, revealing the meanings and aims they conceal and explaining why these two projects stand in stark opposition to each other.

In the case of the Komi Republic, I focus on describing and analysing the diverse forms that Gulag memory can assume. In this region, the various memory actors' differing interpretations of memory have not created a conflict, yet memory is stored in very varied forms. First, by examining the historical exhibitions shown at local museums, I define the main boundaries of Gulag memory in this region. Next, I describe the Gulag monuments and cemeteries located in this area, attempting to establish their meanings and functions.

In my description of the Perm region, the primary emphasis is placed on a presentation of the actions of two memory actors – the Memorial Society and Perm-36 Museum – whose memory projects are grounded in the same ideological assumptions yet deliver different outcomes. Although both memory actors have set themselves the task of creating a museum, believing that this is the most effective form of speaking about the past, they have a very different understanding of the manner in which exhibitions should be constructed and the social function of museums. I analyse the distinctive features of each project while indicating the distinguishing features of these memory actors' proposals for how Gulag history should be comprehended and presented.

In the last study, devoted to Kolyma, I discuss the situation of memory in a region that used to be regarded as 'the Archipelago's capital', because it embodied the worst aspects of the Gulag. First, I analyse the Magadan identity debate that accompanied the process of erecting a monument to victims of the Gulag – Ernst Neizvestny's Mask of Sorrow. I also take a detailed look at the monument itself, the only secular and artistic memorial complex in the Russian Federation. Next, I move on to the manner of commemoration that can be encountered in Debin and Yagodnoye – settlements on the Kolyma Route, about 500 kilometres from Magadan. There are so many memory actors operating at these sites that I refer to them collectively as a 'Kolyma memory repository' and outline the distinguishing features of this memory space.

In the conclusion, in which I summarize my findings, I attempt, on the one hand, to demonstrate the distinguishing features of Gulag memory in the Russian Federation, and on the other, by alluding to the analyses contained in each study, I highlight the various similarities and differences between Gulag sites of memory. My book concludes with a bibliography.

Notes

1. Project No. N11601231/1159, funded by the Polish Ministry of Science and Higher Education.
2. Two projects funded by the National Science Centre in Poland: 'New Martyrdom – The Orthodox Interpretation of the Experience of Soviet Repressions' (No. N N116 696040; 2011–2016) and the 'From Enemy of the People to Holy Martyr – An Analysis of the One-Hundredth Anniversary of the 1917 Revolution and Eightieth Anniversary of the Great Terror in Russia' (UMO-2016/21/B/HS6/03782 (2017–2020)). See http://www.memoryofrepressions.aps.edu.pl.
3. This was before I was in receipt of a research grant, so the cost of the research was partially covered from my own funds and partially from funds allocated by the Consul General of the Republic of Poland in St Petersburg.
4. Travel and accommodation was funded by the Consul General of the Republic of Poland in St Petersburg.
5. A list of all the conversations cited in the book can be found in the bibliography.

Chapter 1
The Solovetsky Islands

Solovki – The First Gulag Camp?

The title of this subsection alludes to the title chosen by Anne Applebaum for the second chapter of her book on the Gulag (2003). In this chapter, which the author titled 'The First Camp of the Gulag' (cf. Solzhenitsyn 1974: 25–70), she writes about the Solovetsky Islands. The *Solovetski lager osobogo naznacheniya* (the Solovetsky special purpose camp, or SLON) was not in fact the first lager, because from the beginning of the revolution, the Bolsheviks had been creating smaller camps to detain their enemies (Applebaum 2003: 31; Courtois et al. 1999: 71–80). However, the common conviction that it was the first camp has some basis in fact. SLON became a testing ground where principles appropriate to the efficient functioning of a camp system were developed. It was here, following the application of rules and directives of various kinds, that the *ispravitelno-trudovoy lager* (corrective labour camp) machine slowly began to grind into action while its 'cogs' settled into their roles as *zeks* (zek is an abbreviation of the word *zaklyuchenny*, or 'prisoner') (Applebaum 2003: 40–58; on the history of SLON see Brodsky 2008; *SLON. OGPU*. 2004). A great deal is also known about SLON because certain documents exist from which the lager's history can be reconstructed by describing its dynamics and dividing it into different periods. In other words, it can be subjected to historical scrutiny. There are many turning points in this dynamic history, which possesses its own sense of internal drama.[1] Well-known figures also made an appearance, including Pavel Florensky and Maksim Gorky, who further enriched potential narratives by contributing interesting moments from this *histoire des mentalités* (Gullotta 2018). This explains why the assertion that it was from here that the system spread out to encompass the whole country, basically a metaphorical notion, eventually embedded itself in common parlance.

Such a generalization is of course a kind of mental shorthand that would theoretically compel historians of the Gulag to write in-depth articles on the events preceding SLON's foundation, while for scholars of memory this conviction would appear to provide the perfect starting point for any analysis of the complexities of the memory forms occurring in both the Solovetsky Archipelago and other parts of the Russian Federation. However, one important reservation should be advanced at this point: the double assertion that the Gulag, conceived as a system of repression, was born here and that memory of its birth grew out of Solovki is false. Nevertheless, the actual process of creating memory projects (i.e. visual forms of various kinds designed to symbolically express how a particular community remembers the notion of the Gulag) is very strongly associated with the Solevetsky Islands.

What is more, this common perception that 'it was there, at Solovki, that the Gulag began' may be singled out as the key to understanding this process. This notion is therefore capable of determining the historical importance ascribed to the site, influencing in turn the conviction that it should play an important role in the process of shaping Gulag memory. Of course, the question then arises as to what extent memorialization activities after 1989 arose from the conscious action of various memory actors, rather than being the outcome of specific meanings being conferred on them in retrospect. Certainly, 'chance' has played an enormous role here. However, the aforementioned notion that 'it was here it all began' not only influenced how the staff at the Solovetsky Museum explained the need to create an exhibition telling the history of SLON, but also defined the actions of Memorial Society members or representatives of the Orthodox Church for whom the Solovetsky Islands had become an important element of the memory infrastructures they had created.

All these processes caused the Gulag memory infrastructure in the European part of the Russian Federation to be semantically associated with the Solovetsky Islands. It may therefore be stated that, much like SLON spread across the USSR, creating the Gulag, many monuments and memory markers in this part of the Russian Federation are either associated with the history of this place or come from there directly. This is the case with the Solovetsky stones and memorial crosses that started migrating from Solovki from the beginning of the 1990s, marking sites that were important to memory actors and creating secular or Orthodox memory infrastructures.

When analysing forms of Gulag memory in the Solovetsky Islands, I shall therefore attempt to reveal the motivations and inspirations guiding the various memory actors erecting the aforementioned markers. My primary aim is to outline the genesis of selected memory projects while attempting to define their contemporary meaning.[2] While focusing on the White Sea Archipelago, I have no wish to reflect on whether the exhibition titled *SLON – The Solovetsky Special Purpose Camp* was the first to tell the history of the Gulag in the USSR or whether Solovki's Victims of Political Repressions Memorial is the first purposefully[3] erected Gulag monument.[4] Although the venerability of these projects is worthy of note, what interests me most about them is that they have afforded me, upon close inspection, the invaluable opportunity to explain important processes influencing the form assumed by Gulag memory in the early twenty-first century. This will be my primary focus in this chapter.

The Awakening of the 'Island of Pain' – The Solovetsky Islands, 1989–1992

> [Gulag history] was banned in the USSR and not until 1988 did this subject come into the open, and before 1988 no information was given

during an excursion, during a visit to the islands, the kremlin or other monuments. Nowhere could this subject have emerged. It was categorically banned, but in 1988, this subject became manifest.

(Olga Bochkareva, Employee of the
Solovetsky Local History Museum [06_OB])

The title of this subsection was borrowed from an article on Solovki's first Days of Remembrance (Chukhin 1989). The Solovetsky Islands, like the rest of the country, stood at a crossroads. Ever more frequent press articles revealing the scale of the Stalinist repressions were simply the final nail in the coffin for the outgoing regime. The desire to uncover this history's 'blank pages' applied particularly strongly to the Solovetsky Islands. As the national press published ever more information on Solovki, interest in its history expanded exponentially. During this period, the *Pravda Severa* and *Severny Komsomolets* newspapers began printing articles written by Antonina Melnik[5] that uncovered the Islands' labour camp past.

They include reports on the museum staff's gathering of materials relating to SLON's history. The manner in which they searched for and located such source materials comprises a separate page in the history of this period and strongly influenced the form assumed by Gulag memory.[6] In one article, Antonina Melnik describes this process, relating how she and some of her colleagues from the museum found a hoard of unsent letters written by SLON prisoners in a lighthouse attic on Sekirnaya Hill. She stresses how surprised they were that they had managed to find such 'treasures'. Many years have passed since the SLON era. During this period, various buildings were being used by the Northern Fleet, and from the sixties, tourists started arriving at Solovki. Until recently, as Melnik writes, museum staff actually used to 'travel to Anzer[7] to destroy traces of the Gulag' (Melnik 1989a). Despite this, these original letters survived.

Museum staff used the materials found in the attic, along with information contained in the *Solovetskiye Ostrova* magazine[8] and other periodicals published in the USSR in this period, to draw up a list of prisoners' names. They then sent this list to the editorial teams of various newspapers across the country, requesting that they publish it along with the information that the museum was preparing an exhibition and would like former SLON prisoners and the families of anyone on the list to get in contact (Melnik and Soshina 1990).

The public response to this request was unexpectedly large. People who had discovered the fate of their loved ones from the list got in contact, as did those who had information about the later fates of SLON prisoners or the people to whom the unsent letters lying in the lighthouse attic for sixty years had been addressed (Melnik and Soshina 1990). Melnik cites two examples demonstrating how the notice placed in the newspapers helped her to determine prisoners' further fates. The first relates to an older woman who identified her father on the basis of his surname and initials. All that this woman had previously known about her father was that he was a cellist in

Odessa before being sent to Solovki. The second story she cited related to the fate of Iosif Gotsiridze, a former SLON prisoner. An extract from his letter was used in *Vlast solovetskaya*, a film directed by Marina Goldovskaya. The *Zarya Vostoka* newspaper helped Gotsiridze's nephew get in contact with the museum, to tell them about his Trotskyite uncle's further fate. He also sent a photograph of him that was taken later (Melnik and Soshina 1990).

There were more similar stories. Information collected in this manner was added to the museum archives, served as material for the creation of the exhibition and, above all, assisted with memory retrieval and the building of a community composed of those who had memory ties with SLON. Many people who had entered into the public dialogue initiated by the information in the newspapers came – like the aforementioned daughter of the Odessan cellist – to Solovki to take part in the First Days of Remembrance.

These were organized by the local history museum, in cooperation with Memorial Society representatives from Moscow and Leningrad,[9] on 6 to 8 June 1989. The date of this gathering was important symbolically, for it marked the anniversary of the first documented transport of prisoners to the Islands, the so-called 'first Solovki transport'.[10] The Days of Remembrance were attended by former prisoners of the Solovetsky camps, their children and grandchildren, Memorial Society members and researchers, journalists and television crews. Those who participated came from different cities and republics in the USSR, arriving from Moscow, Leningrad, Petrozavodsk, Izhevsk, Yalta, Krasnodar, Kaliningrad, Zagorsk (today, Sergiyev Posad), Kiev and Lviv (Chukhin 1989).

On the first day, Melnik showed participants around the monastery and told its history. The following day, everyone went to Sekirnaya Hill. There, in the church that held punishment cells while SLON was operational, Aleksander Panne, an Orthodox priest and member of the Leningrad chapter of Memorial, performed a *Panikhida* (orthodox memorial service) at the request of members of repressed families. Following this, those participating in the ceremony went to Savvatyevo, where political prisoners (mainly socialists, Social Revolutionaries and Mensheviks) were held in 1923.[11] On the third day, the *The Solovetsky Special Purpose Camp 1923–1939* exhibition was opened. The museum's director, Ludmila Lopatkina, related how the museum's staff – Antonina Melnik, Antonina Soshina, Aleksander Bozhenov and Yury Brodsky – had worked together on the exhibition. Finally, the time came to visit the exhibition, express words of gratitude and hand out gifts.

On 7 August 1989, at the site of execution of prisoners convicted of involvement in the 'Kremlin Plot' of 1929, a cornerstone was erected for a future memorial to victims of political repressions (Figure 1.1). Pavel Florensky's grandson and the nephew of another prisoner – the poet Kuzebay – addressed the gathering. Yury Chaynikov's speech recalled the following words Kuzebay wrote to his family: 'How I envy the seagulls flying overhead! I would so like to look upon you, my dears, even once . . .'. Chaynikov proposed that the future monument could take the form of two seagulls.

Figure 1.1. The Solovetsky Prisoners Memorial. Erected on the initiative of the Solovetsky Island administration, the Solovetsky Local History Museum and the Memorial Society at the site of execution of prisoners convicted of involvement in the 'Kremlin Plot' of 1929. Photo by author.

One would have a broken wing dripping with blood, and the other would be soaring upwards (Chukhin 1989). During the Days of Remembrance, one of the new streets in the village centre, on which modern villas had been built, was named, with due ceremony, after Pavel Florensky.[12]

The Days of Remembrance were extremely potent symbolically. Those who witnessed the events, their children and other people interested in the history of the camps had an opportunity to meet, exchange information and share their own experiences. The ceremonies facilitated the creation of a new type of community based on the collective memory of an event consigned to oblivion for sixty years, an event that had tragically impressed itself, or rather cast a slur on, their lives. The Days of Remembrance reversed the situation like a magical force. Suddenly, what had been forgotten or denied for years could not only be expressed, but, at the same time, it became a basis for the building of a new community. The witnesses of the events became the centre of attention. Their special status was reaffirmed during official speeches, when representatives of the museum or members of the Memorial Society, who were public authorities, expressed their gratitude and admiration. For museum staff, Memorial members and anyone else interested in Gulag history, the witnesses' stories were a source of historical information and meanings that helped to explain the surrounding reality during a period that still bore many signs of its labour camp past [27_AS; 28_AS].[13] The official version of history had concealed this reality for years, so there were no keys to understanding its functioning within the community.

During these first ceremonies, memory actors proposed a complete cycle of rituals (for example, monastery visits or excursions to Sekirnaya Hill and Savvatyevo) aimed at satisfying a need to learn the history and remember the departed (for example, the Panikhida on Sekirnaya Hill). Furthermore, the gathering by the cornerstone for the future monument to victims of political repressions and an evening meeting at the Community Centre helped to create the new community. At the same time, all these activities were mapping out memory spaces. It is around these that a secular memory of SLON would form over the years to come. There were also meaning-laden sites like Savvatyevo, where a rebellion took place against the Soviet authorities; Sekirnaya Hill, which contained the punishment cells as well as mass graves on its slopes; and the Solovetsky Prisoners Memorial, erected at a site where prisoners accused of treason were executed by firing squad in 1929. The programme proposed in 1989 would form the basis of the Days of Remembrance that would take place in Solovki over the following years.

Apart from those participating in the ceremonies in 1989, Solovki was visited by other groups of people interested in its history. Melnik recalls a visit by members of the Krug Cultural Centre (Melnik 1989b). Dimitry Likhachev also made an appearance with a director, Vladislav Vinogradov, who shot a film about him. As Melnik writes, at the end of his stay, a meeting took place with museum staff, during which Likhachev reminisced about his time at the lager[14] and took questions from the floor. Solovki also received a visit from the writer Oleg Volkov, the main protagonist in another documentary being shot there. Melnik recalls that his camp memoirs were published the following year in Paris (Volkov 1987). They were mainly devoted to Solovki. In October, a group of Ukrainians from the Ukretelefilm channel came to make a film about the Ukrainian creative intelligentsia in Solovki (Melnik 1989b). Unexpectedly, Solovki was transformed from a forgotten place somewhere in the White Sea to a travel destination for many important personages from the USSR's cultural and political life. In Melnik's articles she senses the excitement caused by the visits of such distinguished guests, on the one hand, but on the other hand, she is greatly pained by her awareness of the meaning of the history that had played out on the territory of her 'small homeland'. Melnik concludes her summary of all the visits that took place in 1989 as follows: 'My poor Solovki . . . What if Germans, Czechs and Chinese start coming [here] for the same reason? After all, there's very little information, as it were, to be found among us about them . . .' (Melnik 1989b).

The next year brought the inhabitants of Solovetsky Islands new questions and doubts, as to their future this time. In October, the Council of Archbishops, which was dedicated to the four-hundredth anniversary of the Russian Patriarchate, took place in Moscow. The Council made a formal request to the Supreme Soviet of the

Soviet Union, asking that Solovki be transferred into the guardianship of the Orthodox Church. This information rapidly circulated around the Arkhangelsk region, giving rise to a whole host of questions: What would be the practical repercussions of this process? Would the Archipelago be handed over in its entirety, and if so, what would become of the school, museum and hospital? (Mozgovoy 1990a). Similar questions and doubts appeared in the articles that followed. On the one hand, they revealed how ill-informed people were, triggering speculation and charges levelled at the Church that were frequently surprising. These included fears that the brothers would 'eat the islanders out of house and home' (*Severny Komsomolets*, 15 October 1990), or destroy the Archipelago's unique flora and fauna by tarmacking over roads to attract thousands of pilgrims (Chebanyuk 1990b) or reintroduce the severe monastic rules that functioned during the revolution and order women to leave the Islands (Annin 1990). On the other hand, these fears point to the lack of dialogue between the islanders and representatives of the Church and their inability to communicate with each other.

When presenting its request for Solovki's return, the Church was particularly keen to emphasize the need to reconstruct the decaying monastery. Its main argument was that the museum would not be able to manage this task itself. The whole of the Russian Church had not only decided to involve itself in the reconstruction work but also seek funding from Orthodox émigrés. In interviews given to the press, Bishop Panteleimon of Murmansk and Arkhangelsk confirmed that although the Church's primary aim was to restore the monastery to its former glory and return it to its position as an important spiritual centre in the North (*Pravda Severa*, 20 October 1990), nevertheless, if the whole process was to be completed at all, it would last several years. He had no intention of ejecting the Islands' inhabitants. He merely wished to improve their lives (Chebanyuk 1990b).

The bishop's assurances failed to placate islanders whose mistrust of the Church and anxiety about their own future were intensifying. In the local government elections that took place in spring 1990, it was Ludmila Lopatkina, director of the local museum, who emerged victorious. As Annin (1990) writes, for the first time in Solovki's history, the control of two local authorities ended up in the hands of a single person. He claims that 'although most islanders are aware that Solovki is a symbol of the Gulag', the islanders themselves were not living and breathing a lager that actually ceased its operations there in 1939. The one-and-a-half-thousand-strong community of Solovetsky islanders were living for the present day, since they 'marry here, give birth to children and live in what used to be monastic cells and camp barracks' (Annin 1990). These people were worrying about their future from the perspective of the present.

However, this tendency to focus on issues relating to the Solovetsky Archipelago's future failed to dampen interest in the Islands' labour camp past. From April 1990, Solovki began publishing its own newspaper, *Solovetski Vestnik*. One of its most important parts was a column titled *Po sledam SLON-a* (On SLON's Trail), in which museum employees, in particular Melnik, pieced together the labour camp history that revealed itself to them as they collected and processed materials. It contained articles telling of the fates and lives of monks or presenting the activities of the Solovetsky Society for Local Lore or local theatre. There were also articles explaining the aforementioned Kremlin Plot of 1929 or telling the story of Easter 1926. Many reminiscences and biographies of ex-prisoners were also published.

The next Days of Remembrance took place the following June. Much like the previous year, they were attended by ex-prisoners (who had a great deal to say as they visited the prison cells in which they had served their sentences) and other guests from all over the USSR (Melnik 1990). Melnik summarizes as follows: 'Different biographies, different characters, differently they remember the past. Yet, generally, they exhibit no self-pity: every one of them was more fortunate than their peers' (Melnik 1990).

During the Days of Remembrance, another event took place that gave rise to a new memory ritual. As they dug new graves in the communal cemetery, the islanders had been throwing the prisoners' bones that they found out of the cemetery enclosure. Melnik decided, with three other people, to remove these bones and bury them in a communal grave, so that those participating in the Days of Remembrance would not see them (Melnik 1993). However, this information found its way to the participants, so, on 8 June, the burial was completed of the 'remains of the unknown prisoners'. Each of the participants threw a handful of earth into the grave, which was then filled in by museum staff and former SLON prisoners. Finally, a tall wooden cross, around which stones were laid, was erected on this communal grave of 'people who died in Solovki'. It was also decided that anyone who visited the communal grave in the future should lay a stone there as a memory marker. This ritual has become a Solovets tradition and the whole grave is currently surrounded by stones (*Solovetski Vestnik,* [2] 1994).

This was not the last time that year that Solovki received guests. In July, an international mission named Istoki, organized by the Lichnost Community, visited Solovki. As the organization's representative, V.M. Kuzmin, explained in an interview given to the weekly newspaper *Literaturnaya gazeta,* the mission's aim was to set in motion Solovki's spiritual renewal and aid the Orthodox Church's revival in the area (Mamaladze 1990). This event was marked symbolically through the laying of a memorial cross at the former site of the Church of the Reverend Onuphrius the Great. It was there that the last twenty-six bishops to be exiled to Solovki after the revolution served (Smolensky 1990). The mission also involved the offering of prayers and donation of money towards the renovation of the decaying monastery.

An expedition from the Moscow chapter of Memorial also visited in July. It aimed to uncover the mass burial sites on Sekirnaya Hill and Kulikovo Marsh (*Solovetski Vestnik,* [8] 1990). A delegation also arrived from the Arkhangelsk organization, Sovest, to collect two Solovetsky boulders. On Political Prisoners Day (30 October),[15] they were erected and unveiled in Arkhangelsk[16] and in Lubyanka in Moscow as monuments to victims of political repression.[17] Finally, in October, the first monks arrived in Solovki to take up permanent residence at the part of the Solovetsky Monastery that had been transferred into their hands (*Severny Komsomolets,* 15 October 1990).

In 1992, on 20 August, the date of the Solovetskiye Chudotvortsy (Solovetsky Miracle Workers) holiday, the Islands received a visit from Alexy II, Patriarch of Moscow and All Russia. During his visit, he thanked the abbot of the Spaso-Preobrazhenski Solovetsky Stauropegic Monastery, archimandrite Yosef, for his contribution to the work returning the Solovetsky Monastery to its former glory. This was followed by the ceremonial return of the relics of Saints Zosima, Sabbatius and Herman – the monastery's founding fathers. During this visit, the patriarch underlined Solovki's importance for the Orthodox Church, visited the SLON exhibition, conducted a Panikhida for the prisoners undeservedly killed on Sekirnaya Hill and consecrated a cross, erected at the foot of the hill, commemorating the murdered prisoners (E. Andrushchenko and N. Andrushchenko 1992). This visit symbolically endorsed the Church's presence in Solovki.

The local newspaper presented the patriarch's visit as an important event in the Islands' history. However, the account it gave failed to view the event as a whole from the islanders' perspective. On reading the various articles, the impression is gained that the islanders were tired by the constant stream of visitors arriving at the island over the previous few years. The guests were beginning to be perceived as foreigners with their own agenda, implementing their own programmes and erecting their own markers, without bothering to ask local residents what they thought about this and what their own expectations were. This is most evident in descriptions of the Days of Remembrance. According to Pavel Rozhin's article summarizing the Days of Remembrance taking place in 1992 in Solovki: 'Unfortunately, the Days of Remembrance were of little interest to the Solovetsky islanders. Apart from the representative from the local authorities, Valentina Viktorovna Nebozhenko, representatives from the museum and newspaper, a few passers-by and women watching what was happening from the window of neighbouring houses, the gathering attracted nobody' (Rozhin in Melnik 1992). This lack of interest in the Days of Remembrance may be seen as the outcome of a gradual decline in interest in the history of the Islands' camps. To a certain extent, inhabitants, by now acquainted with and 'used to' the history of SLON, lost interest in it and increasingly began to focus on their everyday concerns and, first and foremost, the Archipelago's future.

At this juncture, I would like to interrupt my narrative of the reawakening of memory of SLON in the Solovetsky Islands and move on to an analysis of the Gulag memory markers and the meanings they connote. The timeframes adopted in this book are symbolic and simplify the whole memory-shaping process, a process which, after all, began in the past and is essentially continuing to this very day. However, I decided that a detailed description of the events from 1988 to 1992 was needed to define the space around which memory of SLON began to be shaped. I believe that such a definition is essential for the successful comprehension and explanation of the contemporary functioning of memory markers. In the period I have described above, all the main actors – the local museum, the Memorial Society and the Orthodox Church – became involved in the creation of memory markers. These in turn helped to define the spatial and thematic frameworks around which memory of the Solovetsky Islands' Gulag would later be shaped, notably: Sekirnaya Hill, Savvatyevo, the communal cemetery, the grounds of the former Church of the Reverend Onuphrius the Great and the grounds of the mass grave dating from 1929. The first projects also came into being at this time. It was these – the exhibition, the Solovets stone serving as a monument to SLON prisoners, the memorial crosses – that determined the future path of development for the SLON memory infrastructure developed by the various actors.

The events that took place over the following years such as the economic and political crisis in the mid-90s that affected the Archipelago as much as the rest of the Russian Federation,[18] the arrival of President Putin or the administrative reforms had a profound impact on the islanders' lives and how they perceived their future. The Islands' labour camp past that in 1989 had just been discovered and was dominating the Solovetsky islanders' lives now belongs to the past. The story of how SLON's history was discovered also belongs to the past.

Nevertheless, the events that took place between 1988 and 1992 determined the manner in which the Gulag was thought about and commemorated in the Solovetsky Islands over the following fifteen years. The memory infrastructure created in this period by the museum, Memorial Society and monastery was also subject to development and supplementation over the next few years. Despite the mutual mistrust among the actors and the intensifying conflict between the museum and monastery over the management of Solovets cultural heritage, it appeared that the labour camp past would be permanently recorded within the Archipelago's cultural landscape and that an unwritten agreement held between the actors on how spheres of influence should be divided among them when it came to shaping memory of SLON. However, this sense of stability was only superficial. The moment that upset the apparent equilibrium between the memory actors was the seventieth anniversary of the outbreak of the Great Terror, when, as I shall discuss in a later section of the book, participants in a *Krestny Khod* religious procession transported a memorial cross made in the Solovetsky Islands to Butovo, just outside Moscow, and erected it near the Church of the Holy New Martyrs and Confessors of Russia. Unlike the commemorative activities undertaken in jubilee year by Memorial members, which were ignored by the official media, the Solovki-Butovo Krestny Khod became an important media event. The Orthodox memory discourse was thus effectively legitimized by the state authorities, encouraging the Church to undertake further activities directed at the monopolization of Gulag remembrance.

In 2008, the discussion on the establishment of a special legal status for the Solovetsky Islands flared up again. It was provoked by a letter the Civic Chamber submitted to Vladimir Putin that requested that the special status of 'spiritual and historical site' be conferred on the Archipelago (*Solovetski Vestnik*, [3(61)] 2008: 5), arguing that in a place so important for the Russian Orthodox community: 'In the immediate vicinity of the Solovetsky Monastery and a cemetery dedicated to Gulag victims, powerfully amplified festivals of jazz and amateur song and provocative exhibitions and contemporary art actions are taking place, regattas are being held on the Holy Lake and camp sites are being pitched in forest zones'.[19] The letter and the interest it provoked in Solovki's fate led to the Archipelago's problems taking on a national importance. Heritage management in the Islands was streamlined at the end of 2009 through the appointment of the abbot of the Solovetsky Monastery, archimandrite Porfiry (Shutov), as director of the Solovetsky Museum, an unprecedented event in Russia (*Solovetski Vestnik,* [3(79)] 2012: 5). This was the first time a cleric had become the director of a state cultural institution. From this time onwards, the Church and museum implemented a common remembrance policy in the Islands, systematically removing people from positions of influence who had any vision for conferring meaning on the past that differed from that of the Church (Soldatov 2016).

The first person to be dismissed from their post, in January 2016, was Olga Bochkareva, who had been involved with the history of the repressions at the museum, had prepared a new exhibition that opened in 2010 (devoted to the history of SLON and the Solovetsky prison) and was director of the Gulag historical research unit. The unit itself was disbanded. Furthermore, from 2015, the museum and monastery changed the date of the official Solovetsky Days of Remembrance for victims of the repressions to July, hence distancing themselves from the commemorative activities being undertaken by Memorial Society members during the August Days of Remembrance. The boycotting of the secular ceremonies currently prepared by Memorial members and sympathizers, who make a special journey to the Islands, have led to a situation whereby the Orthodox interpretation of the past is beginning to predominate within the Archipelago's cultural landscape. As Evgeny Shtorn and Darya Buteyko have stressed: 'The resultant coalition of state power . . . and the monastery, vested with the authority of the Russian Orthodox Church, became the most significant force and was granted the right to determine the island's cultural and historical meaning. Naturally, in this situation, Memorial's position seemed much weaker' (Shtorn and Buteyko 2016).

What interests me in this chapter is the genesis of the museum, Memorial and Orthodox SLON remembrance projects that came into being during the carnival of memory and continued to shape memory of the repressions in the Solovetsky Islands over the following twenty years. I both explain the meanings and content that formed the original bases for each of these projects and present the distinctive features of each one in turn. In the concluding section, I reflect on how the changes introduced over the last few years will affect the form assumed by memory of SLON in the Solovetsky Archipelago. I ask whether memory of SLON will undergo further transformation and mutation or whether, perhaps, the form currently beginning to dominate the

Archipelago's landscape is set to permanently define the cultural memory of the repressions recorded in the Islands' landscape.

The Museum's Memory Project: From ADSTROY to *The Solovetsky Lagers and Prison '1920–1939'*

> Near the Arctic Circle, a testing ground had appeared, where, far from the [prying] eyes of outsiders ... the possibilities of the mass deployment of forced labour were being investigated. The Solovetsky supervisors who underwent training in the islands later managed camp authorities throughout the USSR. In Solovki, the process of creating citizens with a new – Soviet – consciousness was set in motion. The overseers of this system believed they had created a 'Factory of Humans'. One prisoner, M. Nikonov, named this enterprise 'ADSTROY' [hellbuilding].[20]

When I arrived in Solovki in 2006, Olga Bochkareva informed me that the museum had begun work on changing its exhibition devoted to the history of SLON, the field she was responsible for at the museum. Previously, the main memory project (known as *Solovetski Gosudarstvenny Istoriko-Arkhitekturny i Prirodny Muzey-Zapovednik*[21]) had been a permanent exhibition opened in 1989 in the rooms of the Kremlin's former monastery. These rooms now required reconstruction, as they were to be returned to the monastery, so the exhibition, in its new, modernized format updated with information reflecting what was then the current state of knowledge on SLON was opened in 2010 in a reconstructed former camp barrack located in the village centre. The exhibition was actually supposed to have been opened there, rather than in the monastery, in 1989, but there was insufficient funding at the time to pay for the barrack's renovation [06_OB].

The exhibition that was opened in 1989 was hailed as an extremely significant event throughout the USSR. Firstly, it was the first exhibition devoted to the history of the Gulag. Secondly, its influence was far from local in impact. After its official opening in Solovki during the Days of Remembrance of 1989, it travelled across various Soviet cities for several months, from Moscow, to St Petersburg, Minsk and Kiev, and was very well attended by citizens of the USSR. When it returned to Solovki it became the primary educational site for the history of the Solovetsky lager and Soviet repressions, receiving many visits from tourists and pilgrims touring the Islands. For this reason, when describing the museological memory project telling the camp history of the Solovetsky Islands, I shall focus my analysis on the old exhibition. This will enable me to draw the reader's attention to fundamental features of a museological project that shaped comprehension of SLON's importance to the Archipelago's history for twenty years. The new exhibition opened in 2010 (Bochkareva 2011) differed fundamentally from the first exhibition, both visually and in terms of topic selection, yet they shared common features arising from the specifics of working on a museum exhibition.

The new exhibition always took a stance on its predecessor; either contradicting, complementing or acting as an invariant to it.[22] It often made use of some of the same important or valuable exhibits or relied on the same documents from the museum's collections as well as similar academic studies on various themes.[23] Viewed in this light, the fundamental difference between the old and new exhibitions did not so much reside in the incorporation of newly discovered facts and corrected and replenished information into the museum narrative, but rather in the interpretation and mode of presentation that had been applied, for these reflected changes in the manner in which specific events were being perceived by society. I therefore wished, when analysing the old exhibition, to discover something about the sources of the museological project. However, my intention, when referring to the new conception for the exhibition, was to present the fundamental changes that had occurred over the intervening twenty years.

Melnik wrote, and Bochkareva later assured me, that when the museum staff set about creating a new exhibition in 1988, they were entering unfamiliar territory, where they discovered 'missing pieces of history'. When analysing the old exhibition, I was most interested in the main narrative and the thematic motifs that were being deployed. I hoped to use these to establish what information the museum staff managed to obtain, and hence what historical facts had begun to constitute SLON history. I also wondered to what degree these were indeed completely new, previously uninvestigated topics. Finally, when examining the mode of presentation, arrangement and display techniques that were being employed, I wished to discover what meanings were being ascribed to various historical elements and how the museological memory project aethetized SLON history.[24]

The Memory Project Created by the Museum in 1989

Entering the second floor of the abbot's wing of the Solovetsky Monastery, where the permanent exhibition was presented, viewers initially found themselves in an exhibition telling the Islands' history before the Revolution. The exhibition's form was reminiscent of typical ethnographic exhibitions, where the main accent is placed on the presentation of material culture. It provided information about everyday life and the work the friars undertook. Objects and icons used by the monks could be viewed there. Another smaller room was devoted to a turning point in the Archipelago's history, the transformation of the Islands from the monks' dominion to a place inhabited by zeks.

This moment of transition and transformation was presented symbolically. On the wall, still part of the monastery's history, a bird's-eye view photograph presenting the monastery in all its splendour could be seen. The recollections of prisoners travelling to Solovki positioned next to the photograph were the only harbinger of the coming changes. On the other side, however, some documents provided information about the monastery's fate from when it was requisitioned by the Bolsheviks to the point when the whole Archipelago passed into the management of the OGPU in May 1923. The entire narrative was built around information about a fire that broke out at the monastery at the point when the Islands were relinquished by a sovkhoz,[25] passing into the management of the OGPU. As could be read in the curatorial text, the fire 'not only drastically changed the monastery's appearance, but also became a kind of boundary, beyond which the history of Solovki's special purpose camps began'. The whole display was supplemented by small photographs revealing the scale of the damage to the Kremlin. Thus began the narrative of the Islands' camp history.

When moving on to the room presenting SLON's twenty-year history, viewers were confronted with a signboard containing the exhibition's motto – 'With an iron hand, we will drive humanity to happiness' – and brief curatorial information about what the exhibition would be about.[26] This introduced viewers to the atmosphere of an exhibition that aimed to 'reinstate the historical truth about the mass repressions of the 1920s and 30s', show the sites and importance of the Solovetsky lagers within the Gulag system and discuss the victims of the 1920s' and 30s' repressions using the fates of former Solovki prisoners as examples.[27]

The arrangement of the exhibition room brought to mind the interior of a camp barrack with a wooden frame reminiscent of *sploshnye nary* (barrack plank beds) and rack stands containing information about SLON's history, whose form imitated that of the wooden wheelbarrows once used by labouring zeks (Figure 1.2). Positioned at the viewer's eye level, at the point where the boundary between an upper and lower plank bed would generally lie, there were photographs accompanied by brief information about SLON prisoners. The wooden structure 'imprisoned' viewers inside the narrative, dividing them off from the outer walls, which contained propaganda photographs and posters from the thirties, showing the world to which 'the iron hand had driven humanity'. Apart from the 'world of Soviet dreams', the photographs also contained certain elements of the Soviet reality of the twenties and thirties, like marches and rallies or the faces of people who were famous at the time.

Despite the division between the inner and outer sides of the exhibition, a unique dialogue was taking place that revealed the interpenetration of both worlds. By the entrance to the exhibition, a large format photograph of Lenin had been placed behind the text of a decree by the Central Executive Committee of the USSR on the special purpose lager, unambiguously indicating the decree's provenance. This effectively placed SLON's history on a timeline linking it with the history of the October Revolution. The photograph of Lenin actually appeared to enter into a dialogue with two other large format photographs of human faces that gazed into the interior of the 'barracks' through the cracks between its planks. The first one depicted White Army soldiers and was located on the other side of the entrance to the exhibition, on the same wall as the photograph of Lenin. On the opposite wall were the enormous faces of Joseph Stalin and Genrikh Yagoda, which were perfectly visible from every part of the exhibition.

Figure 1.2. The exhibition titled *The Solovetsky Special Purpose Camp 1923–1939*. It could be visited up until 2008 in the Solovetsky Kremlin's grounds. Photo by author.

This arrangement appeared to explain to the viewer that the White Army soldiers belonged to the same world as Lenin, the leader of the revolution, yet, following the decree issued by the Central Executive Committee, they became the Solovetsky camp's first prisoners. The following information could also be read on a plaque in the photograph's background: 'List of prisoners in Solovki's lagers from 1923 to 1928'. The photograph therefore appeared to play a double role. On the one hand it was showing the process whereby the lager was filled with prisoners, and on the other it was linking the photographs of the SLON prisoners being shown in the exhibition with their pre-Revolution history.

By contrast, the photographs of Stalin and Yagoda were evoking the efficient continuators of Lenin's ideas. At the same time, their piercing gaze, which followed the viewer round the entire exhibition, appeared to bear testimony to the real and persistent influence of decisions taken on the outside on life inside the camp. Furthermore, the eyes directed at the viewer were meant to provoke anxiety in visitors – an important component of the exhibition's atmosphere.

The exhibition's biplanar structure not only rendered the atmosphere of SLON's years of operation, but may also be interpreted as a metaphor of what had until then, Anno Domini 1989, been Soviet citizens' knowledge of history. Viewers suddenly found themselves inside history from which they had been isolated by a wall of silence and oblivion. Furthermore, images that had previously constituted their knowledge of their country's history suddenly revealed themselves to be an illusion of reality invented by their leaders to conceal the truth. The construction of such an atmosphere, which created a sense of being involved in a conflict between the present and past that was taking place in the past, was a deliberately planned and important component of the exhibition. At the same time, the exhibition's construction reflected the atmosphere of '89, a time when the learning of history was really gathering pace, since it was being learned through directly experiencing it (Ankersmit 2004) rather than by attempting to comprehend the past from an intellectual perspective.

Further evidence that the exhibition constituted a kind of dialogue conducted between viewers in the here and now and the historical knowledge that had been conveyed to them is provided by the manner in which the exhibition presents the writer Maksim Gorky, the USSR's most important proponent of socialist realism. His visit to Solovki in 1929 was rooted in pure propaganda, its primary aim being to disclaim the rumours circulating in the West relating to the inhumane conditions prevailing at the Soviet lagers by presenting the merits and achievements of the corrective labour camps (Yedlin 1999). Gorky completed the task entrusted to him with real aplomb, describing the Solovki lager's merits in a series of articles titled 'Po Soyuzu Sovetov' (Across the Land of the Soviets), which were published in the *Nashi dostizheniya* newspaper.[28] It was possible at the exhibition to read extracts from these texts and view photographs Gorky took during his visit to the Islands.

However, the manner in which Gorky was presented suggested that the articles he penned should not be treated as 'objective truth' about the past. Gorky's letters and photographs were presented within the exhibition as a component of SLON's world, while the portrait of the writer was placed on the outer wall, effectively fencing it off with barbed wire. This mode of presentation appeared to be a purposeful rhetorical exercise employing the principle of meaning reversal. Gorky's propaganda writings had been placed within the labour camp reality while he himself, looking out from the window of his Solovki room, had become part of a world of illusion.

On his arrival at the Islands, the writer saw what he wanted to see, but through the prism of his blind faith in an idea, an inner world. In effect, he enclosed himself within a special purpose camp, transforming himself into a writer-zek toiling for the system with his pen. Such reflections are provoked by the manner in which Gorky was presented by the exhibition's creators. They employed Soviet knowledge of Gorky's activities, but conferred new meanings on it, loading it with negative connotations, as if they were 'turning it inside out'. It is fair to say that, in a sense, they were employing the 'dual model' meaning, which, according to Lotman and Uspensky (1993a 17–61), plays an important role in Russian culture. By bestowing a negative meaning on such an important figure as Maksim Gorky, the entire narrative was apparently transformed to such an extent that, rather than being a continuation of the old narrative, it became a completely new entity, a *novum* (Lotman and Uspensky 1993a).

The narrative of SLON's history was actually presented in chronological and thematic order. Even the photographs and biographies of prisoners were arranged in accordance with the order in which various groups of people arrived at the lager: officers and officials of tsarist Russia were followed by representatives of political parties (who had assisted the Bolsheviks with the Revolution but later became SLON prisoners), Orthodox clerics, representatives of the intelligentsia and world of science and, finally, peasants regarded as kulaks. In addition, the rack stands contained more detailed information and memorabilia associated with a few selected prisoners. These included letters written by Pavel Florensky, notes made by Dimitry Likhachev and an article by the agronomist Nikolay Tulaykov.

By placing the main accent on the portrayal and commemoration of people who had been forgotten during the time of the cult of personality, the exhibition's organizers were consistently implementing the objectives set for it in 1989.[29] It is clearly stressed in the topic-based display plan that the reason for reducing the number of documents and objects in the exhibition was to present people as well as possible. The decision to place an accent on the presentation of specific people's fates undoubtedly reflected a clear need, so evident in 1989, to show respect to ex-prisoners. However, the actual information on the selected persons was drawn from material collected following the publishing of a request in various newspapers for readers to provide any data they had on Solovetsky convicts.[30] The exhibition also contained materials only just discovered by museum staff, such as cards containing the numbers and surnames of transported convicts or unsent letters found in a lighthouse attic on Sekirnaya Hill. All these materials were meant to reveal the complexity and uniqueness of the group of people who found themselves in the lager. Although brief information about the prisoners' further fates was placed by the photographs, the exhibition did much more than provide visitors with the sense that they were satisfying their curiosity for historical knowledge. It also provoked feelings of admiration for the whole of this enormous group of people as well as a kind of nostalgia for this lost community.

The period when the exhibition was created was itself filled with an atmosphere of nostalgia. It turns out, from both Antonina Melnik's articles dating from this period and my conversations with Antonina Soshina,[31] that up until the moment the first ex-prisoners were found, nobody had any idea what 'celebrities' had been serving their sentences on 'their islands'. The articles being published at that time reveal how exceptional this community really was. In one of these, Dimitry Likhachev recalls that nowhere else would he have had the opportunity to meet so many splendid people of culture of the kind that he had met here. He also adds that in Solovki, he not only discovered what the 'Solovets life' entailed, but also the life of 'pre-revolutionary Russia' (Likhachev 1989). In all these articles, nostalgic tones can be sensed for the 'splendid' world that existed in Solovki in the twenties.

The topic selection and accentuation of each stage of Solovki's history would appear to confirm my thesis that the exhibition's objective was to show exceptional people – in this case, the prisoners – and their activities under camp conditions. The greater part of the exhibition was devoted to SLON's first period of operation, when some of the prisoners were able to continue their academic work and undertake research. In this period, several newspapers and magazines were being published in Solovki, including *Novyye Solovki* and *Solovetskiye Ostrova*. Some numbers of these newspapers could be viewed at the exhibition. There was even an active Solovetsky Society for Local Lore, which was involved in research into local fauna and flora. Its findings were published in local history booklets (this periodical could also be found amongst the exhibits). Solovki also boasted functioning theatres and a museum at which icons from the monastery and objects associated with life before the Revolution were displayed.

However, only a small part of the exhibition (two panels) was devoted to the physical labour of those prisoners responsible for forest felling and turf extraction or work conditions, malnutrition among convicts and the labour undertaken by women. In addition, the entire narrative was supplemented by propaganda photographs taken by members of the SLON administration,[32] which did in fact give an impression of the primitive work conditions, yet failed to provide confirmation of the crushing brutality of such work. Likewise, the second period of SLON's history, by which I mean the early thirties, when living conditions in Solovki drastically worsened and the theatres, newspapers and the Solovetsky Society for Local Lore were all disbanded, was treated very briefly, even in token fashion. The final stage of the Islands' Gulag history, when, in 1937, the lager was closed down and converted into the Solovetsky Special Purpose Prison was very briefly presented.

The manner in which these topics were selected and presented appears somewhat puzzling, especially when it is taken into account that the exhibition's original aim was meant to 'reinstate the historical truth about the mass repressions of the twenties and thirties'. In fact, apart from the information below the names of ex-prisoners, from which it could be discovered that a particular person died in Solovki or was executed by firing squad in 1937, the other dark episodes in SLON's history were hardly presented at all. The extensive treatment afforded to the history of the Local History Society, theatres and newspapers, showing their development and importance, hindered comprehension of what the repressions actually entailed even more. This therefore begs the question of how the idea for such a topic selection arose.

A response to this can be found in the museum's archives, which indicate that certain topics associated with SLON's history were developed and presented during classes offered by the museum or explained further by guides during tours. This was the case from 1967, when the museum started functioning. A very interesting picture emerges of the first attempts to collect camp stories from the recollections of Nikolay Varakhin, who was working in 1969 as a guide in Solovki. Varakhin recalls that he was in fact barred from speaking about the Islands' camp history, but this was no easy task, because, 'traces [of this history] were evident at every turn, particularly in Bolshoy Solovetsky – crumbling barracks, barred windows . . .' (Chebanyuk 1990a). Tourists also asked many questions. For this reason, following the tour, the guides used to invite people who were interested to an extra gathering, at which they told SLON's history to a smaller audience. As Varakhin writes: 'in their company, one could not but tell the truth, especially as there were many residents of Leningrad among the visitors whose family members had served their sentences in Solovki' (Chebanyuk 1990a).

Varakhin also recalls that a member of the museum's research staff, Evgeny Abramov, was corresponding with a Russian leader of the Socialist Revolutionary Party of the post-revolutionary period who was a former SLON prisoner, Ekaterina Olitskaya (1971). Other ex-prisoners visited the Islands in person. In 1968, as Varakhin notes, Likhachev came to Solovki to tell museum staff the lager's history (Chebanyuk 1990a). Varakhin was not offered a permanent position at the museum and had to seek alternative employment. In the end, he left the Islands. He writes that two other members of the museum's staff, including Evgeny Abramov, who had been corresponding with the former Solovki camp prisoner, left Solovki a year later. The incumbent director of the museum was, by then, Ludmila Lopatkina, who successfully oversaw the organization of the SLON exhibition in 1989.

During the period Varakhin was describing, the period of de-Stalinization prompted by the publication of Khrushchev's secret report was drawing to a close and gradually began to be suppressed as the USSR entered the Brezhnev era (Malia 1998: 351–77). Nevertheless, during the wave of revelation provoked by the discovery of the true extent of Stalin's crimes, it became possible for the first time to share experiences, albeit not on the same scale as was the case in 1989. Yet the circumstances described by Varakhin demonstrated that there was a need – and the opportunity existed – to exchange ideas at the time. This process was, however, stifled from above to such an extent that Alexander Etkind, an expert on Gulag memory, calls this period 'the repression of repressions', a time when some knowledge came to light, but just as much was hidden and denied (Etkind 2009: 634–35). However, it is worth stressing that Khrushchev's thaw enabled museum staff to both collect interesting material on the Islands' camp history and record information ex-prisoners visiting the Archipelago revealed to them about how SLON functioned.

It is also not the case that from that moment on nothing more was said about the Archipelago's camp past. In a script created in 1969 for a tour of the monastery, a brief mention of SLON can be found, confirming that guides were able to inform visitors at the time about the lager's dates of operation and provide information about the newspapers and magazines that were published there. It also mentions the Solovetsky Society for Local Lore, theatres, museum and Gorky's visit in 1929 to Solovki.[33] Furthermore, in 1971, a museum employee named Litvinov prepared a lecture on Maksim Gorky's stay in Solovki, interspersing his description of the writer's three-day stay in the Islands with extracts from his memoirs.[34] Finally, in 1981, Antonina Melnik compiled several pages of information for guides about the activities of the Solovetsky Society for Local Lore, in which she clarified the society's important contribution to Solovki's 'taming' and the development of science on the Islands.[35]

However, the most interesting document in the museum archives contains information Melnik prepared for guides in 1987 and bears the title: 'The Solovetsky Special Purpose Camp'. When preparing this text, Melnik chiefly relied on local newspapers and magazines from the lager's period of operation. According to the beginning of the text, while the sovkhoz continued to function, the Solovetsky Islands fell into decline, but once the Archipelago was transferred to the camp authorities, the various local companies were not only given a new lease of life, but even began to thrive. Melnik devotes a great deal of space to her description of the local economy's development, discussing the harvesting of the forests, peat extraction, road construction, canal clearing and fox breeding. However, she also mentions the scientific and cultural development manifested in the activities of the local theatres and the Solovetsky Society for Local Lore as well as the publishing of the local press.[36] When preparing her reference material, Melnik mainly collected and systemized what she had discovered in previously published guide materials and texts created by museum staff. However, at the same time, she supplemented this with a great deal of new information on SLON's economic activity. Two years later, Antonina Melnik became the chief curator of the first exhibition in the USSR to be devoted to the Islands' camp history.

When the information for guides prepared in 1987 and the materials for the exhibition in 1989 are compared, it becomes clear what the exhibition's creator had in mind when she stated that the lager's history only really began to be discovered in 1988. This did not mean that its entire history had been unknown before then. However, the way this history was viewed fundamentally changed, with much more emphasis being placed on perceiving 'human beings' in prison, noting their innocence and understanding that the state's actions had been truly oppressive.

Despite this change in the manner of perceiving history as a whole, SLON's cultural and scientific activity could be presented as a positive accomplishment, since these successes were, by then, being attributed to exceptional individuals rather than any action of the state. However, it was not yet possible to present such topics as the economy or physical labour in a simplified, schematic manner, even though the controversial nature of these issues had by then become apparent. This explains why this part of the exhibition, as previously mentioned, only warranted two panels. Much the same applied to Sekirnaya Hill and Golgotha,[37] whose histories had only just been uncovered and so were not yet fully comprehended, at least not enough for them to be described and presented. Consequently, these topics were omitted from the exhibition.

The *Solovetsky Special Purpose Camp 1923–1939* exhibition, both in its selection of materials and the manner in which they were presented, perfectly conveyed the atmosphere of the time when it was created. This was not only evident from the decision to accentuate the personal histories of prisoners as people while only showing selected elements of the history as a whole and omitting problematic issues, but also in the exhibition's actual construction. The inner and outer walls on which the entire history was related not only alluded to the times when SLON was a reality, but simultaneously urged viewers to privately examine their own knowledge and faith in history. The exhibition therefore had a great deal more to say about social ideas that were prevalent in 1989 than the history itself.[38] This was even more the case because the hard history revealed in documentary sources was essentially not included in the exhibition. It should therefore come as no surprise that museum staff decided later to make changes to the exhibition.

The Memory Project Created by the Museum in a Former Camp Barrack

The main criticisms levelled at the old exhibition were that it contained nowhere near enough written documents, focused on selected human interest stories and presented SLON's history in selective and unrepresentative fashion. Over the course of a few years, museum staff (mainly Olga Bochkareva) collected documents containing previously unknown facts from the history of the Solovki lager. Some of them demystified some of the ideas and legends that had built up around SLON's history. It was these documents that formed the basis of a new exhibition opened in 2010 that aimed to show the functioning system (Bochkareva 2011). As Bochkareva had stressed in 2007:

> Documents form the basis of historical reality. The creation of the history of an event cannot be based on recollections alone. If there are no documents, anything can be claimed at will . . . Different people, different ways of thinking, different educational backgrounds, different situations; everyone was interpreting things in their own way. The history of the camps should be shaped on the basis of documents alone . . . only then is it real history. [07_OB]

Perception of the exhibition content was also supposedly aided by an exhibition arrangement that constructed a suitable atmosphere and appealed to the viewer's emotions. All the rooms imitated different aspects of the past reality by employing elements typically associated with each one; for example, the part of the exhibition telling the history of the lager contained an interrogation table and wooden floor and the section devoted to the construction of the White Sea Canal featured wooden scaffolding. SLON's history was therefore discovered through the harmonization of intellectual cognition by the emotions.[39]

The new project therefore proposed a manner of presenting SLON's history that was different from that implemented by the old exhibition, in that it arose from different assumptions and had different aims. The previous exhibition had mainly been based on memory and social imagination. It is comparable to early museum collections, which, as Cameron (1971: 15–16) stresses, were authentic in the sense that they were showing how specific individuals perceived and created a vision of the surrounding reality. The old exhibition had created its message in like fashion, since people were shown in prisons serving their sentences in the Islands. The main concern here was to ensure that viewers could identify with the protagonists of the presented narrative, while simultaneously perceiving their own fates in those of the prisoners, since they had all been ultimately cheated by the Soviet system.

As Cameron (1971) points out, with time, private collections became more democratized, and museums were increasingly eager to collect exhibits of various kinds in order that they may be interpreted for the purposes of public education, enlightenment and recreation. This also happened in the case of the Solovetsky Museum. The new exhibition was meant to present scientific facts garnered from historical analyses. It was certainly planned so as to be open to viewers and help them learn the history, yet it was also meant in itself to constitute a very meaningful interpretation of the past (compare Macdonald 1998: 1–24).

The first exhibition was first and foremost meant to create a kind of imagined community (Anderson 1983) uniting former repressed persons and a contemporary generation who had been living for years in ignorance of the Soviet system's crimes. However – as Cesar Graña points out – the 'past is the past' and belongs to the past, so the manner in which it is discerned today depends on socially, culturally and historically shaped perception (1971: 106–7). This had been changing over the preceding years, so the exhibition also had to change, legitimizing its message by becoming more scientific.

Nonetheless, the conception for the new exhibition was strongly influenced by the past way of thinking. Above all, the conception for its spatial form appears to have drawn from the same sources. Although the new exhibition employed many modern exhibition techniques unknown in 1989, both of the spatial designs made use of similar components of the camp reality. In both cases, the imitation of a camp's spatial layout was meant to aid perception of the presented content. While a title was being chosen for the new exhibition, allusion was made to its predecessor, which influenced the conception's final shape. The initial proposal was *SLON – People and Fate*. This was followed by *Solovki: Russia's Golgotha* and finally, the adopted name – *The Solovetsky Lagers and Prison '1920–1939'*. However, the link between the two exhibitions was most evident in the role that their organizers attempted to confer on both by designing them as a kind of *forum*, as defined by Cameron (1971). Although the new exhibition was much more firmly underpinned by scientific authority, provoking the sensation of a temple imposing its own interpretation on the viewer, it is its spatial arrangement and interactive design elements that conclusively show that its primary aim was to draw viewers into a dialogue, inviting them to reflect on the past.

When the messages communicated by the two exhibitions are investigated, it is clear that the museum's memory project fundamentally changed over the twenty years that separated their respective creation. It transitioned from a hot memory (Müller 2016: 64–65, cf. Maier 2000) project drawing from certificates, materials and information acquired from witnesses to a project based on historical documents that aimed to reconstruct history, transmit historical knowledge and examine the myths that arose during the carnival of memory period. The meaning the curators attached to materials like certificates or documents as well as their mode of argument and awareness of the need to favour some presentations over others all indicate that the museum's memory project was largely shaped by the social expectations of its viewers. The design for the 1989 exhibition was informed by a need to become acquainted with human stories, but twenty years later – as is clear from the questions asked by those taking part in the Solovetsky Monastery tour – visitors were much keener on learning the facts.

The museum's memory project is apparently very important for two reasons. Firstly, it is created by people living in the Islands, hence expresses the manner in which the islanders perceive and treat the Archipelago's camp history. Secondly, it is visited by groups of tourists who travel to Solovki and develop their knowledge of SLON on the basis of the information they obtain there. However, some context should be provided at this point. Presenting the history of the Islands' camps is only one small part of the museum's activities. This institution actually offers several permanent and temporary exhibitions as well as a wide range of tours of the Archipelago, from nature and culture tours to history tours. What is more, as far back as 1989, the director of the museum, Ludmila Lopatkina, stressed in an interview given to Olga Slobozhan that SLON's history is a minor episode in the Islands' history and that is how it should remain (Slobozhan 1990). Such a way of thinking about the Archipelago's past is also relevant today.

After the abbot of Solovetsky Monastery, archimandrite Porfiry (Shutov), became director of the museum, the manner in which the Archipelago's camp history was perceived fundamentally changed. Currently, the main narrative of the repressions is an exhibition, promoted by the museum and prepared by the monastery, titled *Solovki . . . Golgotha and Resurrection. Solovets Heritage in Russia's Past, Present and Future*. From 2010, this exhibition toured various Russian cities, like the first Solovetsky exhibition had,[40] acquainting viewers with the Archipelago's history. However, the narrative it presents is not exclusively devoted to the repressions. Instead, the history of SLON has been incorporated into the narrative 'of the five-century history of the development of the Solovetsky Monastery's unique spiritual and cultural heritage from the fifteenth to the nineteenth centuries, its tragic fate over the twentieth century and its reawakening in modern times'.[41] Porfiry (Shutov) has stressed the monastery – like the museum, which he now, as the monastery's abbot, manages – aims to 'revive what we call Solovets civilization' (*Solovetski Vestnik*, [3(79)] 2012: 6).

The Memorial Society's Memory Project – The Solovetsky Islands as a Basis for Remembering the Gulag

> It is actually [the need for] work within this sphere that led to Memorial being founded – as an organization whose mission is to bring Russia out from the world of the Gulag, which it continues to inhabit today, whose language it speaks, norms it lives by and values it adopts. (Ioffe 2002a: 113)

If Russia was to be brought 'out from the world of the Gulag', various actions needed to be taken. The Memorial Society was therefore involved from the beginning of its existence in increasing public awareness and providing material assistance to ex-prisoners. In fact, it was both a human rights social movement and a political organization that sought to influence the authorities (Adler 1993, 2002: 239–67; Smith 1996). Immediately after its foundation in 1987, Memorial was already planning to erect a memorial in Moscow to victims of Soviet terror, and its activities memorializing the era of Soviet repressions became a very important element of its work, enshrined in its statute.[42]

The history of SLON and Solovki itself as a memory space occupied an important place in Memorial's field of interest almost from the very beginning. As the Society began to develop and assume its present shape, Memorial activists undertook the first historical research in an attempt to explain the 'riddles' in SLON's history and initiated the first commemorative activities. In 1989, they undertook field research at Solovki, and then cooperated with the museum on the organization of the first Days of Remembrance. They helped to programme this ritual while also participating in the process of ascribing meanings to it. Later on, they undertook further field trips, managing to find sites important to the history of the camps, which they incorporated into their own memory project. This is how Memorial's memory infrastructure came into being (Mitzer 1992).

I considered Memorial's Solovetsky Island camp history memory project from the perspective of the Islands themselves, focusing on the kind of narrative they were being incorporated into and the meaning that was being ascribed to them. I not only examined the content and meanings concealed within individual memory markers and rituals, but also attempted to describe the semantic network they comprise. By doing so, I hoped to establish the fundamental features of Memorial's memory infrastructure. I also employed, as a basic point of reference, the museum and Orthodox memory projects, hoping to show the similarities and differences between these approaches. This was more important for me than seeking to contextualize Memorial's activities related to SLON's history by contrasting them with the Society's work as a whole. My description of this memory project therefore focuses on a few selected activities, namely those that appeared to be the most interesting and most capable of clearly illustrating this project's distinctive features.

The Origins of the Infrastructure: The Solovetsky Stones

When the idea arose in 1987 to erect a memorial in Moscow to the victims of Soviet repressions, the form it would take and a suitable location for it were not immediately established (Smith 1996: 153–60). It is true that it was initially hoped that it would stand in front of the Lubyanka building, but the decision to erect a boulder from Solovki was in fact somewhat dictated by chance. Nonetheless, it was the kind of chance event that not only acquires meaning over time, but also starts to influence any other actions that are undertaken.

There is no doubt that the visual form of the future monument was very important, so the decision was made to organize a competition (Smith 1996).[43] However, building a monument required time and money. A number of procedural problems also surfaced. It was therefore decided that a so-called 'temporary memory marker' would be erected, the primary objective being to start honouring the memory of ex-prisoners as quickly as possible.

The notion of erecting a rock from Solovki as a memorial to victims of the political repressions was conceived by members of the Sovest Association in Arkhangelsk, an organization affiliated to Memorial. As mentioned by Mikhail Butorin, who was working for Sovest at the time, when some Memorial Society activists in Moscow discovered that an expedition to Solovki was being planned, they asked those that were going on it to choose a boulder from Solovki that could serve as a 'temporary memory marker' for them as well (Butorin 2000). Both monuments were unveiled on the same day – 30 October 1990. The selection of this date was by no means coincidental, for since 1974 it had been functioning in the USSR as Political Prisoner Day, a public holiday that could be observed officially for the first time in 1990. Undoubtedly, its rebranding, in 1991, as the Day of Remembrance for Victims of Political Repressions, was not exactly to the liking of the Memorial Society's membership.[44] Nevertheless, the event that took place in front of Lubyanka in 1990 was immensely significant both symbolically and politically. Effectively, it lifted Gulag memory out of the samizdat underground, depositing it in public space.

The Solovetsky stone played an important role not only as a memory marker around which gatherings could take place and memory rituals be performed, thus marking a transition from the unofficial to the official sphere, but also as a material participant in real historical events. This was explicitly expressed in the inscription on the plinth supporting the stone: 'This stone was brought [here] by the Memorial Society from the Solovetsky special purpose camp and erected to honour the memory of victims of the totalitarian regime'.[45] A link was therefore created between the Memorial Society, SLON and Solovetsky in their respective roles as memory actor, real historical event and memory marker.

Solovetsky boulders currently serve as memorials to victims of political repressions in three cities within the Russian Federation: in Arkhangelsk, at the intersection of Gagarin Street and Obvodny Prospect, on St Petersburg's Troitskaya Square, and in front of Moscow's Lubyanka building. In Moscow, there is one more, by the Memorial Society's central offices on Maly Karetny Pereulok Street, which often serves as a focal point for the civil protests and rallies they organize.[46] One final Solovetsky stone devoted to victims of the repressions – a memorial to SLON prisoners – has stood in Solovki since 1989. These stones together comprise a semantic network of memory markers that are not only interlinked through their provenance, but by the meaning conferred on them by the Memorial Society.

The Memorial Society grew out of the dissident movement, yet from the very beginning had no wish to be limited to the role of a 'combative organization' (Ioffe

2002a: 112). Instead, it intended, by naming and defining long term problems, to act in the future interest. It therefore placed great emphasis on the need to create a language suited to describing the past. Such a language would certainly enable repressed persons to be given their due honour, but its primary purpose was actually to describe the essence of this experience and thereby form the basis for the construction of the civil society of the future (*Uralski rabochi,* 29 October 2005). It was very important because as the Polish memory sociologist Barbara Szacka (2000: 18) writes: 'the transformation within social memory of past figures and events into symbols of attitudes and values creates a symbolic language within a group that becomes one of this group's core characteristics, and the ability to use this language makes an individual a rightful member of this group'. Crucially, the existence of such a language strengthens group ties and provides identification markers that enable group members to be differentiated from outsiders. Consequently, Memorial always used to accentuate the importance of the dates and symbols it was employing. Ultimately, these were meant to comprise a secular collection of days of remembrance and symbols that could be drawn on by a new civil society constructed upon worked-through Gulag history. This not only explains why the Lubyanka Solovetsky stone was unveiled on 30 October, the USSR's Political Prisoner Day, but also the monument's neutral form.

When, in 1990, two stones were transported from Solovki to be erected in Lubyanka and in Arkhangelsk, they were meant to serve as a universal memory marker that would never become a hotbed of conflict based on national and religious differences.[47] And this was also how they were generally perceived. Information in the press on the unveiling of the monuments and the gatherings around them over the next few years confirms that the monuments' form failed to provoke any heated misunderstandings. Memorial's other memory projects were motivated by similar aims.[48]

At the same time, Memorial activists often wish to use particular memory projects to communicate meaningful modern content and ideas. The Solovetsky stones exemplify this process. They do more than commemorate the innocent victims of repression, since they also symbolize their creators' struggle against, and opposition to, a state that strives to restrict human rights. As this struggle has intensified along with changes in the political situation in the Russian Federation, Memorial activists have increasingly used the areas around the Lubyanka stone and small stone in front of their main offices as a space for public expressions of opposition. However, this complex conception is most fully realized on Troitskaya Square, at the site of St Petersburg's Solovetsky stone.

The decision to construct a memorial on Troitskaya Square to victims of political repressions had been made by 1990, and a cornerstone for the new monument was even set in place. However, it was not unveiled until September 2002 – under completely new conditions, both political (the USSR had been supplanted by the Russian Federation) and social (Gulag memory was no longer such a hot topic or such an important part of everyday Russian life). The Memorial Society had also changed. It was now a highly developed organization with clearly defined goals and tasks, which it was implementing with consistency. Furthermore, Gulag memory had materialized in visual form, as evidenced by the many diverse monuments and memory markers that had been erected over the previous twelve years in various cities within the Russian Federation. However, the Memorial chapter in St Petersburg was not seeking a new form for the monument, and simply decided to model it on a classic 'Memorial' memory marker. The St Petersburg stone therefore not only joined the ranks of the other Solovetsky stones scattered across the European part of the Russian Federation, becoming the final element in Memorial's secular memory infrastructure, but also expressed this infrastructure to the full through its very form.

The Solovetsky Stone in St Petersburg

The elements that construct the meaning of a Solovetsky stone are its provenance, location, inscriptions and the history of the monument's erection (Figure 1.3). I shall start with this final element, which at first sight may appear to have little connection with a monument's meaning, yet fulfils an important function in the memory projects Memorial prepares. Memorial not only confers meaning on the projects it creates, but also on the actual process that gives rise to the projects. The story of a given project's creation is not only a legitimization of Memorial's activity, but also a kind of

Figure 1.3. The Solovetsky stone on St Petersburg's Troitskaya Square. Erected on the initiative of the St Petersburg chapter of the Memorial Society in 2002. Photo by author.

secular parable explaining how Russia's continuous 'existence in the Gulag' is manifested in the here and now. Thus, when it comes to Memorial's memory projects, although comparatively distant historical events (from when the Gulag still functioned) retain their significance, more recent history (associated with events accompanying the erection of a given memory project) is often just as important. It is generally easier to communicate content based on more recent history, since it is related to people and circumstances that are more familiar to everyone and therefore leaves a stronger emotional imprint. Consequently, stories of how a given project came into being both complete and supplement its meaning while also making a crucial contribution to the building of a community of Memorial members. The story of the unveiling of the Solovetsky stone on Troitskaya Square perfectly exemplifies this process.[49]

At the end of July 2002, the funding became available to erect the monument, so Memorial decided to act swiftly and send an expedition to Solovki to collect a boulder. This was no simple task. A stone had to be found that would not only meet the artistic but also the ideological requirements. As Flige says:

> It was important to us where the stone came from . . . Sekirnaya Hill is a symbol of sacrifice. It is in itself like a cemetery hill . . . Golgotha Hill also has a narrow and precise meaning. Savvatyevo has multiple meanings . . . [these relate to] the people who died [there] and the political opposition, because from 1923 to 1925, this place was called a 'political refuge'. It was there that genuine opponents of the Soviet authorities were held, there that the toughest hunger strikes took place during the struggle against the regime, so the symbolism is complex. That's why the stone comes from there. [10_IF][50]

After a stone weighing several tonnes had been selected, it had to be transported to the centre of St Petersburg and erected at the designated site. Flige recalls: 'We erected the memorial and quietly departed . . . That was 20 August, and the unveiling was on 4 September.[51] It was impossible to unveil it as a monument because it was not registered, had not received the Governor's approval, and so on' [10_IF].

Next, Memorial encouraged ex-prisoners to send an official letter to the municipal authorities, informing them that they had been waiting twelve years for the city to erect a monument. Not wishing to wait any longer, they had decided to fund such a project themselves and present the monument on Troitskaya Square 'to the city on its three-hundredth anniversary as a gift from political prisoners'. Memorial took such a measure on the assumption that the authorities would not be able to order the removal of a gift from prisoners.

At the same time, a problem arose over the choice of words on the inscription to be placed beneath the stone. As Flige explains, most such memorials contain the words 'To the Victims of Political Repressions', but it was important for them that not only victims, but also oppositionists, be commemorated. The memorial should be dedicated to all repressed persons, and not just those who lived in St Petersburg. Consequently, three inscriptions were eventually chosen: 'To Victims of the Communist Terror', 'To Freedom Fighters' and 'To Gulag prisoners'. The fourth side of the plinth contained an extract from Anna Akhmatova's *Requiem*: 'I'd like to name them all by name . . .'.[52] Each inscription precisely defines what was of most concern to Memorial.[53]

The project initiators tried to envisage potential complications. Flige claims: 'We had already had one case when we were forced to re-engrave a plaque that had "Victims of the Communist Terror" written on it, [and replace it with] another inscription, because the approval [required] for its erection was denied'. The letters were therefore printed on a plotter and stuck to the plaque. Next, each letter was slowly peeled away and engraved on the plaque. This procedure was repeated for each letter until the inscription was completed. Their plan was to first look out for any negative reaction. If no one told them to change the name, they would keep it. However, if someone told them to change something, this could be done quickly and at little cost. The day after the monument's 'public unveiling', Memorial activists approached the city's architect-in-chief, requesting that the memorial be granted official approval and all the necessary documents be issued. They assumed that if any problems arose with the inscriptions they had placed on the monument, the 'peeling and engraving letter game' would enable them to quickly make any necessary changes. However, this turned out to be unnecessary, as they managed to obtain the required approval in December.

The story of the Solovetsky stone's unveiling incorporates two important motifs: the first being the struggle to unveil the memorial, and the second, the construction of a community united by its enthusiasm for Gulag commemoration activities. Both motifs seem to be very important ideas that Memorial wishes to promote via its projects. At the same time, both motifs heavily draw on the history of the dissident movement and ideas associated with its activities. Memorial's activities therefore constitute a kind of continuation of the dissident movement's struggles, thus widening their historical scope, both temporally and semantically. This story is also indicative of the meanings Memorial bestows on plinth inscriptions and a monument's site of origin.

Three sides of the memorial list the three basic categories of repressed person: Gulag prisoners, victims of communist terror and freedom fighters. By contrast, the extract from Akhmatova's poem ('I'd like to name them all by name') lends a human dimension to these categories, while showing that the imposition of three general categories to cover all eventualities, rather than being a symptom of linguistic restraint, was actually caused by a tragic ignorance that will never be remedied. The silence will last forever, like the stone memorial commemorating these people. At the same time, the monument indicates what caused this tragic situation and the loss of these people's names, and it turns out the guilty party was ideology – communist ideology.

The three categories of repressed persons would appear to have equal status, yet the fact that the monument originated in Savvatyevo on Bolshoy Solovetsky bestows special meaning on one of these group – the freedom fighters. In 1923, Savvatyevo was a penal institution for political prisoners (social democrats, social revolutionaries and Mensheviks).[54] Political prisoners possessed special rights in tsarist times and they wanted to force the Bolshevik authorities to honour these as well. However, the Bolsheviks aspired to deprive them of their special status by slowly restricting their freedoms. Psychological warfare ensued between the two groups. On 19 December 1923, some camp guards opened fire without warning on some prisoners who were in the barrack square. Six people died. A year and a half later, all the political prisoners were transported from Solovki to various lagers scattered around the USSR (Applebaum 2003: 56–58).

For members of the Memorial Society, this is a very meaningful event, constituting a turning point in the history of the political repressions in the USSR. The special status political prisoners enjoyed in tsarist times was abolished. A new stage of repressions began during which 'politicals' found themselves on the lowest rung of the prisoner hierarchy. This was also important because, as Memorial activists explain, 'the victims were everywhere, but the opposition up to that point had only been here' [11_IF]. This is precisely why the monument's provenance became so very important.

However, Savvatyevo's history is not interpreted in the same manner by everyone. When I spoke with Olga Bochkareva from Solovetsky Museum about the meanings Memorial activists ascribe to Savvatyevo, she expressed her surprise. First and foremost, the history of the prison for political prisoners comprises only a small part of SLON's history as a whole, let alone the history of the Gulag. The politicals incarcerated at Savvatyevo mainly represented other political parties – like the social revolutionaries and Menshiviks – that took part in the 1917 revolution. They continued to be held under tsarist legislation. As Tołczyk (2009: 85) writes:

> they were being treated in a privileged manner. In the Solovetsky lager, for example, they were living separately in conditions that were much more favourable than those facing the rest of the prisoners. They were being fed better and were not forced to work . . . The leftist political prisoners were behaving much like they had in the tsarist prisons, that is, they were declaring protests, loudly asserting their rights and organizing hunger strikes.

As Olga Bochkareva points out, they were fighting to preserve their own privileged status rather than for the rights of all [07_OB]. The line of argument they employed to justify their claims is clearly problematic, especially when the Savvatyevo prisoners are labelled as 'heroes'.

What is more, the memorial's location on Troitskaya Square seems to reinforce this ambivalence. The stone was erected across from the *Dom Politkatorzhan* (the House of Political Prisoners), a building that was erected in 1929–33 as a reward for former tsarist prisoners who participated in the October Revolution. During the

Great Terror, most of them were executed by firing squad. The monument's hidden meaning, namely the implication that 'the revolution devoured its own', is also reinforced by the fact that the monument is sited on the opposite bank of the River Neva, symmetrical to the Field of Mars memorial park, in which the remains of the heroes who participated in the October Revolution lie at rest. Both monuments are dedicated to the dead, but the Field of Mars is dedicated to those who died while creating the new system, and the Solovetsky stone, to those who helped to create the system but later fell victim to it. The semantic dialogue between these two monuments is brought about by the Neva's physical location.

When Memorial both employed the Savvatyevo motif and erected the monument on Troitskaya Square, it appears not to have noticed the aforementioned ambivalence and in fact evokes a completely different meaning for these two sites. Savvatyevo is both a site and symbol of the 'war between the Russian authorities and the nation' (Ioffe 2002a: 106–7).[55] This history shows the continuation of the tsarist *samoderzhaviye* political system, which relied on autocratic rule and the state's destruction of its own people on the grounds of their supposed disloyalty. The memorial's siting on Troitskaya Square conveys the message that this problem applies not only to the Bolshevik authorities, but to the whole of Russian history. Troitskaya Square is the oldest square in the city as well as its first administrative centre. Its creation also contributed to the construction of the legend of Peter I as a hero who had called the new city into life with a single gesture, a legend that extolled his 'power' without considering the price citizens had to pay to facilitate its constitution.

For Memorial, Savvatyevo is not only an important component of memory of SLON, but also that of the entire Gulag. Savvatyevo is being associated with concrete historical events that took place there. The memorial was erected to honour the memory of Gulag prisoners, yet the underlying idea behind it appears to have more universal appeal, invoking the whole of Russian history. This does not, however, mean that Savvatyevo is being instrumentalized, because only by remembering this and other concrete events can change be given a chance. As Ioffe writes: 'The only thing we can do is to remember and tell the government that we remember this, always have and always will – these victims, this blood, these events. That is the only thing we can do to ensure that we and this government we have gifted ourselves change at least a little' (Ioffe 2002a: 107).

The Solovetsky stone standing on Troitskaya Square in St Petersburg seems to incorporate all these meanings. The semantic network concealed within the boulder is certainly not comprehended by passing pedestrians and mothers walking across the square with their children on sunny days. An explanation would need to be sought from a member of Memorial, since no attempt has been made to offer one on any of the monument's plaques. Yet the Solovetsky stone on Troitskaya Square stands as an invitation to random passers-by, creating the possibility that they may feel a sudden desire to discover its meaning and enter into the narrative it invokes. Marcin Zaborski (2006: 317) describes this phenomenon as follows: 'The stone is a kind of archetype, a means of expression, a symbol denoting the consolidation of memory . . . the stone's interpretative richness . . . clearly determines the scope of its use in the culture of remembrance, defining its place in it'. A similar function is performed by the other Solovetsky stones, located in Moscow and Arkhangelsk. When combined with the Solovetsky Archipelago, they create a kind of semantic network designed by Memorial. An important role in this infrastructure is played by a place equidistant between St Petersburg and the Solovestsky – Sandarmokh Cemetery.

Sandarmokh: A Story of Discovery

When the first Days of Remembrance took place in 1989 in Solovki, the participants included a dozen or so children of SLON prisoners who had been executed by firing squad in 1937. When they began talking to each other, it turned out that the documents confirming the death of their loved ones contained dates that were very close to each other, and also that all of them had been issued by the same governing body. This intriguing fact inspired members of the Society to begin collecting, from that time onwards, all the documents and memoirs they could in the hope that it would enable them to establish what happened at Solovki in the autumn of 1937.

As Irina Flige[56] recalls, until 1993, Memorial activists suspected that the executions had taken place in Solovki itself. However, many memoirs relating the events of 1937 contain the information that prisoners were transported from Solovki. One Ukrainian writes that it was in fact Ukrainians who were being transported, because almost all his compatriots were deported from the Islands. Memoirs written by others contained some dates and names of some of those who were deported. Subsequently, these names did not appear in any memoirs from any other camps in Karelia, Kolyma or Norilsk. In the 'world of the Gulag', prisoners transferred to other camps passed on information about people in the camps they had left, which is how prisoners in the new camp found out where their friends and family were. When information about condemned prisoners disappeared, that meant there had been a so-called 'transport to the firing squad' *(rasstrelny etap)* [10_IF].

The search was given added impetus by the discovery of a batch of *troika*[57] rulings containing the names of 1825 prisoners, which was discovered in an archive in Arkhangelsk. In particular, this document not only enabled the discovery of names, but also some dates: 27 October, 1, 2 and 3 November, 8 December and a final entry indicating a date around 17 February. Attached to the records of proceedings was a document that stated that an NKVD functionary named Matveyev had been dispatched on state business to carry out the order. Establishing Matveyev's identity and the role he played in Solovki would clearly greatly assist further work on the reconstruction of the events that had taken place on the Islands in autumn 1937.[58]

The next clue to solving this mystery was a book published around this time in Leningrad (*Na palachakh krovi net: Tipy i nravy Leningradskogo NKVD* (Lukin 1996)) that related the biographies of various NKVD functionaries. These included a Captain Matveyev and the information that he was originally rewarded for efficiently carrying out his duties only to be later arrested and executed by firing squad. Unfortunately, the Leningrad branch of the Federal Security Service, or FSB, did not have his files. However, a Memorial member from Petrozavodsk came across a document relating to him by chance while working in the local archive on the history of the White Sea Canal. He found the files from a large trial at which several functionaries were tried for 'overstepping their official duties', in this case, harassing prisoners. Matveyev's name was one of those on the trial list. As Flige explains: 'in 1938, wardens and NKVD functionaries were not tried for harassment. They did not charge them in the fifties and sixties either and [wouldn't] today if they were alive. Something is not right' [10_IF]. When they managed to read the complete records for the case, it turned out that the functionaries had carried out a manhunt in Medvezhyegorsk for *raskonvoirovannye* convicts, namely those that were roaming Medvezhyegorsk territory without documents. Afterwards, they shot them. As Flige explains:

> The times were such that raskonvoirovannye, who roamed freely, were not ordinary prisoners caught up in the regime. They were prisoners who received massive support from somewhere above. Consequently, [the NKVD functionaries] had shot someone they shouldn't have . . . and they really arrested them for this. And once they'd arrested them, they created a beautiful bill of indictment, [stating] that they had been harassing the prisoners. [10_IF]

As soon as the case got underway, the accused began defending themselves by incriminating Matveyev, arguing that when he had arrived from Leningrad he had taught them execution procedures. At that point, Matveyev was himself arrested and his name added to the bill of indictment. The records contain the minutes from Matveyev's hearings, which clarify why the execution procedure was designed as it was rather than differently. Flige explains further:

> Why did this bill of indictment interest us? Firstly, this bill could contain geography, geography [telling us] where this took place. In one of the volumes . . . Matveyev explains the procedure as follows: the place to which he took the Solovetsky zeks out was poorly prepared for executions. This place was inconvenient and on 27 October, on the first day of executions, there was an attempted escape, so the executions were stopped, and up until 1 November, Matveyev was working out a change in procedure. He went on to explain: [The distance] from the place where the zeks were being held to the execution site was 19 kilometres. [10_IF]

On the basis of the information they had received, Memorial activists were therefore able to establish that the execution site was located within a radius of about 19 kilometres of Medvezhyegorsk. Other information contained in the bill enabled further details to be established.

On the basis of a statement given by a driver whose car broke down near the village of Povenets while the prisoners were being transported, the road along which the execution site should be sought was successfully established. In 1997, a search expedition was launched. As Flige recalls:

> on the very first day, we found a swathe of forest with very distinctive depressions . . . We don't carry out full excavations, we carry out a surface excavation. We continue until [we encounter] the first bone. That's all we do. The first bones appear and we stop digging and don't remove anything. After this, we summon the prosecutor. The prosecutor arrives and any further work then proceeds at prosecution level. [10_IF]

Memorial was opposed to an exhumation for two fundamental reasons. First, the site they had managed to discover was not only a site where 1,111 Solovetsky convicts had been executed. Other executions were also meant to have taken place there.[59] This is why, as Flige explains:

> All the pits can be dug up, separate people can be identified from their bones. Experts are capable of doing this . . . [But] we don't know all the names, even [when it comes to] our Solovetsky convicts, we know their surnames, but we don't know which pits are Solovetsky . . . [Furthermore], they have been lying together intertwined for 60 or 70 years. They are peacefully lying like that in the earth, the earth has by now long been mingling with their remains. They are together. In any case, this is their grave. [10_IF]

Memorial marked the pits using wooden stakes, and enclosed the cemetery grounds, taking care to keep a suitable distance from its potential boundary. As Flige explains 'it's always frightening to think that some pit will end up outside' [10_IF]. Afterwards, the forestry commission and highway authorities had to be persuaded to hand over the part of the forest containing the cemetery and grant permission for an access road to be built.[60] Flige recalls that when the foresters and highway authorities arrived, they were devastated: '[Their] reaction was close to shock: *We were coming here, collecting mushrooms, yet this was here [all the time]*'. According to Flige: '[They moved the enclosure out by] an extra 5 or 10 metres from each stake, becoming even more scared. This is very important, they really tried hard . . . *If we leave any land out, someone will end up outside the cemetery*' [10_IF].[61]

The Karelian regional authorities were also in shock. This was the first time that mass execution burial sites had been found in their region. They therefore appealed to Memorial to help them commemorate this site. As it was freshly discovered, it could be characterized as a 'shared memory' site. Memorial wanted to see confessional markers erected away from the pits, rather than beside them, and their wishes were respected: 'all the confessional markers stand on land where there were no burials; they stand on empty plots' [10_IF]. However, the pits were supposed to be marked with a universal marker that did not trigger any associations yet clearly indicated that there were mass graves there. The main objective was to ensure that the site was clearly visible, so that no one would walk past it. The artist whom Memorial brought to the site adapted the wooden stakes driven into the pits to create markers for them that assumed the form of wooden stakes surmounted by sloping rooves resembling nesting boxes (Figure 1.4).

Sandarmokh immediately became one of the most important sites of memory not only locally, but internationally. This was due to the 1,111 Solovetsky convicts shot there. As Flige explains: 'the Solovetsky transport contained the Soviet Union's international elite . . . these were people they were remembering and looking for all the time' [10_IF]. The victims of the Sandarmokh firing squads included three hundred members of the Ukrainian intellectual elite, the last king of the Moscow region's Romani community, bishops and many other famous people (Krikhtova 2014). Consequently, the Day of Remembrance is attended annually by official delegations from many consulates as well as representatives of various faiths.

Figure 1.4. Sandarmokh Cemetery. Visible in the photograph are the wooden stakes marking the pits of mass graves. Photo by author.

The story of Sandarmokh's discovery was worth describing because it says a great deal about the distinctive nature of Gulag history, which is very often discovered through the luck and determination of historian-detectives rather than through thorough research in the archives. What is more, this method of discovering sites of memory is the typical working method not only of Memorial but also of anyone else involved in this discipline. The story of Sandarmokh's discovery also not only shows how much time is required to locate some sites – Memorial began looking for Sandarmokh back in 1989, and found it in 1997 – but also how much luck is needed to chance upon materials capable of confirming these discoveries. Such searches are not always successful and many sites will never be found.[62]

History also shows how much energy goes into these searches and how difficult it is to predict what will be found. Memorial was looking for 1,111 Solovetsky convicts, but found a mass execution site containing the bodies of five or six thousand victims shot at different times and under different orders, still mostly unfamiliar to us today.[63] It can also be seen how difficult it is to embark on memorialization work and how quickly action needs to be taken once mass graves have been located, and with what limited resources. This explains why all that can be found at many sites are simple, straightforward markers, often the outcome of some chance event or random association, such as an artist seeing stakes and being reminded of nesting boxes.

This story also confirms that the commemoration process is very difficult for Memorial. The form taken by the monuments they erect is often not determined by factors like choice of material and artistic inventiveness, but rather by the need to conform to the ideological assumptions of a given project's sponsors, assumptions that are supposed to provoke appropriate reactions from the community. Ultimately, I think this story makes it easier to comprehend how important the annual Days of Remembrance are for Memorial's memory infrastructure by showing how closely Sandarmokh is bound up with Solovki and how much work and energy Memorial put into the discovery and preparation of this site.

5 August, Sandarmokh's Day of Remembrance

The first Day of Remembrance at Sandarmokh took place on 27 October, on the sixtieth anniversary of the first executions of prisoners that were on the Solovetsky transport (Merridale 2001: 1–20). However, Memorial felt it was important to somehow combine the remembrance events taking place in Karelia and Solovki. Since it is already cold in both of these places by the end of October, it was decided that the Day of Remembrance in Solovki would take place on 5 August, generally regarded as the first day of the Great Terror's implementation. At the same time, Memorial asked Solovetsky Museum to abandon what was previously an ad hoc system[64] for setting the dates for their Days of Remembrance in Solovki and permanently schedule the event for 6–8 August instead. It would then be taking place immediately after the ceremony at Sandarmokh. The museum consented to this request, in effect agreeing for the Days of Remembrance in both places to be merged into a series of consecutive Days of Remembrance. This arrangement held for almost ten years. Some of the people travelling to Sandarmokh continued on the so-called Remembrance Trail to the Solovetsky Islands, where they participated in the local Days of Remembrance. However, in 2015, the museum rescheduled the Days of Remembrance it organized to 13–14 July, on the pretext of fulfilling its wish to combine the event with an academic conference it was organizing with the local monastery (*Solovetski Vestnik*, [1(97)] 2015: 6). The following year, the Days of Remembrance at Solovki also took place at a different time (23–25 June).[65] During this period, Memorial activists continued to arrive in the Solovetsky Islands from 6 to 8 August, organizing separate Days of Remembrance for themselves and an accompanying delegation. The museum stopped promoting and inviting guests to this event, so it is now attended by few people apart from these Memorial members. The Days of Remembrance at Sandarmokh have therefore become more important for the Society.

Memorial wanted to create a site of memory without any confessional markers in a previously uninhabited area. This explains why the Society decided to mark the site of the pits with markers resembling nesting boxes rather than crosses. However, over time, the cemetery filled up with a wide variety of memory markers, and these included confessional markers.

When, in 1997, the first Days of Remembrance were organized at Sandarmokh, some of the names of the people who were buried there were printed in local Petrozavodsk newspapers. At this point, members of the families of those who had been murdered began carving the names of their loved ones on the wooden stakes, affixing photographs to them, creating symbolic graves and planting crosses. New stakes also began to be erected on the cemetery's peripheries and at sites beyond the mass graves.

The cemetery grounds also contain some monuments. The first one, which visitors encounter when approaching the cemetery from the main road, was created by Grigory Saltup and contains the inscription: 'People, do not kill each other.' Next, there are two stones containing plaques providing basic information about Sandarmokh. The first plaque contains the words: 'Here, in the wilderness of Sandarmokh, the site of mass executions from 1934 to 1941, over seven thousand innocent people were killed: inhabitants of Karelia, prisoners and special displaced persons of Belbaltlag and convicts from the Solovki prison. Remember us, people! Do not kill each other!' The inscription on the second plaque reads: 'Here, from 27 October to 4 November 1937, 1111 convicts from the Solovki prison were executed by firing squad.' It is flanked by a wooden Orthodox shrine dedicated to St George the Victorious. On a plot at the back of the cemetery, Poles, Ukrainians, Jews and Muslims have erected their own national and religious monuments to commemorate their murdered compatriots and co-believers.

The complexity and multifaceted nature of the past narrative latent within the markers filling the grounds of Sandarmokh Cemetery materializes to its fullest extent during the annual 5 August Day of Remembrance, also the anniversary of the first of the mass arrests that took place in 1937. On this day, the peaceful burial ground is transformed into a genuine spectacle of remembrance.

The ceremonies start in Medvezhyegorsk. A cavalcade of vehicles sets off from the local history museum. They stop by the main road, and the participants walk in a procession of pilgrims towards the cemetery, which is opened by an Orthodox priest. As the group reaches the cemetery, it divides into two sub-groups: an Orthodox funeral procession, which continues to the shrine to participate in a Panikhida memorial service, and another group, composed of all the other participants, which takes part in a secular commemoration ceremony by one of the monuments.[66] This opens with official addresses delivered by foreign delegations, in which consuls from various countries remember their compatriots who were murdered at Sandarmokh or in other places. They also lay wreaths by the monument. After this, speeches are given by representatives of local organizations and museums and Memorial activists. All of these emphasize Sandarmokh's historical importance and the need to preserve the memory of the events that took place during the repressions, both there and throughout the rest of the Soviet Union. Very frequent references are also made to contemporary disputes based on different interpretations of history,[67] an axis of conflict between countries whose citizens take part in the Day of Remembrance. Finally, members of the families of people murdered at Sandarmokh make their voices heard. They movingly speak about the effect the death of a loved one had on their later lives.

Afterwards, the participants separate to visit their 'own' sites of memory, where their private recollections can finally begin. Often, they bring plastic flowers, crosses and food, or even national flags or photographs. These are 'mobile memory markers', which either complement the meanings connoted by the sloping rooves of the stakes marking the pits or develop new semantic motifs. This phase of the ceremony reveals the broad diversity of the modes of commemoration on display and the complexity of the meanings different groups of mourners ascribe to various memory markers.[68]

For the families of the people murdered there, Sandarmokh performs the function of a family cemetery. Most of them have chosen to tend to one of the pits marked by nesting-box structures, treating it like their own site of memory. Plaques containing the names and photographs of deceased loved ones have been nailed to the boxes or surrounding trees. Some people have erected tombstones, creating symbolic graves. It is also noticeable that there is usually only one symbolic grave for each pit, so these are clearly being used to commemorate a single family member (except in cases where a particular family lost more than one family member). It is even more unlikely that a single grave would be used to commemorate people of different faiths or nationalities. Very often, newcomers find all the boxes are taken, so need to erect their own boxes in other parts of the cemetery deeper into the forest.

The rituals performed by these mourning families display the distinguishing features of the Orthodox rites observable in communal cemeteries. Nonetheless, Sandarmokh is no ordinary cemetery and pits marked by boxes on stakes are hardly ordinary graves. This is a mass execution site and the pits contain the bones of many unknown people. Families wishing to turn this site into a 'family cemetery' had to take special action to perform such a transformation. When talking to those responsible for tending to particular graves, extremely intriguing narratives emerge, often revealing a link between the histories of these families and that of the Gulag. Three of the narratives I discovered in this way were so interesting that I would like to cite them.

I heard the first of these in 2006 from an elderly woman. She discovered from a newspaper that her father had been shot there. She travelled to Sandarmokh to find a pit, choosing the one she was standing by when I met her. And it was not chosen by chance. Her father had enjoyed looking through a gap between the trees in a forest at a road in the distance. As the woman approached this particular pit, she knew it was the one – 'her heart told her'. Every year, she came there with her son and his wife. Earlier, when she was still unaware of her father's place of burial, she visited a church in Petrozavodsk. However, once she discovered the site of his execution and that he had been buried there, she had never returned to the church.[69]

Another woman mentioned that she had been unaware of her father's place of burial for many years. He had been arrested in April, but she (my interlocutor) had been born in July. Her mother got married a second time, to a Ukrainian, but – as her daughter was keen to point out – she did not love him as much as her first husband, whose photograph she always kept in a wallet. The woman's father appeared to both her and her mother in a dream, in which he asked that his legs be covered, as he was lying by a road. In the sixties, her father was rehabilitated and her mother received compensation. She died in the eighties, but before she did, she asked her daughter to try to find her father's place of burial. In the nineties, the woman read in a newspaper that her father had been shot at Sandarmokh, so she decided to visit the site. As soon as she arrived, 'her heart told her' that he had been buried in one of the pits by the road. She and her children planted a cross by the pit and she had not dreamed of her father since.

That woman also took a little earth from that pit and buried it by her mother's grave. She then took some earth from her mother's grave, burying it by her father's. She hoped, by doing this, to reunite her parents. When I met her, she was visiting Sandarmokh once a year with her family. During these visits, they laid food on the grave and prayed. They also visited the Ukrainian memorial, because her Ukrainian stepfather died later on the front. Earlier, when they had not known the location of her father's place of burial, they had thought that he had probably been buried somewhere in Petrozavodsk and laid flowers on the road to the cemetery. The woman also mentioned that she was the first to ring the pit with flowers. Other people followed her example, starting to do the same. As she spoke, she showed me various pits and listed the first names and surnames of people who visited those places. She called all of them neighbours.

The last story I wish to cite was told to me by a person who made her own cross for her father's grave. Next, she built a symbolic burial mound and nailed the cross to the nesting box that already stood there. When a group of Finns travelled to Sandarmokh to check whether this was indeed a mass execution site, they confirmed that there were people buried in that particular pit, and that was enough for her. It was of no interest to her whether her father was definitely buried in that grave, or another. She had chosen that pit and was tending to it.

For the relatives of those who were murdered there, Sandarmokh is not only a space where they can reclaim the history of their own families, but also a place where they can gain the peace of mind and sense of closure that mourning rituals can provide. As Italian anthropologist of religion Alfonso Maria di Nola (2006) claims, death always disrupts the existing order, creating a sense of chaos. Mourning rituals of various kinds are therefore performed to restore a sense of order and help the bereaved to cope with their sense of loss. For many years, the relatives of those murdered at Sandarmokh not only had to live in a state of ignorance, unaware of what had happened to their loved ones, but also in a situation of ritual non-closure (Domańska 2006: 161–94). When the body and burial site were missing, mourning rituals could not be performed and the deceased lived on in some world-between-worlds (like the father who appeared in his daughter's and ex-wife's dreams). This explains why these people were using substitute methods to honour the dead. These behaviours are typical of those suffering from 'missing grave syndrome', which is sometimes referred to as mourning 'the homeless dead'. Those affected by this syndrome compensate for not knowing where their loved ones are buried by creating symbolic graves and cemeteries for them (Lifton 1967: 492–94; Young 1993: 7). This issue has been thoroughly researched on the example of Nazi concentration camp survivors (Kugelmass and Boyarin 1998: 31–34). A similar permanent sense of uncertainty[70] arising from lack of knowledge and similar methods of coping with this situation (laying lit candles or flowers by a cemetery) are observable among the families of prisoners murdered at Sandarmokh.

Following the discovery of the mass graves, these people regained their peace of mind and the period of mourning could end and funeral rites be performed. Apart from the official rituals, personal rites drawing from family histories (referring, for example, to the father who liked gaps in forests or the father who said he was lying by a road) proved to be necessary. These made it possible to link the past with the present, while granting communal graves the character of individual family graves.

By contrast, for Poles, Ukrainians, Jews or Muslims, Sandarmokh became a site of memory based on national or religious considerations. This explains why they separated from the main group after the official speeches to lay flowers by their own national confessional markers and used their own religious rites and languages to honour their dead. Until 2014, when the War in Donbass broke out, the Ukrainians were particularly noticeable. They formed the most numerous group and had developed their own rituals over the years they had been participating in the Days of Remembrance. Many Ukrainians came dressed in their national costumes. During the procession from the cars to the cemetery, they carried national flags, which they continued to hold aloft during the official speeches by the memorial. They usually also comprised a single compact group. After the official speeches, they formed their own column and walked together, led by a Ukrainian cleric, to the Ukrainian memorial. First, they attached photographs (identified by name) of Ukrainians from the Solovetsky transport on the trees growing around the monument. Next, a Panikhida memorial service was held, which was followed by speeches and recitals by poets reading their own verses. Everyone participated in a ritual meal for the dead and sang songs together. Next, they took photographs of each other as mementos. The ceremony concluded as they slowly began to make their way to their coaches and cars.

Those participating in the international ceremonies returned on their own to the main road, rather than in a group. At this point, in 2006 and 2007, some people took the opportunity to stop at one of the ordinary market stalls outside the cemetery to refresh themselves or quench their thirst. Some of these stalls also stocked a souvenir of Sandarmokh – a stone emblazoned with a hand-painted cemetery monument. Much like other mass extermination sites, Sandarmokh frequently exhibits the traits of a tourist attraction (Cole 1999: 97–120). When I asked a stallholder if what she had to offer was attracting visitors' interest, she answered that many stones had been sold, but she had been counting on higher sales. The year 2006 was the first that such souvenirs of Sandarmokh could be purchased. The woman had come to the cemetery earlier with the express intention of gathering stones and hand-painting crosses, monuments and a church on them. She also informed me about the visitors' tastes. The Ukrainians usually bought stones depicting the Ukrainian monument, while the Finns preferred stones showing the Polish cross or a traditional Sandarmokh nesting box.

During the two or three hours of ceremonies that take place during Sandarmokh's Day of Remembrance, the site is transformed into a genuinely vibrant semiosphere – a space for the manifestation of various kinds of memory languages and rituals. Sandarmokh Cemetery's distinctive nature can be more fully comprehended by referring to Sławomir Kapralski's analysis of Auschwitz. When investigating Auschwitz as a chronotope of Jewish, Polish and Romani identity, he notes that despite variations in content the identities of these groups do somewhat resemble each other insofar as they feel endangered, threatened with elimination and have a need to defend themselves (Kapralski 2000: 163; 2002). Likewise, in Sandarmokh's case, it would appear that Polish, Russian, Ukrainian and Jewish memory of this site is founded on similar content. Nevertheless, those doing the remembering come from different national and religious groups, so they shape what should be remembered and determine what will be forgotten in their own different ways (Misztal 2007: 385). This knowledge is integrated into differing national narratives. This was particularly evident in 2007 from the content of the official addresses delivered by the delegations from various states. The Poles' speeches were dominated by references to Katyn, while Lithuanians and Latvians tended to focus in their speeches on Stalin's deportations of 1941; the Ukrainians, on the extermination of the Ukrainian nation, and the Russians on the tragedy of the Great Terror.[71] This reflects similarities between the situation prevailing at Sandarmokh and in Auschwitz, where ethnic groups tend to divide into national camps, each offering a different vision of what should be remembered (Kapralski 2000: 142). Much like Auschwitz, Sandarmokh is not a universal space telling of crimes against humanity, even though this was Memorial's original intention. Sandarmokh also does not seem to be a chronotope of the identities of these national groups, because the site does not occupy a prominent place in the consciousness of these states' inhabitants.[72] Nonetheless, it should be recognized as a special space, an annual meeting place for delegations from many states affected by the Soviet repressions as well as a forum for the manifestation of different versions of memory.

When the ceremonies draw to a close, those participating in the Day of Remembrance get into their cars and buses and go their separate ways. Just as suddenly as it sprang into life, Sandarmokh returns to its former state – a peaceful swathe of forests hiding a secret. Over the twelve months leading up to 5 August the following year, when the next Day of Remembrance will bring it to life again, few people will visit Sandarmokh. It would appear that the forceful, intense nature of this site's annual transformation into a site of memory perfectly expresses the distinctive character of Gulag memory, not only on a local, Karelian level, but as it is experienced by the Russian and international community.

The Days of Remembrance in Solovki: 6–8 August

On the evening of the 5 August, after the completion of the Sandarmokh ceremonies, Memorial activists continue their journey, following the Remembrance Trail to the Solovetsky Islands to participate in the ceremonies there. In 2014, the last time the Days of Remembrance were jointly observed by Memorial and the local museum, the programme had hardly changed since 1989. The most important event was the ceremony by the Solovetsky stone, erected at the site where, in 1929, the prisoners accused of being involved in the Kremlin Plot were shot. This is one of the Solovetsky stones forming the Memorial memory infrastructure network. For years, it was the only secular monument on the Islands.

As is the case at Sandarmokh, the ceremonies by the Solovetsky stone commenced with official addresses. The first to speak was the museum director, or someone deputizing for him. The next to deliver speeches were a representative of the Solovetsky local authorities and an invited abbot or other monk appointed for the task from Solovetsky Monastery. Later, representatives of foreign delegations, Memorial members and ex-prisoners were given a chance to speak. Everyone laid wreaths and flowers and lit candles. At the museum's behest, a representative from Solovetsky Monastery led a Panikhida for the dead around a memorial cross opposite the stone. This marked the conclusion of the official part and most people departed at that point. Only a group of Ukrainians remained behind. Dressed in traditional costume and holding Ukrainian flags, they organized their own Panikhida in Ukrainian, led by a Ukrainian clergyman. Afterwards, the Ukrainians followed the Avenue of Remembrance to a memorial cross on a nearby hill, where the Church of the Reverend Onuphrius the Great[73] once stood, to perform another Panikhida there for the dead.[74]

The appearance of the Days of Remembrance changed in 2015, when the museum changed the date of the annual ceremonies it organized to 13–14 July. This change was officially dictated by a wish to combine the Days of Remembrance for Victims of Repressions with a conference jointly organized by the museum and the monastery, titled 'The History of the Country in the Fates of Prisoners of the Solovetsky Camps'. However, as Evgeny Shtorn and Darya Buteyko[75] write, the real reason for the change of dates was to respond to the charge that the 'Days of Remembrance are heavily politicized'. The museum thus decided to distance itself from them.

The Days of Remembrance that Memorial and the museum jointly organized in Solovki were increasingly frequented from year to year by representatives of various organizations representing former repressed persons and representatives of various countries and faiths. One of the most visible and recognizable groups participating in the ceremonies every year was composed of representatives of the Vasyl Stus All-Ukrainian Memorial Society. Local residents were unhappy that the Ukrainians displayed their nationality so unashamedly, dressing in national costume and carrying national flags. However, the situation never descended into open conflict. Both sides tried to find a compromise and understand the other side's arguments, as exemplified by incidents that took place in 2006 and 2007. In 2006, during the official ceremonies by the Solovetsky stone, the Ukrainians, as they had done at Sandarmokh, placed portraits of compatriots sent from Solovki to the Sandarmokh firing squads on trees surrounding the Solovetsky stone. Their actions were not to the liking of the Solovetsky islanders. Consequently, the following year, the Ukrainians decided not to display photographs, thus complying with the local community's wishes. However, the situation changed following the outbreak of the Crimean Crisis in 2014. The Ukrainians stopped attending the Days of Remembrance, and any actions associated with Ukrainian commemoration rituals began to be regarded as a manifestation of political viewpoints.[76]

The Days of Remembrance in 2015, despite being attended by representatives of various delegations, were not as formal in character as they had once been. As *Novaya Gazeta* reported, 'the remembrance gathering by the Solovetsky stone was modest – short speeches, words of commemoration and repentance, flowers and lit candles' (Shkurenok 2015). After twenty-five years of jointly organized Days of Remembrance, the ceremony was not attended by any representatives from the museum, the Solovetsky local authorities, the monastery or local community. However, it is worth stressing that local residents had rarely attended the ceremonies anyway in previous years. In fact, the Solovetsky islanders, rather than linking these days with the history of their 'small homeland', treated them as a holiday for visitors wishing to remember their dead. This does not mean that the Islands' camp history is unimportant to them, but they certainly do not regard it as the most important moment in the Archipelago's history (Takahashi 2008). However, for Memorial Society activists, the camp history is of prime importance, determining perspectives of both the past and future. For years, Memorial and the museum were aware of differing attitudes to the past, which is why they attempted to create suitable conditions for dialogue.

Until 2014, the aforementioned round table discussion organized at the Community Centre was an important component of the Days of Remembrance, meant to initiate dialogue and promote mutual understanding.

The participants sat down at a table loaded with cakes and sweets to commemorate the dead and discuss Gulag memory. The round table discussion was also an opportunity to exchange SLON materials found in the possession of various organizations. However, the objectives of these discussions were never successfully realized. While the participants were remembering the dead by reciting poems and singing songs, the meeting proceeded calmly. However, when the time came for speeches and debate, a sharp exchange of views ensued among the participants. Despite attempts made by museum staff and individuals from various Memorial organizations to calm the situation through negotiation, it was very rare that any consensus was reached.[77]

The problem of being unable to communicate is not unique to the people who come to Solovki. In fact, it also surfaces – as William Outwaite and Larry Ray point out – in many post-communist countries. One of the main reasons for this is a shortage of communication structures capable of shaping civil societies. The effects of this problem are felt particularly acutely in debates relating to memory. Since memory was subject to state surveillance and control under communism, struggling to prevent its erosion became a form of opposition. After communism fell and the process of rewriting history began, conflicts also erupted among groups who did not share each other's perceptions of past events. As the authors of the book *Social Theory and Postcommunism* stress (Outwaite and Ray 2005: 176–96), social changes were often accompanied by violence. This could therefore also apply to groups forming varying conceptions of memory. In extreme cases, this violence could assume the form of a civil war, as was the case in the former Yugoslavia, and in milder cases, it could erupt into less serious disputes, such as the conflict over the presence of crosses at Auschwitz (Zubrzycki 2006).

In the case of the associations and societies taking part in the Days of Remembrance in Solovki, the conflict mainly took the form of sharp exchanges and broken off discussions. Both the manner in which various participants comprehended the Gulag experience and their ideas for shaping Gulag memory were so very different that it was almost impossible for them to find a common language. Consequently, the round table discussion's fundamental objective – to create a space for dialogue on the shaping of shared memory – was never achieved. Nevertheless, for a period of twenty-five years, the round table discussion groups met every year in the hope that their objective could at last be achieved. The museum's decision to change the date of Solovki's Days of Remembrance ultimately led to the demise of the only space, however modest, open to shared dialogue.

Secular Gulag Memory

When establishing a role for itself in the late eighties, Memorial wanted to make Gulag memory the basis for a new civil society. From 1990, when the Solovetsky stone was erected in front of Lubyanka, Gulag memory began to play an increasingly important role in this process. Memorial hoped for a network of monuments whose neutral form would create the foundations for shared memory and a holiday – the Days of Remembrance – which would help to bind the community. Memorialization activities, such as those taking place at Sandarmokh Cemetery or in connection with the Solovetsky stones, were subordinated to the ideological assumptions of their creators. They were supposed to express universality and neutrality, while underlining the significance of the individual and the harm being caused by the authorities' failure to take into account the will of its citizens. These assumptions not only underpinned Memorial's mode of commemoration, but were also basic components of its conception of Gulag memory. This explains Memorial's unwavering commitment to the implementation of these assumptions and its determination to achieve its intended objectives at any cost (perfectly exemplified by its attempts to erect a Solovetsky stone in St Petersburg).

However, Memorial's interpretation of Gulag memory does not appeal to everyone. This explains why relatives of the deceased began to erect their own private memory markers at Sandarmokh, expressing what, for them, was the quintessence of the Gulag experience. Likewise, Ukrainians, Poles, Muslims or Jews primarily view Gulag memory in terms of the suffering of their own national and religious groups, so erected their own memory markers in the cemetery grounds. These markers in effect divided a communal site of memory for all SLON prisoners into symbolic national domains, over which they exercised control and which they use as a kind of cultural capital in national and ethnic conflicts (Nijakowski 2006). These monuments symbolize the national tragedies of specific groups, enabling them to communicate what is important to them by using their own history, traditions and understanding of the past as a point of reference. These monuments are primarily meant to be interpreted by their own group, rather than others. In effect, the cemetery space becomes a 'typical manifestation of nationhood' (Krikhtova 2014). The foundations of Memorial's Gulag memory project were therefore undermined. In fact, Memorial continues to claim that Sandarmokh meets its assumptions, fulfilling the role of a site of memory that unites rather than divides. Yet the genuine sense of community between all participants only lasts while they are following the path to the cemetery. Once mourners have entered their own area, the sense of community slowly disintegrates. Orthodox mourners keep away from the secular ceremonies, only participating in their Orthodox Panikhida, and after the official ceremonies, everyone makes their own way to their own national and religious markers, where they speak their own national languages. The community re-bonds once everyone has performed their memory rituals in their own way and is leaving the cemetery.

A similar process involving the disintegration of a community has occurred in the Solovetsky Islands. Much like at Sandarmokh, this process is bound up with the appearance of national and group memory markers on the Avenue of Remembrance. The first memorial to 'SLON prisoners', erected in 1989, was dedicated to every prisoner irrespective of their nationality, faith, social background or political views. However, from 2009, monuments dedicated to different groups of people repressed at Solovki started to be erected on the Avenue of Remembrance, namely, to Yakuts (2009), Poles (2011), Ukrainians (2012), socialists and anarchists (2013) and Scouts (2014). As a result, the memorial complex at Solovki stopped emphasizing the prisoners' shared fate and began drawing attention to the origin of different groups of repressed persons. This change of accent has had a marked effect on the manner in which this site's message is comprehended.

Memorial's creation of sites of memory is bound up with certain expectations and hopes. The Society takes care to ensure that everyone is able to liberate their own memories, believing that this is the only way to genuinely 'free oneself from the Gulag'. The carnival of memory of the late eighties was so successful at encouraging people of different backgrounds and faiths to join forces to remember the victims of the Gulag that Memorial was enervated to undertake more such activities. Consequently, when, in 1989, the first official Orthodox service was meant to take place at Solovki, 'the local authorities, taking fright at these circumstances, demanded that, before they issued an official permit, someone should take responsibility . . . [by] signing that they are responsible for this act of reviving the Orthodox ministry on the island', a signature that was eventually granted by Veniamin Ioffe from the St Petersburg chapter of Memorial (Ioffe 2002b: 54).[78] Permission to undertake separate memorialization activities was also granted to other national groups that appealed to Memorial for the right to commemorate their own victims of the repressions. By returning the Solovki or Sandarmokh sites of memory to public use, the Society renounced its exclusive right to determine their further development. Consequently, these sites currently express a rich mosaic of diverse conceptions of memory, which often conflict with each other and are far removed from the original assumptions behind Memorial's Gulag memory project.

'Solovki – A National Golgotha' – The Solovetsky Islands in an Orthodox Memory Project

> Seventy years ago, in August 1937, a campaign began in the Soviet Union that was targeted at the mass destruction of 'enemies of the people'. The entire Russian nation became a Golgotha on which hundreds of thousands of martyrs testified to their faith in God, devotion to the Orthodox Church and love for the Motherland. Indeed, they endured [their fate] to the end, understanding that, without this sacrifice, Russia's spiritual and moral rebirth had no chance [of coming to pass]. Through the prayers of these devout people, the Russian Orthodox Church is being revived and the edifice of Russian statehood is being re-established. This explains why such attention is being attracted by sites of torment and sacrifice hallowed by the blood and prayers of New Martyrs – in particular, Butovo and Solovki.[79]

When the Orthodox Church returned to the Solovetsky Islands in 1990, Bishop Panteleimon of Murmansk and Arkhangelsk said in an interview granted to *Pravda Severa* that the most important task facing the returning monks was to restore the local monastery.[80] At the same time, he added that he was firmly convinced that, with time, pilgrims would appear in Solovki whom monks 'will serve through prayer. That has always been the case. This is very important, particularly now, during our *smutnoye vremya*'[81] (Mozgovoy 1990b). The bishop thus sought to stress that the main purpose of the Orthodox Church's return was to restore to the Islands their former role as an important religious site and centre of pilgrimage, a status they had held for centuries.

This does not, however, mean that the history of SLON is falling into oblivion or being completely erased from the Archipelago's space. Nonetheless, during the reconstruction of the monastery buildings, any relics of the site's labour camp past – such as bars, barbed wire and prisoners' scribblings on the walls of their cells – are removed. Yet the memory of those who died in Solovki defending the Orthodox faith continues to be preserved and encoded in the increasing number of crosses being erected on the Islands. Their great importance to the Orthodox Church is evidenced by the fact that as early as 1992, when Alexei II made his first visit to Solovki, the patriarch blessed the memorial cross dedicated to the *novomucheniki* (New Martyrs). The cross itself is invested with deep religious symbolism and was constructed in the traditional *russkogo severa* style (that of the Russian North).[82] Alexei II's symbolic act not only revived the old Solovets tradition of erecting memorial crosses on the Islands,[83] but also stressed how important Solovetsky's New Martyrs, and New Martyrdom in general, are to today's Orthodox Church.

The meaning of the Islands' memorial crosses can only be comprehended by examining the inscriptions on them and the spaces in which they were erected.[84] An appreciation is also needed of how the Orthodox Church interprets the period of Soviet repressions and what it means by the 'period when people were persecuted for their faith'. Two dimensions should therefore be taken into account when analysing the meanings of the Orthodox project memorializing the Solovetsky Islands' camp history: the local (Solovetsky) dimension and the universal (Orthodox) dimension. Although these two dimensions are interconnected, I shall investigate them separately. This should enable me to present the different layers of the Orthodox memory project more clearly. While the local dimension makes it possible to understand the form and meaning of individual memory markers, investigating the project from a universal perspective provides insight into the assumptions underlying it.

Examining the project from two angles also has another advantage. In the Orthodox project, the Solovetsky Islands' camp history, rather than being viewed as a component of local memory, is regarded as an increasingly important part of the history of twentieth-century New Martyrdom. Since this phenomenon appears to be key to understanding the Orthodox conception of SLON memory, I shall start with this. However, I would like to stress that it is not my intention to explain the phenomenon in full. Instead, I will provide a general framework that should make it possible to understand the basic assumptions behind the Orthodox Gulag memory project and the place that the Solovetsky Islands' camp history occupies in this conception.

The Universal Dimension

The importance of New Martyrdom for today's Orthodox Church is clear from the words of Hierarch Peter, spoken when deputizing for the abbot of Solovetsky Monastery on 23 August 2006, during ceremonies taking place on the Feast of New Martyrs and Confessors of Solovki:

> In the history of Christianity, there was never such a time [as this] when, over the course of twenty years, several hundred monasteries were opened, when, over the course of twenty years, millions of people accepted holy baptism – this did not even happen in the first centuries or during the time of Kievan Rus'. Much like many centuries ago, when the universal Church grew out of the blood of the first martyrs, in our times, the Russian Orthodox Church has been growing out of the blood of the New Martyrs.[85]

During 'the period when people were persecuted for their faith', 'Russia's best people – very cultural and good people who had big merciful hearts' died martyrs' deaths,[86] so it is hardly surprising that many of these were raised to the rank of saints during 2000's jubilee session of the Local Council of the Russian Orthodox Church (Christensen 2017).[87] According to the Moscow Patriarchate's official website, this elevation of status was meant to acknowledge their great sacrifice while serving as 'a testament to their deep understanding of the nation's tragic errors and its painful straying [from the path of good]'. The article continues as follows: 'This is the first time in the history of the world that the Orthodox Church has elevated so many new heavenly advocates (with over 1000 new martyrs becoming saints)'[88] (Bogumił and Łukaszewicz 2018; Christensen 2015, 2017; Kahla 2010; Rock 2011).

As early as 1991, the Orthodox Church had begun celebrating the annual Feast of the New Martyrs and Confessors of Russia on 25 January (7 February by the Orthodox calendar). On this day, the New Martyrs, saints whose date of death is unknown or whose first names are only known to God are remembered alongside more familiar saints. Separate days are allocated to the remembrance of individual saints and groups of saints. Moreover, since 2000, the Solovetsky New Martyrs and Confessors have been remembered on 23 August, and since 2003, a Day of Remembrance for New Russian Martyrs has been observed for those who died at Butovo. The date of the latter ceremony varies from year to year, as it is held on the fourth Sunday after Easter. Some of these church holidays are local in character, while others are observed by the entire Orthodox Church.[89]

The canonization of New Martyrs is accompanied by the painting, or 'writing', of icons (Christensen 2017). These play a mediatory role, enabling the faithful to worship the saints they present. The year 2000 saw the consecration of an icon that fully expresses New Martyrdom's importance to the Orthodox Church. The Council of New Martyrs and Confessors of Russia icon was painted by *ikonopisateli*[90] from St Tikhon's Orthodox Theological Institute. In 2005, the abbot of Solovetsky Monastery commissioned a first icon depicting The Council of Solovetsky New Martyrs and Confessors, and in 2006 another new icon was dedicated to this group of saints. Both of them are currently kept at the monastery on the Islands. They depict Solovetsky saints and important Solovetsky sites of martyrdom. However, I would like to take a closer look at the Icon of the New Martyrs and Confessors of Russia in order to explain the place Solovki's camp history occupies in the concept of New Orthodox Martyrdom.[91]

The icon[92] (Figure 1.5) was modelled on earlier representations of similar material.[93] The New Martyrs are presented against the background of the Cathedral of

Figure 1.5. Icon of the New Martyrs and Confessors of Russia. Painted by an *ikonopisatel* from St Tikhon's Orthodox University in 2000. Photo by author.

Christ the Saviour in Moscow. In front of the church stands a *prestol* (sacrificial table) covered in a red antimins, which is meant to symbolize victory over death and hell. Lying on the prestol is the Holy Book, opened at the page containing the words: 'And fear not them which kill the body, but are not able to kill the soul'.[94]

The church presented on the icon symbolizes the Kingdom of Heaven, so the decision to depict the Cathedral of Christ the Saviour was not taken by chance. As Dmitri Sidorov notes, this church also symbolizes a break with the Soviet past and the beginning of a new era for Russian society (Sidorov 2000). It is currently the most important Orthodox shrine in Russia, and its history is closely bound up with the concept of a Russian nation. The decision to construct it was made by Alexander I on the day in 1812 when the last soldiers of Napoleon's Grande Armée left Moscow. Its construction coincided with a period of national reawakening in Russia,[95] so its architects not only decided to evoke Christian symbolism, but also presented important events from the nation's history. The Cathedral was meant to embody the idea of Moscow as a third Rome.[96] In 1931, the Soviet authorities blew up the church, hoping to replace it with a Soviet palace. However, this project was never implemented, so, for many years, the site was occupied by a swimming pool. In 1990, the Synod made an appeal for the church to be reconstructed, and in 1998, the new Cathedral of Christ the Saviour was returned to the faithful (Sidorov 2000).

Today's shrine varies little from the original that was destroyed by the Bolsheviks. When the first cathedral was erected, there was no Patriarch in Russia (the office had been abolished by Peter I) and Moscow was not the country's capital. Now, as Russia's most important shrine, it acts as the seat of the Patriarch of Moscow and All Russia and holds the most important services at Easter and Christmas. The church has also changed its own meaning. According to its self-published catalogue (2005: 8), it no longer wishes to symbolize the victory over Napoleon, preferring to be seen as a symbol of the passage from atheism to the Law of God, a kind of memorial dedicated to Russian history, heroism and suffering (cf. Chibineyev and Amaryan 2004).

Returning to my description of the New Martyrs of Russia icon, behind the prestol, in the very centre of the icon, stands a cross, which acts as a horizontal and vertical ordering component.[97] The cross indicates the contribution made to the victory over sin by the New Martyrs depicted in the icon as well as the Orthodox Church's triumph over death. Beneath the prestol stand the family of Tsar Nicholas II, personifying the principle of authority and order sanctified by God. The family is clothed in traditional Byzantine vestments, emphasizing historical links between Russia and Byzantium.[98]

Standing by the prestol are Russia's most important hieromartyrs: Patriarch Tikhon[99] and St Peter (Polyansky), Metropolitan of Krutitsa. Around and above the hieromartyrs, canonical saints are presented hierarchically, and below them, level with the tsar's family, secular saints are portrayed. Even further down, representatives of other social groups can be seen. These groups are not represented by real people. The clothes of these figures attest to their social status. All the saints together comprise the

Russian Orthodox community, while the very centre of the icon (the *srednik*) depicts the victory of the battling Church.

The sides of the icon (the *kleyma*) contain scenes from the martyrdom of individual saints (the right side) and mass martyrdom (the left side). All of these are presented in a concise, sharply outlined manner. The saints' clothes are rendered in intense bright colours to emphasize their membership of the Church. By contrast, soldiers are clothed in uniforms of an earthy colour and their faces are indistinct, symbolizing that they were a blind instrument of the forces of evil.

The first icon on the kleymo depicting mass martyrdom presents Solovki. The composition was modelled on an icon presenting Saints Zosima and Sabbatius of Solovki, founding fathers (along with Herman) of the Solovetsky Monastery, which was converted into a prison during the SLON period. The new icon depicts a scene in which the saints have been locked inside the monastery. An execution by firing squad can be seen on the seashore. To the left are representations of Sekirnaya Hill, which was converted into punishment cells, and the stairs that prisoners were once, according to legend, thrown down.[100] To the right, Golgotha, on the island of Anzer, is depicted. It was here that Peter Zverev died.[101] In the icon, he is depicted lying at rest in the ground. Another important component of the scene is a birch that first appeared on the island of Anzer in the mid-twentieth century. Its cruciform structure has led it to being regarded as a cross erected for the martyrs by God himself.

The other icons on the kleymo depict other places of personal and group martyrdom.[102] I would like to conclude my description at this point, for I believe that the elements I have discussed are indicative, in themselves, of the features of the New Martyrdom concept that are most important to the Orthodox Church. The central part of the composition symbolizes the Church's rebirth through New Martyrdom. At the same time, the icon indicates how this process should proceed. Firstly, the Orthodox faith should be allied to a strong state (symbolized by the tsar's family). Secondly, by virtue of the good example set by its activity and other models that it deems worthy of emulation (like the New Martyrs), it should both unite with the Russian nation (represented by the Cathedral of Christ the Saviour) and participate in its construction.

Solovki plays a very important role in this process, as is clearly expressed by Archbishop Augustine of Lviv and Galicia:

> I believe that every Orthodox person should definitely find an opportunity to visit Solovki ... After all, the New Martyrs and Confessors of Solovki were similar to the first Christians, to those who perished in Rome and other places in the Roman Empire as a result of persecutions. Many accepted their martyrdom with gratitude, because it enabled them to testify their faith and prove to God and [other] people [the strength of] their faith and love for the Lord. During the persecutions, Rome, for Christians, was like a second Golgotha, and the Solovetsky Golgotha

may, in the history of Christianity, be interpreted as a third. Certainly, for the Orthodox Russian nation, Solovki is – their national Golgotha. (Osipenko 2007: 255)

The archbishop's statement shows what an important function the Solovetsky Islands and the twenty-year history of their lagers fulfil in today's Orthodox Church. They are not only the 'Russian nation's Golgotha', but also a kind of third Golgotha for Christianity as a whole. Consequently, the history of SLON, and therefore the entire history of the Soviet repressions (exemplified by Solovki), has been incorporated into a myth, firmly rooted in Russian culture, which presents Moscow as a third Rome. The repressions are interpreted as confirmation of the exceptional nature of the Russian nation, which God chose and appointed to guard the true faith. The New Martyrs' deaths enabled the rebirth and development of the Russian Orthodox Church and are contributing to the building of a better future for the whole nation. This concept is clearly reflected in the form of the Cathedral of Christ the Saviour – the Russian Orthodox faith's primary shrine and home to the original New Martyrs and Confessors of Russia icon.

This Orthodox concept is therefore proposing a universal explanation of events from the recent past that involves their incorporation into a holistically conceived history of Christianity. Such a comprehensive and multifaceted model makes it possible to provide answers to many of the questions troubling today's inhabitants of the Russian Federation ('Why?', 'How was that possible?'). What is more, this model can assist the process of understanding and working through the traumatic past by providing signposts (Bogumił and Łukaszewicz 2018).

The Solovetsky Islands are one such signpost. Their meaning expresses itself on many levels. On the one hand, this place's camp history could be generalized to serve as a figura symbolizing broader meanings – it could, for example, be a kind of warning for the future or provide models of heroism based on the fates of the Solovetsky saints. On the other hand, the Solovetsky memorial crosses appearing around the Islands are very concrete, tangible memory markers, which is why they are being increasingly used to mark sites of Soviet repressions in the Russian Federation. Much as was the case with the Solovetsky stones, the Solovetsky crosses have been leaving the Archipelago since 2000. In effect, the Orthodox infrastructure commemorating the Soviet repressions is being enriched with Solovetsky memory markers.

The Solovetsky Memory Markers – Memorial Crosses

By the time the local monastery was shut down in 1920, the Solovetsky Islands contained about three thousand crosses (Kopylova 2001). These fulfilled various functions. Some performed a thanksgiving role, while others commemorated important events, marked sacred sites or protected against evil. As Georgy Kozhokar, who works at the monastery workshops, explains, making crosses is: 'an old tradition, in fact a Greek tradition, when a cross is erected for the purposes of religious remembrance or [to mark] a historical event . . . In those days, a cross received a name' [15_GK].¹⁰³ The first cross to be erected in Solovki was planted by the local monastery's founding fathers, Saints Sabbatius and Herman, shortly after they arrived at the Islands. The Solovetsky crosses are characteristic for their *bogoimenny* nature – that is, they use the language of symbolism to communicate a narrative of sacrifice in the name of global salvation. God reveals himself to man in these crosses through the inscriptions and symbols – or 'names of God' – they contain. When examining these signs, it should be remembered that they are designed to be read and understood not only as icons but as prayers.

The cross planted in 1992 at the foot of the stairs leading up to Sekirnaya Hill was the first contemporary cross to be made in this tradition. As Georgy Kozhokar, its creator, recalls, the idea of erecting this cross occurred to him when he was studying the history of the Solovetsky crosses:

> I took measurements of crosses in Solovki, especially those on the island of Anzer, on Verbokolskaya Hill . . . According to a description, there was a 9-metre tall cross on it. And I was reading that description. We were looking for it and they told us where it was . . . We found this cross to be in a really bad state. It had subsided and was overgrown with berries . . . Imagine – through the greenery, pieces of wood were visible. And there [an inscription]: 'Glory to the Tsar, Jesus Christ' . . . I was shocked that the Church [had been] so desecrated, forgotten, abandoned . . . Then I wanted to make a one-to-one copy of this cross and erect it somewhere, so that it could live a new life. When we discovered what had happened [on Sekirnaya Hill] we [decided] with our loved ones that we had to repair this [situation] . . . I suggested . . . to the abbot of the monastery that I'd make a cross and we'd erect it at the site where they killed the people and threw them down the stairs. Right there at the bottom, where their legs met their end. [15_GK]

The cross on the island of Anzer was not the only memorial cross, but its height and location on one of the islands' tallest hills led to it performing the function of a navigation marker for the Archipelago's inhabitants. In 1992, as he blessed the copy of the cross erected at the foot of Sekirnaya Hill, Alexei II emphasized that the conduct of the holy New Martyrs should serve as a model for future generations to emulate. The new Solovetsky cross is meant to guide the Orthodox community's further spiritual development, much like the original cross in Anzer, which was used to show passing fishermen the way home.

This was how the tradition of Solovetsky memorial crosses was renewed. In 1994, a second cross was erected on a small hill in front of Golgotha Hill on the island of Anzer. As Kozhokar explains: 'it is dedicated to the New Martyrs and Confessors of Russia and Solovki, and first and foremost, the hierarchs – that is, the bishops and metropolitans who died here in great numbers. Why? Because many bishops and hierarchs were being held right here in Anzer.' This explains why the cross was meant to, on the one hand, commemorate the hierarchs and, on the other, show that: 'here, there is a cemetery, all of the land on Anzer and Solovetsky and the entire Archipelago is one huge miserable cemetery, which we're walking around with you, where we live' [15_GK]. This is why Kozhokar decided to decorate the cross using *polystavros*, a design formed of many smaller crosses. The idea was taken from pontifical vestments decorated in this manner:

> The idea came to me from an icon; specifically, the iconography of St Nicholas, whose omophorion is decorated with such crosses. I even executed such a composition [at a ratio of] one to one . . . that is, I engraved a cluster of crosses of two or three types . . . And there, a large cross appeared amid the small crosses. This is symbolic. First, this is a polystavros, and second, the cross of a hallowed person. [15_GK]

As I mentioned earlier, the cross, rather than being erected on Golgotha itself, was planted on a smaller hill in front of it. This site was actually chosen by the monastery's abbot. As Kozhokar told me, 'it's good it's not on Golgotha, as Golgotha is Golgotha [and should remain so]' [15_GK]. The cross was situated in such a manner as to afford a panoramic view of Golgotha, creating a space for reflection and contemplation, a role it still performs today. When, in 2007, I took part in a tour of the island organized by the museum, our group paused by the cross. An intriguing discussion on twentieth-century history ensued. As they gazed at Golgotha, tour participants asked the guide many questions about the site's history and the symbolism of the cross.

All of the symbols on the Solovetsky crosses have religious meanings. The skull carved below the lower crossbar of the cross in front of Golgotha connotes Adam's resting place,[104] while the iconic inscription on the crossbar itself ('GA') stands for Adam's Hill, and the letters 'NI' and 'KE' inscribed, respectively, on the left and right arms of the crossbar symbolize victory over death (Kuznetsov 1997). However, Kozhokar emphasizes that there is no point in approaching this cross' symbolism from a Kabbalistic perspective, for no deeper meanings are concealed in the cross' numerical dimensions or the number of small crosses it contains. The intention behind the cross' erection and the function it is meant to perform are important, but, for the cross' creator, the most crucial factor to remember is that 'this is the cross of Christ, who became a tool of salvation' [15_GK].

Anyone investigating the crosses on the Solovetsky Islands dedicated to the New Martyrs can not only expect to discover allusions to local traditions relating to the production and erection of such Christian symbols, but also certain elements associated with Solovetsky crosses created before the Revolution, when they were signs of the Archipelago's Orthodox spirituality. In fact, such allusions and elements, which one would expect to be evident in the cross Kozhokar modelled on the cross erected on Verbokolskaya Hill, are also visible in a cross erected in front of Sekirnaya Hill in 2003, which is not overtly dedicated to the New Martyrs. However, as Georgy Kozhokar explains, in fact 'all the crosses are devoted to the New Martyrs and Confessors of Russia, all of them' [15_GK]. However, this is not always directly expressed in their iconography.

The cross that was built in 2003 is located by a path leading to the top of Sekirnaya Hill that affords an expansive view of the whole hill. It was modelled on a cross that once stood on the hill's summit. Following the closure of the monastery, it was chopped down and removed from the island. Georgy Kozhokar had an old photograph of this cross. The date '1437' could be seen on the left arm of the upper crossbar, and on the right, the letters 'гг' (a double 'g' stands for 'years' in Russian). On the central, vertical bar, there was an inscription, illegible in the photograph. As Kozhokar explains:

> I added the year 1937, the approximate date, as it were, of this cross' death. We have no way of knowing what the date of 1437 was dedicated to. Quite possibly . . . to the appearance of the monastery in 1437. Not to the date of [the monks'] arrival in Solovki, just to the foundation of the monastery. Quite possibly, it was to this that this cross was dedicated. Anyway, that is what has survived of the staurography. There was also a long text engraved into the cross . . . The photograph was old and it was difficult to make out what was written there, so I reconstructed all the kleyma, only I substituted the date [1937] for [the word] 'year', and a description of the cross' history, for the text at the bottom. [15_GK]

The cross fully articulates the idea of New Martyrdom for a number of reasons. Firstly, it presents a symbolic date for the cross' death that coincides with the onset of the Great Terror. Secondly, the historical text engraved on the main bar provides information about the original cross' demise. Finally, the symbols on the horizontal crossbars (representing the instruments of Christ's torture – a spear, a lance and a vinegar-soaked sponge) prominently feature on *skhimnicheski* (Golgotha) crosses (Kuznetsov 1997: 19). It could even be said that this cross symbolically expresses the suffering of the entire history – spanning centuries – of a monastery that was finally destroyed in 1937, yet is now undergoing a rebirth.

Clearly, the new Solovetsky crosses are helping to restore the Islands to their former glory as a centre of religion, by serving as vehicles for the sense of religiosity that developed in the Solovetsky Islands over many centuries. It is this that the Orthodox Church intends to return to the Islands after a period during which the nation 'strayed' off course. Nevertheless, their primary role should be seen as 'memory marking', or the commemoration of tragic events. Most of the crosses directly referencing the history of repressions are located on or near Sekirnaya and Golgotha Hills, indicating which events from SLON's history are most important for the Orthodox memory project (martyrs' deaths) and which sites are becoming spaces allocated to the history of the Archipelago camps. It is worth remembering that it is Sekirnaya and Golgotha Hills with their churches and attributes (the stairs, the cruciform birch) that were presented on the New Martyrs and Confessors of Russia icon.

The importance of the Archipelago's history and symbolic power acquired by the Solovetsky memorial crosses ever since the Orthodox concept of New Martyrdom reached its full crystallization at the beginning of the twenty-first century have led to the crosses being transplanted from the Islands. This is effectively creating a network of Solovetsky memory markers that is, in turn, enriching the Orthodox Gulag memory infrastructure. In 2001, a Solovetsky cross was erected in front of the Solovetsky Monastery's Moscow offices to indicate that this was a place to which people could come to pray for their loved ones who died at Solovki or at other Gulag sites (*Pravoslavny tserkovny kalendar,* 2002: 166).[105] In 2007, another Solovetsky cross was erected at Butovo, a site near Moscow where mass executions by firing squad took place from the mid-thirties to the early fifties (Christensen 2017; Dorman 2010). During the Great Terror alone, 20,761 people were shot there (Shantsev 2007: 144), explaining why this place has become a symbol of the Soviet repressions. From the mid-nineties, when Butovo passed into the hands of the Orthodox Church, the former shooting range slowly began to assume the shape of an Orthodox memory project (Fedor and Sniegon 2018) and is currently the most important site of cult worship for the New Martyrs. It has also been named a 'Russian Golgotha'.[106] The site now contains the purpose-built Church of the Holy New Martyrs and Confessors of Russia, by which the aforementioned Solovetsky cross was erected (Figure 1.6). The official union of Solovki and Butovo took place on the seventieth anniversary of the Great Terror, assuming the form of a symbolic yet meaningful Krestny Khod procession (Dorman 2010).

Butovo-Solovki: 'Two Russian Golgothas'

In the curatorial notes for the *Stations of the Cross – Solovki-Butovo* exhibition organized in the monastery grounds in 2007, the decision to erect a Solovetsky cross at a mass burial site near Moscow was explained as follows:

> Butovo and Solovki are not only bound together by the magnitude of the evil that took place there. They are invisibly bound together by the fates of the New Russian Martyrs. Many SLON prisoners, saved by some miracle from a camp torture chamber, were rearrested in 1937–38. They offered up their lives at the Butovo shooting ground. Their path was followed by prisoners of many other subchapters of Gulag [history].

The Solovki-Butovo Stations of the Cross began on 25 July 2007 with a service at a church in the Solovetsky Monastery compound (Dorman 2010). The following

Figure 1.6. The Solovetsky cross at Butovo, near Moscow. Erected next to the Church of the Holy New Martyrs and Confessors of Russia in 2007. Photo by author.

day, celebrants went to Sekirnaya Hill to say prayers for the dead at the site of mass graves that had been recently discovered there. Next, they sailed to Anzer to remember the dead at Golgotha. Only after the prayers at these two places did the cross make its journey to Moscow, first, by sea and then, by following the White Sea Canal to the capital. It made stops along the way at places 'where New Russian Martyrs and Confessors had made their [ultimate] sacrifice and defended Faith and Truth, at former lagpunkts and sites drenched in the blood and tears of the innocently slain' (Bogumił 2016). At some stops, locals came to do obeisance to the cross and pray with the Stations of the Cross pilgrims, who decided to make a few further stops at such places as Medvezhyegorsk, from where they visited Sandarmokh. As Kirill Kaleda recalls, 'We had the impression that the whole path we were following was a path through burial sites, through one endless cemetery.'[107]

When the cross reached Moscow, it sailed along the River Moskva, past the Cathedral of Christ the Saviour and the Kremlin, before being transferred to a vehicle at the South River Terminal, which followed the Moscow Ring Road to the Church of the New Martyrs and Confessors in Butovo. There, on the morning of 8 August, on the seventieth anniversary of the first mass executions, the cross was consecrated.

The entire event attracted great media interest. The Krestny Khod itself expressed a sense of contrition and was meant to cleanse the Russian nation of errors committed in the past. This was meant to be achieved through a multiple reversal of meaning. In fact, the Stations of the Cross can be seen to exhibit a kind of 'anti-behaviour', as defined by Boris Uspensky (1985: 326–340.). For example, rather than travelling by land, the cross sailed to Butovo, and rather than sailing down the river, it sailed upstream. It was dedicated to zeks, who had died for their faith, yet while they were alive, these same zeks not only built the canals along which the cross was sailing all those years later but also the lagpunkts where the Stations of the Cross pilgrims were taking breaks and praying. This event not only united the two Russian Golgothas, Solovki and Butovo, but also gave the Orthodox Gulag memory concept its final shape (Bogumił 2016).

This idea has been most fully realized in the symbolism and design for the Solovetsky cross erected at Butovo. According to Georgy Kozhokar, this is not only the largest memorial cross in the world, but it is also unique in that: 'This was the first time we made a cross composed of three different kinds of wood ... Just like the cross of Christ' [15_GK]. In fact, the three parts of the cross – the main bar and two vertical poles – were constructed from three different kinds of wood imported from Siberia, Karelia and Abkhazia. However, it is the cross' symbolism that is most intriguing. This, as Kozhokar points out, is inextricably bound up with the New Martyrdom concept:

> We made use of the iconography of the Forty Martyrs of Sebaste, in which the forty martyrs are depicted with the garlands [hanging] over them that Jesus is placing on them from heaven.[108] Forty people can be counted at the bottom [of the cross], and forty garlands at the top. This is a double-sided cross – that's very important ... The front symbolizes the victorious Orthodox Church, the celestial Orthodox Church, where the angels are, the Archangel ... we do not see any objects familiar to us from our world there. On the other side, I have presented the earthly Orthodox Church, the battling Orthodox Church, the Orthodox Church that is battling sin. The symbol I have presented here is basically crosses, symbolizing that Butovo is a cemetery ... this is why the whole of this side is covered in crosses. And I have presented the crown of thorns. I wanted to portray this as naturalistically as possible ... And there's an additional element there – the thorns are intertwined with barbed wire. This was an instrument of death for the New Martyrs and Confessors of Russia in the twentieth century. On the front of the cross ... in the centre, is Christ's crown. That's his crown. I built it up from the New Martyr's tiny garlands. This [represents their joint] participation in the victory. [15_GK]

The Butovo cross is complemented by a replica that was erected in 2008 on the summit of Sekirnaya Hill in the Solovetsky Islands, on the path leading to the mass graves. The cross was to be unveiled in autumn 2007, but it was not actually consecrated until 2008, on 21 August, the date of the feast day marking the 'translation' (or transferral) of the relics of Saints Zosima, Sabbatius and Herman. The front of the Sekirnaya cross contains the same representation that is on the back of the Butovo cross, including the crown of thorns intertwined with barbed wire and the instruments of torture – the spear, lance and nails. Furthermore, some of the symbolic representations are meant to recall events that took place in Solovki during the SLON period.[109] The cross is red in colour, which, on the one hand, symbolizes a martyr's death and, on the other, alludes to Solovets tradition, because originally 'all Solovetsky crosses were red' [15_GK]. According to the Solovetsky Monastery's website: 'This cross, given the symbols used on it, can be called a martyr's cross, because it symbolizes the sufferings of Christ and the death of the New Martyrs and Confessors, who kept their faith during the persecution of the Orthodox Church and the Cross of Christ.'[110]

The Solovetsky crosses – on Sekirnaya Hill and in Butovo – thus comprise a kind of axis linking the two Golgothas. This connection operates at a historical level (both sites are marked by the presence of mass graves and their linkage implies that any intervening space is one 'endless cemetery'), but also on the basis of their status as memory markers (the symbolism they share facilitates dialogue between the two sites). The inscriptions on the cross on Sekirnaya Hill reference the repressions that occurred in Solovki, particularly there, on Sekirnaya Hill, the Archipelago's most lethal site. The fact that one side of the Butovo cross also references the repressions seems to imply that the system of repression developed in Solovki swept across the whole country, culminating in the Great Terror, which is most potently symbolized by the site of Butovo. However, in this case, the victory over the repressions prevailing in the 'earthly world' is represented by the symbolism on the front of the cross. Therefore, although the Butovo cross undoubtedly commemorates the repressions, its main role is to bear testimony to Christ's victory over death and evil, a victory in which the New Martyrs depicted in the staurography on the front of the cross participate.[111]

Finally, it is worth emphasizing that the Solovetsky Islands' and Butovo's importance in the history of mass martyrdom is not only evidenced by the fact that they are delineating an axis on which other sites of mass martyrdom are located, but was also expressed in the New Martyrs and Confessors of Russia icon I analysed earlier. In this icon, Solovki can be found at the very top of the kleymo that shows scenes of mass martyrdom, while Butovo, which is located in the bottom left corner, closes off this vertical strip. Both sites are therefore linked not only geographically (thanks to the Solovetsky crosses), but also mystically, in an icon illustrating part of the heavenly world (Alekseyev 2007: 7–27).

Orthodox Gulag Memory

The arrival of a Solovetsky cross at Butovo and the symbolic linking of the two martyrdom sites heralded the end of the next formative stage of the Orthodox project memorializing the Soviet repressions. The concept had crystallized of a 'Russian Golgotha', on which the New Martyrs and Confessors had laid down their lives, so that the Orthodox Church could be reborn and enter the twenty-first century. The church in Butovo dedicated to the Church of the Holy New Martyrs and Confessors of Russia is notable for its architectural symbolism, vaults reminiscent of Greek crypts, icons of Butovo saints and holy Councils of New Martyrs, and an exhibition devoted to Butovo's history and the people who were shot there (Christensen 2017; Fedor and Sniegon 2018). Clearly, this church is in itself a full realization, on many levels, of the 'Russian Golgotha' concept, which also actively participates in this concept's further development.

The Solovetsky Islands also firmly contribute to the furthering of the New Martyrdom concept. This is not only clear from the Solovetsky cross standing by the church in Butovo, but also from the so-called 'small Solovetsky cross', which accompanied the large memorial cross on the Krestny Khod to Butovo and is currently being used by Butovo pilgrims during Krestny Khod crucessions to other sites of mass and personal New Martyrdom scattered across various parts of the Russian Federation.[112] The small Solovetsky cross not only goes on pilgrimages, but also participates in prayers for the dead spoken at sites of mass and personal martyrdom, symbolically joining the network of Orthodox infrastructure whose axis is delineated by Solovki and Butovo.

On the Islands themselves, the 'national Golgotha' concept is being implemented through the erection of memorial crosses as memory markers. Since they are located in places whose camp history is associated with death and suffering and their symbolism is rooted both in religion and Solovets tradition, they are becoming part of the Golgotha concept, while also granting it a distinctive, local dimension. What is more, the memorial crosses, by virtue of their religious dimension, are not only contributing to Solovki's rebirth as an important centre of Orthodoxy, but also serving as a reminder that this rebirth is only possible thanks to the Solovetsky New Martyrs who died martyrs' deaths at the sites marked by memorial crosses.

Since 2010, the concept of Solovki as a Russian Golgotha has been promoted by an exhibition prepared by the monastery and Solovetsky Museum, titled *Solovki. Golgotha and the Resurrection. Solovetsky Heritage in Russia of the Past, Present and Future*. The decision to prepare this exhibition was taken by Kirill, Patriarch of Moscow and All Russia, to whom the Solovetsky Monastery is directly answerable. During his first visit to the Islands in 2009, the Patriarch emphasized that: 'This marvellous place in which we now find ourselves is immensely significant for our country and the whole world. And it is very important that the Solovetsky Monastery regains its former glory' (*Solovetski Vestnik* [4(71)] 2010). At the same time, he drew attention to the Solovetsky Islands as a refuge and the history of SLON, saying: 'this is not only a subject worthy of veneration, but also of deep and thorough study' (*Solovetski Vestnik* [4(71)] 2010).

The following year, at the Cathedral of Christ the Saviour in Moscow, the most important shrine in Russian Orthodoxy, an exhibition devoted to the Solovetsky Monastery and its importance for the contemporary Orthodox faith and Russia was opened on the twentieth anniversary of the Solovetsky Monastery's return to the Solovetsky Islands.[113] Since then, the exhibition has been shown at various Russian cities, including Moscow, St Petersburg, Nizhny Novgorod, Arkhangelsk, Sochi, Sebastopol and Oryol. Looking at comments left in the visitors' book,[114] as well as the visitor attendance records and the importance of the venues at which the exhibition has been showing,[115] it is clear to see that this travelling exhibition is an important propaganda tool for the Orthodox Solovetsky Island memory project.

By incorporating the Solovetsky Islands into the New Martyrdom concept, the Orthodox Church is transforming this resting place for human bones of various nationalities and faiths into a Russian Orthodox place of worship. In 2007, one of the monastery's monks pointed out during a conversation I had with him that the Russian Orthodox Church: 'cannot pray for Jews or Catholics . . . but if a rabbi comes here wanting to pray at these burial sites, nobody can forbid him from doing that' [A4_AO]. Of course, the question of whether such a situation will still be possible in a dozen or so years remains open. After all, by then, Sekirnaya Hill will show all the hallmarks of an Orthodox cemetery and the Solovetsky Islands will have recovered their former glory as a place of Orthodox cult worship. Yet this does not stop the Memorial representatives leading groups of pilgrims around Sekirnaya Hill during the Days of Remembrance from asking themselves the very same question. This also explains why it is so important for them to create a universal memory project at Sandarmokh.

However, the Solovetsky Monastery is implementing another SLON memory project. Its most important aim is to honour the memory of those who laid down their lives in defence of the Orthodox faith, while also explaining the essence of the Soviet repressions by using the same faith. In the Orthodox memory project, Solovki, much like Butovo, is perceived as a 'Russian Golgotha'. It is thus becoming part of the concept, firmly rooted in Russian culture, of Moscow as a third Rome. The repressions are being interpreted as confirmation of the exceptional nature of the Russian nation, which God has chosen and appointed to the position of guardian of the true faith. The New Martyrs' deaths have facilitated the rebirth and development of the Russian Orthodox Church and are contributing to the building of a better future for the entire nation.

The Orthodox Church is thus proposing a holistic and multifaceted concept equipped to respond to many questions and doubts. The Soviet repressions, rather than being perceived as a phenomenon defying description, have assumed the important status of a creator of culture. This phenomenon is clearly illustrated by the Solovetsky crosses, the Councils of New Martyrs icons or the architecture of the church at Butovo. All of these render the essence of New Martyrdom by supplementing the tradition they have drawn from with new elements. In this way, they are reshaping contemporary Orthodoxy.[116]

Solovetsky Vlast: Repeating the Past

The Solovetsky Islands undoubtedly occupy a unique place on the map of Gulag sites of memory.[117] No other camp centre can claim a history that has attracted so much interest from so many different memory actors or that formed the basis for the implementation of such diverse memory projects during the carnival of memory. Over the twenty-five years since the collapse of the Soviet Union, the Archipelago's meaning and its attitude to its camp history have undergone substantial transformation. Initially, three memory actors operated on the Islands: the museum, Memorial and the monastery. In fact, as late as 2007, despite these actors' mutual distrust, it appeared that there was an unwritten agreement dividing their spheres of influence over the shaping of Gulag memory. However, later events have shown that this sense of equilibrium was nothing more than an illusion. Despite the fact that the Orthodox interpretation of the Archipelago as a 'Russian Golgotha' only really assumed its final shape during the commemoration of the seventieth anniversary of the Great Terror and the Solovki-Butovo Stations of the Cross pilgrimage, it is this concept that is increasingly making its presence felt in the Archipelago's cultural landscape. What is more, it has supplanted or appropriated the roles of the other memory projects.

The first memory actor to undertake memorialization work was the Solovetsky Museum, which created its first exhibition providing information about the history and significance of the Solovki special purpose camp in 1989. Following the appointment of the abbot of the monastery as the museum's director in 2009, this cultural institution became a vehicle for conveying the Orthodox memory project. As a consequence, instead of promoting *The Solovetsky Lagers and Prison '1920–1939'*, the museum now recommends that visitors view the exhibition that opened in 2010 as the most important Gulag memory project: *Solovki. Golgotha and the Resurrection. Solovetsky Heritage in Russia of the Past, Present and Future*, which is the exhibition the monastery prepared itself.

The monastery not only appropriated the museum's memory project, but also the history of its foundation. When the museum and monastery decided in 2015 to stop organizing joint Days of Remembrance with Memorial and rescheduled the commemoration ceremonies to another date, this was done under the pretext of a desire to combine the Days of Remembrance with an academic conference. The conference itself was organized in memory of the recently deceased Antonina Soshina, one of the curators of the first exhibition devoted to SLON history. For years, Soshina researched the repressions while working at the Solovetsky Museum, and later at the monastery's museum department. Antonina Soshina and Antonina Melnik were not only the first staff members to commit themselves to researching the Islands' camp history, but also persuaded Ludmila Lopatkina, the incumbent director of the museum, to create the first exhibition devoted to the history of SLON and wrote articles in the local press explaining to local inhabitants why the camp history of their Islands is so important. By dedicating its conference to Soshina, the monastery was incorporating the memory of this important researcher, and thus, by implication, the meaning of the first acts of commemoration she undertook, into the history of its own memory project.

The next memory actor to undertake commemorative work on the Islands was the Memorial Society, which actually became involved before the Orthodox Church and initially supported the religious way of life's return to the Archipelago. Nonetheless, the paths chosen by Memorial and the monastery quickly diverged. The first conflict rooted in differing approaches to the memorialization of the Islands' camp past occurred in 1999, when the Doctors and Anaesthetists of North-West Russia Organization erected a memorial cross by the Solovetsky stone in Solovki, to commemorate the sixtieth anniversary of the closure of the Solovki camp prison. After the organization asked the monastery where the cross could and should be erected, the abbot indicated a plot of land by the Solovetsky stone. This seemed to be an obvious choice. After all, there was a cemetery there. Moreover, it was there, in 1929, that prisoners had been executed by firing squad, and not far from there that the Solovki camp hospital had been located. Nevertheless, Memorial interpreted this as an assault on their memory project. As Veniamin Ioffe said in 1999 during the Days of Remembrance: 'Our non-confessional memorial to all victims of the Solovki repressions is now overshadowed by a religious sign . . . Every day, this cross' shadow is being cast on a stone commemorating people, many of whom would never approve of such symbolism. This is an act of spiritual violence' (Ioffe 2002a: 54).

Over time, Memorial itself began to change the meaning of the Solovetsky stone in Solovki. In 2015, it used the memorial cross to express its opposition to the Ukrainians' absence at the Days of Remembrance by hanging an embroidered rushnyk on the cross, thus changing the meaning of the cross and the shadow it casts on the Solovetsky stone. At the same time, Memorial has granted permission for memorials to various groups of prisoners to be erected on the Avenue of Remembrance around the 'memorial to all of Solovki's victims'. These markers in effect exclude outsiders from particular communities, thus weakening the overall effect of the Memorial memory project.

The monastery was the last memory actor to make its presence felt in Solovki and, much like the other two, it quickly set about creating its own memory project based on the history of SLON. Despite the Orthodox Church facing the persistent charge that it is trying to erase the camp history from the Archipelago's cultural landscape, the monastery is very heavily involved in preserving precisely this. However, rather than working to preserve the lager's historical remains, it primarily focuses on erecting memorial crosses and writing New Martyrs icons, all the while making abundantly clear how important the camp history is to contemporary Orthodoxy. It is worth adding that the monastery's rescheduling of the Days of Remembrance to the

Victims of Political Repressions from August to June or July ensured that the central place in the Islands' cultural event calendar for August would now be occupied by Orthodox holidays. These start on 19 August, with one of the twelve most important Orthodox holidays, the Feast of the Transfiguration, which is followed by the first and second translations of the relics of the Venerable Zosima, Sabbatius and Herman (21 August), the Feast of the Council of Solovetsky Saints (22 August) and, closing the cycle, the Feast of the New Solovetsky Martyrs and Confessors (23 August). The Solovetsky holidays are becoming increasingly important events in the life of the Orthodox Church, attracting Orthodox dignitaries, government representatives and pilgrims.

Memorial's primary objective is to develop a universal, neutral memory project capable of bonding people of different faiths and nationalities together. By contrast, the Orthodox Church is focused on developing a project forming part of the Orthodox tradition that would be capable of uniting the Orthodox faithful. Pierre Nora's *lieux de mémoire* concept (Nora 1989: 7) can be usefully evoked to justify the claim that Memorial intends to create a kind of network of archives preserving memories that will remind citizens that the state could conceivably conduct a repressive policy against them. However, the Orthodox Church's primary concern is to reconstruct environments where memory itself constitutes a genuine part of the experiencing (Nora 1989) of a setting typical of Orthodox spirituality.

This spiritual setting is more in tune with the feelings of the islanders themselves. One museum employee described her attitude to the Islands' history as follows:

> I was brought up here, so my attitude to this place is completely different. This is my home. This is the place where I felt comfortable when I was a child. I want to show Solovki to the people who come here – not only those sites where people were dying. I want to show [them] places, exalted by their spirituality, that testify to the splendid culture and history. [01_AA]

It is worth stressing that the grandeur of the Islands' religious past has always been a source of admiration for their inhabitants Takahashi points out in his analysis of the Solovetsky Museum's activity during Soviet times, 'Although, in 1965–1985, nobody spoke about this openly, within the specifics of the local landscape, religion continued to exert a definite, albeit hidden influence' (Takahashi 2008).

Not everyone regards the history of the Gulag as their own. One Russian who took part in a festival of bardic song I attended claimed that he visited cemeteries and war memorials: 'A lot more people died there than in the Gulag. None of our own died in the Gulag; our own died on the front – that's why we go there [instead].' His comment displays the influence of a quite important aspect of Gulag memory; namely, its strong connection to the memory of the Great Patriotic War and the fact that a heroic myth is much more attractive than victimhood.[118] This also explains why not everyone wishes to identify themselves with the history of the labour camps. During an organized excursion I took to Anzer in 2007, I asked the guide how interested tourists are in Gulag history, and received the response that foreign tourists are much more interested in this history than Russians are. According to the guide, this was an outcome of Western propaganda that wanted Stalin's crimes, rather than anything else, to be remembered. This comment reveals an important dimension of Gulag memory; namely, how markedly perceptions in certain Russian circles differ from those predominating in the West. The guide's comment clearly indicates that many Russians are unprepared, despite the West's insistence, to accept that there is any need to make the Gulag a fundamental component of both local and national identity.

Over recent years, religion has become the dominant element in the Archipelago's landscape, determining the way in which the past is perceived. As late as 2007, a museum employee stressed during an interview with me that everyone who come to the Islands defines them differently: 'For some, it's . . . the cabin boys' school,'[119] and with respect to them, to the boys who studied there when they were sixteen or seventeen, they have their own history and their own memory . . . Everyone has their own Solovki' [01_AA]. However, images of the past are becoming more uniform as time passes. This has been very aptly expressed by Roman Balashov, Vice Governor of the Arkhangelsk Region, who said during an interview for the *Pravda Severa* newspaper: 'I would like to evoke the words of Patriarch Kirill: From the way Solovki lives one can assess how Russia will live . . . Currently, a new attitude is forming to the theme of the repressions . . . the New Martyrs theme is taking precedence.'[120] Not everyone, however, would want this to happen, which is why Memorial activists, among others, are attempting to save Gulag memory from being absorbed into the history of Russian Orthodoxy by creating an alternative, secular SLON memory project.

Notes

1. For problems related to the creation of historical narratives, see Frank Ankersmit (2001, 2004).
2. By 'contemporary', I mean the years 2006–2008, when I carried out my field research.
3. I draw this distinction here, because Gulag monuments have not always been purposefully erected as such. As I will make clear later (in the chapter devoted to the Komi Republic), the meaning of some monuments erected in communist times to commemorate particular events or people was transformed during the period of the awakening of Gulag memory, leading to them currently being regarded as Gulag memory markers.
4. Although it was not in fact the first, because the Victims of Political Repressions Memorial in Vorkuta (whose meaning I analyse in the next chapter, devoted to the Komi Republic), was erected in December 1988.
5. Antonina Melnik had a curatorial role at the Solovetsky Museum, where she researched various themes from the Islands' history. From 1988 to 1990, she developed a deep interest in the Islands' prison camps.
6. My conversations with people engaged in uncovering the Gulag past in other parts of the Russian Federation indicate that the manner in which Solovetsky Museum staff sourced materials is typical of methods commonly used for acquiring information about a specific place's labour camp past. See later parts of this text.

88 | GULAG MEMORIES

7. One of the Solovetsky Archipelago's islands.
8. *Solovetskiye Ostrova* was published in the Islands from 1924 to 1930, a period during which SLON was operating there. For the newspaper's history, see www.solovki.ca/camp_20/magazin.php (retrieved 2 September 2016).
9. 'Memorial' is a name used by a number of organizations working on Gulag memory. The Days of Remembrance in Sandarmokh were attended by representatives of a Ukrainian Memorial, as well as the MEMORIAL: An International Historical, Educational, Human Rights And Charitable Society (NIPC) and Moscow Memorial. When I mention 'Memorial' in this book, I am referring to NIPC Memorial. All the people I quote come from this same organization. When I am referring to other organizations called Memorial, I specify which one I am referring to, for example, Ukrainian Memorial or Moscow Memorial.
10. Information about this transport was found in the *Solovetskiye Ostrova* magazine. It subsequently turned out that this was actually the first transport of so-called political prisoners. The Solovetsky Islands actually functioned as a deportation site from the moment the monastery was closed.
11. For the history of the political prisoners' camp in Savvatyevo, see Applebaum (2003: 42–43, 56–57).
12. Pavel Florensky was a distinguished Russian humanist, writer and expert on icons. He was exiled to Solovki, where he became involved, as a prisoner, in chemical experiments, during which his accomplishments included the discovery of iodine. He was executed by firing squad in 1938. His name had sunk into oblivion in the USSR. It was not until the wave of transformations in 1989 that the Soviet Culture Foundation set about restoring the unjustly forgotten names of those active in culture and the sciences. It was decided that Pavel Florensky should be the first person to have their name restored to the pages of history (Melnik 1989a).
13. During this period, one could still come across barbed wire, barred windows, the remnants of barracks and other objects that were part of camp life.
14. Alternative term for a forced labour camp.
15. In October 1974, Sakharov announced at a press conference in Moscow that 30 October would thenceforth be the 'Day of Political Prisoners, the Day of Struggle and Freedom'. On this day and over the following days, political prisoners being held in camps organized hunger strikes and published special newspapers. The date of 30 October was selected purposefully, as it was not associated with any other political or historical event, so did not connote any other meanings or provoke any doubts.
16. Information obtained from: www.sakharov-center.ru/asfcd/pam/pam_card.xtmpl?id=254.
17. For the history of the Solovetsky stone in Lubyanka and the competition organized by the Memorial Society at the end of the eighties for a design for an official memorial, see the virtual exhibition titled *Unimplemented Memory Project*. http://project.memo.ru/#stones (retrieved 18 December 2017).
18. People are reluctant to speak about this period. The everyday reality can be reconstructed from information appearing in local newspapers. However, this is also selective (Wilk 2007).
19. Cited after an article titled 'Solovkami zaymetsya Minkultury': www.oprf.ru/ru/about/structure/structurenews/newsitem/14989?PHPSESSID=nim1acq08q43t9s7blo6ojphc3 (retrieved 30 December 2016).
20. An extract from a text positioned at the beginning of the exhibition *The Solovetsky Special Purpose Camp 1923–1939*, which could be visited until 2008 in the Solovetsky Kremlin's grounds.
21. The Solovetsky State Historical-Archeological and Nature Museum-Reserve.
22. Many articles investigate the motivations behind changes in museum expeditions and the problems caused by a new manner of presenting material. Every change to an exhibition aims to accommodate the latest specialist knowledge and the manner in which a particular event or phenomenon is perceived. However, such changes often cause problems and dilemmas, as Teslow Lang (1998) points out in an interesting article. In this, she shows how sculptures created by Malvina Hoffman in the thirties, which presented people of different cultures, were perceived as being representative of various races. They were treated by some as confirmation of the existence of a natural hierarchy. In the sixties, the exhibition started to be seen as problematic and out of tune with the prevailing social and political correctness, so the sculptures were taken from the exhibition halls and deposited in the corridor, where they became *Portrait of Man* – an art collection presenting people 'from one or other corner of

the world'. This may be viewed as an attempt to break free from an earlier typologization. Another interesting analysis of a change in the mode of presenting material triggered by changing societal perceptions of a particular phenomenon is James Clifford's article (1988: 117–51) on the Museum of Man in Paris. Susan Crane (2004: 325–27) in turn shows in her analysis of two German museums – the Haus der Geschichte der Bundesrepublik Deutschland in Bonn and German Historical Museum in Berlin – how museums made various attempts, following German unification, to combine the history of East and West Germany. I think these three examples show the problems accompanying the changing of an exhibition extremely well.

23. In the case of local history museums, this last aspect is particularly important and exerts a profound influence on the work methods applied to specific exhibitions. These museums aim to document and present a region: its nature, history and ethnography. At the same time, museum staff undertake research themselves, publishing their findings in articles or presenting them at conferences (see, for example, the articles by A.J. Kotylev and G.L. Mosse, both published in 2005 in the journal *Muzey i krayevedeniye*). They also form the basis for future exhibitions. More often than not, the papers they write are the only existing studies of particular topics. For more on local history museums, their missions and aims, see E.A. Shulepova (2005: 178–214).

24. Many experts on museum exhibitions draw attention to the fact that placing objects in museum display cases confers a special new status on them – often the status of works of art (Cameron 1971: 11–24). When curators remove objects from their natural context, the meaning they confer on them is only partially related to them, since its primary purpose is to legitimize a narrative (Kavanagh 2005: 6). At the same time, it is difficult to imagine them in their natural context. Take, for example, weapons in war museums. It is difficult to imagine a restored and polished gun being used by soldiers or being found, damaged and rusting, on a battlefield (Jones 2005: 154–55). In the case of exhibitions telling the story of tragic events such as the Holocaust, the selection of exhibits and their mode of presentation becomes even more problematic (Young 1993: 123–33).

25. A Soviet state farm, as opposed to a collective farm, or kolkhoz.

26. See the citation that begins this subsection.

27. My summary of the exhibition's aims is based on the topic-based display plan created for it in April 1989, listed in the bibliography (Other Materials) as Solovetsky Local History Museum Archive 2_1_34.

28. Nos 5 (September/October) 6 (November/December). These were eventually incorporated into a book (Gorky 1964) that collected together some of Gorky's articles describing his impressions of various places responsible for the building of socialism.

29. Solovetsky Local History Museum Archive 2_1_34.

30. Some of the photographs shown at the exhibition were sent by families of ex-prisoners, and some of the information about convicts contains facts from their later lives.

31. Interviews [27_AS] and [28_AS].

32. Photographs depicting the Gulag, much like photographs of the Holocaust, are very problematic. Experts on Holocaust photography are keen to stress that many photographs presenting the Shoah were taken by the perpetrators, so the manner in which the viewer perceives the victims is from the perspective of the perpetrators, rather than that of the victims. As one Holocaust photography researcher writes: 'Photographs are fragments. They illustrate stories rather than telling them. How they are interpreted has been left to curators, film-makers, historians and propagandists ... Photographs and interpretations of them do not always allow us to gain a better understanding of the historical event that we call the Holocaust; instead, they remind us of how the world was organized later. The present always exerts an influence on reconstruction of the past' (Struk 2007: 35). For broader discussion of the presentation of victims in photographs, see Sontag (2003). Tomasz Kizny, creator of an album entitled *Gulag: Life and Death inside the Soviet Concentration Camps* (2004), has also paid frequent attention to the controversial nature of Gulag photography.

33. Solovetsky Local History Museum Archive 2_1_480_5.

34. Solovetsky Local History Museum Archive 2_1_34.

35. Solovetsky Local History Museum Archive 2_1_490_2.

36. Solovetsky Local History Museum Archive 2_1_501_1.
37. A holy site on the island of Anzer converted in the early 1920s into a Bolshevik concentration camp.
38. For more on the fact that exhibitions say more about society in the here and now than about how it was in the past, see Bogumił (2011a); Bogumił, Wawrzyniak et al. (2015); Bogumił and Wawrzyniak (2010); Ernst (2000: 25); Graña (1971: 98); Macdonald (1996: 1–18).
39. From a document providing information about the new conception of the exhibition devoted to the Solovetsky Islands' labour camp history. Unpublished materials presented at the exhibition.
40. See http://solovki-monastyr.ru/exhibibtion/golgofa-and-anastasis/ (retrieved 4 January 2017).
41. http://solovki-monastyr.ru/exhibibtion/golgofa-and-anastasis/ (retrieved 6 January 2017).
42. See Memorial's official site: www.memo.ru/about/index.htm.
43. The Memorial Society cooperated with the Ministry of Culture of the USSR, the Artists' and Architects' Union of the USSR and the USSR Academy of Fine Arts on the organization of a large design competition for a memorial to victims of repression, which received applications from many famous artists and architects. For more on the first stage of this competition for the 'best memorial to victims of the travesties of justice and repressions that took place during the years of the cult of personality', see Baranov (1989); Fuks (1990). The competition was criticized for being badly prepared because the requirements were imprecisely defined. It was unclear whether this was meant to be a design for a memorial or an architectural structure, and, in particular, where the future monument was to be erected. The competition was never brought to its natural conclusion, so the best design was not chosen. For more on the competition, see a virtual exhibition titled *Unimplemented Memory Projects* http://project.memo.ru/#stones (retrieved 18 December 2017).
44. The USSR's Political Prisoner Day/Day of Struggle and Liberation was introduced by political prisoners on 30 October 1974. At the camps in Mordova and Perm and prison in Vladimir, political prisoners went on hunger strike and Andrei Sakharov informed Western journalists at a conference in Moscow that political prisoners, by doing this, had effectively established their own holiday. Official recognition of this day was greeted by universal public euphoria, yet, as mentioned, its later name change (to the Day of Remembrance for Victims of Political Repressions) did not meet with the general approval of Memorial members, because it was felt that this changed the day's original message. For the history of the Day of Remembrance for Victims of Political Repressions, see Grabinova (2007).
45. The original inscription reads: 'Etot kamen dostavlen obshchestvom "Memorial" iz Solovetskogo lagerya osobogo naznacheniya i ustanovlen v pamyat zhertv totalitarnogo rezhima.'
46. See article '"Malyy" bolshoy Solovetski kamen, www.solovki.ca/events/stonemos_02.php (retrieved 19 December 2017).
47. For more on the symbolism of stones, see Eliade (1958: 216–17, 437–40).
48. I discuss one of these projects – the Sandarmokh Cemetery – below.
49. I heard the story below in 2006 in Medvezhyegorsk. Accompanied by students from Poland, England and Germany, I was taking part in the Days of Remembrance at Sandarmokh and Solovki. In the evenings, Irina Flige passed on her knowledge to us of both places. She told us about Memorial's activities, while also explaining the meanings being ascribed to particular places. The stories she told included that of the St Petersburg Solovetsky stone's unveiling. This story and the story of the discovery of the cemetery at Sandarmokh really intrigued me. Firstly, they revealed how Memorial works. Secondly, the story's construction was in itself deserving of separate attention. Stories do not just convey information, but also employ repetition and rhetorical questions to build an atmosphere. After getting to hear a few more such stories the following year in such places as Sekirnaya Hill and Savvatyevo, I came to the conclusion that both the stories themselves and their form are very important components of any Memorial memory project. For more on the distinctive features of orality and oral expression, see Ong (2002).
50. All the quotes relating to the history of the Solovetsky stone that follow have been taken from this same interview [10_IF] with Irina Flige.
51. The choice of 4 September for the date of the memorial's unveiling was no coincidence. On 30 July 1937, the USSR Politburo ratified NKVD Order 00447, effectively launching the mass repressions.

The document provided for the number of people that were to be subjected to two kinds of repression: execution by firing squad and deportation to a forced labour camp. On 5 August, the arrests of people condemned to death began, and on 4 September the first deportees were arrested (Gregory 2009; Okhotin, Petroc and Roginsky 1993).

52. The original inscriptions read: 'zhertvam kommunisticheskogo terrora', 'bortsam za svobodu', 'uznikam Gulaga' and 'Khotelos by vsekh poimenno nazvat . . . .'
53. Irina Flige informed me in August 2006 that Memorial's main concern was to ensure that 'communist terror' was used rather than 'Soviet repressions'. The first option made the oppressive character of the ideology more explicit.
54. As Tołczyk (2009: 84) writes, the Bolsheviks' aim was to liquidate all competing political parties. Initially, however, they counted on the support of Western leftist circles, so gave 'arrested social revolutionaries, Mensheviks and anarchists the official status of political prisoners. This status was not enjoyed by members of any of the non-revolutionary political parties the Bolsheviks liquidated first or former aristocrats, landowners, entrepreneurs, Orthodox priests, White Guards, tsarist officials and all of the other de facto political prisoners – often so by complete chance. They were simply "class enemies"'.
55. Ioffe is in fact writing about another event from the time of the Revolution, but his judgement is also applicable to Savvatyevo's meaning.
56. This subchapter is based on an interview with Irina Flige [10_IF], and a book edited by I.A. Reznikova (1997).
57. 'three Soviet officials who, in lieu of courts, sentenced periods during periods of mass arrest, starting in 1937' (Applebaum 2003: 592).
58. It subsequently turned out that the 1825 prisoners had been executed in three different places: near Leningrad (December 1937), in Solovki (February 1938) and the largest group, containing 1,111 people, at Sandarmokh. It is the last group that is called the 'Solovetsky transport' (Reznikova 1997).
59. It is supposed that between five and six thousand people were executed by firing squad there; see Krikhtova (2014).
60. The cemetery is about 1.5 km from the main road.
61. This fear provoked by the possibility of some grave being located outside a cemetery can be explained by referring to Mircea Eliade's research (1958: 370). As the Romanian scholar writes: 'The enclosure does not only imply and indeed signify the continued presence of a kratophany or hierophany within its bounds; it also serves the purpose of preserving profane man from the danger to which he would expose himself by entering it without due care.'
62. On 4 August 2007, during the Day of Remembrance, there was a round table and panel discussion titled 'Vyyavleniye, uchet i memorializatsiya mest zakhoroneniya zhertv terrora' (The Discovery, Registration and Memorialization of Burial Sites of Victims of Terror). In his talk, Arseny Roginsky, the representative of the Memorial Society, explained how difficult it was to establish the sites of the 1937 executions due to documents either not being available or containing fragmentary information (e.g. the personal details of someone who was shot and the date the sentence was carried out are given, but the execution site is not revealed). Moreover, not all the materials are released from the archives. As Roginsky stressed, only 20 to 25 per cent of the 1937–38 mass execution sites are known, so it could even seem as if they are not as 'tragic' as the execution sites from the early twenties or civil war. These sites were shrouded in even more secrecy, so establishing their whereabouts is practically impossible.
63. Not everyone was executed under orders issued during the Great Terror. Many of the victims of these murders could have been condemned by local orders. It is assumed that most of the convicts buried at Sandarmokh could have died building the White Sea Canal (see Krikhtova 2014).
64. The date 6 June 1923 was regarded in 1989 as the date of the first prisoner transport to Solovki. However, it later turned out that this, rather than being the date of the first transport, was actually the date of the first documented large-scale transport of political prisoners. By this time, the lager was already functioning, so the Days of Remembrance could be scheduled for any other date. Until 1997, they were organized on various dates in June and July. The Museum accepted Memorial's proposal to permanently schedule the event to 7 August, despite this date not being connected with any meaningful event on the Islands.

65. www.solovky.ru/reserve/ties/releases/2016/06/22/414.shtml (retrieved 6 January 2017).
66. In 2006, the commemoration ceremony took place by the 'People, do not kill each other' monument, and by 2007, by the boulder containing information about the Solovetsky transport.
67. In 2007, for example, reference was made to Katyn.
68. In this respect, Sandarmokh resembles other mass grave sites, where various kinds of national and group memory intersect, perceiving and transforming specific places in their own way.
69. None of the information I presented earlier was recorded at the time. Instead, I wrote it down after the conversations. I walked around the cemetery grounds after the official ceremonies in August 2006, talking with those who were tending the graves.
70. Joost Merloo writes that the worst thing for those who outsurvived loved ones who had been murdered in the camps was that they could not lament their loss. 'Not the torture, not the famine, not the humiliation kept them down now, but this lack of cathartic ceremonial' (Merloo 1968: 74).
71. The delegations seemed to perceive these particular events as the most tragic moments of the Soviet repressions for their respective nations in 2007, so granted them special status, thus turning them into important components of their national memory.
72. Sandarmokh is not well known in Poland. When I asked some Ukrainians who had not participated in the ceremonies if they had heard of Sandarmokh, none of them were able to tell me anything about the site.
73. A cross that was erected in 1990 by members of the Lichnost Community.
74. I have described here my impressions of the ceremonies that took place in 2006 and 2007, which I participated in, but have also drawn from the following sources, which describe the ceremonies from later years: *Solovetski Vestnik* 3(70), August 2010, pp. 1–2; *Solovetski Vestnik* 4(76), August 2011, p. 3; *Solovetski Vestnik* 5(94), August 2014, pp. 1–3.
75. www.intelros.ru/readroom/nz/nz4-2016/31027-borba-za-ogranichennoe-prostranstvo-pamyati-na-solovkah.html (retrieved 6 January 2017).
76. Since the Ukrainians who had been attending Solovki's Days of Remembrance in rising numbers abruptly stopped coming from 2014, Memorial activists took over one of the Ukrainian customs on their behalf in 2015, hanging an embroidered rushnyk on the large memorial cross near the Solovetsky stone. See http://novayagazeta.spb.ru/articles/9878/ (retrieved 6 January 2017).
77. In 2006, the situation was successfully brought under control. Following a sharp exchange of opinions, the participants returned to listening to the songs and poems. However, in 2007, when a great number of people came to the Islands to mark the seventieth anniversary of the Great Terror, a fierce conflict arose. A comment made by one of the members of Moscow Memorial offended the Ukrainians so much that they left the room, bringing the round table discussion to a de facto conclusion. Afterwards, people sat down in small groups in various places (often in the company of representatives from other organizations) to discuss the conflict situation and share their opinions on that year's round table topic.
78. Ten years later, he already regretted this decision and wrote in his memoirs that he would like to divest himself of the responsibility of taking this action.
79. From the materials for an exhibition prepared by Solovetsky Monastery, titled *The Stations of the Cross – Solovki-Butovo*, which was presented in the monastery grounds in August 2007.
80. The title of this section quotes the name of a chapter in M.V. Osipenko's history of SLON (2007: 50) and expands on an article previously published on the same subject (Bogumił 2011b).
81. The phrase 'smutnoye vremya' alludes to the Time of Troubles (1605–1612), a period of multiple uprisings provoked by internal conflicts within Russia and interventions by the Polish and Swedish armies.
82. I discuss the meaning and importance of this cross below.
83. Before the Revolution, Solovki was famous for its crosses and the workshop, owned by the monastery, where they were manufactured. See www.solovki.ca/history/crosses.php.
84. For more on Orthodox staurography, see Kuznetsov (1997).
85. www.solovki-monastyr.ru/propovedi_2006_08_23.htm (retrieved 15 May 2011).
86. www.solovki-monastyr.ru/propovedi_2006_08_23.htm (retrieved 15 May 2011).

87. In August 2000, as part of celebrations marking the 2,000[th] anniversary of the birth of Christ, a Council of Bishops was held in Moscow at an Orthodox shrine by the Cathedral of Christ the Saviour (the seat of the Patriarch). The process of canonizing the new martyrs had started in 1989, when a permanent commission was appointed to make the necessary preparations (Christensen 2017).
88. '8 fevralya – Sobor novomuchenikov i ispovednikov Rossiyskikh', www.patriarchia.ru/db/text/194754.html (retrieved 19 December 2017).
89. See the calendar of Orthodox holidays.
90. Lit. 'icon-writers'.
91. Investigating the New Martyrdom concept through the analysis of an icon is legitimated by the role and importance the icon possesses in the Orthodox faith.
92. A precise description of the icon can be found at www.pravmir.ru/article_1152.html.
93. The method of using earlier representations to create new icons enables the preservation of a sense of continuity and the Orthodox tradition of depicting saints.
94. The Gospel According to Matthew 10:28 (quoted from the St James Bible).
95. The war against Napoleon is called the Patriotic War in Russia. When the Germans invaded the USSR in 1941, the conflict between the two nations was called the Great Patriotic War to emphasize its national importance. The decision to evoke the war with Napoleon indicates that this military conflict also possesses an important meaning for the creation of the nation.
96. For more on the concept of Moscow as a third Rome, see Duncan (2000); Lotman and Uspensky (1993b).
97. The arrangement of elements and perspective are very important components of icons.
98. As W. van den Bercken (2003: 202) writes, depictions of Nicholas II in icons, including that of the New Martyrs and Confessors of Russia, were an important component of his family's canonization process.
99. Patriarch Tikhon stands on the left rather than the right side, because an icon is read from its centre rather than from the viewer's perspective. In this case, the spiritual centre is the prestol.
100. The information that prisoners were thrown down these stairs appears in Solzhenitsyn's *The Gulag Archipelago*. This story can also be heard during tours of Sekirnaya Hill. According to Memorial, this is only a legend, which has not been confirmed by any documents or first-hand accounts.
101. Peter Zverev, once Bishop of Voronezh, was born in 1878 in Moscow. He was arrested for the first time in 1921, but, having made a successful personal request for Patriarch Nikon to be released, he was also freed himself. He was arrested for the second time in 1926. Having been charged with undertaking counter-revolutionary activity, he was sentenced to ten years at the Solovki camp. He worked there as an accountant. After Archbishop Hilarion (Troitsky) was transported from the Islands, Peter Zverev became head of the Orthodox clergy, who were being detained at Solovki. In 1928, he was transported to the island of Anzer, where he contracted typhus, dying on 7 February 1929.
102. A description of all the kleyma can be read at www.pravmir.ru/article_1152.html. For more on the icon of New Martyrs and Confessors of Russia see Kahla (2010: 197–99 and Thon 2000).
103. All the other quotes in this subsection are drawn from this interview.
104. Christians believe that Jesus was crucified over the site where Adam's skull was buried.
105. See *Pravoslavny tserkovny kalendar* (2002: 166).
106. Butovo is widely known as such. This is clear, for example, from a brochure detailing the history of the Butovo firing range and church titled *Butovski poligon, Hhram Svyatykh novomuchenikov i ispovednikov rossiyskikh 1937–2000*.
107. Quotation from the website of the Butovo Polygon – Russian Golgothas: www.martyr.ru/content/view/85/15/.
108. For the history of the Martyrs of Sebaste and their icon, see http://days.pravoslavie.ru/Images/ii6972&629.htm.
109. www.solovki-monastyr.ru/news_2008_08_29_2.htm (retrieved 15 May 2011).
110. www.solovki-monastyr.ru/news_2008_08_29_2.htm (retrieved 15 May 2011).
111. Unlike Western Christianity, which stresses, after the teachings of Augustine, mankind's sinfulness and immorality, Eastern Christianity primarily proclaims Christ's victory over sin and death.

112. In 2008, I encountered some pilgrims from the Butovo Monastery travelling with the 'small Solovetsky cross' around sites of Soviet repression in the Urals.
113. The exhibition was opened on 26 November 2010, on the anniversary of the first meeting of the Board of Trustees responsible for the restoration of the Solovetsky Transfiguration Monastery.
114. During the presentation of the exhibition in Nizhny Novgorod, one of the visitors commented: 'We thank the museum organizers from the bottom of our hearts. Having acquainted myself with [the exhibition's content], I have begun to view Russia's history and the accomplishments of monasticism differently.' By contrast, a tenth-grade school pupil wrote, 'a few words of gratitude for restoring the memory of the national tragedy of the Russian nation' (*Solovetski Vestnik,* [1(83)] 2013: 8).
115. These include the Smolensk State University and the Church of the Smolensk Icon of the Mother of God in St Petersburg.
116. For New Martyrdom's importance to the contemporary Orthodox Church and the issues associated with this cult (Christensen 2012, 2015, 2017).
117. The title of this subsection alludes to an article published in *Novaya Gazeta* that can be found at http://novayagazeta.spb.ru/articles/9878/ (retrieved 4 January 2017). The Russian word *vlast,* which is used in the title, relates to political power. As Arkady Ostrovsky stresses, "In Russia and its former republics, *vlast'* is inseparable from *sobstvennost* or ownership, property, assets. Lacking legal property rights, Russian ownership can be backed only by state power" (2017: 239).
118. I develop this theme in the next chapter, devoted to the Komi Republic.
119. After the closure of the Solovki camp prison, the so-called Northern Fleet Cadets School, which trained future sailors, operated from the same premises.
120. http://novayagazeta.spb.ru/articles/9878/ (retrieved 3 January 2017).

CHAPTER 2

THE KOMI REPUBLIC

> By the will of Fate, the Komi region became one of the core islands of the sweeping 'Gulag Archipelago'. Over one-hundred thousand exiles and special displaced persons and no less than one million prisoners charged with political crimes passed through it. Their slave labour built our northernmost cities, railways, coal mines and oil industry, and felled our forests. Many of them settled our northern lands for good.
> —From a brochure published in 2007 by the Pokayanie Foundation

An Island of Coal Mines

The decisive moment in the history of the Komi region was the year 1929, when members of an OGPU (Obyedinennoye gosudarstvennoye politicheskoye upravleniye[1]) geological expedition discovered oil deposits after disembarking on the banks of the River Chibyu. This exerted an irreversible impact on land inhabited by the Komi peoples, a Finno-Ugric ethnic group that had until then been subsisting on fishing, hunting and reindeer husbandry and lived in traditional wooden huts. In 1929, the Komi region (from 1936, the Komi Autonomous Soviet Socialist Republic) started to be transformed into an area utilized for the industrial extraction of coal, oil and other useful minerals as well as prime logging territory. The main group inhabiting the vast expanses of the Komi Republic was an international community of special exiles and zeks (Rogachev 2002: 3).[2]

As a matter of fact, the Komi region was also a site of deportation in tsarist times. The Soviet administration's first political prisoners (Rogachev 2002: 3) appeared here in 1923, but it was not until 1929 that the Komi Republic truly entered Gulag history.[3] In Chibyu (now Ukhta), a camp was founded that was named Ukhtpechlag in 1931.[4] Successive geological expeditions were organized for the purposes of discovering useful minerals. In 1930, Georgy Chernov discovered coalfields along the River Vorkuta, and in 1931, Gulag prisoners started extracting this natural resource at Rudnik (Getsen 2004: 107–17). In the same year, construction began on a mine in Inta (Malofeyevskaya 2004: 30–34). Construction also began on a network of roads and railways, facilitating the transportation of raw materials and ensuring a constant supply of prisoners to the various camps (before then, transportation had been primarily seasonal and river-based) (Azarov 2000b). In the Komi Republic, more and more '-lags' responsible for road construction, coal and oil extraction, water haulage and logging came into existence, undergoing continuous transformation.[5] After a number of years, some of these developed into local towns such as Vorkuta (Barenberg 2014), Inta, Pechora and Ukhta (Rogachev 2002), or villages such as Abez.

The specific nature of the local history powerfully determines the shape of Gulag memory. As Mikhail Rogachev – historian and representative of the Pokayanie Foundation – writes in his preface to Evgeniya Zelenskaya's book *Lagernoye proshloye Komi kraya* . . . , the early history of the town of Ukhta had two dimensions. On the one hand, this was 'the history of the zone' and the thousands of prisoners who passed through it, labouring like slaves in the mines and on the construction of roads and bridges as well as felling forests. On the other, this was the history of the foundation of a fuel and energy complex in the European North: 'the history of the most magnificent geological expeditions, scientific surveys and discoveries, and the development of new industrial technologies. This was the history of the construction of a town in the taiga, a history bound up with the creative labours of talented architects . . . This was the history of the camp theatre' (Zelenskaya 2004: 3). Rogachev's words may be applied not only to Ukhta, but the whole Republic. From 1929 to the end of the fifties, Komi possessed two histories developing in parallel, the tragic one – that of the Gulag – and the heroic one, manifested in the taming of the nature of the North and construction of cities by coal and oilfields. The intertwined memories of these two histories also mutually determine them.

Another element imparting special meaning to memory of the Gulag in the Komi Republic is the fact that after the lagers were closed, many ex-prisoners stayed behind to work and live on these lands. In the early nineties, ex-prisoners and their children became a genuine political force, holding high-ranking positions in municipal structures and at Republic, or even national, level. Branches of the Memorial Society mushroomed in all the cities that were once camps. Many people supported them. Almost everyone sympathized with this environment. Special newspapers were published, and meetings, evenings and Days of Remembrance were organized. The Komi Republic was experiencing a true carnival of memory. Every town had its local colour and unique atmosphere. As one of the participants in those events mentioned, 'In '89, every day was a Day of Remembrance' [20_AN].

The awakening of memory in each town originated from different sources and had its own heroes – in Ukhta, these were Alexey Terentyev and Arkady Galkin; in Vorkuta, Dmitry Mamulayshvili; in Inta, Olga Molenya and Viktor Demidov; in Pechora, Vladimir Chivanov; and in Syktyvkar, Revolt Pimenov. What these cities shared was a desire to tell the truth, venerate the repressed and create a new, better state. A full picture of the atmosphere of this period could only be given through detailed reconstruction of the prevailing circumstances at each of these places and the thorough presentation of all of Memorial's founders, for they were the primary driving force that shaped it. But such a reconstruction would require a separate book, so I shall only provide one example that, in my view, partially renders this atmosphere.

This is the story of the origins of the awakening of memory of the Gulag in Syktyvkar, as told to me by a member of the Syktyvkar chapter of Memorial. It is a story that is bound up with the figure of Revolt Ivanovich Pimenov. As my interviewee relates:

> Revolt Ivanovich Pimenov came from a very orthodox communist family. They called him 'Revolt' . . . This was no coincidence. His parents, his mother and father were 100 per cent communists. Anyway, in 1957, Revolt Ivanovich Pimenov, a young student of the mathematics department of a Moscow university, became embroiled in dissident activity. This was Khrushchev's Thaw of '57 [sic],[6] when there were many physicists, mathematicians, scholars, artists, poets . . . there was such a movement. They arrested Revolt Ivanovich Pimenov a first time, then a second time, then sent him here to Syktyvkar . . . and he worked, washing the dishes; there was no work anywhere else. At the Komi Science Centre, where it was possible to work as a mathematician and there was a shortage of mathematicians, they didn't give him any work. [20_AN]

Pimenov's trials were attended by Andrei Sakharov, who had befriended him. In the end, he managed to write a doctoral thesis, and then a habilitation thesis. He worked at the Komi Science Centre.

In October 1988, following a decision by the state authorities to resume the process of rehabilitating unlawfully repressed persons, a meeting took place at the Builders Community Centre in Syktyvkar. As my interviewee recalls:

> Some friends telephoned me and asked if I was going to an evening being held in memory of Nikolay Bukharin . . . The decision had just been taken to rehabilitate Bukharin . . . This was the first ever meeting of the repressed in Syktyvkar. It was organized by Revolt Ivanovich Pimenov and a group of young scholars who had organized themselves around him. [20_AN]

At the meeting, Party representatives read out the communist authorities' decision regarding Bukharin's rehabilitation, after which 'a woman came out, a completely humble woman, and started talking about her family – this was a humble family from somewhere in the Volga region, ordinary peasants – and how they had confiscated their kulak lands there, how they had sent them here, all of which they had survived' [20_AN]. As my interviewee recalls, the hall contained around three hundred people and all of them cried after hearing this woman's story: 'No one shed any tears on

Bukharin's account' [20_AN]. Afterwards, several more people took to the floor and, finally, Revolt Pimenov presented a paper on the history of Russia.

Thus began the Syktyvkar carnival of memory. For the whole winter, Pimenov gave lectures on nineteenth- and twentieth-century Russian history, which were well-attended. The participants recorded what he said and disseminated it to others. A first student newspaper appeared, which was followed by another, in effect breaking the information blockade. As my interviewee recalled:

> These waves spread. And in Vorkuta, they had already risen up, and in Inta, miners were burning their Party badges and throwing them out of their homes. Right before our very eyes, the Communist Party, Komsomol and all those pro-union organizations[7] collapsed like a house of cards . . . and they couldn't do a thing about it, neither the Party nor the KGB, . . . nobody could do anything. This was the Truth and it had to be heeded, and it was heeded, in '89, in '90. [20_AN]

In 1990, during the first Congress of People's Deputies, Revolt Pimenov received majority support and was elected as deputy for the Komi Republic. The carnival of memory had reached its apogee. On 30 October 1990, Days of Remembrance took place. As my interviewee who participated in one recalls:

> Now it's hard to imagine several hundred people; that's how many gathered around the Komi Science Centre; and with lit torches, some dressed as political prisoners, they went up to the building of the MVD, previously the NKVD, and held a meeting to commemorate the departed. MVD officers were running and shouting, "Just don't burn anything, . . . get on with it, we won't interfere". They gave us microphones and people said anything they wanted. . . . After that, there were no more such Days of Remembrance. [20_AN]

Days of Remembrance organized with the approval and assistance of municipal authorities and the militia also took place in other cities. On 25 December 1988, during the Day of Remembrance and unveiling of a memorial to 'victims of Stalinist repressions'[8] in Vorkuta, Vitaly Troshin (the incumbent Head Architect of the town of Vorkuta) recalls the participation of:

> the First Party Secretary . . . Deputy Mayor of Vorkuta, the actual mayor being out of town at the time and the camp commander; a salute was fired by the VOKhR – that is, those who guarded the camp, . . . also the first clergyman was there. At the time . . . we didn't have an Orthodox *batushka*, and a young cleric arrived from Pechora with his assistant. That was Father Petelin. [30_VT]

Much as in Syktyvkar, the origins of Memorial in Vorkuta are closely associated with one particular person; in this case, Dmitry Ulich Mamulayshvili, a former repressed Party member enjoying considerable authority in Vorkuta. Mamulayshvili cooperated with a journalist from the *Zapolarye* local newspaper in 1988 to create a social movement called U Pamyati v dolgu (The Debt of Memory), whose aim was to collect money for the building of a memorial (*Zapolarye*, 15 September 1995). The newspaper began to publish articles uncovering little known episodes from Vorkuta's history. As Troshin recalls, there were only two of them at the outset, but, 'everyone believed we had thousands behind us' [30_VT].

With time, many more people began to get involved. In April 1989, a Vorkuta chapter of the Memorial Society appeared. This incorporated the Poisk group, responsible for listing names and collecting information about former Vorkutlag prisoners. Expeditions to former camps were organized (Rogachev 2002: 3). The Days of Remembrance were important events of cultural, social and political significance. Initially, they lasted a whole week. In 1990, they began on 23 November and finished on 2 December. The programme featured meetings with former Vorkutlag prisoners, the opening of a new exhibition prepared by the local history museum, a two-day coach trip to historical sites in Vorkutlag, a meeting with religious activists of various faiths, a film screening, concerts and a Krestny Khod religious procession. There was also an opportunity to accept holy baptism (Petrov 1990).

One of the core tasks the Vorkuta chapter of Memorial set themselves was to build the Victims of Stalinist Repression Memorial Complex. The monument erected in 1988 on a riverbank facing the mine was meant to be the first step – the cornerstone of the future complex (Troshin 1989). In September 1989, sculptors from Moscow, Leningrad and the Baltic States arrived in Vorkuta, as later related in a chronicle of important dates and events published by *Zapolarye* (23 March 1991). Responsibility for the organization was taken by Vitaly Troshin, Vorkuta's Head Architect and a representative of the local chapter of Memorial. As he recalls, the artists came for a few days, a tour of the Vorkuta Ring Road was organized for them, and they were shown the most important sites, the 'remnants of the Gulag'. Next, the sculptors created their own designs. Every design expressed something different and they were all embedded in the national culture of the individual artists who had designed them, so it was decided to build all these memorials. As Vitaly Troshin explained to me: 'Vorkuta is a place in which many nationalities died, a continent containing all the nations. . . . [so – ZB] every nation should erect its own memorial. I then proposed to the administration that a complex should be built consisting of all these monuments, and this would be paid for by all these nations' [30_VT].

All the designs for the future complex were shown to the public during the Days of Remembrance taking place from 8 to 10 December 1989 (*Zapolarye*, 23 March 1991). The inhabitants of Vorkuta also had an opportunity to meet the sculptors (Mitin 1989). The actual concept for the memorial complex continued to evolve. As Vitaly Troshin wrote in the *Zapolarye* newspaper (Troshin and Usenko 1990):

The memorial complex is not only a monument to the victims of repressions. It is a huge complex consisting of architectonic–artistic compositions . . . an open-air museum, a memorial dedicated to the memory of those who died in the War in Afghanistan, the Inturist Hotel, an exhibition hall, a centre of spiritual culture, a Far North art restoration school, an Orthodox church, an Evangelical church, a reconstruction of burial sites and the international Road to Purification trail.

A schedule for this international trail was developed. Over a dozen days, tourists were to travel by train, boat, horse-drawn cart and aeroplane from Syktyvkar to Vorkuta, acquainting themselves with the history of the Komi Republic's lagers en route. The programme envisaged opportunities to visit former lagers and memorial cemeteries, meet former victims and also visit local history museums and learn about the culture of the Komi people and other peoples and nations of the Far North.[9] The route was jointly created by all the Memorial chapters, in Syktyvkar, Pechora, Ukhta, Inta, Abez and Vorkuta. Each one was responsible for preparing a part of the route.

The memorial complex in Vorkuta was supposed to be the most important item on the programme. Vitaly Troshin even recruited a separate Memorial organization, which was to be responsible for the construction of the complex. The shape of the designed architectonic project was constantly evolving, and his vision was influenced by the conceptions of the artists arriving in Vorkuta. One of the monuments planned for the complex was supposed to be Ernst Neizvestny's Kurgan of Suffering. In 1990, the famous Russian artist and sculptor, who had been living since 1976 in the USA, arrived at Vorkuta to choose a site for the future monument (*Zapolarye*, 23 March 1991).

He chose a bank of the River Vorkuta, where the residential area of Timan lies. It is clearly visible from Naberezhnaya (Waterside) Street on the facing bank, where the town centre is located. The monument was to point towards the pole star. Besides its gigantic scale, it is particularly notable for its simplicity. The form he designed is a huge mask composed of many other, smaller masks. It lies face up on the ground with its eyes flooded with tears. It was supposed to be executed in its entirety from concrete. The objective was to create a huge monument surrounded by 'northern nature – austere, stern, beautiful' (*Krasnoye Znamya*, 13 May 1990).

As Vitaly Troshin explained to me, the monument is gigantic because the artist wanted to show: 'the absurdities of tragedy. And the absurdity of this notion found its expression in this grandiosity . . . Secondly, he wanted to execute it in concrete to demonstrate the artificiality of people finding themselves here' [30_VT]. Ernst Neizvestny was particularly concerned to emphasize by means of his monument that people should not be living in such a place. This was to be symbolically stressed by means of the material from which it was planned to construct the monument – concrete, which, unlike stone, is an artificial material. The naturalness of the landscape would thus be violated, while the monument would express its creator's premise that this region was not suited to human habitation. The inside of the monument was to contain museum spaces where surviving tools from the lagers would be presented.

The memorial complex assumed its final shape after the arrival in Vorkuta of a group of students from the Academy of Fine Arts (ASP) in Warsaw. They arrived in 1994 with Professor Bogusław Smyrski to select a site for the planned Polish monument to the Prisoners of Vorkuta. The initial intention was to build two memorials: a cross by the entrance to mine No. 40 and the Crown of Thorns – a symbol of convict labour – which they planned to construct around the Memorial to the Victims of Stalinist Repressions on Naberezhnaya Street. This was designed by ASP student Klaudiusz Daczka. The thorns, which were cast from concrete, were to protrude from the earth around the monument and were linked by a steel cable resembling barbed wire, as mentioned by Smyrski (1998: 34–38).

Klaudiusz Daczka's Crown of Thorns sculpture enabled Vitaly Troshin to work up a final vision for the memorial complex. It was incorporated into the conception for Russia's Crown of Thorns, which became a crucial component of the project to transform Vorkuta into a Town-Memorial of international importance. The entire project was to be implemented within the framework of the *Rehabilitation – Town, Man, Culture and Ecology* programme. The programme was developed by the Council of Ministers of the Russian Federation. Its primary objective was to transform Vorkuta – a place where prisoners of various nationalities and faiths had died – into a 'symbol of the unification of cities, republics, states and nations that experienced suffering at the hands of totalitarian regimes'.[10]

Russia's Crown of Thorns was planned as a set of spatial-architectonic-artistic sculptures placed at significant sites in Vorkuta itself and on the Vorkuta Ring Road. The conception merely contained the assumptions behind the project and set a framework for it. The monuments were to be prepared by artists representing various countries and nations. As they held the initiative, Russia's Crown of Thorns underwent continuous modification. Some monuments were incorporated into it, while others were excluded based on the contemporary notions of various memory actors, in this case, delegations from the various countries.

The erection of some monuments forming part of the complex was essentially unrealistic from the very outset. Some projects, such as the German or Lithuanian memorials, began to be implemented. However, this was during a period in the mid-nineties when the Russian Federation was plunging into a worsening economic crisis (Service 2003: 137–51). This was felt all the more keenly in the Komi Republic, where towns, such as Vorkuta or Inta, kept afloat by their coal output turned out to be so unprofitable that they stood on the verge of bankruptcy. Rising inflation and prices made the erection of all the monuments essentially impossible. A similar fate was met by the international Road to Purification. As Troshin says, airline tickets rose in price so much that implementing the project became completely unrealistic.

This does not mean that no memory markers were erected. From 1988 to 1991, memorials, plaques or crosses were put up in the Komi Republic that were meant to constitute the beginnings of a memory infrastructure. The first acts of Gulag commemoration were performative in nature and should be perceived as what Jack Santino (2004) calls 'spontaneous shrines'. Such commemoration is unofficial and characterized by a duality that means that such shrines 'both commemorate deceased individuals and simultaneously suggest an attitude toward a related public issue' (Santino 2004: 367). This, within the context of the crumbling Soviet Union, may be seen as a struggle to democratize the country and memorialize forgotten victims. As Santino points out, spontaneous shrines compel visitors to personally engage with this issue rather than viewing victims as nothing more than regrettable statistics. They require viewer participation and, even more importantly, interpretation. That explains why the first Gulag monuments were neutral in form and mostly made of stone. Rather than imposing a meaning on viewer-participants, they invited reflection and discussion.

When these monuments were erected in the late eighties and early nineties, they were clear markers of the past. Firstly, because they commemorated a clear-cut category of deceased persons (victims) and marked the most important sites in Gulag history (cemeteries, shooting sites, former death hospitals), since their role was to turn past terrors into an instrument of group identity, as Paperno argues (2001: 109). Secondly, because, rather than being perceived as completed monuments, they were seen as the cornerstones of gigantic future memorials. They were treated and perceived as temporary memory markers. This had the drawback of interrupting the process of transforming soft into hard memory. This process was further interrupted by the economic crises and political changes of the mid-nineties. As a result, many of these temporary memory markers still stand in the Komi Republic today.

When inhabitants of the Komi Republic's northern territories discuss the mid-nineties economic crisis, they stress that it was a dramatic period in their lives. Their salaries were not paid for months. Today, they still do not know how they survived. Since basic life needs were not being met at the time, interest in the process of memorializing the Gulag past also decreased. People were focused on their daily lives. As a matter of fact, for some, the very idea of erecting monuments was controversial from the outset. In 1988, critical opinions on this subject could still be encountered in the pages of the *Zapolarye* newspaper. One dramatic example is a letter (17 December 1988) from ex-prisoner Mikhail Zabotkin, who wrote:

> I have to write, because twice in my life I have been gravely wronged: the first time – in 1937, when I was arrested, and the second – now, even more so. I have heard that they want to erect a memorial to the rehabilitated. But I'm alive! A monstrous injustice! I'm alive and want, by way of an apology, a pension supplement.

Mikhail Zabotkin was not alone in this opinion. Many former repressed persons shared the motto 'the living for the living'. The notion of memorials therefore caused conflict from the outset. This was compounded by the death of such figures as Mamulayshvili (1989) or Pimenov (1991), which led to a dearth of important authorities and people able to organize the movement. Other people appeared in their place. Hundreds of people swept through Memorial, but – as my interviewees stressed – this phenomenon offered no benefits to Gulag memory. Anyone who wanted to could become a member of Memorial, and this led to the appearance of the kind of people who believed that membership of Memorial would help their political careers. These people therefore joined the movement before moving on to pursue their own private interests.

However, the most important factor (as stressed by Mikhail Rogachev, Vitaly Troshin and Viktor Lozhkin, the people engaged in the creation of the memory projects in Syktyvkar, Vorkuta and Abez, respectively) is that this was a social movement. All the undertaken activities would not have been possible without determination and social engagement. Following the period of euphoria at the end of the eighties, the initial curiosity had been satisfied by the early nineties and interest in Gulag memory began to tail off. The economic crisis only served to exacerbate the situation. Realizing that social interest can sometimes wane, Vitaly Troshin founded a separate Memorial organization tasked with creating the memorial complex. In turn, Viktor Lozhkin sought to grant the cemetery in Abez the status of a memorial cemetery listed on the Republic's List of Objects of Cultural Heritage. He achieved his objective. And in 1998 members of the Memorial chapter in Syktyvkar set up the Pokayanie Komi Respublikanski Blagotvoritelny Obshchestvenny Fond Zhertv Politicheskikh Repressiy,[11] an organization funded from the Republic's budget that is involved in historical research and the process of memorializing the victims of Soviet repressions.

From 1999 to 2001, within the framework of this programme's implementation, a memorial complex in Abez was partially completed and the cemetery in Ukhta was cleaned up. In Pechora, the Pokayanie Kedrovy Shor Museum came into being. Budgetary resources for further memorialization work were, however, limited. As Antonina Kargalina, the former Mayor of Ukhta, has stressed, Pokayanie, rather than being the law, is only a programme. Based on this programme created on the Foundation's initiative and supported by the Republic's government, each town prepares its own action plan for memorializing the Gulag. The towns do not possess separate funding for these purposes, so when financial support from the Republic's budget is lacking, it is difficult to continue the work. In fact, certain funds are earmarked for these purposes every year, yet what the cities manage to accomplish is only a fraction of what should be done [14_AK]. One event that is successfully organized every year and in which the Komi Republic municipal authorities participate is the Day of Remembrance for the Victims of Political Repressions, celebrated in every large town on 30 October. It features the participation of representatives of towns and cultural institutions like local history museums. Everyone takes part together in an official meeting by the main memorial to victims of repression in a given town, but they also help to organize buses for a ceremonial tour of sites of memory and a commemorative light meal with tea (a *chayepitiye*) for ex-prisoners.

Gulag memory in the Komi Republic forms part of this region's identity. This is not a taboo topic, but it is also not a topic that dominates its inhabitants' everyday lives. The Day of Remembrance is widely celebrated, yet there are hardly any separate local holidays inextricably linked to the history of repression in these particular places (the exception being Vorkuta, whose inhabitants separately observe 1 August, the day in 1953 when prisoners from twenty-nine mines were shot). As stated by Mikhail Rogachev at the beginning of this chapter, Komi has two histories and these two histories exert their presence within its space and identity. Before 1988, all that was spoken of was heroic memory. Similarly, in 1988, the discourse was dominated by Gulag memory. Today, both are talked about. They would appear to complement each other and jointly comprise what is understood by the term 'the history of the Komi Republic'.

I began this chapter by sketching out the atmosphere of the late eighties because the manner in which Gulag memory is manifested at the former sites of the Soviet lagers in this region of the Russian Federation is deeply embedded in the activities being undertaken there. In the following part of this chapter, I focus on the Gulag memory projects being implemented there in an attempt to grasp their meanings. The Komi Republic contains many sites of memory, so my intention is not to catalogue them – especially as such lists already exist.[12] My primary concern is to explain how monuments and architectonic constructions manage to evoke the meanings that constitute multifaceted Gulag memory.

The issue of how certain sites and monuments achieved the status of Gulag memory markers can be better understood by considering how two histories – one telling of the heroic taming of the wild nature of the North and the other, of the tragic death of thousands of innocent people – combine to form a coherent story of the Komi Republic's past. I shall therefore take a look at the history exhibitions at the Komi Republic's local history museums. Each of them can tell us about what a given community wants to remember and how it confers meaning on its past. Comparing these history exhibitions should therefore facilitate the naming of the fundamental components of Gulag history constituting the Komi Republic's identity, which, in turn, will enable a better understanding of the meanings concealed within Gulag memory projects.

Komi, The Pioneers and the Zeks – The Portrayal of Twentieth-Century History at the Komi Republic's Local History Museums

> The Russian regional museum is a typical phenomenon of the country's culture... Over the last century, the museum was, in turn, an educational institution, a centre of agitation and propaganda, and a site for the revival of national culture. (Kotylev 2003: 26–36)

While travelling through the Komi Republic, I visited the local history museums in Syktyvkar, Ukhta, Pechora, Inta and Vorkuta. The conclusions I present in this subchapter are mainly based on my analysis of three museums: the Ukhta Local History Museum, the Inta Local History Museum and the Vorkuta Interregional Local History Museum. My decision to focus on these museums was not a coincidence. They are located in towns that grew out of former Gulag centres, developed throughout the Soviet era and, in the case of Vorkuta and Inta, experienced an economic crisis and slow decline at the beginning of the twenty-first century. These museums also share a very similar structure. They contain rooms devoted to nature, ethnography and history. The common features they share make it possible to compare and view them as a composite space for the creation of meanings of the past.

This does not mean that I shall not be referring to exhibitions at the Pechora Local History Museum and National Museum of the Komi Republic in Syktyvkar. It should, however, be stressed that these museums are fundamentally different to the museums in Inta, Ukhta and Vorkuta. The museum in Pechora is much smaller and does not contain all the components that generally constitute a Russian local history museum. To use Max Weber's terminology, it is not an 'ideal type' for a Komi Republic local history museum. The museum in Syktyvkar possesses a much larger collection. Despite its structure being the same as that of the museums in Ukhta, Inta and Vorkuta, it nevertheless presents much more expansive material, not only from the Syktyvkar region, but also from all the other areas making up the Komi Republic. Moreover, the city of Syktyvkar, rather than growing out of the Gulag, had already been founded in Catherine II's reign. Up until that point, it had been a settlement inhabited by the Komi people.[13] What is more, there was no labour camp at this site during the period of Gulag administration. All that could be found here was a local seat of administration and transit point.

As Sharon Macdonald writes (Macdonald and Fyfe 1996: 7):

> Like anthropology and sociology, museums are also technologies of classification, and, as such, they have historically played significant roles in the modernist and nationalist quest for order and mapped boundaries. In particular, like anthropology and sociology, museums have been supremely important in what Richard Handler refers to as "cultural objectification".

By systemizing knowledge, museums create a coherent and logical whole. When examining museum exhibitions at local history museums, I initially tried, therefore, to establish what vision of the world order they were proffering, using this as a basis for understanding how their structure influenced the interpretation of history as well as how history (both heroic and tragic) was being presented and, ultimately, what motifs were appearing and which were being omitted.

Modern Russian local history museums are reminiscent of a kind of library or encyclopaedia, presenting topics from various disciplines of knowledge from archaeology through nature to ethnography, art and history. The logic governing the construction of these exhibitions is reflected in these museums' structure. The starting point is always nature. This is followed by the appearance of sections devoted to ethnography and, finally, history. The arrangement of the various rooms also follows its own logic. Nature exhibitions first take up geological topics before presenting flora and, finally, fauna. It may therefore be stated that such an exhibition narrative is dominated by Darwinian evolutionism. This is most evident at the museum in Inta, where the exhibition starts with the formation of the world and the first primitive organisms. Only then can other animals be seen, mostly those currently inhabiting the terrain of the North: reindeer, bears and wolves. The nineteenth-century history and ethnography sections follow, and only after these does the twentieth-century section introduce the viewer to the contemporary reality in Inta.

Such a manner of presentation is reminiscent of nineteenth-century anthropological and ethnological works describing ancient peoples or the evolution of civilization (Morgan 1887). The standard version begins with a description of the most primitive (or archaic) forms of organization, before the appearance of more complex structures and, finally, the inhabitants of Europe – exemplifying the highest stage of human development. Such an approach may seem naïve these days, yet it is governed by certain assumptions. By showing the evolution of the world based on the example of a particular region, an attempt is made to locate the place in question within the historical order. The manner in which this material is presented places the foundation of Ukhta, Inta or Vorkuta within the wider context of the region's development. In effect, the history of the 1930s – i.e. the de facto moment of these towns' creation – appears to represent little more than another stage of this process. The construction of such exhibitions lends weight to the conviction that the intensive development of the European North was the simple outcome of an inevitable evolutionary and civilizational process occurring over millennia. This museum narrative reveals a concrete and carefully conceived conception of the cosmic order and aims to respond to every possible question relating to the course of history.

An important component of this conception is the notion of development. Even the ethnographic sections of the museums are not reminiscent of typical ethnographic collections (Riegel 1996). Instead they are governed by their own unique logic. The metal objects, samovars and colourful costumes in display cases are presented by the guide as objects of luxury that only the wealthiest or most resourceful of Komi's inhabitants could afford. At the same time, these ethnographic expositions are partially historical exhibitions, telling of the lives, work and customs of the Komi people in the pre-revolutionary era. Twentieth-century history begins with the events that gave rise to today's towns. In Ukhta, these are bound up with the actions of the first successful oil prospectors back in the seventeenth century; in Inta, with the October Revolution and 1918–1921 intervention of Western states; and in Vorkuta, with Chernov's discovery of an oilfield in this region. It should, however, be stressed that not only in Vorkuta, but also in the expositions in Inta and Ukhta, it is the moment when the geological expeditions arrived that is emphasized. In Ukhta's case, this is the 1929 OGPU expedition, and in the case of Vorkuta and Inta, Chernov's expedition.

This is followed by a description of the intensive industrial development of this terrain – from the first, very primitive mines to the latest generation of machines used in mining today. The last display cases provide information about the modern mining industry. It may therefore be stated that both the entire construction of the expositions and the manner in which history is presented are evidently subordinated to the notion of development. Whereas for the exhibition as a whole this is represented by evolutionism, for the historical part, this is development ideology in its typical Soviet form.

Another prominent feature of the Soviet discourse within the exhibitions' history sections is the strong emphasis placed on the presentation of heroes of the Great Patriotic War. Wartime actions are presented in great detail at Syktyvkar and Pechora. The emergence and rapid development of these towns is closely linked to the outbreak of the Second World War. By contrast, the other museums mainly focus on displaying heroes of the Soviet Union. Both the manner of their presentation (portrait photographs presenting the heroes with a multitude of medals) and the descriptions accompanying the photographs (the information always contains detailed data, including when and for what achievements a hero was awarded a medal) are rendered in the Soviet style.

This does not mean that local history museums exclusively reflect the Soviet historical discourse. After the social awakening of memory of the Soviet repressions (at the end of the eighties), local history museums swiftly began to incorporate new Gulag motifs into their narrative.[14] Museum employees were often members of Memorial and actively participated in social processes as they occurred. As creators of exhibitions, they were the first to become involved in the creation of a language of communication that was to enable the presentation and discussion of the history of the forced labour camps. The local history museums played and continue to play a significant role as important institutions during the Day of Remembrance. It is here that temporary exhibitions devoted to the labour camps are organized and also here that remembrance conventions are often held for former repressed persons. However, I was more interested in how the Gulag-themed material was being incorporated into the main expository narrative. What motifs had been accounted for and which omitted? To what degree was this a new manner of presenting the history of a given region, and to what degree were the new motifs integrated into the previous narrative? These questions could be most easily answered by analysing what the exhibition at Vorkuta was attempting to communicate. The present exhibition was prepared in 1987 to mark the anniversary of Great October. It was shown at the local Miners Community Centre. As can be discovered from the thematic-expository exhibition plan, it aimed to present Vorkuta's history from 1930 to 1959, rendering the atmosphere of those times, but above all to place an accent on the presentation of 'the town's development and character'.[15] As can be read in the original programme for a tour of the exhibition, 'our town's history dates back over 25 years and reads like a book portraying the heroic history of our country and its arduous, and occasionally tragic, path to building socialism in the USSR'.[16]

A year later, the exhibition was moved to the local history museum, and because the period when Gulag memory was being intensively rekindled had started by then, the exhibition was supplemented in 1989 by a memory wall presenting famous people – artists, writers, painters and actors who had served out their sentences in the lagers of Vorkuta. Over the following years, some documents were replaced by new ones, but no changes were made to the actual exhibition. It is an old version of an exhibition devoted to Vorkuta's development from a primitive settlement to a modern mining town, supplemented by information about repressed persons. The memory wall forms a discrete unit that is sectioned off from and has no influence on the original narrative relating the progress made during the taming of the European North. The main emphasis has been placed on the region's development, which commenced with the arrival of the first geologists and the opening of the first mine. This moment is portrayed at the exhibition by means of a sculpture presenting a geologist – the discoverer of the Vorkuta coalfield – above a scale model of Rudnik (the first mine and first camp). Any photos of zeks, if they appear at all, present anonymous figures, frequently engaged in the kind of hard labour that characterized the first stage of industrial development in these lands. However, information about the prisoners' daily lives, the conditions they faced in the barracks, how they were fed and reasons for their detention at the camp has been omitted.

However, another topic that is important and well developed, occupying a central position within the exhibition space, is that of the theatre. Unlike ordinary prisoners, prisoner actors have been listed by name and surname. The theatre appears as a space of dance and song, full of smiling young people. Such a display of a camp theatre is typical of local history museums. The phenomenon of the camp theatre serves as a summary of the entirety of a given town's twentieth-century intellectual life, and prisoner artists are presented as honorary residents of these cities.[17] Such a mode of presentation, arises, on the one hand, from the fact that under the terms of Article 58 of the USSR criminal code, many intellectuals ended up at the lagers, which influenced the formation of the popular assumption that 'in almost every concentration camp, there could be an open university' (Sherbakova 1992: 107). On the other hand, such a mode of display is firmly bound up with the mission of Russian local history museums, which are meant to show the positive aspects of a region (Kotylev 2003: 26–27; Shulepova 2005: 178–96). Within such a context the Gulag theatre activities symbolize the republic's cultural and civilizational development.

It is worth comparing the manner of displaying the Gulag prisoners who formed Vorkuta's cultural elite with that of the heroes of the Great Patriotic War. Whereas the photographs of the former are displayed on a separate wall and their history has somehow been separated off from the general narrative (Figure 2.1), the latter are entirely embedded in it. This is evident as soon as the exhibition discusses the year 1945. This duality of presentation is typical of every exhibition in the local history museums. Those who participated in the war are always placed inside the narrative and portrayed as members of the local community – they are 'our heroes'. Moreover,

THE KOMI REPUBLIC | 109

Figure 2.1. History exhibition at the Vorkuta Interregional Local History Museum. Part of the exhibition presenting the lager's former prisoners, which is displayed separately from the general narrative and located on the opposite side to the history of the camp's theatre. Photo by author.

the description accompanying a photograph of a hero often transcends the exhibition's main narrative by providing the separate story of heroic deeds on various fronts. Gulag prisoners representing the cultural elite of lager towns are portrayed differently. In addition to being separated off from the narrative in its entirety, the information about these people revolves around their cultural and academic activity in a particular place. The only biographical facts related to their life in the camps are based on dates: the dates they were arrested and exiled to the Komi Republic, the date they were shot or released from the camp, or maybe the date of their rehabilitation. An important piece of information that museum guides are often keen to stress is that some intellectuals decided, following their 'liberation from the camp' (i.e. upon completion of their sentence), to stay in the town and continue working there. The Gulag's cultural elite are therefore presented as a piece of positive local history, whereas war heroes are mediator-links melding local history to the heroic history of the whole country.[18]

When examining contemporary local history museums, it should be stressed that, despite the transformations that occurred post-1991, they have always continued to reflect their erstwhile Soviet mission – to sustain the taming of the North myth as well as that of the civilizational leap that coincided with the Soviet Union's emergence as a power. The lager is indeed no longer a taboo topic, but only those of its components that form an inherent part of the history of the region's cultural and industrial development are presented. Moreover, any talk of tragic events fails to shatter the illusion of the taming of the North. Sometimes the impression may be gained that the Komi Republic not only possessed two histories, but that they were running in parallel and exerted no influence on each other.

This is confirmed by the programmes of two tours that visitors to the museum in Syktyvkar can book. The first bears the title *The Development of the Komi Region from 1917 to 1940* and the second, *Repressions in the Komi Region from 1929 to 1956. Journey into the Whirlwind*.[19] The exhibition informing visitors about the repressions begins with the general observation that the eventual outcome of the revolution was the formation of a totalitarian state. It goes on to present well-known figures from the history of the Komi Republic and the whole of the USSR who became the victims of the Soviet repressions on the Republic's territory. This is the story of people and their fates. However, the tour devoted to the development of the region attempts to 'objectively' convey history 'as it actually happened', by telling the history of the Komi region from the outbreak of the October Revolution to the commencement of the Great Patriotic War. The route taken by both tours leads through the same exhibition and visitors often pause at the same exhibits, yet they are essentially presenting two different stories: one focusing on development and the other on the repressions.

During the *The Development of the Komi Region from 1917 to 1940* tour, the viewer becomes acquainted with two different histories in parallel. In an attempt to preserve a sense of objectivity, the guide first speaks of the atrocities of the Red Terror before informing visitors about civil war heroes who were awarded the Order of the Red Star. After receiving information about dekulakization and the difficult, primitive living conditions of special displaced persons, the viewer learns about the advantages of the mechanization programme introduced by the Soviet authorities to aid collectivization and the creation of kolkhozes, and can also admire 'the museum's most precious exhibit' – the HTZ[20] tractor on which the tractor driver Petr Aleksandrovich Velayev worked for over twenty-five years. The guide moves from one display case to the next, pointing out exhibits and listing one historical fact after another. Visitors curiously ask questions, such as why people were charged with being kulaks and how many tractors were being used in kolkhozes in the thirties. Apparently, shifting from the first to the second narrative is neither problematic or internally contradictory for them. Both appear equally interesting and important, and both represent a piece of the Komi Republic's history.[21]

My main findings on the local history museums I visited are encapsulated in the words of the famous German museum scholar Hermann Lübbe (1991: 7–29). In his view, despite the openness of museums to new trends and their incorporation of these into their narratives, these institutions mainly shape and materialize perceptions of the past in such as manner as to help contemporary humans living in a continuously changing world maintain their cultural identity. The fact that the narrative in these local history museums is predisposed toward the preservation of the old progress and development myth confirms that it is still relevant today and meeting a social demand. As Mieke Bal notes (1996: 3–4), myth models (see Obeyesekere 1992: 8–15) that allude to powerful and paradigmatic myths – such as the progress myth, in fact are preserved by discourses that neutralize them, conferring on them the status of objective truth. Museum narratives employ myth models for their stories of everyday life, thus legitimizing and objectivizing their communicative content.

Furthermore, the example provided by the local history museums demonstrates that no other equally realistic and convincing narrative has been produced that could replace the existing one. The history of the Gulag only partially constitutes a fragment of this narrative. It is mainly presented in parallel on a separate wall or an adjoining display case. It is no longer passed over, yet also exerts little significant impact on the old progress narrative, which still enjoys the continuous interest of the public. What is more, in the face of the economic crisis that Inta and Vorkuta are experiencing (both towns are unprofitable, the mines are closing down and people are being displaced to other regions of the Russian Federation), the progress and development narrative is increasingly attractive and even more of a social need. The comprehensive vision of the world presented by the local history museums makes it possible to determine Inta and Vorkuta's place in this system. Breaking the spell cast by this myth could send the message that there is nothing else to hold on to apart from this fiction. Moreover, the functioning of these towns was not only not historically necessary but should be given a radical rethink. Such opinions also appeared in the late eighties, and it was these that Ernst Neizvestny was attempting to express in his design for the 'Kurgan of Suffering' mask for the town of Vorkuta. However, not everyone concurs with this approach, and not only because it shatters their ideals. Their main reasoning is that it destroys a coherent system of explanation without proposing anything in return.

Gulag Monuments – What Is Commemorated at the Former Sites of Soviet Lagers

> A society's culture is expressed in the care with which it treats its spiritual treasures – monuments of history and art. They . . . present themselves, as it were, as the face of a city. (Minina 1994)

The Gulag memory projects found in the Komi Republic are diverse. From basic memory markers that communicate condensed information to expansive multi-component memorial complexes with multifaceted messages; from markers of local significance to those of national importance; from monuments erected in artificially demarcated space conveying the assumptions of the memory projects' creators to those located in situ at the site of an important historical event; from markers possessing an artistic dimension to those purely confessional in form; and finally, from monuments constructed with the express intention of remembering the Gulag to those erected earlier that have later been designated as Gulag monuments. When we investigate these diverse forms of commemoration more closely, it turns out that general assumptions exist on a regional scale when it comes to the selection of site and form as well as the functions ascribed to memory markers. I therefore attempt in this chapter to characterize various kinds of monument. This should enable me to create a catalogue of issues pertinent to Gulag memory projects in the Komi Republic.

Initially, it is worth collecting and naming those elements that most powerfully influenced the form of the memory markers found at these sites. Crucially, the Gulag was not a taboo topic here, enabling memory actors to function relatively free of constraints. However, financial problems have meant that any projects requiring significant funding were impossible to implement, making it necessary to create other alternative monuments requiring a modest budget as well as utilizing and transforming elements of the cultural landscape that already existed.

It was crucially important to decide where a monument should be erected and what it would commemorate. Antonina Kargalina drew attention to this issue in our conversation. When she was Mayor of Ukhta, she planned to place commemorative plaques at sites with some link to Gulag history. With this aim in mind, she asked a former Ukhtpechlag prisoner and local tour guide to indicate such sites in the town. After two days of visiting potential sites together, it turned out that commemorative plaques deserved to be placed on every second building in Ukhta [14_AK]. The realization of such an undertaking was obviously not possible, mainly for financial reasons. Apart from this, nobody wanted to transform the town into a museum. It was therefore necessary in Ukhta as well as other towns in the Komi Republic to make choices about what should be commemorated and where and decide what was more important – commemorating the Gulag or protecting what remained of it (for example, the crumbling and overgrown cemeteries).

Apart from this, another factor influencing the form of monuments in the Komi Republic was the fact that the memory actors functioning there were a relatively homogeneous group – namely members, former members and sympathizers of Memorial closely cooperating with the Pokayanie Foundation. They have very similar views about how memorialization should take place and also cooperate closely with each other on various projects. All the aforementioned factors determine the meaning of the Komi Republic's Gulag monuments, but they can also be divided into several basic categories.

Monuments to the Pioneers – Remembering the First Zeks

At a first glance, it would appear that memorials to the first prospectors have little in common with Gulag memory. However, since some of the expeditions were manned by prisoners and it was zeks who had to be brought in to extract the minerals following the discovery of oil or coalfields, these monuments have acquired new meanings with the passage of time. Apart from providing information about the 'founding fathers' of local towns, they have also become important Gulag memory markers. The best example of such a monument is the Pioneers of the North Memorial in Ukhta (Figure 2.2).

It was unveiled in 1974 on a bank of the River Ukhta on the forty-fifth anniversary of the arrival of the OGPU expedition from Solovki (the 'Ukhta Expedition') that provided the impetus for the development of the oil industry in this region. The memorial's unveiling was an important social event that the municipal authorities participated in, and members of the 1929 exhibition also contributed to the speeches (*Ukhta*, 24 August 1974). Nobody said anything about the Gulag prisoners. The monument quickly became part of the infrastructure of sites of memory with oil and gas links, an infrastructure meant to commemorate the 'magnificent people' who managed to construct a 'town of industry and culture in the heart of the taiga'. As can be read in the edition of *Ukhta* marking the fiftieth anniversary of the expedition's arrival (Yuryev 1979): 'our state, our region has a superb and heroic history. That is why we solemnly honour the memory of the first adventurers, those who initiated the oil and gas industries.'

Today, the monument still performs its original function as a memory marker linked to the development of the Komi Republic's oil industry. However, for some of the town's residents, it has another meaning. As Evgeniya Zelenskaya, a representative of the Ukhta chapter of Memorial, explained to me, 'Ninety-eight per cent of the

Figure 2.2. The Pioneers of the North Memorial. Photo by author.

discoverers of the North were prisoners, so it could in fact be said that this memorial was erected to honour the memory of prisoners' [31_EZ]. Those participating in the Day of Remembrance of the Victims of Political Repressions actually come to this place on 30 October every year after attending the official ceremony in front of the Memorial to Ukhtpechlag and Ukhtimzhemlag Prisoners, thus honouring the memory of former prisoners – Ukhta's first zeks – while they walk around the sites of memory associated with the repressions. The Ukhta monument is therefore an example of how both memories – the heroic one and that of the Gulag – are directly expressed by this one block of stone.

Similarly, the memorial to Vladimir Rusanov, an expert on the Pechora region, which stands on a riverbank in Pechora, has a dual meaning. Firstly, it is a symbol of the town and, secondly, Rusanov's words that were inscribed on it ('The time will come . . . when a beautiful town shall flourish here and the working folk shall delight in this splendid view') played an important propaganda role for many years. However, the monument's location (from 1938 to 1941, the embarkation point for barges from Arkhangelsk bringing prisoners used on the construction of the Kotlas-Vorkuta railway) makes it a Gulag site of memory as well. This explains why it is here that Tatyana Afanasyeva – a Memorial representative and employee of the Local History Museum – begins her Pechorlag Sites of Memory walking tour.[22]

Memorials to the first pioneers can also be encountered in Inta, Abez and Vorkuta. All of them stand at historical sites – either the arrival point of an expedition or the foundation site of the first settlement. On the one hand, they speak of the origins of a town, and on the other, they reveal a piece of labour camp history. The monuments to the first pioneers would thus appear to fully express the Komi Republic's dual history.

The Pushkin Memorial in Ukhta – Remembering Famous Zeks

The Pushkin Memorial standing at the site in the centre of Ukhta where the Ukhtpechlag began its existence is one of the most precious of the town's objects of cultural heritage. It was completed by a famous artist – Nikolay Aleksandrovich Bruni, an Ukhtpechlag prisoner – in 1937, on the hundredth anniversary of the poet's death. The sculpture has a dual meaning: on the one hand it is dedicated to Russia's greatest poet, and on the other it commemorates its creator – a person who suffered during the repressions.

After the monument was unveiled, it changed location many times. According to an *Ukhta* report from 1994, it had not been adequately conserved, so had fallen into a very bad state of repair (Minina 1994). However, in 1999, 'Pushkin' was restored by local artists and re-erected at its original site at the intersection of Pushkin and Oktyabrskaya Streets. As the former Mayor of Ukhta notes, the monument's re-unveiling was a significant cultural event, and it quickly became a symbol of the Gulag and one of the sites visited during the annual Day of Remembrance. It is so important that when, in 2007, countrywide meetings commemorating the seventieth anniversary of those murdered during the Great Terror took place on every first Thursday of the month in front of Gulag memory markers, members of the Ukhta chapter of Memorial chose to meet by the Pushkin Memorial rather than by the one commemorating the Ukhtpechlag prisoners. As Evgeniya Zelenskaya explains, it was easier to gather around 'Pushkin' to commemorate the deceased. However, this response is not really very convincing, because the Day of Remembrance every 30th of October does actually take place in front of the Ukhtpechlag Prisoners monument. What is more, these two memory markers are separated by fewer than five hundred metres. The fact that the Pushkin Memorial is regarded as an important space for remembering the Gulag and the site of meetings commemorating the Great Terror would appear to have another cause.

Gulag memory seeks out its own heroes, or exceptional people. While the heroes in Orthodox memory are martyrs, in secular memory they are artists, singers, painters or writers, who become part of the myth of the intelligentsia and artistic bohemia. I wrote earlier about the powerful need to find prisoner heroes for exhibitions at local history museums that devote a great deal of space to exceptional life histories and little information to ordinary zeks. In such a town as Ukhta or other places that have grown out of the Gulag, there would appear to be a stronger emphasis on valuable roles and exceptional heroes, because these towns do not want to perceive their existence as the outcome of a tragic catastrophe. They therefore seek out positive moments in their history. Their attitude towards the Pushkin Memorial would appear to be an attempt to meet these expectations.

When the Pushkin sculpture began to be perceived as a monument to Bruni the zek, this memory marker attained a new, additional meaning. It is worth stressing that this monument is unique to the Komi Republic. Most other famous zeks and groups of zeks are remembered by way of commemorative plaques on the walls of buildings. These are either dedicated to individuals – like the plaque on a building on Ostrovsky Street in Pechora, providing the information that from 1953 to 1955, G.M Danishevsky, a professor of medicine and Pechorlag prisoner from 1943 to 1948, lived there – or to groups of people, like the plaque on the rail workers' community centre in Pechora placed there to honour the memory of Pechorlag prisoners, cultural and art activists who appeared on the local theatre stage from 1940 to 1956. Whereas these plaques directly communicate that the people in question were prisoners, many others suggest this fact in a less transparent manner. This approach is exemplified by a plaque on a hospital building in Ukhta dedicated to the founders of the hospital that functioned in Ukhta between 1930 and 1960. It lists the names of fourteen people, some of whom were repressed, though this has not been recorded. However, Memorial members make it very clear that this memory marker can be found on the website developed by the Sakharov Centre devoted to monuments of political repression.[23]

The plaques not only commemorate famous people, but also communicate information about historical sites, and events that took place in a given space. A plaque on a wooden building in Pechora provides the information that from 1950 to 1957 it fulfilled the function of a Pechorlag isolation cell. By contrast, it can be learned from a plaque placed on a monument on Bushuyev Street in Ukhta that it marks the site of a drilling rig that was flowing with oil from 25 October 1930. It might therefore be said that these markers constitute a kind of encyclopaedia of the Gulag, explicating the past of their 'small homelands' to the inhabitants of these towns.

Monuments to Victims of Political Repressions – Remembering Anonymous Zeks

The Victims of Political Repressions monuments erected by Memorial Society members in various towns in the Komi Republic are the most important Gulag memory markers. Most of them were funded from voluntary donations collected from former repressed persons and the inhabitants of the towns in question. It is in front of these monuments that the official Day of Remembrance ceremonies take place. Let us therefore take a look at some of these monuments.

The Pechorlag Prisoners 1940–57 Memorial was constructed in Pechora in 1992 on the site of mass graves for prisoners from lazaret No. 1 at Pechorzheldorlag (a lager responsible for the construction of a railway line). It can be found in front of the entrance to today's communal cemetery, and was constructed from an ordinary gravestone. Another monument, unveiled in 1990, has been erected in Inta on the site of a former labour camp cemetery. Much like the monument in Pechora, its basic building material is a gravestone. The monument is shaped like a cemetery grave. The stone is inscribed with the inscription 'To the victims of Stalinism'. It was a temporary memory marker that was meant to stand there until the point when a large memorial complex was to be erected, yet it still stands there today. A similar inscription – 'To the victims of Stalinist repressions' – was initially placed on another memorial in Vorkuta (Figure 2.3). In 1988, when attempts were being made to gain approval for its unveiling, the authorities would only accept content such as this. As Vitaly Troshin recalls, at one of the first meetings by the stone, one participant, wishing to draw attention to the fact that Stalin, Lenin and Trotsky belonged to the same group of criminals, pulled out a banner that read: 'not Stalinist, but Stalinist and Leninist'. However, the other people participating in the meeting were afraid that this gesture could provoke the authorities into dispersing the gathering, so they tried to silence the protestor. In 1988, it was not possible to openly discuss every dimension of the Soviet repressions. It was only a few years later that the name of this monument changed to *To the Victims of Political Repressions* [30_WT]. However, this history in its entirety shows that the first monuments only appeared to be neutral. In reality, they expressed social opposition to what had until then been the official position on the past.[24]

A monument was placed on a riverbank opposite Rudnik – the first mine and lager. It was a temporary memory marker meant to be replaced in the future by a memorial complex. However, *Zapolarye* (25 December 1998) reported that: 'there is

Figure 2.3. The Victims of Political Repressions Memorial erected in 1988. Visible in the background, on the opposite riverbank, is a Polish Catholic cross – a memorial to victims of Soviet repressions erected in the former grounds of Rudnik, Vorkuta's first mine and lager. Photo by author.

nothing more permanent than the temporary. By now it can certainly be said that if someone ever builds a memorial complex, it is our grandchildren, God willing, who will live to see it'. The stone still stands today.

In 1997, a rock bearing the inscription 'Dedicated to the Memory of Innocent Victims of Repression' was placed in front of the National History Museum in Ukhta. It was brought there from Mount Vetlasan, because – as Evgeniya Zelenskaya explains – when the lagers were still operational, there was a hospital there where prisoners died in their droves. Nothing survives of this building today. The very existence of this place is only apparent from a cross erected in 1929 by members of the Ukhta chapter of Memorial in the hospital's cemetery grounds [31_EZ]. The monument was located in front of the museum, because – as Zelenskaya explains – it is a place popular with local residents. People pass this way on their way to work.

It is clear from a closer inspection of the above examples that these monuments share features in common. First, they are very simple, neutral and non-confessional in form. Their names are also succinct and in most cases associated with the word 'victim', which clearly indicates that they are commemorating those who died there, especially when their locations or provenance are also taken into account (for example, the grounds of former labour camp cemeteries). The gravestones at Pechora and Inta additionally emphasize the main message of memory markers: these objects commemorate the dead.

In the case of the monument in Ukhta, it also worth paying attention to its surroundings, which reveal a fresh dimension of Gulag memory – namely, its link to the history of the Great Patriotic War. The stone faces the Local History Museum, and is therefore on the periphery of a monument constructed in 1980 commemorating inhabitants of Ukhta who died between 1941 and 1945 on the fronts of the Great Patriotic War. An analysis of both monuments based on their location, scale and artistic form clearly demonstrates the place and function the Great Patriotic War and Gulag occupy in social memory.

Since the sixties, when the Great Patriotic War's meaning became fully apparent, it has grown into the most important event in the country's modern history (Gudkov 2005). The monument therefore speaks eloquently through its artistic form, stressing the heroism and ultimate victory of the fallen soldiers. Gulag memory has not yet been worked through, and this is symbolically expressed by an unhewn stone.[25] Modern publications by Russian historians contain the information that the forced labour system was necessary for final victory, and the zeks' slave labour was the only possible solution at that particular time (Morukov 2006). Such an interpretation of both events forms the backbone for a positive history of the Komi Republic's towns, whose period of most intensive development coincided with the war. The country's central regions were occupied by the enemy at the time and the 'the republic behind the battle lines' was tasked with providing essential energy resources required by heavy industry. This explains why many Russian scholars believe that the zeks' labour and death were a 'necessary factor' that facilitated the achievement of final victory in the Great Patriotic War.

As a matter of fact, the repressed persons themselves want to be treated as part of the memory of the Great Patriotic War.[26] As Evgeniya Zelenskaya says, the former repressed persons living in Ukhta want to be perceived as combatants in the Great Patriotic War and receive flowers and good wishes on this day. Their desire to be perceived as part of this significant event leads to former repressed persons appearing to ignore that fact that the war accelerated the Gulag's development, and it was actually at this point that they ended up in the camps. They also fail to reflect on the cost of a victory that, in the form that it appeared in the official discourse, could be regarded as a kind of false tradition (Grzybowski 1998). What seems to be of most importance to them is the fact that the war is perceived as an important binding agent uniting the national community of Russians, and this is actually why they wish to be perceived as part of this history.

The surroundings of the monuments throw light on one other important issue. Both commemorate the dead, but one commemorates prisoner-victims and the other, victor-heroes. The scale and location (the centre and periphery) of both monuments not only seem to explain what place both events occupy in social memory, but also display the cultural valorization of both kinds of death. Dying in defence of one's homeland is a heroic act unequivocally positively rated in Russian culture, while an ordinary death unaccompanied by sacrifice has no loftier meanings (Lotman 1990: 239). By placing the stone on the periphery of the Great Patriotic War monument, the Gulag's victims are granted heroic deaths, resulting in the stone acquiring positive connotations.

The Water Tower in Inta – Memory of the Zeks Preserved in the Town's Cultural Landscape

One of Inta's most valuable architectural treasures is a water tower designed by Artur Tambelius, a Swede by extraction who was accused of spying for the Germans and sent to the lager at Inta. He worked here in the fifties as an architect, designing municipal buildings. His most famous and intriguing work is the water tower. It became a symbol of the town, even being portrayed on its coat of arms. The prisoners themselves called it the 'Tower of Babel'.[27]

For many years, no one spoke about the contribution made by zeks to the tower's construction. But today, people taking part in a tour of Inta's objects of cultural heritage hear such information from the guide. When it turned out that the building had ceased to fulfil its original function, much thought was given to its future fate. The idea of organizing a planetarium or café in the tower was discussed, but the Inta Local History Museum's proposal to create a Victims of Political Repressions in the North Museum emerged victorious. In 2011 the tower was reconstructed and on 4 October 2014, on the sixtieth anniversary of Ukhta being granted city rights, a new museum was opened. The museum's current appearance conforms to the plans I was shown in 2007. The museum's collections are housed on several storeys, and present the political and economic situation in the USSR in 1930–1940, as well as Inta's industrial potential, and the village's architectural layout. The main goal of the exhibition is to show 'how the destinies of people – former political prisoners – joined together by the Gulag have created the history of the city, leaving an indelible mark on its fate and largely predetermining it'.[28] As Mikhail Rogachev stressed in his speech during the opening of a new exhibition:

> Of course, this museum is extremely important, since the Gulag in fact played an extremely important role in the history of our region, [especially] in the economic, social and cultural processes of the thirties, forties and fifties. Moreover, this is the third museum in Russia devoted to the history of the political repressions to be opened at a site of memory associated with the history of the Gulag, as there are similar museums in Perm and Tomsk. This is a good exposition, as it examines many issues, but it is modest in size.[29]

Despite these space constraints, the inhabitants of Inta still managed to construct a Gulag museum in a Gulag object of cultural heritage. The water tower stands on

Inta's main square and can be seen on its coat of arms. It not only reminds its inhabitants of to whom they owe their origins, but also that the most important local architectural treasure was designed by a zek and that their small homeland is a remnant of the Gulag.

The Zinaida Khorol Memorial – Remembering the Gulag's Women

In 1990, Zinaida Khorol's son came to Inta to search for his mother's grave. In 1952, she had been sent to Vorkuta, but was left behind in Inta due to her poor state of health and placed in a lazaret located on land occupied by the lagpunkt's fifth department. Here she died and was buried in this southern settlement's cemetery.

Most of the former cemetery is currently occupied by a chicken farm and allotment gardens, where people grow potatoes, cabbages and other vegetables. The surviving part is modest in size and difficult to access due to their being no road. As a matter of fact – as Nikolay Baranov explained to me – Zinaida Khorol's son never found her place of burial:

> They came here from Moscow and abroad and looked for their loved ones, but did not find real graves. During this period, it was not possible to erect monuments and put surnames, first names, father's name, date of birth, date of death on a prisoner's grave. There was just a plaque with his number on it on a wooden post. [05_NB]

That explains why the monument stands on a crossroads at a site visible from the main trail. It resembles a cemetery gravestone. The main stone contains the inscription 'Khorol Zinaida Osipovna 1908–1954. To the sacred memory of my beloved Mum, inhumanly slain by the Gulag'; and the plinth below, the inscription 'To unknown and uncountable women – victims of the Stalinist terror. Your names are immortal'. The second inscription has led to this object being treated as a symbolic grave for all the woman of the Gulag. On 30 October, the Day of Remembrance for Victims of Political Repressions, when those participating in the ceremony walk around all of Inta's memory markers dedicated to the Gulag, they also stop at this place to light candles and lay flowers, at which point many women make their voices heard.

Zinaida Khorol has become famous in Inta. Legends have circulated relating the reasons why she was condemned to be sent to Vorkuta, including how she refused to yield to Beria's amatory advances. For some time, the reading room in the town's library bore her name. However, most importantly, following the erection of the gravestone, other repressed women have found a place they can look upon as their site of memory. They not only come here to remember mothers and grandmothers who died in the lagers. They can also bemoan their own fate and that of other repressed women and children deprived of their mothers by the Gulag.

The Victims of Political Repressions Chapel in Syktyvkar – Gulag Memory in the Komi Republic

The most important Gulag monument in the Komi Republic is the Victims of Political Repressions Chapel constructed in 2000 by the Pokayanie Foundation (Figure 2.4). As the Foundation's chairman Mikhail Rogachev says [23_MR], it is no coin-

Figure 2.4. The Victims of Political Repressions Chapel. The central monument in the Komi Republic, designed by A. Neverov. Photo by author.

cidence that a monument was created in the form of an Orthodox chapel oriented to the East, as an attempt was made to emphasize that Gulag history took place on Orthodox land. Nevertheless, members of the Pokayanie Foundation add that this marker commemorates all the deceased, and not only those of the Orthodox faith.

Despite its simple form, the monument is rich in symbolism. The walls at the centre of the chapel contain the names of prisoners who spent time in the Komi Republic's lagers. Here can be found the first names of representatives of various nationalities, including Russians, Germans, Lithuanians and Arabs, all of which are interwoven and presented in alphabetical order. These names were taken from the *Martyrology* – commemorative books published by the Foundation. As Mikhail Rogachev explained to me: 'We took . . . the first two volumes and wrote out all the first names, not the surnames, just the first names, and put them into alphabetical order on steles. All of them are in order. There's the Russian, Patak, and after him the Lithuanian, Pranas . . . here's the Muslim, Radim . . . the German, Raymond' [23_MR]. This manner of presentation (using first names rather than surnames) was meant to demonstrate that all the prisoners, regardless of their nationality, stood in the face of death as a single community. The plaques on which the names are engraved were made from a special blackened metal to ensure that the inscriptions on them were not visible from afar and could only be read after walking up to the steles.

Another important component of the monument is the listing on the chapel's outer walls of all the Komi Republic's lagers along with the names of the main lagpunkts. The list was prepared in a very meticulous and diligent manner to ensure that no names contain errors and the record itself is notable for its historical accuracy. The composition is complemented by illustrations presenting scenes from life in the Gulag. Some of them were created from diagrams and drawings by artists who served time in the Gulag, while others present how the artists creating these portrayals imagined their past lives in the lagers.

It would be instructive to compare the prisoner names inside the chapel with the names of the lagers on the external walls. Whereas the latter refer to historical places, the former are not associated with specific people. Instead they represent a kind of imaginary prison community. Despite none of them being here by chance (all of them appeared in the Pokayanie *Martyrology*), this artistic composition has detached them from actual prisoners to create its own world of Gulag names. This nuance is reinforced even further by the fact that they have been placed in the inner – mystical – part of the chapel, while the walls on the exterior reveal historical facts (the names of actual lagpunkts that existed in the past). Such a manner of presentation, in my view, reveals another aspect of Gulag memory very well. Whilst we are capable of reconstructing the history of the Gulag as a state institution on the basis of documents, the essence of this experience escapes our view because it belongs to a community whose world we will never be able to fully comprehend.

It is worth drawing attention to one more element; namely, the metal relief located on the chapel's back wall portraying a 'night arrest'. At the very top is a carving of the Virgin Mary watching over the figures below. The artist next cut the figures off from each other by interposing an image of the hammer and sickle. This is a sign that communist ideology was an illusion concealing its true repressive nature. At the very bottom, the night arrest scene can be seen. The man was a devoted communist, as is clear from a badge with an image of the hammer and sickle in the child's outstretched hand. The Soviet authorities rewarded him for his loyalty and then killed him. The whole scene is reminiscent of Christ's crucifixion, with the two Marys – his mother and Mary Magdalene (here, his wife) – standing in front of the cross. The man himself appears to be humbly accepting his fate, and his gaze, which is directed at the hammer and sickle, expresses regret for his sins and repentance.

In front of the monument, a gravestone has been placed bearing the inscription 'In Eternal Remembrance to Victims of the Repressions'. Beneath this gravestone there is a mixture of soil from various post-Gulag towns in the Komi Republic. As Mikhail Rogachev explained to me, representatives of some towns wanted to place separate urns there containing soil from their districts, but in the end, earth from all the places was mixed together: 'We buried everyone together to ensure there was no division between what is ours and yours' [23_MR].

The monument clearly alludes, not only through its form but also its symbolism, to Orthodox depictions, but rather than violating them in any way, it merely becomes an artistic interpretation of them. This is why it has not provoked great controversy and was consecrated by the Orthodox priest. It is also approved of by the spiritual representatives of other faiths who congregate together in front of the chapel on 30 October to say prayers for the dead in their own tongues and according to their beliefs. An Orthodox clergyman enters the chapel alone while the others pray by the tombstone and lay flowers there. Anyone can enter the chapel and, according to Orthodox rite, light a candle. The chapel is also not closed on workdays, so anyone can come whenever they wish to light a candle and ring a bell to honour the memory of their loved ones.

The monument being discussed here clearly illustrates the basic function ascribed to sites of memory in the Komi Republic. The sites of burial of many victims of the repressions and their names and surnames are not known and will probably never be established, so the monument first and foremost fulfils the function of a tomb for all those who died on the Republic's territory. (This is expressed by both the names listed on the chapel walls and the gravestone mounted on soil and ashes from the lagers). The monument's main purpose is to honour the memory of the dead and the cemetery art is distinctive for its conservatism (Kolbuszewski 1995: 25), explaining why the building has the form of a traditional Orthodox chapel resembling those that often stand on Russian cemeteries. The monument therefore draws from the old Orthodox tradition of commemorating the dead, and by commemorating all the deceased prisoners at the same time it seems to allude to the tradition of tombs of the unknown soldier[30] but constitutes a curious invariant – the 'tomb of the unknown prisoner'.

The ideas presented in the Komi Republic's various memory markers manifest themselves synthetically. This monument is dedicated both to every prisoner and to specific groups, for example women (one of the reliefs on the chapel's interior walls commemorates the women and children of the Gulag) or individual national groups (names in national languages). Also, by basing the relief depictions on the interior walls of the chapel on drawings by Gulag prisoner artists, famous people from the Gulag and their creative output are evoked. The relief itself was partially executed by Neverov – a famous artist from Syktyvkar – transforming it into real art. The monument is physically located at a historical site, the point from which a road runs to a transit point on the River Sysola, but given the fact that the soil from various former labour camp towns has been laid beneath the gravestone in front of the chapel, it could be said that it has been erected on 'all' of the Komi Republic's territory. At the same time, it is located on the outskirts of a town, which also seems to express something about the place the Gulag occupies in Komi Republic memory. It has not been forgotten, but also cannot be said to constitute the heart of the local inhabitants' identity.

The Gulag Cemeteries – Texts of a Forgotten Culture in Contemporary Translation

> Here there is a world apart, unlike everything else, with laws of its own, its own manners and customs, and here is the house of the living dead – life as nowhere else and a people apart. (Fyodor Dostoevsky, *The House of the Dead*, quoted in Herling [1951])

This Dostoevsky quote is used by Gustav Herling to open his account of his experiences of the realities of the Gulag, where both the world of the living and that of the dead had been completely redefined.[31] Within the Gulag system, the dead did not count as much as the living, so they were 'got rid of' by being buried in mass graves or – as Nikolay Baranov from Inta says – being laid to rest by the embankment of the Kotlas-Vorkuta Railway (on a riverbank to ensure the spring floods would carry off their bodies) [05_NB]. There are many similar accounts of the desecration of human remains. They form the basis of the widespread conviction that the entire Komi Republic organically emerged from the 'bones of prisoners'.

Not until 1946 was an order sent out to bury the deceased in separate graves marked with a special number allocated to each body (Applebaum 2003: 314). It was prohibited to place signs of confession or any other symbols on the graves that would enable a corpse to be identified. What is more, as Anatoly Smilingis says, the dead were buried by strangers rather than their kith and kin [24_AS]. A brigade composed of people who attached no significance either to burial methods or the marking of burial sites was specially appointed for the task.

With time, the lager cemeteries passed into oblivion. They became overgrown, decayed or were even purposefully demolished, either by the authorities when they closed the camps or by people desecrating them in the belief they were the burial sites of 'enemies of the nation' (Merridale 2003, 2000). They were rediscovered during the political transformations that occurred in the USSR at the end of the eighties. The contemporaneous rekindling of Gulag memory was accompanied by a desire to learn more about the markers preserved within the cultural landscape. As the cemeteries became more visible, those who were alive at that time began to feel similar fear to that which continued to haunt ex-prisoners.[32] Their ignorance as to the purpose of these sites, the identities of those who had been interred there, when these people had been buried and the meaning of the markers and symbols preserved on the graves struck horror into them. As I walked with Anatoly Smilingis and Mikhail Rogachev through the Lokchimlag[33] cemetery near Kortkeros, Smilingis commented:

> You see, here there are people everywhere and we don't know anything about any of them. It's good that someone is still tending to them and someone's still living, yet there is nobody left here. Here there are people everywhere, we're walking [around their graves – ZB] . . . how many of them are here is anyone's guess. [24_AS]

Gulag cemeteries are sites at which the dead themselves demand to be remembered, striking fear into us with their skulls and shinbones. Mikhail Rogachev told me one such story that took place in Nidz Vychegodskaya. In 1994, a man arrived from Moscow to look for his father's grave. The records indicated that he was buried in Nidz Vychegodskaya. Unfortunately, when he got there, it turned out that the cemetery was located on a steep riverbank, and most of it had been inundated. The only part that had survived was on a hill:

> This too had been partially destroyed and the sand contained many bones. For half the day – there were four of us – we walked across this embankment collecting bones, and then we laid them all in one place . . . We established that one of the pits would be his father's symbolic grave . . . Then, some locals arrived, dug up the graves, laid all the bones there and gave them a humane burial in the new grave . . . they erected a cross and consecrated it. [23_MR]

Thanks to their actions, the lager cemeteries and mass burial sites no longer allow anyone to forget that the 'world apart' really existed. The dead would appear to be appealing to the living to afford them the respect they were deprived of during their lives, while the living are trying in various ways, by either creating memorial cemeteries or destroying those that already exist, to deal with a past reality that terrifies them.

In Nidz Vychegodskaya, the people from the village adjoining the cemetery decided to honour the memory of the dead. In order to do this, they made a wooden cross, the women baked commemorative dumplings, the men took some vodka and they all went to the cemetery [23_MR]. Nobody had known about this cemetery's existence before because it was located by a lager that was liquidated before the district's current residents had moved there. Apart from one exception – the father of the man from Moscow – the identity of the dead is not known. But this did not stop the villagers and local authorities tidying up the cemetery and erecting a memory marker (Sivkova 1997). Now metal crosses tower over two symbolic graves. The Komi Republic contains many similar sites.

The primary aim of memorialization activities in the Komi Republic is to pay homage to the dead by marking burial sites. The areas occupied by former cemeteries or mass burial sites would essentially appear to be the only spaces where a dialogue takes place between the past and present, the dead and the living.[34] Not only do they mark the landscape with the remnants of the Gulag, uncovering its 'otherness' to the fullest possible extent, but they also – by means of the commemoration processes being undertaken today – show what local communities continue to remember.

They can be viewed as peculiar kinds of text of culture (Kolbuszewski 1981) recorded in a language that is incomprehensible today and whose content has been largely disfigured by the bulldozers of post-Gulag history. There is therefore a need to translate the Gulag 'transcript' into a language of symbols and meanings that are comprehensible today. As far as most sites are concerned, little more can be said than that they are the locations of lager cemeteries or mass shootings during the Great Terror. All that is known are the victims' names. Some cemeteries' existence is evidenced by documents in the possession of members of Memorial or the Pokayanie Foundation. However, most of them can only be discovered from the recollections of former prisoners or so-called 'elders' – that is, the oldest inhabitants of the surrounding villages.

It is difficult to determine how many cemeteries there are, but if my interviewees' claims are accurate, and they claim that the Komi Republic's lagers contain the ashes of hundreds of thousands of people of various nationalities and faiths, then they certainly number in the thousands. The primary aim of the school trips sponsored by the Pokayanie Foundation and led by Memorial members is to find these sites and fund symbolic memory markers. Enthusiasts such as Viktor Lozhkin (in Abez) or Anatoly Smilingis (in Kortkeros) actively participated during the carnival of memory, erecting crosses and monuments on lager cemeteries on their own initiative and using their own money. The number of former cemeteries and the lack of funding for large memorial complexes mean that very simple memory markers are erected on most burial sites. They are cruciate in form, because – as memory actors say – crosses are the most typical and widely recognizable method of commemorating the dead. They enable swathes of wild northern nature to be demarcated in such a way that mushroom pickers can recognize when they are straying into land marked by a gloomy history. The erection of simple universal symbols is also dictated by the fact that the people resting here are not known to the people living in the surrounding area. The locals are much more likely to visit today's Christian cemeteries where their kith and kin were buried. Due to the relative inaccessibility of these remote sites, they receive few visitors. Apart from the aforementioned Muscovite who placed a cross on his father's grave in Nidz, Khorol (the Israeli who erected a monument to his mother in Inta) and Józef Dzięgielewski, who built a symbolic grave for his father at the Inta cemetery, there are few other private memory markers in these remote places. As a matter of fact, even those people usually go there only once, to symbolically mark the burial sites of their loved ones.

Apart from the local population, enthusiasts and families of the dead, Lithuanian, Latvian, Polish and Ukrainian organizations responsible for memorializing the burial sites of their compatriots are involved in the erection of crosses on the grounds of former cemeteries. For example, Poles have erected a cross at Rudnik (see Figure 2.3), another one has been erected in Ezhva by Lithuanians, and another by Ukrainians at the cemetery of the fifth division of the Inta lagpunkt. Six Ukrainian crosses can also be found at former lager cemeteries on the Vorkuta Ring Road, including Zapolyarny, Yur-Shor and Rudnik. Very often, the local population regard these crosses as communal memory markers. This is best exemplified by their attitude to the Lithuanian cross in Ezhva.

It has been executed in the traditional Lithuanian style, preserving the appropriate symbolism, yet its inscription ('To the exiles of '41') has been rendered in three languages – Lithuanian, Komi and Russian. The cross commemorates the Lithuanians deported here, yet the local authorities and inhabitants of Ezhva regard the cemetery as a communal memory marker and so come here every year on 30 October to observe the official Day of Remembrance of the Victims of Political Repressions. Given such communities' belief that all nations shared similar experiences, being harmed as much as each other by the regime, and that deportations or forced labour in the mines were just another stage of the political repressions, such transferrals of meaning are widespread.

Erecting the Lithuanian cross in Ezhva caused this site to assume an important role. The living began to treat it as an important local memory marker of the victims of Soviet repressions. Since other graves had also survived in this cemetery, not only the monument but also the whole of the cemetery grounds have been tended to. Weeds have been pulled up, subsiding gravestones steadied and fences added. The cemetery has returned to its former status as a social space. The Lithuanian cross has triggered a dialogue between the dead and living, and the commemorative work being carried out today is directed at 'allocating' space to be adapted for the needs of the cemetery. Such programmes, which generally involve the erection of a monument by representatives of other countries, the steady reconstruction of the site by the local population and the conversion of a cemetery into an important place for the remembrance of political repressions, are also typical of other sites.

The Komi Republic also contains cemeteries whose history or location has led to them becoming a space for dialogue between the dead and living, akin to that described above. Memory actors are compelled by the surviving remains to take a stance on the Gulag 'transcript'. People then attempt to confer on these places a form that will best express the social conceptions associated with the history of a given site, transforming them enough to enable them to begin to fulfil the role the living intend them to have. Some places, by virtue of the lager-related relicts they contain, the memorializing activities taking place there or the function they are currently beginning to fulfil, seem to be exceptionally intriguing, so I would like to take a closer look at them now.

The Vostochnoye Cemetery in Inta

The cemetery was created in 1941, when a second lagpunkt was established and the prisoners began working in a new coalmine. Most of those buried here were Latvians and Lithuanians living in the village of Vostochny. In June 1956, following the death of Oskar Putni – an extremely well-known and respected Latvian – the idea arose to construct a monument to 'all Latvians exiled to Inta'. This was during Khrushchev's Thaw, when the prisoners began to sense the impending changes, so they set about realizing their intention.[35]

The monument presents the figure of a woman – a mother in Lithuanian national dress. Her gaze is directed to the south-west, towards her home – Latvia. In her right hand she holds an oak branchlet – a marker commemorating everyone who never made it home. In her left, she holds a ball of thread. According to Latvian tradition, a mother who sends her children away for a while gives them a ball of thread to enable them to return home. The thread symbolizes their unbreakable bond with their home – their mother country. Alongside the statue is an urn of ashes, a symbol of the pain of bereavement, emblazoned with three stars – an *Auseklis* denoting Venus, the morning star, and symbolizing an awakening from the darkness.[36] It was not possible at the time to dedicate a monument to 'The Victims of Stalinism', so it was engraved with the word *Dzimtenei,* which means 'To the Motherland' in Latvian. As Nikolay Baranov says: 'The Latvians who were exiled and imprisoned here, and those who died here . . . were passing on their final regards to their fatherland' [05_NB].

Following the camp's liquidation, many Latvians returned home and civilians began to be buried there. With time, the cemetery began to become overgrown and the monument subsided. It was restored in 1989, with official delegations from Latvia and Lithuania arriving to mark the occasion of its re-unveiling. This was also attended by people who took part in its first inauguration. It was underlined during the official speeches that this monument, rather than belonging to Latvians, belongs to all the nations harmed by the repressions.

Not far from the Dzimtenei memorial, a Lithuanian monument depicting Christ as the Man of Sorrows has been erected. It is inscribed with the following words in Lithuanian, Komi and Russian: 'Lithuania . . . to those who did not return'. Both monuments are surrounded by crosses: Orthodox crosses with their distinctive low crossbars, straight Catholic crosses and Lithuanian crosses containing typical national ornamentation. Most of these were erected when this place ceased to function as a camp cemetery, becoming a communal cemetery instead. Some of them have been restored and the cemetery's entrance has been marked by two memorial crosses. As Nikolay Baranov says: 'Such was the tradition in this region, memorial crosses were erected at the cemetery entrance . . . This was how the Komi people used to mark the cemetery gates. In the centre, they placed an icon of Mary, Mother of God, and a candle. [The construction offered protection – ZB] from the wind and rain' [05_NB]. Komi's indigenous inhabitants and those of Inta always erect crosses with rooves, explaining why this type of entrance was created at the Vostochnoye Cemetery by drawing from local tradition.

This is one of the most important Gulag sites of memory in Inta. Every year, after the official Day of Remembrance ceremonies in front of the monument to the Victims of Stalinist Repressions, the inhabitants of Inta come here to remember the dead. The most important element in the cemetery is the Latvian *Dzimtenei* monument, which – much like the Lithuanian cross in Ezhva – has become a meaningful symbol of the lager past to the town's inhabitants. It has become a very important local object of culture due to its artistic form. The round anniversaries of its unveiling are solemnly observed by the town.[37]

Inta's inhabitants, much like other human communities, wish to save their past from oblivion.[38] The town's history is bound up with the tragic history of the Gulag. The cemetery has therefore come to denote the 'ruins of civilization' from which Inta grew. It also marvellously reflects its history while providing information about today's inhabitants. It could be treated as a kind of mirror in which Inta can be viewed.[39] The space itself is divided into camp and communal cemeteries. Likewise, the progeny of both repressed and free people can be encountered at the same site. Those who inhabit Inta today settled the ancestral lands of the Komi, so the cemetery grounds (and gate) were given the form and elements typical of the autochthonous cemetery culture. Furthermore, the Lithuanians' and Latvians' national monuments found inside the necropolis and the crosses of various faiths attest to the international community laid to rest in the cemetery, while also informing visitors that those who inhabit the town today are the progeny of many different cultures.

The Yur-Shor Cemetery in Vorkuta

As late as 1989, members of the Vorkuta chapter of Memorial set about cleaning and reconstructing the camp cemeteries (*Zapolarye,* 23 March 1991). One of the first places they tended to was the Yur-Shor Cemetery, where prisoners who took part in a rebellion in August 1953 at mine No. 29 were buried (Applebaum 2003: 438–43). Over the years, the cemetery became overgrown, yet the memory of the rebellion endured among Vorkuta's inhabitants, especially as some of those who witnessed this series of incidents were still alive. This was such an important event in the region's history that every year since the nineties, witnesses of the rebellion, former repressed persons, the mayor and Vorkuta's inhabitants have participated in a Day of Remembrance held on 1 August in the Yur-Shor grounds (*Zapolarye,* 18 November 2003).

The central monument by which all the official meetings take place is a shrine dating from 1994 designed by the Lithuanian sculptor Vladas Vildžiunas. This is one of the monuments originally planned to be incorporated into the Russia's Crown of Thorns complex, the only one to date that has been successfully completed. For a long time, the shrine was incomplete and anonymous. Not until 1 August 2003, on the fiftieth anniversary of the rebellion, was the following inscription added: 'To those who died in the Vorkuta camps and the victims of the executions at mine No. 29 Yur-Shor 1 August 1953'. The hanging of the plaque not only marked the completion of the monument's construction, but also became a symbolic sealing of the formation of the cemetery's contemporary meaning as a space for commemorating the rebellion's participants.

Even though the monument commemorates all the deceased buried in the cemetery, the plaque's inscription clearing distinguishes the victims of the rebellion from the other Gulag victims, conferring a special status on the former. Other communal memory markers found in the cemetery explain what this exceptionality entails. The inscription of one of the monuments explains that it was erected 'In internal remembrance to those who died for freedom and human dignity'. On a Ukrainian cross can be read: 'In internal remembrance to the victims of the communist terror. To fighters for Ukraine's freedom'.

Plaques have been hung on the insurgents' graves containing the names and surnames of those who were murdered. Twelve of them were buried in a mass grave, so plaques containing the names of all of those buried there have been placed on a communal cross (Figure 2.5) (*Zapolarye*, 18 September 2003). This has the advantage of distinguishing the insurgents' burial sites from the other graves that are surmounted by anonymous crosses or only display camp numbers. This results in the insurgents' graves becoming the dominant element in the cemetery's landscape. Such individualized commemoration of the insurgents and the erection of communal memory markers that directly or indirectly highlight the importance of their deeds have led to the Yur-Shor Cemetery assuming the role of a site of memory for heroic freedom fighters. There are no other similar sites in the Komi Republic that commemorate a single group of repressed persons. The fact that only one such cemetery has been created and this honours the memory of the insurgents, and not, for example, the dekulakized peasants, would appear to be significant, as would the fact that the local Day of Remembrance is held on 1 August (the only day commemorating the victims of repressions in the Komi Republic associated with the local history).

The cemetery's uniqueness arises from the fact that it expresses opposition to the system, a notion of importance to Memorial. This explains why the Society's members attached special significance to the reconstruction of this site from the very outset. Moreover, the international memory markers erected there (there are many more of these than in the Komi Republic's other cemeteries) demonstrate that it is also important to these nations to not only commemorate the ordinary victims, but also those who paid for their opposition to the communist ideology with their lives. The

Figure 2.5. The Yur-Shor Cemetery, Vorkuta. Visible in the photograph is the grave of twelve of the rebellion's participants. In the background, a shrine can be seen, which dates from 1994 and was designed by the Lithuanian sculptor Vladas Vildžiunas. Photo by author.

Yur-Shor Cemetery is therefore not so much a site of memory as a space for holding a contemporary debate on it. Although most people who died in the camps were ordinary people – i.e. victims par excellence – when choosing a site to commemorate them, it was decided to use the Yur-Shor Cemetery, where victims of the sacrificial type are buried. These countries' desire to erect their own national monuments in this particular cemetery seems to indicate that 'victim nationalism', as described by the Korean Historian Jie-Hyun Lim (2008), is also applicable to Gulag memory.

The Memorial Cemetery in Abez

In the forties, Abez contained a stadium, theatre, bank, airport and several factories, and the settlement was even granted the opportunity to obtain town privileges (*30 Oktyabrya,* Vol. 45). In 1949, around thirty thousand people lived here, but today there are no more than seven hundred (Povolayev 1999). The only remains attesting to the 'world apart' that once existed there are the cemeteries. Only two of the several dozen that once existed there have survived, but they are so huge that they make us aware of what this place once was.

Visitors heading towards a local cemetery known as the Memorial Cemetery come across a Lithuanian cross – a memory marker commemorating repressed Lithuanians.

The chasm in the cross and plinth serves as a kind of symbolic gate through which the world of the dead can be entered. The Memorial Cemetery can only be reached by passing through three communal cemeteries. It is like walking through three consecutive bands of history to reach the early 1940s. Up until 1989, the local population were not interested in the cemetery, so it became overgrown and dilapidated. As Viktor Lozhkin recalls, the people believed that this cemetery contained the buried remains of criminals and 'enemies of the nation', who deserved to be forgotten and have their graves desecrated [19_VL]. All of this changed following the visit of a Leningrad journalist (Zhavoronkov 1989) who arrived in Abez on an expedition to find the grave of Lev Karsavin.[40] It was at this point that Abez's inhabitants discovered for the first time that it was the USSR's intellectual elite, rather than their enemies, that had been buried in the cemetery grounds.

This began what could be called a period of dialogue with the burial space. Attempts were also begun to decipher the letter and digit code that could be seen on plaques by the graves. The cemetery functioned from 1949 to 1959, by which point prisoners were being buried in separate graves marked with letters and numbers. After some time, the burial site of some of the deceased was successfully established. This task was aided by the lists of the buried obtained by Lozhkin from the archives. As the search progressed, various riddles surfaced; for example, how three tiny crosses someone or other had erected over the graves at some point (erecting signs of confession was prohibited at the time) had survived until the nineties. Viktor Lozhkin placed them in the museum he had been running for many years in Abez, replacing them with large wooden crosses.

The first modern memory markers had appeared on Lev Karsavin and General Jonas Juodišius' graves by 1989. At this point, various delegations began coming to Abez to erect memory markers on the graves of famous people – for example, that of Nikolay Punin – or to honour the memory of their compatriots, whether they be Ukrainian or Lithuanian. Thanks to their actions, visitors to the cemetery can encounter graves of exceptional form, such as those belonging to Karsavin or Punin, as well as others that are uniform, such as the Ukrainian graves provided with plaques of one particular kind.[41] The family members of the prisoners buried here came in person or asked Viktor Lozhkin to tend to the graves of their loved ones. New structures appeared in the cemetery, including a pyramid with a red star over the grave of Chekist and colleague of Dzerzhinsky, Aleksandra Andreyeva-Gorbunova (Zhavoronkov, 1989). Lozhkin added a star, because, as he explains: 'This person was a non-believer . . . We erect crosses for believers . . . In Soviet times, a pyramid with a star was erected. And rightly so. People have a right to their own beliefs [19_VL].

When erecting a new memory marker, the stakes containing the camp numbering were not removed, so that the cemetery's original form could be preserved. As a result, there are two memory markers on some graves: an old one erected by the camp and a new one constituting a contemporary translation (Figure 2.6). Lozhkin also introduced signage to the cemetery that was meant to transform it into a meaningful

Figure 2.6. The Memorial Cemetery, Abez. Photo by author.

modern site of memory. He placed a bell in front of the entrance so that anyone could ring it, as is the Orthodox custom, to honour the memory of their loved ones. He also erected a pyramid within the grounds informing visitors about the necropolis' history and undertook further work directed at transforming the cemetery into a large memorial complex. An avenue along which every nation could erect their own cross or monument was supposed to run through the middle section. The Lithuanian and Ukrainian delegations gave some impetus to this avenue by bringing their own memory markers. A museum telling the story of the Abez camp, which would initially be based on Lozhkin's collection of camp objects as well as the cemetery remains, was to be a permanent feature of the cemetery. However, these plans were never implemented.

The cemetery is currently falling into disrepair again. However, thanks to the intensive memorialization processes of the nineties, its original appearance as a camp cemetery has been superimposed by several layers of modern interpretation. The old text, represented by graves numbered by camp, is spatially juxtaposed with its contemporary translation; in this case various kinds of memory marker. Some of these, like the markers standing over famous people's graves, are unique in form, while others, like the crosses over the Ukrainian graves, greatly resemble each other. Furthermore, the choice of a cross or star expresses the respect of the living for the beliefs of the dead. The cemetery landscape also contains part of the planned memorial complex that was meant to be based on the avenue of national monument. The project devised by Lozhkin, more of a memory actor than a caretaker, has also left its clear imprint. The acts of commemoration he undertook (the aforementioned bell and pyramid) strongly influence the contemporary shape of Abez's site of memory, conferring on it a unique, local atmosphere.

The Makarikha Cemetery in Kotlas

The town of Kotlas belongs to the Arkhangelsk region, but the Makarikha Cemetery, which is located here, is strongly associated with the Komi Republic semantically. I therefore decided to include it in the section devoted to this territory. Kotlas was the gate through which all the condemned (lager prisoners, special displaced persons) had to pass on their way to the North, while Makarikha was the central transit camp at which prisoners stopped on their journey (Smolina 2001).[42] The mortality among the convicts was very high, so the cemetery quickly expanded. Initially, people were buried in mass graves; later, permission was granted for individual burials and graves. Makarikha functioned until 1959.

The cemetery's modern history began in 1995, when the Polish consul-general in St Petersburg decided to erect a cross there commemorating the Poles who died in this area. It contains the following inscription written in Polish and Russian: 'To the Poles, Russians and all the others tormented to death in the Kotlas camps: mothers, fathers, sisters, brothers, daughters, sons . . . Eternal rest. Eternal remembrance. Compatriots from Poland'. The cross became a communal monument from the outset, because – as Irina Dubrovina, who tends to the cemetery, explains – the 'To the Poles and Russians' inscription encouraged Orthodox clerics to accept this place and say prayers to the dead here. As a matter of fact, someone painted a small Orthodox cross in oil paint on the back of the monument's concrete plinth. Dubrovina explains, 'Let there be religion. This is one, Christian religion' [08_ID].

The graves were almost bare, so tiny saplings were planted to mark the deceased's resting places. These are the first authentic memory markers and important living witnesses to history.[43] Today, they are enormous pines growing out of the graves. The cemetery contains both individual and communal burial sites. There are also symbolic graves; for example, plaques and headstones erected here to honour those who died in the northern lagers and *spetsposelki* (special settlements) – people whose resting place is unknown or whose remains were buried in cemeteries that were later liquidated. Many of the plaques have been attached to trees. The tradition of placing information about the deceased on trees was borrowed from Levashovo Memorial Cemetery.[44] When Irina Dubrovina was visiting this place, this custom appealed to her. Since she is Makarikha's caretaker, she recommended this form of commemorating loved ones to many people.

The cemetery's diversity is immediately evident to visitors. There are areas dominated by anonymous graves covered in trees functioning as memory markers. However, plaques containing Polish names are clustered around a Polish cross, and markers commemorating dekulakized peasants have been erected in front of the monument to peasant victims of the 1929–33 collectivization programme (Figure 2.7). A monument in the form of a triptych draws attention to the other groups of repressed persons. Each part of the grave has been devoted to a different category – clerics, children and foreign citizens, respectively. In effect, all the most important groups of repressed persons have been named and commemorated.

The erection of the peasant monument and triptych was initiated by the Sovest Association, so they fully express the ideas of their creators and those tending the memorial cemetery. Apart from the simple, modest form of the graves, the distinguishing feature of these monuments is the poetic language in the epitaphs they contain. The inscription on the peasants' monument reads: 'They loved . . . They believed . . . They lived . . . The saintly and sinful here – in this large common grave – have found eternal shelter'.[45] A passage from the Gospels has been engraved on the triptych: 'For there is nothing hidden that will not be disclosed'.[46] The inscription dedicated to children reads: 'In eternal remembrance. To children deprived of blood and food; children wandering with tiny beggarly sacks. To children who died while being transported and deported. To infants cold in death in their mothers' arms'.[47] And the one dedicated to foreigners reads: 'To all who left their country against their will. To all who found eternal peace here. Let the earth be light upon you'.[48]

Figure 2.7. The Makarikha Cemetery, Kotlas. The memorial to peasant victims of the 1929–33 collectivization programme. Surrounding the monument are symbolic graves, built by the relatives of peasants who died in the lagers.

The cemetery's uniqueness arises from the fact that this is the place through which all the prisoners travelling north had to pass, which explains why, for people today, Makarikha has become a kind of symbolic cemetery for all those laid to rest in unknown places in the North. The custom, borrowed from Levashovo, of hanging plaques on trees has led to the languages of commemoration used in other cemeteries having as much an impact on Makarikha's form as local tradition. Just as the people laid to rest here came from different countries, the cemetery landscape currently displays the influence of manners of commemoration typical of other sites of memory. If the poetic language in the peasant monument and triptych epitaphs is also taken into account and this is jointly interpreted with the pinewoods surrounding the graves, Makarikha can be seen as a kind of sentimental park whose semantics are reminiscent of nineteenth-century cemetery parks imbued with an atmosphere of reflection and meditation on life and death (Kolbuszewski 1985).

Makarikha's uniqueness can be also be explained by its role as an important site of memory for Kotlas inhabitants. Every year, on 30 October, they arrive in coaches to remember lost loved ones. Furthermore, this microregion's primary school contains a museum that presents the cemetery's history. Children and young people also tend to its grounds, collecting branches and washing the headstones. As one of their teachers explains, 'The children understand that this is a sacred place and this needs to be done' [26_AS]. The school's headteacher believes it is self-evident that the cemetery should be tended to, while parents are happy with the work their children do and the knowledge they are acquiring. As the teacher explains: 'Parents who grew up in this microregion say, "Wow, we grew up here and didn't know anything. It's great that at least our children know this" . . . Parents believe that this attitude towards a cemetery is normal and it should be preserved in this way' [26_AS].

What If the Gulag Had Never Existed?

After the carnival of memory period, which gave rise to various projects grounded in unrealistic assumptions whose form and scale expressed universal social upheaval, the emotions subsided. It was followed by a period marked by a steady appraisal of the history and decoding of the Gulag markers contained within the cultural landscape. Simultaneously, in all the Republic's lager towns and cities, memory markers were erected, enabling suitable rituals to be performed. There was a lack of funding, so new meanings were being bestowed on already existing monuments (like the monuments to the pioneers) as they began to be treated as Gulag memory markers. Likewise, some elements of the cultural landscape (the water tower in Inta or the Pushkin Memorial in Ukhta) gained new nuances. However, the memorialization work mainly focused on the marking of lager cemeteries and paying homage to the dead.

The fact that special weight was being attached to the cemeteries is indicative of an important transformation that was taking place in society. Clearly, prisoners were now being perceived as victims rather than being treated as 'enemies of the nation'. At the same time, monuments and cemeteries are material testament to the fact that the inhabitants of the Komi Republic's towns and villages were attempting to understand and interpret the lager past of their small homelands. This is not an easy task, because Gulag history is comprised, on the one hand, of tremendous suffering and pain and, on the other, of development and new culture forming on the crossroads of civilization (Smolina 2001: 49); on the one hand, dying of starvation, exhaustion and inhuman labour, and on the other, living in the towns that emerged in the North and providing assistance to a country at a difficult moment of the war. This ambivalence was an inseparable component of the historical Gulag and continues to form an indelible part of Gulag memory.

Below I quote extracts from a conversation with a history student living in Pechora on the lager history of his town. It may be treated as an emblematic picture of Gulag memory in the Komi Republic.

> A.A.: The attitude of many people, including myself, to the Gulag is ambiguous. On the one hand, it is of course really bad – thousands, tens of thousands of lost human lives, wasted human lives, and so on, yet at the same time . . . in many spheres, it was thanks to the Gulag that our territory developed . . . If it wasn't for the Gulag, would there be anything here at all? In this place? In this Republic? Of course there would. There were already people living here when the Gulag arrived. But everything would be at a low level of development.
>
> ZB: And if it hadn't existed, would that be a problem?
>
> A.A: Interesting question. Would that be a problem? I'd say that my approach to that question is ambiguous . . . If I approach it from an egoistic point of view: If there was no town here, I wouldn't have been born here. [02_AA]

This comment did not, in my view, show my interviewee to be an egoist. It instead indicates that he is bound to his homeland by an emotional bond. The changes that occurred in the late eighties led to many people asking themselves similar questions: 'Was the foundation of Pechora, Vorkuta or Inta necessary?'. For many, the response they found for themselves diametrically changed their lives and mode of perceiving the world. They not only began to perceive traces of former lagers appearing in space, but also their assessment of these places, previously self-evident to them (lager cemeteries hold the graves of enemies of the people undeserving of our respect) became ambiguous and problematic. It could therefore be said that, just as my interviewee is taking his first tentative steps on a quest to find a response to the questions that are vexing him, the Komi Republic began to work through various memory issues during the carnival of memory period.

The establishment of the Pokayanie Foundation was meant to assist this process. It is engaged in professional research in the archives and supports the publication of history books as well as research expeditions. Every year, groups of young people go on field trips to look for former lagpunkts, record oral histories and analyse documents. They then use the material they have collected to write dissertations, articles or papers to be presented at academic conferences regionally and across the country.

The material acquired during expeditions often becomes the basis for memory projects. This certainly applies to an exhibition created in 2002 at the Pechora Local History Museum, which used documents found in a former lagpunkt of Kedrovy Shor (a lager engaged in cereal cultivation and livestock and pig farming (Azarov 2000a)) to tell of its past. Likewise, in many school museums exhibitions on a Gulag theme can be viewed. They were prepared by teacher enthusiasts and students frequenting history clubs who set out on their own research expeditions in their microregions. All of these activities aimed to provide more information about the history of the Gulag and Gulag sites. However, they failed to answer a fundamental question; namely, 'What can I learn from Gulag history?'. The catalogue of Gulag memory issues presented in this chapter demonstrates how difficult this task is and how diverse responses can appear.

Notes

1. The Unified State Political Administration – i.e. the political police in the USSR, active from 1923 to 1934, when it was incorporated into the NKVD.
2. For the history of Soviet repression in the Komi Republic, see Morozov (1997); for the construction of the railway line to Vorkuta, see Azarov (2000b: 9–37).
3. The year 1929 was a turning point for the whole forced labour camp system. It was then that it was decided to reorganize it to take advantage of the free labour of prisoners while implementing the assumptions of the first Five-Year Plan for industrializing the country. During this period, changes were also made to the actual nature of the OGPU, which assumed a portion of responsibility for the country's industrial development. It started organizing its own research and geological expeditions, one of which was the 'Ukhtinskaya Expedition of 1929' (Applebaum 2003: 59–72, 89–90).
4. Applebaum writes about the foundation of Ukhtpechlag (2003: 86–102).
5. Morozov (1997) writes about the history of the development of the Gulag system and the roles of the various lagers.
6. The Thaw actually took place in 1956.
7. Social and political organizations of various kinds that operated within the Soviet Union and were answerable to the state.
8. The inscription was later changed to victims of political repressions.
9. Based on an interview with Vitaly Troshin and the map/schedule for the memorial trail. The map is kept in Vitaly Troshin's private archive.
10. Quoted from a document passed to the Council of Ministers of the Russian Federation. A copy of this document is kept in Vitaly Troshin's private archive.
11. The Pokayanie Komi Republic Charitable Society Fund for Victims of Political Repressions. Read more about this organization at www.pokayanie-komi.ru.
12. I wrote about catalogues of this type in the Introduction.
13. For the city of Syktyvkar's history, see I.B. Berkin (1980).
14. As Sharon Macdonald stresses, a museum represents a kind of consensus reached between experts and bearers of vernacular knowledge (1996: 1–18). American culturologist and musicologist Tony

Bennett (1998: 30) is keen to stress, in turn, that a museum does not necessarily have to be a space for the representation of a dominant culture, for it can also become a centre for social exchange. He pointed out in his analysis of nineteenth-century museums in the West that not every museum acted at the time as an instrument of the conservative hegemony facilitating the preservation of the existing order. As he explains, many museum employees were theorists studying new transformations and liberals viewing the museum as a force that could possibly contribute to the facilitation of the planned and controlled transformation of existing social rules. When museums are viewed in this light, it becomes apparent that they need not always support the existing social order. They can also establish a roadmap for a new order or instruct visitors how to take a fresh look at the existing system.

15. From the archive of the Vorkuta Interregional Local History Museum, NA913/1, a thematic-expository plan for the *Vorkuta zapolarnaya* exhibition, designed by E.B. Galinskaya.
16. From the archive of the Vorkuta Interregional Local History Museum, NA913/2, programme for a tour of the *Vorkuta zapolarnaya* exhibition, designed by E.B. Galinskaya, 1/XI/87.
17. For more on the Gulag theatre, see, among others, A.N. Kaneva (2001).
18. For more on the portrayal of war in local history museums, see Z. Bogumił (2014) and E. Melnikova (2015).
19. The text of the programmes for both tours were made available to me by their author M. Morozova, a museum employee responsible for exhibition content at Syktyvkar. The title of the *Repressions in the Komi Region from 1929 to 1956. Journey into the Whirlwind* exhibition was taken from the title of Eugeniya Ginzburg's book that was translated into English as *Journey into the Whirlwind* (2002 [1967]).
20. Kharkiv Tractor Works.
21. Based on my observation of a tour group visiting the exhibition, September 2007.
22. Information from the text prepared by Tatyana Afanasyeva for the programme for the Pechorlag Sites of Memory tour, Pechora 2004. The text was made available to me by its author.
23. www.sakharov-center.ru/asfcd/pam/pam_card.xtmpl?id=849.
24. I have written more expansively on this in an article published in the *Polish Sociological Review* (Bogumił 2012).
25. An unhewn stone can also have a secondary meaning. As Janusz Skoczylas and Mariusz Żyromski (2005: 101) write, in ancient cultures unhewn stone was a symbol of freedom.
26. As stressed by Joanna Wawrzyniak (2015: 31–32), combatants in a nation state become the embodiment of that country's values. The Great Patriotic War is seen as the binding agent that cemented the Russian Federation as a nation, so the fact that former repressed persons wish to be perceived as combatants in this war should be understandable.
27. The Archive of the Inta Local History Museum (1992), NA 444 (a), Ekskursiya po sledam "Pamyatniki Inty kak otrazheniye istorii", authored by V.A. Aduyeva.
28. V Inte otkryli pervy v Komi muzey istorii politicheskikh repressiy, https://7x7-journal.ru/item/48162.
29. Ibid.
30. For the history, symbolism and social meaning of tombs of the unknown soldier, see G.L. Mosse (1990).
31. Passages from this chapter were previously published in Bogumił (2010b).
32. As Herling (1951: 198) writes, anonymity and 'the awareness that no one would discover about their deaths and where they were buried was one of the greatest psychological tortures for the prisoners'.
33. A logging camp.
34. For the cemetery's role as an important social space, see S. Tanaś (2008: 59–76).
35. The Inta Local History Museum Archive, NA 336, Istoriya sozdaniya intinskogo pamyatnika "Rodine", V.A. Aduyeva.
36. Ibid.
37. In 2006, the fiftieth anniversary was observed. A delegation came from Latvia. The museum organized a special exhibition providing information about the monument's construction. A meeting took place at the cemetery (*Iskra*, 2 August 2006).
38. As S. Sikora (1986) writes, cemeteries are a record of a given community.

39. For more on what cemeteries can tell us about those who are living today, see D. Francis, L. Kellaher and G. Neophytou (2005).
40. A famous Russian philosopher and historian. From the end of the 1920s, he lived and worked in Lithuania. At the end of the forties, he was sentenced to ten years in a camp for spreading anti-Soviet agitation. He died in Abez.
41. Viktor and Inna Fedushchak (2006: 189–284) describe how they erected the Ukrainian crosses.
42. For the history of the cemetery, see A. Klapiyuk, T. Rodionova and M. Shnyakova (2007) and *30 oktyabrya* ([5] 2000).
43. For more on living monuments, see J. Małczyński (2009).
44. The Levashovo Memorial Cemetery, which is just outside St Petersburg, was established in 1937. Prisoners were executed by firing squad here during the Great Terror. The cemetery functioned as a mass burial site from 1937 to 1964. Up until 1990, it was secret and under the guardianship of the army. In spring 1989, the site was tracked down by members of the Memorial Society and a year later it was transferred into the care of the city of St Petersburg. It currently contains a wide array of memory markers, including individual graves, symbolic graves, national monuments and memory markers dedicated to particular groups of repressed persons, e.g. a tombstone commemorating power engineers from the local Lenenergo electrical plant. By the entrance is a monument representing the Moloch of Totalitarianism and on the cemetery grounds there is a museum. For more on the history of the Levashovo Cemetery, see a brochure published by Memorial (St Petersburg, 1999) titled 'Nam ostayetsya tolko imya'.
45. 'Lubili . . . Verili . . . Zhili . . . Svyatyye, greshnyye tut – v velikoy obshchey mogile – vechny nashli priyut.'
46. 'Net nichego taynogo, chto ne stalo by yavnym.'
47. 'Vechnaya pamyat detyam, lishennym krova i pishchi. Detyam, brodivshim s sumoyu nishchey. Detyam, v etapakh i ssylke pogibshim. Mladentsam, v rukakh materey ostyvshim.'
48. 'Vsem, kto po vole chuzhoy pokinul rodnyye kraya. Vsem, kto nashel zdes posledni pokoy. Da budet pukhom eta zemlya.'

CHAPTER 3
PERM KRAI

There are various ways of remembering. There's dutiful remembering. This is awakened immediately on the Day of Remembrance and reminds us to lay wreaths and carnations by a memorial . . . Then there's selective memory. This perceives and stores only the good. In our country, there was neither a Gulag, nor dekulakization, nor mass repressions . . . There is also the other extreme: memory transfixed by evil, continuously returning to the tragedy. Memory that stopped yesterday, unaware of the present and incapable of seeing the future. This is constructive memory, directly and openly gazing into the eyes of the past. Only this memory offers any hope that the Gulag was shut down. (N. Kluchareva, *Pervoye sentyabrya*, 30 October 2004, p. 5)[1]

The Island of Political Camps

The camp history of Perm Krai merits special attention for two reasons. Most importantly, it was here in 1929 that Vishlag – the first OGPU industrial camp – was opened in the city of Berezniki (Gladyshev 1998; Shmyrov 1998b: 70). This undertaking was organized by Edward Berzin, who completed this assignment so commendably that he was later tasked, in the very same year, with setting up and managing Dalstroy, which expanded the Gulag's reach into the remote Kolyma region.[2] Secondly, it was here in 1972 that the 'Perm Triangle' was established – three lagers, known as BC-389/35, BC-389/36 and BC-389/37 (Deberdeyev 1998: 2–4), into which political prisoners began to 'disappear' (Hutchins and Vietzke 2002; Shmyrov 1998a: 250–66). When the penal code was reformed in the sixties, a new category of prisoner appeared: 'offenders dangerous to the state', who were to be detained in Mordovia (Applebaum 2003: 471–91). From the end of the sixties, these were mainly dissidents, so the Mordovia lagers began to be called political camps. Despite being isolated, the convicts communicated with the outside world by bribing the guards. This led to special lagers being created for them with heightened security. These were colloquially known as Perm-35, -36 and -37 and functioned until the end of the eighties.

Perm Krai was therefore one of the Gulag's 'cradles' as well as its last bastion. Traces of the Stalinist Gulag and dissident past have been preserved in the former lager Perm-36.[3] By the nineties, thanks to the involvement of activists, this site had attained its current status as the Perm-36 Memorial Complex of Political Repressions, the Russian Federation's only fully functioning open-air museum of camp buildings (Adler 2002: 261–63; Williams 2007: 14, 82–84). For years, Perm-36 functioned as a social organization with an educational role commemorating and archiving political repressions in the USSR. At the same time, this place was heavily involved in the kind of pro-democratic activities best expressed by the Pilorama Festival, organized at the Perm-36 site from 2005. However, in 2014, the state took over the former lager's grounds, replacing it with an autonomous state cultural institution named the Memorial Complex of Political Repressions (Giesen 2015). The Perm-36 social organization ceased to exist. The resultant clashes in the media over the museum's role and its seizure by the state granted Perm-36 a new meaning. It became the symbol of the cultivation of a new state policy on how the repressions should be remembered.

However, the present and previous museum authorities are not the only memory actors functioning in this area. Since the late eighties, the Memorial Society has been implementing its own memory projects in Perm. Although the people who launched the Perm-36 Museum and the Memorial Society representatives shared the same roots and initially held similar ideological assumptions, their paths diverged over time as they began to create projects that differed significantly from each other. When I carried out field research in 2008 in Perm Krai and participated in Pilorama at the Perm-36 Museum, this conflict was very apparent. I have therefore chosen in this chapter to describe the differences in the memory projects created by both groups while presenting the arguments used by both sides to justify the importance of their activities. The Perm-36 Museum no longer exists in the form in which I analysed it in 2008. Not only have the museum authorities changed, but most of the exhibitions I was viewing in 2008 have also been closed. Even so, my description of the Perm-36 Museum's appearance before it was taken over by the state would still appear to carry weight. Firstly, this is an analysis of the meanings of the Perm-36 Memorial Centre of the History of Political Repressions memory project, which Viktor Shmyrov created over a number of years. Secondly, every new exhibition either contradicts or complements the earlier exhibition. It was initially thought that the new authorities appointed in 2014 to take charge of the Memorial Complex of Political Repressions would create a new narrative. However, they are largely continuing the previous museum's activities and new exhibitions tend to draw from those that Viktor Shmyrov created earlier. Thirdly, my description of the appearance and operation of the memory project created over a number of years by a non-governmental organization strongly allied to the Memorial milieu[4] facilitates comprehension of the policy changes that have been taking place in Russia following the introduction of the State Policy on Commemorating the Memory of Victims of Political Repression (Nechepurenko 2015). Fourthly, by demonstrating differences in approach to the commemoration of political repressions displayed by various people affiliated to Memorial, I hope to elucidate the specific nature of the memorialization of political repressions. However, I shall begin this chapter with a short profile of the carnival of memory in Perm.

'Stirrings of Conscience' – The Onset of Perm's Carnival of Memory

Officially, the Memorial Society first became active in Perm in 1989, but as its local representative, Aleksandr Kalikh,[5] relates, 'Memorial was born earlier in my soul and those of others' [13_AK]. In fact, as early as the late sixties, some young students in the city of Kirov found the diary of a former repressed person in an attic. They uncovered some hidden history by reading it together. This was followed by the establishment of the first Parus student organization, whose members discussed the past and the contemporary domestic political situation. After some time, Parus was disbanded, its members started their own families and Aleksandr Kalikh was expelled from Kirov for dissident activity. At this point, he moved to Perm, where he continued his historical research.

Riding the wave of transformation occurring in the late eighties, journalists at the *Zvezda* newspaper, for which Aleksandr Kalikh also worked, began to slowly collect the reminiscences of former repressed persons. This was quite an arduous process, because people were reluctant to speak. The first public meetings at which Perm's inhabitants had the opportunity to express their opinions were actually devoted to ecology rather than the repressions. As Aleksandr Kalikh explains, there were many munitions factories in this city. The rivers were overflowing with sewage, and people were breathing in polluted air and falling ill. Consequently, in 1987, the meeting that took place in the hall of the local community centre was called to protest against air and water pollution.

Memory of the Gulag began to awaken in November 1988, when Aleksandr Kalikh published a conversation in *Zvezda* with the regional public prosecutor. This focused on legislation relating to the rehabilitation of victims of political repression. At the end of the article, he asked former repressed persons to write to the editorial team, describing their lives from the moment they left the lager to the present day. They received a massive response. The wall of silence had been breached. Many of these reminiscences were published in the newspaper and *Zvezda* journalists began corresponding with some of these letters' authors. As Aleksandr Kalikh emphasizes, despite being involved with this topic from his youth, he had not realized how many victims there had been: '[the fact] there were millions had never even occurred to me' [13_AK].

On 12 December 1988, a meeting took place in the Builders Community Centre during which former repressed persons shared their experiences and discussed what should be done to ensure that the Gulag could never be re-established [13_AK]. Thus, in Perm, as was the case in other cities, open discussion sessions began to be organized. Sometimes, Party members also participated, even drafting in their own experts to convince people of the veracity of the official Party line. This gave rise to social dialogue.

The first important social rally was a march on 1 May 1989. Memorial members walked through the city centre in silent procession fronted by an enormous Memorial banner. They held photographs of those who had been murdered. When the column, mainly composed of older people, passed a parade stand containing representatives of the Communist Party committee celebrating International Workers' Day, the 1 May music was switched off. The Party representatives silently and helplessly observed the former repressed persons and their family members.

Initially, Memorial's activities focused on fighting for the rights of, and compensation for, former repressed persons, the main objective being to improve these people's material circumstances. There was also a plan to create a site of memory by which people could gather to remember their loved ones. From 1991, Perm's inhabitants congregated to this end at the Yegoshikha Cemetery, not far from former NKVD prison No. 1, where prisoners had been executed by firing squad. However, this was nothing more than an empty plot of land without any memory marker.

The history of the erection of the Memorial to Victims of Political Repressions in Perm replicates the scenario of the erection of many similar monuments in the Russian Federation. The main objective was to erect a marker commemorating all former repressed persons and uniting the local community. The Perm chapter of Memorial did not, however, have sufficient funding at its disposal. Moreover, it had to play a protracted game with the municipal authorities, who multiplied the legal obstacles to such an extent that the construction work ground to a halt. There were also heated discussions about what shape the monument should take (Zemskova 1995). In the end, in 1996, a Memorial to the Victims of Political Repressions was erected in the Yegoshikha Cemetery grounds. It was created by Lev Futlik, a sculptor from a former repressed family (Figure 3.1). It was funded from contributions to public collections. The KGB also allocated some funds. As Aleksandr Kalikh relates, on being faced with funding problems, he wrote two letters: one to the Party authorities and another to the KGB. They contained the passage: 'You did not personally participate in the repressions, but you represent the institutions that organized these repressions. Stand by your nation. Raise some money to construct the monument' [13_AK]. The KGB sent a considerable sum; the Party did not even reply to the letter.

The monument is located within the vicinity of the NKVD prison and the Mourning Mother Statue (commemorating the Great Patriotic War). For the Memorial members, it was crucially important to ensure that the two markers would stand alongside each other 'to remind people that not all victims were war casualties; people also killed each other' [13_AK]. The Great Patriotic War Memorial stands by the entrance to the cemetery grounds and the Memorial to Victims of Political Repressions is at the cemetery's edge. However, they are of similar size and both are notable for their intriguing architectural form.

Figure 3.1. The Victims of Political Repressions Memorial. Erected in the Yegoshikha Cemetery grounds in 1996. Photo by author.

The Memorial to the Victims of Political Repressions has a simple but imposing form. Five fence posts shaped like those once used in the lagers rise out of a star. Hanging between them is a bell engraved with the dates 1917–1991, which commemorates the victims. The tips of the fence posts are interwoven with barbed wire.

The whole structure was executed in concrete, and two tablets containing inscriptions were placed alongside it. One of them contains the information: 'In Remembrance of the Victims of Political Repressions'. The other contains the following passage from a poem by Anatoly Zhigulin: 'O people, people with numbers! You were people – not slaves. You were more exalted and tenacious than your tragic fate'.[6]

Despite its simple form, the monument's symbolism is clear. By rising out of a star – a symbol of communist ideology – the camp fence posts unambiguously indicate that ideology was the source of the tragedy. The bell engraved with dates both describes the timeframe during which communist ideology held sway and the duration of the repressions. The bell symbolizes the honouring of the dead and – as Aleksandr Kalikh emphasized – it has nothing to do with the Orthodox tradition. It symbolizes Russian culture as a whole. The passage quoted above from Zhigulin's poem further enriches the evoked meaning. What is being emphasized here is death rather than life as well as the exceptionalness and individual heroism of the convicts who refused to surrender to fate.

Nevertheless, if the bell is treated as a typical Orthodox symbol representing the commemoration of the dead and is interpreted in conjunction with the barbed wire interwoven around the tops of the fence posts (much like a crown of thorns), then the monument will begin to have religious connotations. From this perspective, the convicts' martyrdom becomes more akin to the suffering of Christ. Such an interpretation of the memorial's meaning is bolstered by the fact that this monument was placed on a hill, a symbolic Golgotha towering over the NKVD prison – a site of torment and mass execution. The manner in which primeval signs function in culture lends further weight to this interpretation. As Yuri Lotman wrote, the bell or cross constitutes a 'simple' symbol that possesses a much larger culturo-semantic capacity than more complex symbols, enabling this symbol to enter into unexpected relationships that transform its essence and textual environment. The Russian scholar adds, however, that 'simple' symbols form the symbolic nucleus of given cultures while attesting, at the same time, to their stability and continuity. Therefore, even though bells or crosses possess a universal meaning, this meaning is situated within a contemporary Russian landscape that is increasingly saturated with Orthodox symbols (new churches, chapels and memorial crosses), forcing it to adapt to and support this sacred cultural context (Lotman 1990: 38–43). The argumentation employed by Kalikh and other memory actors that any bell or cross they have erected is a universal sign used in European culture to mark culturally important sites would not appear to be entirely convincing.

Since the Perm monument can in fact be interpreted as a symbol of Orthodox worship, the Orthodox Church has not come out in opposition to it.[7] It did, however, provoke great controversy among communists, who were unhappy that the camp fence posts rise out of a star. As Aleksandr Kalikh says, the matter was eventually referred to the Governor, but he refused to assent to the star's destruction. Consequently, the marker standing in Yegoshikha Cemetery has become a monument central to Gulag memory in Perm. It is here every year that people gather on 30 October to remember the dead. The Mayor and Governor of Perm always participate in these meetings.

Not far from Perm is another memory marker to which former repressed persons make a pilgrimage by bus every May; namely, the Victims of Political Repressions 1930–50 Memorial Complex, which is located 12 kilometres along the motorway linking Yekaterinburg with Moscow. During the Great Terror, inhabitants of Yekaterinburg and Perm (then part of the Sverdlovsk region) were executed by firing squad there (*Uralski rabochiy,* 29 October 2005).[8] Every year, in mid-May, memorialists from Perm go there to honour the memory of their loved ones.

In the mid-nineties, when the material circumstances of former repressed persons had stabilized and memory markers had been created where they could meet each other, Memorial appreciated the importance of attracting young people. The main objective was to interest them in the Gulag and find people to carry on the memory work already begun. This entailed devising activities that would be attractive in form and involve more than just listening to lectures. Someone came up with the idea of a youth-led support service for former repressed persons. Young people would visit them, assisting them in their homes but also, more importantly, talking with them in order to learn about and memorialize their stories.[9] Great emphasis in this enterprise was placed on volunteer youth labour camps to be modelled on the former Perm-36 camp.

Depending on whether one is talking to Aleksandr Kalikh (a local Memorial representative) or Viktor Shmyrov (the museum's director), two different stories accounting for the discovery of Perm-36 may be heard. But both agree that the lager was discovered by chance during a kayaking trip for tourists. Viktor Shmyrov gave me the following version:

> I have visited dozens of lagers surviving from the seventies or eighties. When I arrived at this one for the first time, I was transfixed by its archaism. The buildings were different to those that had been preserved in other cities . . . I wondered whether this lager's buildings had been built in Stalin's time. As I have travelled a great deal around the region, I have seen many lagers and know the kind of state in which Stalin's lagers have been preserved. They are ruins, but here buildings had survived. This was my primary motive. These are Gulag buildings, which are not so often encountered, so they should be preserved. Therefore, my first objective, rather than creating a museum, was the preservation of the Gulag buildings. [29_VS]

Work was therefore begun on the restoration of Perm-36's buildings and the creation of a museum based on Perm-35, which was located in the village of Tsentralnaya, not far from Perm-36. As Aleksandr Kalikh recalls:

This was a provisional idea. There was some hospital, a small hospital from which the last political prisoners were freed.[10] . . . We regard it as a historical site. We erected a commemorative board in the centre of the zone. This was a completely unique situation. The inscription read as follows: 'It was from here that the last prisoners of the Communist regime were freed.' . . . The first conference took place there as well. We invited all the surviving dissidents and those who had been imprisoned in these zones. Many people came and we recorded their reminiscences. [13_AK]

A small museum displaying documents and collected objects was also opened within the zone. It functioned from 1991 to 1993, but had to be closed down because the whole lager was still operating as a detention centre for criminals and the village of Tsentralnaya had become a forbidden zone.

From then on, the primary focus became the reconstruction of Perm-36. This was undertaken by enthusiasts who had discovered the lager and decided to become involved with it. Shortly afterwards, further groups of volunteers began to arrive from home and abroad. They became involved in the construction work, mowed the lawn and painted the barracks. In 1995, the first exhibition devoted to prisoners of the maximum security unit was opened. More or less around the same time, Viktor Shmyrov and Aleksandr Kalikh's paths diverged. Viktor Shmyrov, as director of the museum, continued the reconstruction work on the former lager of Perm-36, while Aleksandr Kalikh became involved in running the local Memorial chapter and youth work.

The Perm-36 Museum – 'Freedom Begins in Prison'

As the new museum's director notes (Shmyrov 2001: 26), when he was setting the museum up, the legal regulations pertaining to land ownership were in a highly disorganized state in the Russian Federation. It was enough to 'come to an agreement' with the mayor of the local village regarding the reclamation of the land for the purposes of the future museum. The buildings appeared to be derelict and did not appear on any land registries, so it was possible to take the buildings into use. An agreement was reached with the authorities and space allocated for the purposes of the future Political Repressions Memorial Centre, known in abbreviated form as the Perm-36 Museum. Initially, all reconstruction work was undertaken by self-funded enthusiasts. Subsequently, Viktor Shmyrov and Tatyana Kursina, founding director of the Perm-36 Museum, started attempting to raise funds more efficiently by applying for external grants from the Governor of the Perm Region, the federal budget and the West. They facilitated this process by establishing a special body through which they could operate (the Perm-36 Memorial Centre of Political Repressions Autonomous Non-Commercial Organization, or ANO Perm-36). In 2004, the Perm-36 Museum was entered on the World Monuments Fund list[11] and attempts were also made to get it entered on the UNESCO World Heritage List (Giesen 2015). The work progressed slowly, because the museum had to contend with funding problems, and it was important for the management for the buildings to be reconstructed professionally. In Kuchino, where Perm-36 is located, two types of camp building had survived: a Maximum Security Unit (MSU) for especially dangerous prisoners and a strict regime camp (Shmyrov 2001: 26), where prisoners with lighter sentences were detained. The grounds of the MSU contain single-purpose barracks in which prisoners sentenced to 10 years of a special regime and 5 years of exile for 'anti-Soviet propaganda and agitation' were held (Figure 3.2). Visitors to this part can see what the prisoners' cells and enclosure looked like. The latter was an area with a width of two square metres surrounded by a high wall surmounted by a mesh of barbed wire. The whole MSU was enclosed by a high wooden fence with guard towers at all four corners and a checkpoint at the entrance.

The Strict Regime Camp is much larger. It is composed of two parts: a living area and a work zone. Visitors entering the camp premises need to walk past the camp administration building and the next gate to reach the work zone. Besides the administration building, the boiler house and the forge chimney have also survived. The renovated accommodation barracks house an exhibition devoted to the history of Perm-36 and the entire Gulag. The camp administration building, which was built in 1972, contains the museum's management office and a screening room known as

Figure 3.2. The Perm-36 Museum, Kuchino village, Chusovskoy region. Photo by author.

the Soviet Club. Further on, a medical centre dating from 1946, a toilet constructed in 1972 and the ruins of a bathhouse and two barracks can be found. Trees planted in 1948 grow along an avenue running through the centre of the living area. Behind the accommodation sector is a punishment block. The Strict Regime Camp is surrounded in its entirety by a wooden fence with guard towers. The living area and work zone are also divided from each other by a wooden fence.

Since most of the buildings date from the forties, Viktor Shmyrov wanted to reconstruct a camp layout dating from this period. His idea was to recreate a Stalinist camp presenting the history of the entire Gulag. As he said when I spoke to him:

> On the site of these ruins [i.e. the ruins of one of the barracks in the living area of the special regime – ZB] we are going to construct a building that will look like barracks from the outside. And inside, as it will not be an authentic building, there will be one enormous room dedicated to an exhibition. What is more, we will set it 4 or 6 metres into the ground . . . it will be possible to slowly descend to the bottom. Anyone will be able to follow a twisting path down to the bottom. In this building, we will create a Gulag exhibition. [29_VS]

By 2008, the *Gulag, History, Work, Life* exhibition, which was supposed to act as a starting point for a permanent exposition, could be viewed in the barracks. The exhibition provided information, according to Viktor Shmyrov, about selected key moments in the history of the Gulag (Figure 3.3). Documents relating to prison life were displayed at the beginning and end of the exhibition and in display cases in the central part of the room. Important dates and information about turning points in Gulag history were given on red display boards hanging from the ceiling. The starting date was 1918, when the VCheka[12] was established, and the end date was 1948, when the MVD Special camps of the Gulag (osobyye lagerya, osoblags) were established for a 'special contingent' of political prisoners convicted under Article 58 for treason, espionage or terrorism. The exhibition also contained the information that, following Stalin's death, the camps began to be liquidated. Information panels contained archival photographs, documents, extracts from indictments and certificates, graphs relating to how camps had performed and maps showing the distribution of the largest industrial centres, as well as drawings completed by prisoners. The upper panels displayed photographs taken by museum employees during a trip to Kolyma in 2002.

The curatorial texts located at the beginning of the exhibition suggested that the reason for the establishment of the Gulag and its swift development was the need to implement the first of Stalin's five-year plans and industrialize the country. The graphs and locations of the Gulag's main industrial centres appeared on the next panels, yet the story that emerged from the narrative as a whole made no attempt to either defend or contradict the initial thesis. While progressing through the exhibition's various parts, it was difficult to find the key to the selection of the displayed

Figure 3.3. The *Gulag, History, Work, Life* exhibition. This exhibition was closed by the new museum's authorities. Photo by author.

documents and photographs. They appeared to have been chosen at random as if they had arisen from different agendas. Alongside documents of national significance were documents relating to local issues. Various parts of the exhibition contained extracts from the memoirs of Varlam Shalamov. Alongside objects from the Stvor or Perm-36 lagers were objects from Kolyma (in this case, the geographical name was given rather than that of the relevant lager). These were collectively meant to depict the prisoners' lives. Alongside archival photographs, mainly of a propaganda nature (information about their origin was not given), were contemporary photographs taken by museum employees (mainly from Kolyma). The Kolyma photographs alluded to content presented on the panels, but constituted a kind of reportage on the remains of the lager. This was a separate 'narrative within a narrative'.

Parts of the exhibition served as a pretext for the guide to tell intriguing micro-stories, yet, collectively, they failed to constitute a macro-narrative that would enable visitors to comprehend what the Gulag was, how it changed and what the distinguishing features of each of the camp regions were.[13] The following words, contained on the last red board hanging from the ceiling, served as a summary of the preceding narrative: 'The Gulag became a synonym for the Stalinist era, the Gulag was a way of life for the great nation, the Gulag created an ever-thriving camp subculture, the Gulag still lives on in us . . .'. Yet the exhibition failed to explain how the Gulag's continuous existence was manifested in everyday life. The viewer was forced to attempt to respond to this question herself.

Opportunities to reflect on this issue were granted by the classes and discussions the museum organized in its education room. It was there that organized groups met with a guide before departing on tours of the former lager's grounds and there that they encountered the problem of interpreting the past for the first time. The interior of this room was furnished in the style of a club from the Stalinist period, which was meant to help visitors to enter into the atmosphere of those times (Figure 3.4). The walls were adorned with propaganda posters and photographs from newspapers depicting the reality created by those who controlled the USSR. The room's most interesting component was an 'iconostasis' presenting a 'collective portrait of the Soviet era'. The top row contained photographs of leaders and theorists of the system of repression, including Joseph Stalin, Vladimir Lenin, Lev Trotsky and Felix Dzerzhinsky. The next row down was constituted of victims of political repressions (the intelligentsia) and the next, the executors of the leaders' commands, including those who later became victims themselves, such as Lavrenty Beria, Nikolay Yezhov, Grigory Zinoviev and Lev Kamenev. The bottom row contains images of ordinary people affected by the repressions.[14]

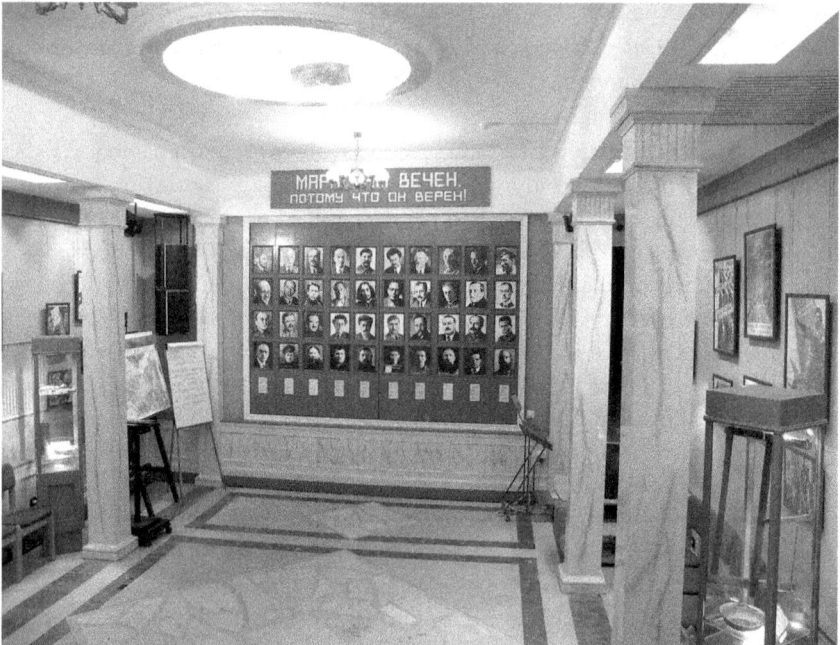

Figure 3.4. The screening room known as the Soviet Club. Its 'iconostasis' presented a 'collective portrait of the Soviet era'. This arrangement was abolished by the new museum's authorities. Photo by author.

As I reflected on the iconostasis' message, it was difficult for me to understand the logic behind the choice of political figures for the first and second rows. While NKVD Heads, Beria and Yezhov, were presented as executors, Yagoda, who also headed the NKVD, was presented as a leader. Furthermore, Bukharin, who headed the politburo, was presented as a leader, yet Zinoviev and Kamenev were presented as executors. What is more, the group of executors and leaders both contained repressed persons (like Yagoda or Bukharin). The iconostasis therefore appeared to be saying that this era appears to continually elude any attempt to fully examine or comprehend it.

The impossibility of presenting a coherent and complete vision of the political repressions was also evidenced by the *The History of a Single Lager* exhibition, which was opened in 2003 and was devoted to the history of Perm-36. Even though it aimed to tell the entire history of the lager, it was primarily based on the biographies of dissidents held in Perm-36, such as Sergey Kovalev, Vasyl Stus, Ivan Gel, Balys Gajauskas or Levko Lukyanenko. The exhibition presented many facts about their lives, yet failed to explain the complexity of the entire dissident period. Much like the aforementioned exhibitions, it was like a tentative design for a future comprehensive narrative.

The Perm-36 Museum created by Viktor Shmyrov in 2008 presented Gulag history much as other museums in different parts of the Russian Federation did in this period. As was the case with the Solovetsky Islands or the Komi Republic's museums, the problem also arose of how to conceptualize and present history in such a manner as to make it comprehensible for the viewer while preventing it from becoming an invariant of Soviet[15] history. Although Shmyrov planned to reconstruct the Stalinist lager, the dissident period became increasingly evident in the lager's space. The fact that former dissidents came to Perm-36 to help museum employees conceptualize the past was not without import. Consequently, the museum began to metamorphose into a forum targeted at shaping civic awareness (Bogdanova 2006; Doldina 2006: 2; Kluchareva 2004: 5) and its Pilorama Festival became the key event.

The festival was organized from 2005 to 2012. Apart from concerts of bard songs and theatre performances, discussions took place involving former dissidents and human rights advocates. Every edition of the festival had a main theme. In 2008, Pilorama was devoted to the sixtieth anniversary of the Universal Declaration on Human Rights and the fortieth anniversary of the foundation of the Human Rights Movement in Russia. The festival also featured open debates. The discussions, in which the public were also allowed to have their say, mainly related to the contemporary political situation in the Russian Federation, the most recent parliamentary and presidential elections and cases of human rights abuse. Andrzej Wajda's film *Katyń* was screened during the festival and discussions on historical topics also took place.

The Perm-36 Museum wished to be an institution supporting democracy in the Russian Federation. Viktor Shmyrov wanted it to become a European centre of culture and democracy at which seminars for young politicians would take place. It was meant to be a space for free liberal discussions.[16] In 2006, a Sakharov Forum was even organized during which representatives of liberal parties collectively reflected on Russia's future.[17] This involvement in the contemporary domestic political situation was also reflected in an important memory project the museum implemented – the Memory Park.[18] The idea to create a memorial park where anyone could plant a tree commemorating someone killed in the Gulag harked back to the period of the museum's foundation. Viktor Shmyrov wanted the park to resemble a map of the USSR in form. In this space, he wanted to erect 580 stones marking every Gulag administration site. These were to be accompanied by plaques with information about each lager. Visitors were supposed to learn about the history as they walked through the park. They could also plant trees in remembrance of repressed persons.

In 2008, the park's first avenues could be seen. As Viktor Shmyrov says:

> the first avenue was planted with trees on the museum's jubilee day . . . the trees were planted by people who had been involved in the museum's creation or this lager's ex-prisoners. They were planted to commemorate the victims of repression. There are trees that were planted to honour particular victims of repression, those who had died . . . Modern day political prisoners also have their trees there. There are pine trees for Khodorkovsky, Lebedev, Bakhmina. [29_VS][19]

Every year on the day after Pilorama, invited guests, mainly ex-dissidents, representatives of foreign organizations or nations, human rights advocates and people working closely with the museum, went to the former park's grounds. On this day alone, plaques were erected, alongside freshly planted trees, informing visitors to whom particular trees had been dedicated and who had planted those green monuments.

The planting itself was of a ritual nature. Viktor Shmyrov commenced proceedings by giving a short address before reading out the names of the people who were to plant pines on that day and announcing to whom they would be dedicated. Once a sapling had been planted in a hole and watered, short speeches or poetry recitals were given. The first tree – a cedar named 'Forum of the Parliamentary System, Democracy and Law' – was planted to honour the memory of Andrei Sakharov.[20] Several avenues, including Jubilee and Festival Avenues,[21] were planted with pine trees. Most trees commemorate all the victims of political repressions. Only a few are dedicated to particular people such as Osip Mandelstam, Vasyl Stus or Anatoly Marchenko. It was also possible to discover who had planted particular trees. These included figures such as Sergey Kovalev, Arseny Roginsky and Aleksandr Daniel. Some people planted trees several times, so their names appear on plaques placed beside different trees. Four pines were planted to honour the memory of modern day political prisoners – three in memory of those convicted in the Yukos case (see note 19) and the fourth tree to pay tribute to Igor Sutyagin, convicted in 2004 of high treason under Article

275 of the Criminal Code of the Russian Federation – for alleged espionage for the British and Americans. In 2008, pines were planted by representatives of Poland, Germany and Sweden in remembrance of victims of political repressions, mainly citizen of the countries concerned.

The park was conceived as a space that would contain markers commemorating selected victims of political repressions. However, in 2008, it became a space for the manifestation of symbols and contemporary political opposition-related content. Some of the green monuments, by virtue of whom they were dedicated to or who planted them, symbolize certain ideas and values of importance in today's political situation. There are also both oppositionists of the Soviet system, like Osip Mandelstam, and former dissidents, with Sakharov in the centre. These figures served as signposts representing models of conduct to be emulated on the path to Russia's democratization.

The Perm-36 Museum placed so much emphasis on promoting democratic ideas that it attracted many supporters from among the dissidents. However, this was not the case from the outset (Adler 2002: 261–63). As Shmyrov explained: 'Initially, the former dissidents were distrustful. They could not understand why we were getting involved in this. They suspected that we were involved in this for commercial reasons . . . to bring people here and make money from that' [29_VS]. This explains why the centre was only supported in its first stage of operation by Ukrainian former dissidents. Subsequently, when it turned out that the museum was beginning to function as, or fulfil the role of, a civic education centre, it began to receive the support of the Moscow-based international chapter of Memorial.

There were also people who believed from the outset that the museum was exploiting Russia's weaknesses and taking American money for this. The inhabitants of the village of Kuchino initially had a similar opinion of the museum. Consequently, when the idea arose of transforming a former lager into an open-air museum, people were opposed to the construction of a Memorial Centre. As one inhabitant of Kuchino recalled:

> [At the time – ZB] no one understood what having a totalitarian regime meant. Everyone thought that political activists had set themselves up here and they would now be making a museum for them. I didn't understand this. It wasn't the best time for a museum. It was a very tough time for the country – perestroika and now they were making a museum here . . . They were asking us if it was necessary . . . Everyone was opposed to it . . . Some were saying, 'Do it, just do it, then we'll come by and smash it up.' There were such situations. Later on, now the people have come to understand what has been going on here, they see things quite differently. [16_AI]

Despite their initial distrust, people were beginning to become interested in the museum's activities and became accustomed to it as time passed.

Perm-36, though it was not a museum in the strictest sense, wished to function as such an institution. The reconstruction and conservation of objects of material cultural heritage was being undertaken under the watchful eye of architecture specialists. The design for the permanent exhibition was prepared by a professional firm from the West. The museum was collecting and preparing archival materials. It also set itself a broader objective – the construction of a civil society. In this, it resembled many other historical museums, such as Yad Vashem in Israel, the United States Holocaust Memorial Museum in Washington or the Warsaw Uprising Museum. These were in fact based on different strands of history, yet their mission, aims and activities were very similar. In all these cases, it was important to base the building of the social bonds associated with civil or patriotic societies on lessons drawn from a tragic past. Perm-36 wished to be the first museum of this type drawing from the history of the Gulag. As Paul Williams wrote: 'Perm-36 understands the Gulag as an example of a politically unnatural institution, foreign to a universal culture of human rights. Aiming to host wider programs and workshops concerning current state repression and political imprisonment, it communicates an idea that might be resumed as: *it's an alien history to be condemned, for the global good*' (2012: 118). This aim could only be achieved through progressive professionalization and institutionalization of the kind that would force changes in working styles and a departure from ventures dependent on the labour of enthusiasts.

The Perm-36 Museum created by Viktor Shmyrov was transformed into a kind of ritual site, where, as Carol Duncan (1995: 7–20) wrote, visitors find themselves in a liminal space that differs from their everyday life, a space offering another kind of experience that accords with a script prepared by the employees of a museum. Visitors are tasked with playing the role envisaged for them; they are meant to follow a route planned by the museum's curators and experience moments of elation at designated places. The Perm ritual was supposed to transform viewers into aware citizens of the Russian Federation supportive of the processes democratizing the country.

The 'Stvor Lager' – A Museum Without a Guide

It was difficult for the Memorial members in Perm to reconcile themselves with the Perm-36 Museum's progressive professionalization and institutionalization. According to Aleksandr Kalikh – a Memorial representative – Gulag history should be learned through action. Consequently, from the nineties, he organized summer camps at Perm-36 for young people from the Russian Federation and beyond (Feraposhkin 2006). During the day, camp participants worked together in the museum grounds, and in the evenings, they met with well-known people, including former dissidents, who discussed historical and political topics. Over time, the work undertaken by young people in the museum grounds became increasingly unimportant. Initially, they became involved in the reconstruction of the camp grounds, erecting fences or painting the barracks, but later they were only allowed to mow the grass and collect rubbish. The progressive professionalization led to fewer and fewer tasks being entrusted to volunteers. Furthermore, the young people stopped having any influence over decision-making. This was accompanied by a lack of dialogue and any attempt to mutually understand differing stances. All these factors influenced the emergence in the Perm chapter of Memorial's milieu of the notion of creating an alternative memory project offering a contrast to Perm-36. Since 2006, the Perm chapter of Memorial has been developing a new project, the Museum Without a Guide, which fully embodies the notion of education and commemorating the Gulag through action promoted by the Perm chapter of Memorial.

The notion of creating a museum without a guide develops the Along the Rivers of Memory project that Memorial has been running since 2000. It was initiated and largely implemented by Robert Latypov, who was initially a representative of the youth division of the Perm chapter of Memorial and currently represents the entire branch.[22] For many years, Latypov has been organizing kayaking trips along various rivers in Perm Krai, during which young people record oral histories and assist former repressed persons living in remote settlements with renovation work, but first and foremost, learn about the local history. This is immensely important, because, as Robert Latypov stressed to me, 'we know more about what went on in Perm Krai in the eighteenth and nineteenth centuries than in the thirties to fifties' [18_RL]. The kayaking trips are supposed to facilitate the learning of this history via direct contact with the lager's remains, both those preserved in the cultural landscape and those living on in people's memories (Feraposhkin 2006).

During the kayaking trips, young people erect memory markers. As Robert Latypov relates: 'sometimes we place them in a cemetery, sometimes on the edge of a village, sometimes in the village itself and sometimes in a field, because there is no village . . . I want people to see these signs' [18_RL]. These are temporary signs created from the materials – wood or stone – available at a given site. Most of them are crosses but, as Latypov stresses:

> I don't feel completely comfortable about erecting confessional markers. In the thirties and forties, there were basically many atheists in the USSR, yet I'm erecting a cross in their memory . . . Even so, a cross, as our European, not just our Russian, tradition shows, indicates that a particular place is a memorial site . . . it attracts attention and provides the information that it was erected to honour someone's memory. That's why I usually erect crosses. Catholic ones too. [18_RL]

At other sites, he constructs ordinary non-confessional steles or posts.

A memory marker is often accompanied by brief information explaining what the marker represents, to whom it is devoted and who can be contacted to acquire more data relating to the site in question. Over the course of a dozen or so years, Robert Latypov has managed to travel with young people along all the most important rivers in Perm Krai, marking the most important sites associated with the history of the lagers. As he says, 'the memorial markers enable us to express ourselves and urge others to begin talking [about history – ZB] as they look at some marker' [18_RL].

Making it possible for young people to express their opinions on the Gulag by creating commemorative projects is an essential component of the manner of approaching the history of the repressions promoted by the Perm chapter of Memorial. This is particularly important, as very few hard sources enabling this history to be grasped on an intellectual level have been preserved. Consequently, Gulag history is mainly discovered via direct contact with what remains in the field and in human memory. It was evident from my conversations with Robert Latypov and Aleksandr Kalikh that, in their view, the museum, rather than aspiring to acquire the reputation of an institution promoting the objective truth, should stimulate and encourage the viewer to learn and interpret the history in her own way. Emphasis is placed on signposting rather than the imposition of one particular interpretation. This is the role the Stvor camp, or Museum Without a Guide, is meant to play.

The Memorial members have known about Stvor for a long time. The lager was created during the war, when many companies and factories were evacuated to Perm Krai following the German occupation of central regions of the USSR. These needed electrical power to operate, so the decision was made to safeguard wartime production by constructing hydroelectric plants on the River Chusovaya. One of these was built by convicts living in Stvor.[23] This lager was a special kind of self-sufficient camp that even had its own coal mine on site. However, the power plant was never completed. After some time, the lager was liquidated as well. Later, the site became a settlement for special displaced persons. Today, according to Latypov, 'nothing has survived of the lager. There is a large green space there' [18_RL].

Memorial purposefully selected this particular site for its museum experiment. As Robert Latypov stresses, Stvor lies on this region's most popular waterway. Every year, thousands of people travel along the River Chusovaya, unaware of this site's history. It was necessary to come up with a concept that would attract the attention of tourists, encouraging them to disembark from their vessels and take a walk around the former lager's grounds. Expedition participants therefore painted a 'Stvor Lager' sign in red paint on the remains of the building's walls and constructed a wooden frame around a concrete post alongside the walls that contained a plaque giving information about this site. As Robert Latypov says: 'We planned the frame, but managed to create a stylized camp guard tower. We found some leftover barbed wire and objects from the camp and created such a guard tower' [18_RL].

In 2008, a few tours of the Museum Without a Guide were designed by erecting signposts informing visitors, for example, that a particular path led to what had been the punishment block and this could be reached by walking about 600 metres. It had been difficult to see the buildings from the marked trail, so the area in front of them was cleared of brushwood and weeds. The central point of this unusual open-air museum is occupied by the tower. The Memorial members envisaged that people would be able to lay flowers there, but, as Latypov says, passing kayakers prefer to use various metal camp objects they find in the former lager's grounds instead (barbed wire, mugs, bowls and spoons and remnants of work tools, like a hoe or shovel parts).

The work undertaken by the young people is of a collective nature. In fact, as they complete their tasks, a kind of community is forged with a collectively authored mission statement. Many solutions are born through action due to ideas appearing on the spur of the moment. Some of the kayakers may express themselves in their own way, throwing further light on the purposes of the exposition. Most of the museum elements are created from materials (like wood) available in Stvor or from very cheap, easily replaceable raw materials that have been brought to the site (paper, plywood, string, nails).

As Robert Latypov says:

> The Stvor Lager is an experiment. The construction of a museum without a guide, a museum in the open air where anyone can interpret the history of the political repressions . . . We're not forcing anything on anyone. We're just providing information and proposing a short walk around this site. It's also an experiment. I don't know what will come of this. [18_RL]

As things stand, it seems that the project is beginning to function and live its own life. Stvor can only be reached by kayak. Even so, the many tracks that were visible there in 2008 indicated that many people do in fact stop there to visit the place. These visitors, who lay metal elements found in the lager's grounds under the tower, are themselves becoming participants in the process of memorializing Stvor.

The Stvor Lager is an intriguing memory project, displaying features of a performance involving both the project's creators and the public – that is, the tourists visiting the museum. As Marvin Carlson, referencing Lyotard, writes, the postmodern condition is characterized by a mistrust of metanarratives. It was precisely this mistrust that the members of Memorial's Perm chapter felt toward the Perm-36 Museum, which was trying to create a metanarrative. An attitude of mistrust, as Carlson writes, causes general intellectual or cultural structures to lose their power, which is acquired by single actions that allow improvised experiments tailored to the needs and desires perceived and felt in a unique concrete situation (Carlson 2013). This is the exact type of experience proposed by the Stvor Museum.

The former lager's grounds have been transformed by collective action. Stvor therefore seems to embody the idea of a 'museum without walls'. As Kelvin Hetherington writes, this type of museum destroys the disciplinary authority of the classical museum and proposes an alternative method for creating a social order. Rather than supporting a single interpretation, it creates a polyphony of different viewpoints. It is a kind of space for which various actors can develop their own ideas and conceptions. Such museums function on a similar principle to festivals, markets or carnivals. They therefore propose an alternative method for constructing a social order, while the resultant image of 'what a society should be' arises from the convictions, judgements and actions of all visitors (Hetherington 1996: 153–76).

Stvor, conceived as a cultural message, on the one hand, incorporates the individual interpretations of the project's participants (these are expressed in the commemorative work they undertake), and on the other, a kind of synthesis of them. Individual activities enter into a relationship with the work undertaken by different actors, being transformed further in the process. There are no barriers in the open-air museum's grounds, so visitors can also enter into the role of memory actors, transforming the site. Consequently, a contemporary interpretation emerges from the historical space and these ruins – the remains of a Gulag camp (which also, on its part, defines a framework for action). This territory thus becomes a space for the manifestation of collective memory shaped by those participating in the performance's negotiation of meanings.

'Why Know History?'

Encouraging members of the public to reflect on the past is extremely important for preserving Gulag memory, especially since – as a history teacher in one of the local schools who was involved in the Perm-36 youth camp claimed – young people are not interested in this history: 'they don't read much . . . They don't need this. It happened so long ago. [They ask] why they should get involved in this – or even remember it. I tell them that they should know about this all the same, so that it'll never be repeated. One needs to know one's history . . . And they ask: "Why know history?"' [03_AJ]. This opinion is also shared by many adults. However, as my interlocutor adds: 'When you start speaking about Perm-36, how they [the prisoners – ZB] ate, how they lived, how they worked, [the young people – ZB] get scared. They listen, but they're scared . . . It's hard for them to understand the process of political repressions – and why it happened. This is not clear to them [03_AJ]. This statement demonstrates the power of the social interaction integrated into the Perm-36 Museum, a project capable of provoking people seemingly uninterested in history into reflecting on the past. It also explains why milieus with differing views on the past, such as the patriotic pro-Kremlin organization Sut Vremeni or the youth wing of the CPFR, so fiercely opposed the museum.

The conflict over the museum began in 2012 after Viktor Basargin was elected as governor of Perm Krai, and escalated in 2013, when he commenced the process of transforming the museum into a state cultural institution. Nationalist and communist organizations began to come out against the museum, accusing it of heroizing Ukrainian fascists and terrorists and being part of a foreign spy network acting to the detriment of Russia (Cichowlas 2014). The main accusation levelled against the museum was that it was distorting history. This idea was most fully articulated in a report by Ilya Ushenin, which was transmitted by NTV, the Russian state television network, in June 2014. The documentary included contributions by former camp guards, who were presented as experts on the past. One of the scenes from the report shows an MVD veteran, Colonel Anatoly Terentyev, looking at the *sploshnye nary* standing in the barracks. Terentyev says that the prisoners never slept on these and he does not understand why the museum is purposefully falsifying the past. However, he fails to mention that the guide said during his visit that these *nary* served the needs of prisoners during the Stalinist period from 1946 to 1956, but not during the dissident period, when he served there himself. The fiercest criticism, however, was reserved for the manner in which the Ukrainian and Lithuanian dissidents were presented.

One of the Ukrainian dissidents referred to in the documentary was Levko Lukyanenko, whose biography was presented at the *The History of a Single Lager* exhibition. As the NTV journalist points out, Lukyanenko was a Ukrainian nationalist, Bandera supporter and fascist, one of the most dangerous prisoners, yet the museum presented him as a 'freedom fighter'. As Ushenin explains, 'the museum keeps silent about the crimes he [Lukyanenko – ZB] committed', thus 'deceiving visitors' and distorting history. The reportage produced the words of a tenth-grade pupil as evidence for the efficacy of the museum's propaganda; after visiting the Perm-36 Museum, she called the Ukrainian dissidents, whom Ushenin labelled 'UPA criminals',[24] heroes. The reportage also referred to another controversial figure presented at the exhibition, Balys Gajauskas, a Lithuanian nationalist who, as Ushenin explains, 'complained, in his post-war memoirs, about not managing to kill more Soviet soldiers'. Finally, the reportage included the opinion of Pavel Gurianov, a lecturer at the Perm State Pharmaceutical Academy,[25] who underlined the dangers of the museum heroizing Banderites in the face of the conflict in the east of Ukraine, itself provoked by 'today's nationalists' – the living descendants of the Banderites commemorated in the museum.[26]

The report was just one episode in a conflict over the museum lasting a few years (Batalina 2017; Kozlov 2014; Sokolov 2016a), yet it played an important role in it. It was prepared using simple, accessible language. The aggressive tone and clear examples evoked in the documentary did not leave any doubt as to how its producers evaluated the museum's activities and the role it played in the armed conflict just beginning in the east of Ukraine. In effect, the propaganda report provided officials with the 'conclusive' arguments they needed to justify the state takeover of the museum.

Viktor Shmyrov and Tatyana Kursina, who had been shaping the museum's development for years, were relieved of their roles and the Regional Ministry of Culture appointed Natalia Semakova as the new director. In 2015, the conflict over the museum reached its apogee with the new director of the Memorial Complex of Political Repressions being strongly criticized by various circles associated with Memorial. She was accused of seeking to whitewash the past by telling the story of the system and the camp authorities, rather than that of the victims, and implementing a policy directed at the complete destruction of the only surviving open-air museum of camp buildings in the Russian Federation (Giesen 2015; Tumakova 2016).

However, the museum was not destroyed and, as time passed, attitudes to it began to change. This transformation is splendidly illustrated by the reports of *Zvezda* journalist Vladimir Sokolov, who has regularly published materials devoted to Perm-36 (Sokolov 2016a, 2016b, 2017). In 2016, Sokolov travelled twice to Kuchino. His first visit to the new museum left a very negative impression on him, but after his second visit, he wrote that everything was changing for the better. An asphalt road now led to the museum, a body of experts and scholars headed by Julia Kantor, Doctor of Historical Sciences, had been appointed, research work was being undertaken in the museum and new exhibitions were being opened (Sokolov 2016b). Although the museum still has its unrelenting vehement critics (Batalina 2017), positive assessments of the museum's activity have been increasing.

The Memorial Complex of Political Repressions, rather than telling the history of NKVD functionaries, as it was originally accused of, tells that of the political repressions in the USSR. New exhibitions have been opened in the museum that tell about different periods and different aspects of the political repressions. The exhibition *Broken by the Axe,* prepared in 2015 to mark the seventieth anniversary of the end of the Great Patriotic War, tells of the forest felling and logging industry in the Chusovskoy region during wartime (1941–45). In 2016, an exhibition was opened titled *Literature Banned in the USSR,* which included works published in samizdat. The same year (18 October 1991), another exhibition was prepared, titled *Long Way Back,* which marked the twenty-fifth anniversary of the Law on the Rehabilitation of Victims of Political Repression and told of the inquiry process and stages of rehabilitation of political prisoners freed in the USSR. Furthermore, in 2017, on the eightieth anniversary of the Great Terror, an exhibition entitled *Material Evidence* was prepared, which was based on documents from the Perm State Social and Political History Archive relating to the Stalinist repressions, with particular emphasis on the Great Terror. These exhibitions are just some of those that can be viewed at the Memorial Complex.[27] It is clear from all of these exhibitions that the museum, rather than proposing a re-evaluation of the past, is following the path adopted by Viktor Shmyrov (Tumakova 2016). However, he was not himself invited to serve on the museum's board of experts and scholars headed by Julia Kantor. Finding himself unable to reach an understanding with the new authorities, he began to create a new project devoted, as he explains, to: 'the history of Perm's political camps. The material will be used in a virtual museum we are currently creating. The project's working title is the Perm Political Camps' (Shmyrov, quoted in Batalina 2017).

Shmyrov's new venture is not the only project in Perm Krai providing an alternative Gulag narrative to that of the Perm-36 Museum. Also worthy of attention is the museum established in the village of Tsentralnaya by former camp guard Vladimir Kurguzov. Kurguzov worked at Perm-36 as deputy commander of a guard division and currently runs this private museum (Sofonov 2006). In 2008, Robert Latypov told me about this museum. Initially, Kurguzov wished to create an exhibition extolling the NKVD functionaries who had worked there, but when he started collecting material, 'he almost started to become a memorialist himself' [18_RL]. Kurguzov has managed to assemble a unique collection of objects. His exhibition contains uniforms used by the secret police from 1918 and a weapon made by prisoners. As Robert Latypov says, 'he has a scale model of a special regime barrack ... with human figures made from bread. The prisoners made them themselves. He then bought them, painted them and placed them here' [18_RL].

When, in 2008, I was told the story of Kurguzov's project, I found it very intriguing, for it seemed to suggest that it is possible to alter interpretations of the past. Since Kurguzov, a former camp guard, had begun to perceive political prisoners as victims of the system, rather than criminals and traitors, a broader social transformation in Russia in attitudes to the past also seemed possible. However, during the conflict over the Perm-36 Museum, Kurguzov supported the viewpoint of those opposed to the museum, returning somewhat to his original views and departing from the roadmap for perceiving the past that had been proposed by Memorial.[28]

Both the Kurguzov example and the entire history of the conflict over the Perm-36 Museum show that memory about the political repressions in Russian is not a closed topic. Although the narrative about the past shaped by the Memorial milieu has never been at the centre of Russian social memory, when I was conducting my research in 2008, its existence did not appear to be endangered. However, once the state became actively involved in shaping memory of the repressions, it became clear how fragile an existence the Memorial-created memory had been leading. At the same time, the activization of memory actors with varied stances on the past indicates that the state does not have a monopoly on memory of the repressions, while the circle of memory actors interested in making sense of the past is expanding. After his visit to the Memorial Complex, the film director Alexander Sokurov stated that the conflict over the museum reflects what is currently happening across the whole of Russian society. There is therefore a need for everyone wishing to avoid tragedy and divisions in society to support the new museum together. As Sokurov says: 'Russia needs this museum. Our national consciousness needs this museum as a marker commemorating those who suffered here, accepted death and reconciled themselves to being ridiculed. This has become a problem in the Russian Federation, especially that part that is not indifferent to what was happening and is going to happen in the Motherland' (Sokolov 2017).

Notes

1. I have also quoted the title of this article ('Svoboda nachinayetsya v tyurme'/ 'Freedom Begins in Prison') in the title of Subsection 3 of this chapter.
2. I write about Dalstroy in the next chapter, which is devoted to Kolyma.
3. The literature contains two dates when this lager ceased to function. Viktor Shmyrov, former director of the Perm-36 Museum, gives the date as 1987 (Shmyrov 2001: 25), and this date could also be seen on the Perm-36 Museum's website until it was shut down in 2014 and the national Memorial Complex of Political Repressions was created in its place. The date currently given on the website is 1988 (http://itk36-museum.ru/about/history, last accessed 20 August 2017). The same date is also

given by L.P. Hutchins and G.E. Vietzke (2002: 65), whereas the date of December 1987 is given by A. Stanley in a *New York Times* article (1997).
4. Perm-36 was strongly supported by NIPC Memorial and was powerfully promoted and later defended by former Perm-36 prisoner, Sergey Kovalev.
5. I have taken the 'stirrings of conscience' in the title of this section from an article penned by Aleksandr Kalikh (1998).
6. The original reads: Pamyati zhertv politicheskikh repressiy, O, ludi!, Ludi s nomerami. Vy byli ludi, ne raby. Vy byli vyshe i upryamey svoyey tragicheskoy sudby.
7. An Orthodox priest consecrated the monument and regularly participates in the 30 October Day of Remembrance ceremonies (*Molodaya gvardiya*, 2 October 1996).
8. For the monument's unveiling and meaning, see Y. Kutuzuv (1996) and A. Pastukhova (2006).
9. More can be read about the social work of volunteers from the Perm chapter of Memorial at: www.pmem.ru/index.php?mode=volonteer&exmod=volonteer/slujba/vol_slujba.
10. Perm-35 was the longest-running political camp. It was not closed down until 1991.
11. www.wmf.org/project/perm-36.
12. The All-Russian Extraordinary Commission for Combating Counter-Revolution, Speculation and Abuses of Power.
13. Based on my observations as a viewer-participant accompanying three different groups.
14. An explanation of the iconostasis is contained in the tour guide prepared by D.A. Tretyakov – 'Razvernuty plan ekskursiy po Muzeyu politicheskikh repressiy Perm-36'. The text is presented as a printout and does not contain a catalogue number.
15. Yuri Lotman defines the term 'invariant' as 'a sign-based "text construct" that will allow for realization of a given culture in all its potential variations' (Andrew 2003: 4).
16. From the text 'Programma razvitiya muzeya na 2007-2013 gg', which does not possess a catalogue number.
17. '18-20 maya v Permi proydet forum "Parlamentarizm. Demokratiya. Pravo. 1906-1956-2006"', www.reporter.perm.ru/news/obwestvo/details_198.html.
18. The Memory Park project was included in the museum's development programme for 2007–2013.
19. Mikhail Khodorkovsky, Platon Lebedev and Svetlana Bakhmina were charged in the so-called 'Yukos case' and subsequently sentenced by a court to several years' imprisonment. They are regarded as political prisoners in Putin's regime.
20. The murdered are commemorated with pines. Only Sakharov has a cedar dedicated to him. It is located in the very centre of the park and serves as an important orientation point – the park's axis mundi.
21. Two other avenues already marked out in 2008 did not receive their own names.
22. More can be read about all the Perm chapter of Memorial's projects and activities at: http://volonter59.ru/project.php?category=16.
23. From a text on the history of the Stvor lager prepared by Memorial. The text was placed on a special information stand – a guard tower in the Stvor lager grounds.
24. The Ukrainian Insurgent Army, or UPA, was created by the Bandera faction (the OUN-B) of the Organization of Ukrainian Nationalists. At the end of 1942, the UPA fought against Nazi Germany (although it collaborated with the Germans in the guerrilla war against units of Soviet partisans) and Czechoslovakia, but its primary enemies were the Soviet Union and Poland. Some UPA units continued fighting until the 1950s.
25. Pavel Gurianov is a representative of the Perm chapter of Sut Vremeni, yet this was not mentioned in the reportage. He was simply presented as an expert and lecturer.
26. http://gurianov-pavel.livejournal.com/40294.html (last accessed 29 September 2017).
27. Based on an analysis of the Memorial Complex of Political Repressions (http://itk36-museum.ru/about/history/).
28. Based on a comment made in the film *Who Does the Past Belong to?*, directed by Kerstin Nickig: www.youtube.com/watch?v=ksHHmN7yYT8.

Chapter 4
Kolyma

> Russia's Auschwitz. If Kolyma isn't a name as chillingly recognizable as Auschwitz, Belsen or Dachau, it is not because the horrors there were any less awful, but because they were perpetrated by a secretive government on its own citizens and because they took place in an isolated ice-located region, 9000 km from Moscow.
> —Russia and Belarus, Lonely Planet (2003, p. 614)

The Island of Gold Mines

Magadan is not only known as the Soviet Auschwitz in the West, but also in the Russian Federation. The names Vorkuta and Magadan (Raizman 1999) – the two camp centres mired in the most profound ignominy and with the highest mortality rates – made a similar impact on the history of the Russian Federation as Buchenwald and Auschwitz did on the history of Europe. This metaphor clearly indicates that Magadan, rather than anywhere else, has become the synonym par excellence for death in the popular imagination. This reputation was not only gained from the murderous work regime imposed on those labouring in this region's gold and uranium mines, but, first and foremost, from the biting cold that killed off workers during the long and dark Kolyma winters. In many prisoners' memoirs, the winter is portrayed as their greatest foe (see, for example, Shalamov 1994).

Kolyma's history greatly resembles that of the Komi Republic. Much as Chernov discovered coal deposits in Vorkuta and forecast in 1930 that this basin would become a uniquely rich source of the 'black gold', in 1928, the geologist Yury Bilibin discovered deposits of pure gold in Kolyma. He stated at the time that Kolyma could yield four times more gold than the output of all the country's other gold mines combined. Back then, Kolyma was a complete wasteland. The decision was therefore taken in November 1931 to establish Dalstroy (Biryukov 1999; Nikolayev 1998; Nordlander 2003; Pilyasov 1998), a company that was meant to tame this wilderness and mine the local minerals. It was headed by Eduard Berzin, who had just completed work on the creation of the industrial lagers in Perm Krai. This time he faced a much tougher task. At a site several thousand kilometres away from Moscow only accessible by sea at the time (and even then, only when the sea route was not frozen over), Berzin was supposed to build factories, mines, roads and towns. He was provided with hired hands and special displaced persons, but, first and foremost, zeks. In 1932, Sevvostlag *(severno-vostochny ispravitelny lager)* was established in Kolyma. Thus began Magadan's camp history.

The manner in which Kolyma's Gulag past manifests itself in the local landscape is also reminiscent of the situation observable in the Komi Republic. Material remains of the lagers and camp cemeteries can be found in areas that were once mining centres, road construction sites or transit camps. The primary difference between them is their accessibility. Whereas the camp ruins sought out by school field expeditions in the Komi Republic are several dozen kilometres away from each other, the equivalent distances in Kolyma are measured in hundreds of kilometres. What is more, though these are difficult to reach in the Komi Republic, in Kolyma, most of them are completely inaccessible. They are far away from the Kolyma Route (this region's main transport route) and the road that used to run there has been destroyed by atmospheric factors. Some sites can only be reached using a suitable off-road vehicle or helicopter. The costs of such an expedition are prohibitive in today's economic climate.[1] It is therefore hardly surprising that, despite the location of many former lagers being known, many people involved in researching their history have never visited them. As one employee of the Magadan Local History Museum told me, in the early nineties, when large numbers of foreign guests with the financial resources to hire a helicopter began to arrive in the city, they managed to get to sites that museum employees researching the Kolyma lagers had never been to [34_AS]. Consequently, knowledge about most of Kolyma's lagpunkts flows in from secondary sources, written records and, above all, witnesses' memoirs.

The reawakening of Gulag memory in Magadan followed the typical scenario manifested in other areas of the USSR. Suddenly, the wall of silence was broken, memoirs and publications relating to the Gulag began to appear, and the process of rehabilitating and campaigning to secure the financial security of ex-prisoners commenced (Damanskaya 1998: 65–66). There were also discussions on commemorating the victims of Stalinist repressions.[2] However, what really set Magadan apart was the dynamic nature of the social polemics revolving around the form that the main monument, which was meant to stand in Kolyma's capital, would take. The polemics became an element of the wider debate on the history of this region and the monuments that should be erected there.

As one of the moderators at the Magadan Community Centre told me, for years the only monuments in Magadan were 'standard-issue', by which he meant statues of Lenin and Party comrades. No other monuments were erected, because very few other people wished to stay in Magadan for long. In general, people were planning to stay there for a short period, motivated by the opportunity to make some money. They therefore attached little importance to monuments acting as cultural identity markers. In the late eighties, however, they realized that they would not be leaving the region. Some of them, including my interviewee, stayed of their own free will, because they fell in love with the area and, as they attest, were unable to live without Kolyma, while others had no choice. As one inhabitant of Debin says, 'We are voluntary zeks. We can't leave here. We can't even go to Magadan. We can't afford to' [33_AV]. This explains why the discussions in Magadan on the memorial to victims of the Gulag ran in parallel with the debate on other monuments that should be erected in the city. The plan was to create a network of stone monuments expressing the identity of Kolyma's inhabitants.

Consequently, the debate devoted to monuments was transformed into a discussion on Kolyma's inhabitants' identity. Those who participated in it wondered what events and figures should be erected in the city's space to mark its identity. The discussion was all the more difficult because the awakening of Gulag memory changed the manner in which the region's history had been perceived. The likes of Eduard Berzin, hitherto regarded as unquestioned authorities, suddenly became ambiguous figures. Much attention was also devoted to the artistic form of future monuments. The actual erection of these monuments was not the only issue under consideration. It was also important to reflect on what message they would be sending to future generations and what they would say about Kolyma's past. Ernst Neizvestny's design for a Victims of Stalinist Repressions Monument provoked the most controversy due to its artistic form and symbolism, becoming the focus of the harshest polemics.[3] This continued for several years, right up until the moment his Mask of Sorrow was erected and unveiled.

These protracted discussions led to the first monument to victims of the repressions being erected, not in Magadan, but several hundred kilometres away at Serpantinka, not far from Yagodnoye, at the site of the former prison of Sevvostlag, where prisoners were executed by firing squad during the Great Terror. Much as was the case in other parts of the Russian Federation, this monument was not sponsored by the local authorities. The initiative came from two of Yagodnoye's inhabitants, Svyatoslav Timchenko (a journalist working for local newspaper *Severnaya Pravda*) and Ivan Panikarov. With time, other memory actors began to become involved in Yagodnoye, and Debin, 30 kilometres away. They erected markers commemorating the history of the local lager. As a result, Yagodnoye and Debin, once gold mine basins, now collectively constitute a 'Gulag memory repository', sites of special significance on today's map of Kolyma.

In my view, Kolyma's discussions on monuments, especially the Mask of Sorrow in Magadan and the memory repository in Yagodnoye and Debin, very clearly illustrate the manner in which its inhabitants comprehend and interpret Gulag history. I shall therefore devote the next part of this chapter to the distinctive features of these discussions, as I believe them to be social phenomena important for the shaping of memory.

'On Memory and Monuments' – The Magadan Identity Debate

The quote in the title of this subsection was taken from a column in the *Magadanskaya Pravda* newspaper devoted to the discussions on the Magadan monuments. These not only involved the local intellectual elite, who were reflecting on the monuments' artistic form and social function, but also ordinary inhabitants of the city, who shared their opinions in letters to the editor. Various memory markers were considered, including a monument to the geologist Yury Bilibin, discoverer of Kolyma's gold reserves, one to Eduard Berzin, the head of Dalstroy, who was primarily responsible for Kolyma's construction, and finally, monuments to the Great Patriotic War and Victims of the Repressions.

The Bilibin Monument did not provoke any great controversy and was erected in front of the North-East Scientific Research Institute in Magadan. However, some doubts were raised about the Eduard Berzin Monument. As my interviewee explained:

> [Berzin] began to be perceived as an ambiguous figure, because he was signing [death warrants] . . . He had to do it . . . He was obligated to sign them. . . . At the same time, he was improving the lives of the prisoners, and those of the politicals too. And he paid for that. They arrested, judged and shot him. They blamed him, among other things, for his humanitarian attitude toward the prisoners. How can this be split into black and white? It can't. [25_AV]

In the end, a bust of Berzin was erected on a square in front of Magadan's local government building.

Even more discussion was provoked by the Great Patriotic War Monument. For many years, the cornerstone of the future monument lay in a square in front of the Cultural Centre on Karl Marx Street, but it was not until the end of the eighties that the decision was finally taken to construct it. The design was approved by a small group of officials. When the *Magadanskaya Pravda* printed a sketch for a monument depicting a rifle-wielding soldier with his arms raised aloft above his head, the editor began to receive masses of letters expressing local residents' opposition to the enterprise. This erupted into a full-blown public protest (*Magadanskaya Pravda*, 14 January 1989).

The discussion was so lively that in 1989, Miron Etlis, a university professor and member of the Magadan chapter of Memorial, conducted a survey among Magadan's inhabitants that was designed to reveal their expectations regarding the city's monuments and the preservation of its architecture (*Magadanskaya Pravda*, 18 February 1989). At the same time, the pages of local newspapers were filled with discussions about what shape the Great Patriotic War Monument should take. Members of the local intellectual elite argued that the simplistic style of the presented design was steeped in the past and failed to correspond to any meaningful contemporary interpretation of events. Its questionable artistic value was also pointed out. The accusation also surfaced that it could have been erected in any other city because its form failed to draw attention to the special wartime circumstances prevailing in Kolyma. Relatively few people from Magadan fought on the front. This region contained a 'labour front' mainly staffed by prisoners. As my interviewee adds:

If a monument of this kind had stood in the centre of Berlin, every Russian, or former citizen of the Soviet Union . . . would have understood it. This was a soldier who had arrived in Berlin, this was a sign of victory. But the associations were different here . . . He was perceived as a convoy officer . . . That was the main charge. This monument was never erected. [25_AV]

Instead, in March 1991, the Memory Knot, a monument symbolizing the contribution of Kolyma's residents to the war effort, was erected. It depicts three intertwined bodies: those of a fighting soldier, a mine labourer and a dying convict. The figure of Mother Russia emerges from the bodies with a child in her arms.

When the debate over the Great Patriotic War was reaching its apogee, a new idea appeared to erect a monument in Magadan to the victims of Soviet repressions. As Miron Etlis recalls: 'I took advantage of the situation and appealed, along with the Mayor, to Ernst Neizvestny. It turned out that he was designing a triptych at the time that was supposed to be erected in Magadan, Yekaterinburg and Vorkuta' [09_ME]. Thus began the history of the construction of the Mask of Sorrow. The new debate, over this monument, also became heated.

The notion of creating a Russian Triangle of Suffering and Redemption, which would be composed of three monuments – masks located in symbolic sites associated with the history of the USSR – arose from the sculptor's deep reflection on the country's past. In 1989, Ernst Neizvestny took part in a conference organized by Moscow State University and delivered a paper titled *Art and Society*. It made a huge impression on those who heard it, and Neizvestny received a proposal to construct a monument to victims of the Gulag spread across various cities of the USSR. He decided on Yekaterinburg, Vorkuta and Magadan (Leong 1998: 67–71). Yekaterinburg was chosen because it was there that Tsar Nicholas II was executed, an event that became the starting point for twentieth-century Russia's 'troubles' and the period of Soviet repression. Standing on Asia's border with Europe, the monument would resemble a 'point of transition, a gateway to the Gulag'. In turn, the monuments standing in Vorkuta and Magadan would symbolize the two Gulag camp centres with the worst reputations (Leong 1998: 67–71).

It was envisaged that all three monuments would take the form of a mask. In Yekaterinburg, there were to be two masks with European and Asian features gazing in different directions. It was planned that the Vorkuta mask, which resembled an island in form, would be erected on a riverbank. Magadan's Mask of Sorrow was supposed to glance sadly towards the inlet where the ships arrived in Kolyma with their cargos of prisoners. Ernst Neizvestny planned that all three monuments would be executed from the same material – concrete. Another connecting element would be the use of fire (the sun) and water (tears) motifs in their construction – symbols respectively of destruction and eternal remembrance (Leong 1998: 67–71).

The idea of creating a Triangle of Suffering developed systematically (Leong 1998: 68). Ernst Neizvestny first employed the crying mask motif in a monument to victims of the repressions he created in 1956, following the secret publication of Khrushchev's report on Stalin's legacy. The Soviet authorities even allocated the funds necessary for its erection, and the poet Robert Rozhdestvensky wrote a poem about it titled *Creativity* (1960).

However, the monument was never constructed and a model of it was destroyed in 1976, when Ernst Neizvestny was forced into exile (Leong 1998: 68). In the early nineties, the sculptor designed three new monuments – the aforementioned masks for the cities of Yekaterinburg, Vorkuta and Magadan. He only managed to build the last of these.

Mask of Sorrow – A Monument to Utopian Consciousness

At the foot of the monument, stone blocks, resembling camp barracks in form, were erected containing the names of all the Kolyma lagers with the worst reputations (Figure 4.1). The monument combined two sculpting styles: Classicism, referencing the ancient tradition, and abstraction, alluding to Cubism. The latter is considered to be a marker of the technocratic civilization of the nineteenth and twentieth centuries that gave birth to totalitarian systems (Raizman 1999b: 7). The right side of the mask respects the principles of Soviet academic art the painter had to master during his studies. This is evident in the form of the nose, eye or mouth. However, the left side is a synthesis of sculpting styles. The classical and abstract parts of the mask are separated by a cross. This by no means symbolizes faith. Instead, it delineates the contours of the face, dividing them into horizontal (the brow line) and vertical (the nose line) parts (Raizman 1999b: 7). The left part of the brain is responsible for memory, so it was on this side that the sculptor placed small face masks that slowly flow downwards, imitating human tears. They symbolize the prisoners' community. Evidently, they are people of various ages and nationalities experiencing pain in various ways.

The right side, which is angular and severe in form, is distinctive for its avant-garde stylistics. The empty eye socket contains bars and a bell – symbols of camp life. The camp number (ZK[4] 937) under the eye is a symbol of the totalitarian society comprised of descendants of the Great Terror of 1937. There is also a staircase there leading to a museum room – an isolation cell in which an exhibition has been organized of objects brought from two lagers: Dneprovsky and Butugychag. Neizvestny wanted everyone who crossed the Mask's threshold to feel as if they were in prison, explaining why the entrance and exit are so narrow. Visitors have to pass through in single file. Such an arrangement is meant to provoke feelings of enslavement, because while the Gulag functioned, all members of Soviet society were de facto prisoners. Visitors entering the space are supposed to feel as if they are in a real cell before they can take the stairs down towards the cross – and purification (*Vecherni Magadan*, October 1990). Consequently, the Mask of Sorrow refuses to allow the viewer to become a passive recipient. She is drawn into a paratheatrical game in which it is assumed that she should become a co-author experiencing what the creator and director of this curious spectacle has proposed for her.

Figure 4.1. The Mask of Sorrow Memorial Complex. Designed by Ernst Neizvestny and erected in 1996. The monument was placed on Krutaya Hill, the site of the former Tranzitka transit camp. Photo by author.

As visitors descend, they come across the figure of a kneeling, weeping woman – a symbol of the descendants of repression victims lamenting the loss of their loved ones. On the Mask's back wall, there is a figure of a man stretched out on a cross. The composition may be interpreted as an allegory for rebellion. The captive, rather than yielding to the cross, is attempting to wrest himself away from it, so it is not a symbol of sacrifice or reconciliation that is being presented, but rather one of fury and being at odds with one's fate. The Orthodox Church interpreted this allusion to Christian symbolism as a profanation. Ernst Neizvestny's monument provoked a huge storm of controversy as it became the focus of intense public debate (Raizman 1999b:7).

'Idol or Symbol' – The Discussions on the Mask of Sorrow Monument

The title of this subsection quotes the title of a press article (*Magadanski komsomolets*, 7 October 1990). For some time, the Mask of Sorrow became the main topic of public discussion in local newspapers and on television. I shall now render the shape and dynamic of this debate by alluding to the most meaningful arguments that appeared in what I am treating as a complex cultural statement.

The monument was criticized on several levels. Firstly, there was some opposition to it being located in the old Marchekanskoye Cemetery, because – as its critics explained – there are no graves of victims of Stalinism there and 'a monument should stand at a site where people died' (Raizman 1999b: 7). An Orthodox clergyman Anatoly Sharov, abbot at the Svyato-Pokrovsky Church, wrote in a letter to *Vecherni Magadan* that he was categorically opposed to the construction of a monument on this site, because the church that already stood there would become part of a memorial complex, which, in his view, was a symbol of pagan cult worship (*Vecherni Magadan*, 16 November 1990). Therefore, rather than being erected in the cemetery, the Mask was placed on Krutaya Hill, the site of the former Tranzitka transit camp.

The main wave of criticism was reserved for the sculpture of the man stretched across the cross. It was argued that this was blasphemous and offended the religious sensibilities of Orthodox believers (*Vecherni Magadan*, 12 January 1996). Andrey Kurayev – a deacon as well as Dean of the Philosophy and Theology Faculty of the Russian Orthodox University and one of the fiercest opponents of the monument's construction – was cited in *Vecherni Magadan*. He explained that in Christian culture, a body stretched on a cross is associated with Christ and expresses assent to the acceptance of suffering. In Neizvestny's sculpture, rather than the Saviour – a symbol of sacrifice and reconciliation – it is an insurgent who is stretched across a cross. He was thus comparing him to Prometheus. A monument to the victims of Bolshevism is in effect imbued with a notion of this doctrine that transforms it into an apotheosis of hatred. A man nailed to a stake appears to be ready, with his outstretched arms, to slay anyone daring to oppose him (Raizman 1999: 7).

The alleged profanation of Christian symbolism prompted Magadan's Orthodox community to gather about 500 signatures of people opposing the investment and petition the local authorities to halt the construction of Neizvestny's monument. The main argument was that he was not answerable to the Orthodox faith and was standing in opposition to the spirit of the Russian people (*Vecherni Magadan*, 30 April 1993). The protest was joined by the Archbishop of Yekaterinburg, who gave a comprehensive explanation of why this monument was so problematic.

Firstly, he emphasized that a monument should serve the needs of the living rather than the dead. Such a marker enables a community to express itself. Furthermore, given it is erected in remembrance of the dead, it is, by definition, sacred, so should accord with the cultural traditions of the nation and become an inseparable part of the national spirit. Ernst Neizvestny's sculpture did not express these values, and future generations would not discover much about the Russian people by looking at it (Raizman 1999: 7).

Secondly, the monument could offend the sensibilities of Orthodox believers. As the archbishop writes, most victims were from the Orthodox community. Many of these people were exulted as New Martyrs and confessors, worthy of the company of saints, so using such a marker to honour their memory is inappropriate. The traditional Russian manner of commemorating the dead is the symbolic erection of a church, chapel or cross. In the end, the archbishop reflected on the memorial's title – Memorial to the Victims of Stalinist Repressions – and asked if that meant that other victims from other periods – for example, the revolution – did not deserve to be remembered.

The monument was also criticized for its aesthetic form. Some were of the opinion that 'Chimaeras resemble Chimaeras, but what is [this monument] supposed to resemble?' (Raizman 1999: 7). It was stressed that a monument should provoke positive feelings in the viewer and express a profounder notion, whereas a mask obscures the truth and is associated with hypocrisy, deception and duplicity (*Vecherni Magadan*, 10 February 1995), hence it is not appropriate for a monument. What is more, the mask's abstract form denies the dead any opportunity for atonement while misleading the living. The mask represents nothing more than the desecration of the Orthodox Church's thousand-year tradition (*Vecherni Magadan*, 24 March 1995).

There was also some speculation over who needed such a monument: the living or the dead. It was underlined, when referring to the latter, that those sentenced to imprisonment in Magadan were members of a traditional culture, most of whom were raised in the Orthodox faith. The monument's creators should have empathized with their circumstances and considered whether they would wish to be laid to rest under 'Ernst's cross' or 'would prefer to be laid to rest in the open air' (*Vercherni Magadan*, 12 January 1996). However, the monument was also poorly equipped to serve the needs of the living. 'Remembering' was equated with relating to the past and one's elders with respect and how could one speak of respect if many human remains from the wars and repressions were still not buried? What is more, how could the memory of the dead be honoured if the living – including war veterans – were treated with disdain? It was argued that respect could only be learned through education and such a monument had nothing to contribute to this process. It was therefore redundant (*Vecherni Magadan,* 23 April 1993).

Doubts also surfaced as to what extent those being commemorated as victims of repression were innocent people rather than common criminals. One reader of *Sovetskaya Rossiya* (Glushchenko 1996) complained about the ongoing transformation of meanings. He pointed out that in Prague there is a monument to those who participated in Vlasov's Russian Liberation Army;[5] in Lviv, one to Bandera's supporters; and in Lithuania, one to the Forest Brothers.[6] Yet in Russia, there are memorials to people – supposed victims of repressions – who were bandits. However, such voices of dissent were few and far between.

The most heated discussions not only revolved around the issue of offending the sensibilities of Orthodox believers, but also the question of funding. The project was extremely costly at a time when the local economy had stagnated. This led some of the monument's opponents to ask why it should be built at all. They wondered whether it would not be better to give this money to former repressed persons and erect a less costly monument able to fulfil the same function (*Magadanski komsomolets,* 7 October 1990).

Some of the opinions offered as counterarguments stated that the cross in the Mask had nothing to do with Christianity and was nothing more than a kind of torture instrument (Shalimov 1996). It was stressed that not every secular artwork need be removed from God. Secular art can in fact carry a profound evangelical and biblical message. The monument's power resides in the sense of contrast it evokes – the chasm between the mask's passionless, indifferent visage and the sense of tragedy expressed by the composition as a whole (*Magadanski komsomolets,* 7 October 1990). It is this aesthetic strand that is laden with meaning. This mask is not only a monument to the victims. It also draws attention, through its form and expressive force, to the intellectual and moral inadequacy of the Gulag's inventor (Medovoy 1996). It was stressed that the monument is not so much an idol as a symbol expressing remembrance and that people should honour such a symbol (*Magadanski komsomolets,* 7 October 1990). Furthermore, it is also a symbol of faith in Russia's democratic future (Raizman 1999: 7). The monument itself also commemorates the victims of other totalitarian states that adopted the Marxist ideology (Leong 1998: 67). Ernst Neizvestny characterized the monument as follows:

> I perceive what happened in the Soviet Union as an anthropological crime against humanity as a whole. This is not the tragedy of individual social groups; this is not the tragedy of individual nations; this is not even Russia's tragedy. This is like the catastrophe in Germany, like fascism. It ranged so widely that it cannot be viewed on a local scale. (Neizvestny 1989)

It is this that the Mask of Sorrow is meant to remind us of while bringing our attention to the possibility of a 'utopian consciousness' being born within us that could lead to a catastrophe comparable to those that occurred throughout the world in the twentieth century.

Given that the main wave of misunderstanding related to the monument's visual form and the meanings it concealed, it is fair to say that the conflict that erupted between those who supported the construction of the Mask of Sorrow and the Orthodox Church was a typical conflict over signs. As Boris Uspensky (2002: 313–60) writes, a good example of this situation was the Raskol (or schism) in 1653 between the Russian Orthodox Church and the Old Believers. The changes Patriarch Nikon introduced focused on form rather than dogma, relating to: the sign of the cross (two- or three-fingered), the number of bows when saying Lenten prayers, the liturgy (*mnogogolosiye* or *odnogolosiye*)[7] and the translation of liturgical texts. Even though the conflict was over nothing more than signs, it caused bloody fratricidal battles and divided Russians for centuries. Quite possibly, if the memory of this conflict had not still lived on, then discussions on signs and symbols in the Russian Federation – in this case, in Magadan – would not have provoked such strong emotions.[8]

Nonetheless, in 1996, when the Mask was unveiled, the opposition of the Orthodox Church failed to endanger its status as an object of symbolic significance. The change of perspective on thinking about the past that had occurred among Kolyma's inhabitants meant that the Mask had already become an identity marker for them, long before it was erected. The monument was unveiled during the Day of Remembrance of the Victims of Political Repressions, specially organized on this occasion on 12 June 1996 in Magadan. Many foreign guests arrived in Kolyma's capital. During the ceremony, the Mayor of Magadan, Nikolay Karpenko, emphasized that the monument commemorated people who had died during one of the most tragic periods in Russia's history. The choice of Russia's Independence Day (12 June) as the Mask of Sorrow's unveiling date was no coincidence. The monument was supposed to serve as a warning that the times of lawlessness should never recur (*Magadanskaya Pravda*, 19 June 1996).

The unveiling was accompanied by a number of cultural events. Visitors could view exhibitions at the Local Museum and Pushkin Library and participate in meetings devoted to famous people. There was also a conference titled *Kolyma. Dalstroy. Gulag: Pain and Fate*,[9] and Magadan's eparch recommended that prayers be said for the dead in all the local churches and sites of mass executions in Kolyma (*Vecherni Magadan*, 14 June 1996).

The Mask of Sorrow has become a symbol of Magadan that the city's inhabitants and local authorities show visitors. It is visited by numerous groups, and on Russia's Independence Day (12 June), City of Magadan Day (13 July) and Day of Remembrance of Victims of Political Repressions (30 October), the local authorities organize free excursions for anyone interested in viewing the monument.[10] The Mask also no longer provokes outrage among Orthodox believers. In 2011, it was even visited by Patriarch Kirill on his first pastoral visit to Kolyma, during which he laid flowers under one of the stones commemorating the Orthodox dead. He also entered the Mask and descended towards Neizvestny's cross, which had provoked so much controversy in the nineties. This does not, however, mean that the Mask is treated as a communal memory marker uniting Orthodox and secular memory. The patriarch was in Kolyma to honour the memory of victims of the repressions, including his father, who was exiled there, but he did this at the Holy Trinity Cathedral (erected in the centre of Magadan in remembrance of New Martyrs) rather than at the site of the Mask of Sorrow. While blessing this shrine, which towers over the city, Patriarch Kirill stressed that this, for Orthodox believers, is the main site of memory for victims of the repressions in Kolyma.

Yagodnoye and Debin – A Contemporary 'Memory Repository'

The first monument commemorating prisoners repressed in Kolyma was erected at Serpantinka, not far from the settlement of Yagodnoye (*Territoriya*, 6 September 1996) in June 1991. In the thirties, this was the site of the Sevvostlag prison, where people were executed by firing squad during the Great Terror. The search for this site began in 1988. The earlier mentioned Svyatoslav Timchenko and Ivan Panikarov searched various sources and documents for information (Smolyakov 2000). The data they uncovered indicated that the site had to be in the Yagodnoye region, but it was not clear exactly where. They were eventually assisted by the recollections of two former Serpantinka prisoners who were spared by some miracle from execution. They not only confirmed the site's existence, but also explained where it was. The investigators subsequently managed to attain a secret map of the region, which had Serpantinka marked on it, enabling them to precisely establish the site's location.

The money needed for the required materials was collected from Yagodnoye's inhabitants and local companies (Smolyakov 2000). As Ivan Panikarov relates: 'In May we erected a stone. And Slavko [Timchenko] ... published material in *Severnaya Pravda* and the *Territoriya* newspaper about Serpantinka, [announcing] that on 22 June, we would be unveiling [the monument]' [22_IP]. The local authorities were unhappy about this, yet did not cancel the monument's unveiling. A few days before the ceremony, Panikarov received a telephone call from a KGB officer whom he and Timchenko had helped, in their own time, find information about his dead grandfather. He informed Panikarov that the CPSU was planning to unveil another monument to victims of the repressions in Debin. The local authorities in Magadan were so unhappy that none of their representatives were involved in the process of erecting the monument that they decided to erect their own and unveil it on the same day, but at an earlier time.

Once people had assembled to travel to Serpantinka, the first secretary of the *raykom* (district committee) proposed to Panikarov that everyone should go together, first to Debin, and then to Serpantinka, so that they could all take part in the unveiling of monuments. However, the organizers of the Serpantinka ceremony declined his offer, because the two places were relatively far from the raykom. Consequently, as

Panikarov says: 'The first secretary went with us to Serpantinka, and he sent a regional representative to Debin for the unveiling of the local monument' [22_IP].

Unlike the Debin ceremony, which was very modest, the Serpantinka unveiling attracted many guests from Magadan and Moscow as well as former repressed persons and their loved ones. Young people from a school in Debin were also in attendance (Smolyakov 2000), as were the descendants of NKVD operatives. As Timchenko subsequently wrote: 'A paradox, but that's the way it is now' (Naimushin 1991). The monument was consecrated by Arkady – the Bishop of Magadan and Kamchatka (Smolyakov 2000). Alongside the memorial stone, a symbolic grave was constructed, at his son's request, for Fyodor Nikolayevich Zhdan, who died at the Nizhny At-Uryakh lager (Smolyakov 2000). This was followed by addresses and speeches. As Panikarov recalls, many agitators arrived, vociferously calling for the authorities of the time to be 'dissolved' and the building of a democracy.

From that time onwards, Serpantinka has been an important site of memory on which war veterans and former repressed persons always converge on 22 June. Initially, the local authorities in Yagodnoye were opposed to the Serpantinka ceremony taking place on 22 June, because that date was associated with the beginning of the Great Patriotic War and the Great Victory, rather than the tragic history of the repressions. However, in 1996, the President of the Russian Federation established the Day of Remembrance and Sorrow on this date, so the authorities' argument lost its force. As Panikarov proudly notes, people in Yagodnoye had been already observing this day in 1991.

Ivan Panikarov continued his historical research on the Gulag and collected documents of various kinds. His primary objective was to assist former repressed persons. To this end, he founded the Poisk Nezakonno Repressirovannykh (Search for Unlawfully Repressed Persons) social organization. The materials in his archive facilitated the rehabilitation of over twenty people (Khits 1999). He has also written several books on Kolyma's history (Panikarov 1997, 2005, 2007) and for some time, he published the *Chudnaya planeta* newspaper, which contained historical articles on the region. For a number of years he has run a museum – first, in an apartment in a block, which he purchased himself, and then in a former bus depot, and finally, from 2008, in a private apartment again (Panikarov 2009).

Panikarov is not the only memory actor involved in memorializing the history of the repressions in Yagodnoye. In 1996, Sergey Golunov, who works as an artist at the local Community Centre, erected a monument on the part of the Kolyma Route leading into Yagodnoye from the settlement of Susuman (Figure 4.2). He told me that the idea was born in 1995 during a meeting with male colleagues: 'We were sitting with our companions, chatting, reminiscing on who had been where, who had encountered which burial site . . . in any event, everyone had come across [some of these], whether they had been gold panning or mushroom picking. The idea arose that something ought to be erected' [12_SG]. Sergey Golunov worked up a concept for the monument himself, executing sketches and creating a scale model.

The monument's main motif is an Orthodox cross shooting upwards from between chained hands. The whole structure is presented against the background of a Gulag wall. In the bottom left corner, there are bas-reliefs of a sickle, hammer and rifle – symbols of the system the Gulag created. Above the weapon, in the upper part of the wall, there are prison bars – a symbol of the Gulag itself. Part of the right side of the wall is being prised apart by a sprouting flower symbolizing the Orthodox Church. As Golunov explains, this denotes the nation's conversion to the Orthodox faith. As people begin to reflect on what happened, they are converted and this spiritual reflection destroys the Gulag wall. This part of the wall is much lower, and the flower looks as if it is about to completely rupture it and thrust its bud up toward the sun. The monument was created from red stone and brick, because – as the design's creator says – Kolyma is covered in snow for the greater part of the year. Thanks to this choice of colour, the memorial complex is more noticeable and forms a contrast with the surrounding landscape.

A long time was spent searching for potential sites for the monument. Eventually, a spot was chosen where people often stopped on their way to and from Susuman. Golunov constructed it himself, though he received some assistance from inhabitants of Yagodnoye, who brought him free cement and stone. The town's local authorities

Figure 4.2. Sergey Golunov's memorial to the victims of political repressions. Erected in 1996 on the part of the Kolyma Route leading into Yagodnoye from the settlement of Susuman. Photo by author.

chose not to get involved in this enterprise, arguing that the region already contained two monuments of this kind. However, Golunov claims that monuments to innocent prisoners killed in Kolyma's lagers should be erected on every hill in the region (*Severnaya Pravda*, 1996). He was therefore prepared to create the Memorial to Innocent People Killed in Kolyma himself and mainly from his own funds.

In 1996, the memorial was ceremoniously unveiled, and in 1998, it was consecrated by an Orthodox priest (Panikarov 1998). Golunov also planned to build an Orthodox shrine alongside the monument. He even completed its foundations, but it was never completed due to lack of funding. As he emphasizes, if the money had been available, he would have finished off the monument and built several more. He showed me his designs for these during our conversation. However, the local authorities in Yagodnoye are reluctant to allocate funding for such a purpose. To make matters worse, the existing monument requires reconstruction. As Golunov says, the Gulag wall was used by an inebriated man as a shooting target. Part of the monument has already been shot off and the bullet holes can be found in the wall.

Another memory actor – Vladimir Naiman – is active in Debin, where he erects memory markers. The manner in which he discovered this kind of activity for himself exhibits certain features of a religious conversion. As he says: 'I am a geologist and get around quite a bit. As the Bible says: there are things an eye doesn't see and an ear doesn't hear. When certain events led me to God . . . when this faith in God appears, you become more reflective' [21_VN]. Naiman's conversion became a turning point in his life. From then on, he began to view the history of the repressions in a different light. An important role throughout this process was also played by the books and articles on Gulag history that appeared in the nineties. As Naiman reflected on these issues, he developed his own interpretation of the events that had taken place in twentieth-century Russia, which in turn inspired him to undertake his memorializing work. As Naiman explains:

> Every nation was involved in the destruction of tsarist Russia: the Russians, Ukrainians, Belarusians, Poles, Jews, Germans, Italians. A great deal of thought was of course needed to destroy such a huge country . . . Nonetheless, the task was completed. In March 1917, when the tsar abdicated, everyone was celebrating their grand victory. Then three years passed, and in March 1921, half of those who had been celebrating were no longer among the living, and the half that had survived were left destitute, without a motherland . . . As the Bible says, four generations will bear responsibility for the sins of their forefathers. The next generation was the one that tamed Kolyma and all the other barely accessible places. The children of those who provoked the revolution, most of them were imprisoned here . . . Things were getting out of control in Russia . . . so Comrade Stalin and the kind of policies pursued back then were needed to restore a sense of order. I'm not singing Stalin's praises, but such a leader was needed for

a sense of equilibrium to appear in the world. Afterwards, a logical system was already in place. If some humility were to be restored to the nation and foreign powers were to be stopped from thinking about how to carve Russia up, a strong country was needed, so that's why it became necessary for a million people to be imprisoned and a hundred to be executed by firing squad every day. That's why special laws were adopted that led to that million serving their time every day . . . This was payment for the sins of their forefathers. This resulted in the appearance of the Gulag. The only way to support this million was to force these people to work. They would only work if they were afraid. The only way to scare them was by increasing the length of their sentences and executing them. This was pure human logic . . . 30% were incarcerated for real crimes, and the rest had committed crimes from that world's point of view: they had said something bad about Stalin, about the Party. These people were a little bit too clever, knew too many languages, had a smattering of education. And what does all this tell us? Russia should be repenting for killing the tsar and his family. [As for the] crosses, I have thought long and hard about why I plant them. I'm certainly repenting for the sins of my parents, my father's and mother's. I think that, since I was born in Kolyma, my grandparents also got up to some mischief during the revolution . . . So this is my penance. [21_VN]

For Naiman, the best way to pay penance for the sins of his ancestors was to erect crosses at sites associated with Gulag history, mainly on the former sites of camp cemeteries. He planted the first one in Debin, next to the monument Yagodnoye and Debin's local authorities had constructed in 1991. It is on the former grounds of a camp hospital's cemetery. He erected more crosses on the former grounds of a lager in Spokoyny and camp cemeteries in Sporny and Dneprovsky. Naiman also erected two memory markers in cemeteries located 323 and 237 kilometres along the Kolyma Route. He knew about some of the places earlier, but discovered about others, like the cemetery 323 kilometres along the Route, from lorry drivers. He had to search for other sites, like the cemetery in Sporny, for several years (Panikarov 2004). Naiman self-finances all the crosses he erects. Usually, an Orthodox cleric blesses one of Naiman's markers after some time has passed, or – if he cannot do this himself – he performs a special anointing ritual. As Naiman says: 'I hope to erect kilos of crosses while I'm still alive and then these can be used to raise the young generation in [the tradition of taking] responsibility for the future' [21_VN]. Naiman would like so many crosses to be so frequently erected that Krestny Khod processions could pass through them, educating young people and shaping a Russian national community.

Apart from the monuments standing on the former grounds of the hospital cemetery in Debin, there are two other memory projects in the town, taking the form of historical exhibitions. The first can be viewed in the local hospital and is dedicated to

Varlam Shalamov. Since the writer once worked in the local hospital, in 2005, on the fiftieth anniversary of this facility's foundation (Panikarov 2005), the manager there decided to prepare an exhibition in the form of a room devoted to the famous writer. The exhibition contains documents and texts telling of Shalamov's life and his work in Debin's hospital. Visitors can read extracts from his short stories and view camp objects collected in Kolyma's camps.

The second exhibition is in a school museum. It was prepared by pupils under the supervision of Danuta Bernadiyevna Tamayeva, who taught history there for many years. The exhibition, which is titled *Memory of Kolyma*, contains information on camp operations in Kolyma and lists the memory markers to be found in the region. It is also possible to view a design prepared by local resident Viktor Korchinsky, in 1991, when the town's local authorities were planning to erect a memorial in the hospital cemetery.

The story of this project and its creator also offer a clear impression of the way in which memory projects come into being in this region. Viktor Korchinsky arrived in Debin in 1961 looking for work. As he recalls, the camp *zona* was still operational at the time, and prisoners were building a school. When walking around the area, he came across a bulldozer churning up the earth over a former camp cemetery. Human bones were strewn around. He recalls returning to the place at night and tying part of a skull to the bulldozer with barbed wire as a sign of protest against construction work being undertaken where human remains had been laid to rest. He was reprimanded by the foreman, but no action was taken against him. The next day, the builders working on the construction site buried the bones.

In 1991, Korchinsky submitted the model of the monument he wished to erect in the cemetery to the Debin local authorities. Much as was the case with native of Yagodnoye Sergey Golunov's design, Viktor Korchinsky's concept expressed his reflections on Gulag history. Korchinsky explained to me that his monument is shaped like a hand, because when people were buried, only their hands remained above ground. The hand also symbolizes the power that 'grabbed hold of these people'. He planned to place a human skeleton in the central part of the composition, because – as he explains – the hill containing the cemetery is one large funerary mound. There was also supposed to be a cross, a memory marker for the dead. However, the authorities chose another, simpler monument – a granite boulder that can still be viewed in the cemetery. Korchinsky's design ended up in the school museum. Much like Golunov's sketches for monuments, it serves as an example of an unimplemented memory project. However, it also demonstrates how sensitive local residents are to the Gulag past and how they interpret the history of the repressions.

The Yagodnoye and Debin region contains so many memory projects exhibiting such diversity that it deserves to be known as Kolyma's true memory repository. Memory markers have also been erected at other sites, but only in this region do they collectively constitute a genuine monument/museum infrastructure. And only there have so many memory actors been actively involved in self-funded memorializing work for some time. Undoubtedly, the fact that it was there that a particularly intensive awakening of memory took place in the late eighties, and there that the first of Kolyma's memorials to victims of repression was erected, contributed to the community's activization. However, this was also accomplished thanks to the presence in the local community of such figures as Panikarov and Timchenko, whose efforts 'paved the way' for others, prompting them to reflect on the past and erect their own memory projects offering their own distinctive interpretations of history.

All the memory actors know each other well, are on friendly terms and help each other. Nonetheless, they act as individuals, creating their own memory projects. Panikarov calls the crosses Naiman erects 'Naiman's crosses', the monument on the road connecting Yagodnoye and Susuman, 'Golunov's monument' and the museum in Yagodnoye, 'Panikarov's museum'. All the memory actors, when commenting on projects prepared by others, use wording based on a 'we-you' dichotomy. Each project should therefore be viewed as expressing its author's views on Gulag history rather than collective memory. They visually represent reflections on the past. Highlighting each memory marker's authorship is therefore considered to be of the utmost importance. What is more, for some people – like Naiman – the crosses they erect are a penance, their own *pokayanie*.

The Yagodnoye-Debin memory basin is therefore a special kind of memory infrastructure arising from the actions of independent memory actors within a single geographical space. When creating their projects, each of these people worked on different assumptions and set themselves different goals for their own memory markers. However, today, all the local monuments and museums collectively constitute a kind of common semantic network, drawing attention to the region's significant sites and explaining their history.

The Paradox of Memory?

The marked similarities between Kolyma and the Komi Republic, so evident in the early history of their lagers, still persist today. Kolyma, like the Komi Republic, is grappling with profitability issues. The villages and settlements situated on the Kolyma Route are being torn down, and their population displaced to Magadan or central regions of the country. Much like in the Komi Republic, former repressed persons became important participants in the process of awakening Gulag memory in Kolyma. History saved from oblivion set the tone for local discussions on the future. However, different scripts were followed depending on where these discussions were held. In the Komi Republic, the debate chiefly focused on the political future, while in Magadan, it was devoted to identity, oscillating between two key questions: 'who are we?' and 'who should we become?'. There where lively discussions on the monuments, focusing on where in the city they should be erected and whom they should commemorate, so as to, on the one hand, express 'who we are' and, on the other, help to define 'who we will be'.

In Magadan, all the monuments that were erected – Bilibin's and Berzin's, the Memory Knot and Mask of Sorrow – were the focus of a public debate, as they express values of importance to the local community. Since the inhabitants of Kolyma had different experiences of the Great Patriotic War to those of the country's central regions, the local Memory Knot also presents this period of history differently to thousands of other monuments found in the Russian Federation. On account of this difference of experiences, every year, on 22 June, when the whole country is observing the Day of Remembrance and Sorrow, which commemorates the beginning of the War, the inhabitants of Kolyma travel to Serpantinka or the Victims of Repression Monument in Debin to honour the memory of those who died defending the motherland at sites where Gulag prisoners were slaughtered.

In Kolyma, individual memory markers have also been erected on former camp grounds, in camp cemeteries or on the Kolyma Route. Despite some memory actors originally wanting every hill to contain one, they are generally found in places inhabited by people for whom Gulag memory is a sacrosanct component of their local identity, a source of reflection on the most important of questions: 'where do we come from?' and 'where are we headed?'.

The comments and actions of memory actors I have quoted and described above suggest that Kolyma's inhabitants are attempting to define who they are by undertaking memorializing work. This is no easy task, because the local history – as the moderator from Magadan's Community Centre said – is not 'black and white'. This ambiguity is visually expressed in a swathe of the local landscape: the Mask of Sorrow on Krutaya Hill is within viewing range of the Eduard Berzin Monument, located in the city centre in front of a local government building. Although Magadan's inhabitants perceive how controversial a figure the head of Dalstroy was, they still decided to erect a monument to him and still appreciate him for the effort he invested into the taming of Kolyma. However, they have not forgotten about the victims of the murderous work regime implemented for the benefit of the Dalstroy project, so in 2011, a church was erected in memory of the new Kolyma martyrs. The Holy Trinity Cathedral is situated in Magadan's Central Square, lying along an axis with the local government offices and Berzin's monument.

The historical exhibitions at the Magadan Local History Museum demonstrate how difficult it is to unambiguously evaluate the past. Since 1992, it has been possible to view the *Kolyma. Sevvostlag. Years and Fates. 1932–1956* exhibition (Figure 4.3), which tells of the difficult living conditions, exploitation and death of convicts. However, in 2001, on the seventieth anniversary of Dalstroy's foundation, a new exhibition titled *Dalstroy*, which was devoted to this period of history and told of the firm's accomplishments, was opened. This telling of the same history from different perspectives greatly resembles the manner in which history is presented at local museums in the Komi Republic, as described in the chapter devoted to that region. This does not, however, mean that the exhibition's creators had returned to the old Soviet rhetoric of progress and development. In 2008, I spoke to Sergey Bakarevich, the incumbent director of the Magadan Local History Museum, about the exhibitions being shown at the museum and the message they were communicating. I also asked him about the dissonance between the manner in which the two exhibitions presented the history. Bakarevich explained that Dalstroy had completed the task assigned to it. It was meant to construct roads, towns and mines and extract minerals, and that is precisely what happened. When we view Dalstroy from such a perspective, we have to acknowledge that it successfully completed its mission. However, the question also arises of whether the costs incurred by the enterprise were justified and whether its operations were economical. When Dalstroy is viewed from a market force perspective, it was not a profitable company. Yet this is not an appropriate argument to use for the purposes of evaluation, for surely an institution's activities cannot be assessed in such a manner when human lives are staked on its success. This explains why plans were already being made that same year to prepare a new exhibition on the Gulag. It was to take a more rounded look at this period, most importantly, from a new perspective.

However, the new exhibition had still not been opened by 2017 and will probably never be created in the form Bakarevich described to me. Since 2015, the principles of the official state policy on the commemoration of victims of political repressions have been being implemented in Kolyma. A plan approved in March 2017 envisages,

Figure 4.3. The *Kolyma. Sevvostlag. Years and Fates. 1932–1956* exhibition. The Magadan Local History Museum, showing since 1992. Photo by author.

among other projects, the opening of a new memorial complex devoted to the history of Dalstroy and Magadan Oblast in the repression years – in a building previously housing the Sevvostlag transit prison.¹¹ The Mask of Sorrow, which is not far from the building's ruins, will form part of this complex. Moreover, as the Governor of Magadan Oblast, Vladimir Pecheny, announced in June 2017, there are plans to open an exposition devoted to repression victims and New Martyrs in the city centre, in the grounds of the Holy Trinity Cathedral, as well as a museum complex and History and Culture Park on the banks of Nagaev Bay, where ships carrying prisoners sailed into Kolyma from 1932 to 1956.¹²

The Magadan Local History Museum's involvement in the implementation of the state policy on the commemoration of the victims of political repressions led, in July 2017, to the closure of the *Dalstroy* exhibition opened in 2001. It is due to be re-opened in 2018.¹³ The Magadan museum has also started cooperating with Moscow's Gulag Museum on the creation of a virtual walk around the grounds of Butugychag, one of the best preserved yet most inaccessible of Kolyma's lagers.¹⁴ It is difficult to say whether all the projects planned for 2017–19 will be successfully implemented. Nevertheless, it is worth emphasizing that in Magadan – unlike other regions, where fierce conflicts are evidently breaking out between memory actors – the implementation of state policy not only involves the employees of the Local Museum, but also figures like Ivan Panikarov from Yagodnoye or the Orthodox Church authorities in Magadan. It is clear from these proposals to create fresh new museum interpretations that the dialogue with the past has not ended and the issue of establishing one all-embracing vision of Kolyma's history is still being negotiated. The dialogue is ongoing, yet is taking place within the framework defined by the state policy on remembering the victims of political repressions.

Notes

1. During my stay in Yagodnoye, I wanted to travel to the former lager of Dneprovsky, which had been preserved in a reasonably good state. I could only have reached my destination by hiring a special vehicle. The trip would have taken two days and cost the equivalent of over £600. Dneprovsky is also one of the most accessible former camps.
2. At the end of the eighties, all the talk was of the Stalinist repressions. Only in 1991, when 30 October became Victims of Political Repressions Day did the term 'political repressions' start to come into use.
3. Lively discussions over whether artists were entitled to create monuments commemorating the victims of a historical event also took place in other countries. As James Young (1993: 8–9) writes in reference to monuments commemorating the First World War or Holocaust victims, artists were rarely invited to erect monuments, and abstract depictions provoked a great deal of controversy.
4. The abbreviation (of *zakluchenny*) from which zek is derived.
5. Andrey Vlasov was a Red Army general who went over to the German side and, in 1944, created the Armed Forces of the Committee for the Liberation of the Peoples of Russia, which aimed to liberate the USSR from Stalin's rule. After the war, he was sentenced to death for his anti-Soviet activity.
6. The Forest Brothers were partisans based in Estonia, Latvia and Lithuania who fought a guerrilla war against Soviets during the 1940–41 Soviet invasion and occupation of the Baltic states, and after the Second World War.
7. Polyphonic or monophonic.

8. Discussions on the Ernst Neizvestny monument in Yekaterinburg were even stormier, and the Orthodox Church protested much more forcefully. As a consequence, even though the monument was basically ready, it was never erected (Bogumił, Moran and Harrowell 2015).
9. The conference papers can be read in a volume published following the event (Biryukov 1988).
10. The Mask is a few kilometres from the city centre. Those wishing to visit it should turn off the main road and follow a metalled road to Krutaya Hill, where the monument was erected.
11. www.kolymastory.ru/glavnaya/eho-dalstroya/u-pamyati-v-dolgu/.
12. www.49gov.ru/press/press_releases/index.php?id_4=25643.
13. www.magadanmuseum.ru/index.php?newsid=1718.
14. www.magadanmuseum.ru/index.php?newsid=1715.

Conclusion

In this book, I have described a formative period for Gulag memory, from the collapse of the USSR to 2015, when the Russian Federation became actively involved in the formation of memory of the repressions. My discussion has primarily focused on the distinctive features of Gulag memory in each region, so I shall now attempt to find some common ground between this material. In the first section, I shall treat the four regions I have presented as a unit, both highlighting any similarities between them and focusing on what makes their memory projects different from one another. By taking into account any factors determining the form of the memory markers erected in these places and the functions their creators aimed to grant them, I hope to demonstrate to what extent they evoke similar meanings and to what extent their meanings vary from one another.

In the second section, I evoke Foucault's concept of counter-memory to reflect on the meaning of the Gulag memory-shaping process. I refer to the facts and events I have mentioned earlier to develop a global picture of them in summary form. As I have written, the late eighties saw the appearance of many memory actors aspiring to delineate a framework for Gulag memory. However, in this final chapter, I shall be focusing exclusively on the actions and projects created by the Memorial Society and Russian Orthodox Church. It was these organizations in particular that most actively participated in the process of forming that memory. In my view, the interpretations of the labour camp proposed by these institutions are the only ones that could be labelled as counter-history in the Foucauldian sense. This conclusion is thus devoted to two aims. On the one hand, it is a summary of the analyses I have conducted. On the other hand, it poses certain questions about the language, broadly conceived, used for speaking about the Gulag experience and its history, language that was shaped during the carnival of memory yet continues to influence memory of the repression today.

Similarities and Differences between Gulag Sites of Memory

The carnival of memory was a time of universal awakening and truth-seeking. This search mainly assumed the form of granting witnesses to past events a voice and looking for documents and certificates that provided information about the history of the repressions. Attempts were also made to establish the meaning of traces of the Gulag contained within the cultural landscape. It was at this time that the first memorials commemorating victims of the political repressions came into being. They were erected as temporary memory markers in the hope that they would be replaced over time by large memorial complexes. They were mainly located at sites where mass killings had taken place or in the grounds of former camp cemeteries. They are simple and austere in form, while simultaneously alluding to religious and national symbolism. This was due to the fact that both Russians and groups of Ukrainians, Latvians or Poles making pilgrimages to these sites placed national and religious symbols of remembrance on their ancestors' graves. The basic function of these monuments was therefore to remember the deceased and pay tribute to them rather than commemorating the Gulag as a whole. As the Russian scholar Alexander Etkind writes:

> Bare stones convey the memory of bare life, constructed from the perspective of the victims. . . . Russian monuments do not give any hint of the solidarity of political prisoners, their fights with criminals and administration, their numerous camp rebellions and escapes. . . . these monuments do not tell us much about techniques of torture, incarceration, or execution. (Etkind 2013: 188)

The crosses and tombstones commemorate every death and not necessarily those that resulted from the actions of a criminal regime, so these monuments neither assign blame nor protest nor make any attempt to explain the past (Etkind 2004c: 68–70).

It is also worth stressing that the space of former camps was not marked in such a manner as to clearly denote that they formed part of a cultural landscape. The memorialization process of this period can itself be interpreted as a manner of reclaiming memory of the dead and paying them the honour that was their due. There was no emphasis placed on preserving the memory of the Gulag's historical dimension. What is more, the fact that most of these memory markers are located in the grounds of former cemeteries makes them difficult to access, especially as many of these cemeteries are far from inhabited areas and often possess no dedicated access road. The monuments erected in cities also do not play a significant role in the living space of these region's inhabitants. Only during the Day of Remembrance for Victims of Political Repressions (30 October), local Days of Remembrance (5 August in Sandarmokh, early July in the Solovetsky Islands, 1 August in Yur-Shor) and the Day of Remembrance and Sorrow in Kolyma (22 June) do they become spaces for memory rituals. At these times, inhabitants of particular regions, the kith and kin of people murdered at a particular site, or visiting guests make pilgrimages to selected sites of memory to pay tribute to the deceased.

The majority of the monuments were erected at burial sites, so apart from the fact that they themselves mean something, they also had to adapt to the existing spatial context. This context was marked by both camp cemetery space and the first memory markers that appeared. These first memory signs mainly possessed religious or national characteristics (e.g. the Polish cross at Kotlas). At the same time, the fact that similar, simple forms of remembrance were created – for example, crosses, monuments and commemorative plaques – would appear to be an outcome of there being no secular language capable of conveying the experience of the Gulag (I will develop this further in the second part of my conclusion).

A separate group of Gulag monuments consists of those erected during the Soviet period. However, these began to be given new meanings connected with the history of the Gulag after 1989. A good example are the sculptures of the first pioneers in the Komi Republic. Zeks began to be perceived as discoverers of oil or coal who contributed to the foundation of cities, and their images started to be treated as memory markers of the Gulag. Likewise, many buildings built by the prisoners, such as the water tower in Inta or Pushkin Memorial in Ukhta began to be regarded as Gulag monuments.

The next group of memory markers are history exhibitions in towns, cities and former lagers. The first exhibitions (in Vorkuta, Ukhta, Inta and the Solovetsky Islands) mainly only revealed those aspects of camp history that had formed part of the process of a given region's cultural and industrial development. Frequently, the central component of these narratives was the functioning of a theatre or the scientific research conducted at a particular camp. They comprised a kind of synonym for the whole of a given city's twentieth-century intellectual life, while convict-artists serving out their sentences were depicted as honorary residents of these places. Such a mode of portraying the Gulag was a natural consequence of the stated mission of local history museums, which was to show a region's positive aspects.

Very few museums or exhibitions devoted exclusively to camp history appeared in this period, but there were some; namely, Perm-36, the *Kedrovy Shor* exhibition at Pechora and the exhibitions in Solovki, Magadan and Yagodnoye. The conclusion could be drawn, on inspecting these more closely, that each of them was unable to deal effectively with the presentation of the past for one reason or another. The main problem was that they had no comprehensive language at their disposal that would enable them to render the experience of the Gulag from both an objective and subjective perspective, so the interpretations they proposed always possessed certain shortcomings. The research Nikolay Vukov undertook on museums presenting the communist past in Bulgaria would appear to suggest that the category that may assist comprehension of the manner in which history was presented at the first Gulag exhibitions is the *unmemorable*. Vukov analysed Bulgarian museums at the point when the previous (communist) system of meanings had ceased to apply, and a new system had not crystallized enough to facilitate the creation of a museum narrative. According to this Bulgarian scholar, unmemorable experiences are those that are: 'not subject to forgetting but face restraints in representation, that are stored in the mind but not employed in narratives, that are preserved as memory traces but not embodied in materialized forms' (Vukov 2008: 313). Consequently, the unmemorable is not so much a conflict between what is remembered and what has been forgotten, as between what is remembered and the manner in which it is represented.

This category illustrates perfectly the manner in which Gulag history is presented at the first museum exhibitions. Rather than suggesting that content had been forgotten, the absence of a coherent presentation language and these exhibitions' allusions to old narratives attested to the impossibility of representing certain issues using a narrative. As I have shown, continuous attempts to modify or develop existing exhibitions not only aimed to present the Soviet repressions in such a manner as to correspond to a vision of the past that was crystallizing along with the large-scale discovery of new documents. They also sought to incorporate certain traits of increasingly profound widespread reflection on the USSR's repressive past. Consequently, the camp history was present in memory, but granting it the physical form of a representation was still problematic.

The clear conclusion can be drawn from the material presented in this book that Gulag history was understood differently in each of the regions I have discussed, and these differences were translated into the form assumed by their local memory projects. After the carnival of memory period, which followed a similar script throughout the former USSR, there was a period of differentiation, which was influenced by several factors.

First of all, the local camp history developed differently in each of these places. The realities of the Solovetsky Islands' SLON in the 1920s were quite different to those typical of the Komi Republic's Stalinist camps of the thirties and forties, and the situation was different again in the case of Kolyma's Dalstroy. The Solovetsky Islands camp had long ceased to function when the first forest camp was established at the village of Kuchino in 1946, which later became the Perm-36 political camp in 1972. Given these places' different histories, even though the memory markers in all of them are similar in form, completely different meanings are bound up with them. These meanings grow out of the local history of these areas and depend on how Gulag operations were manifested there.

Another important factor is how significant the Gulag past of a given place was from a wider historical perspective. The Solovetsky Islands possess a centuries-old history as a centre of religion, and SLON constitutes a mere fragment of their twentieth-century history. We are dealing with a different situation in the Komi Republic or Kolyma, where the labour camps gave rise to local towns and villages. If it is accepted that Stalinism did indeed produce its own civilization (Kotkin 1995; Webb and Webb 1936: 1119–43) populated by *homo sovieticus* (Kozlova 2005; Tischner 1992), the Komi Republic and Kolyma are the remnants of this. It should be stressed, however, that certain meaningful differences are also evident here, and it is these that determine the various ways in which history is perceived. These differences are most evident in the form assumed by the central memorials of both of these regions: the Victims of Political Repressions Chapel in Syktyvkar and the Mask of Sorrow in Magadan.

Other factors that influenced the appearance of differences between all the regions I have analysed were the changeable political situation at the end of the eighties and the variable strength of social support granted to the various memory actors. Another important factor in cases where there was more than one memory actor was the relations prevailing between them. These could either be conducive to cooperation, or be of a passive or conflictive nature. The complexity of this situation is very clearly illustrated by the example of the Solovetsky Islands. As I have shown, fundamental ideological differences arose between the memory actors that operated there, so the projects they created were different from one another. Only the Church sanctioned the erection of Orthodox memorial crosses, while Memorial and the museum dissociated themselves for a long time from this mode of commemoration. By contrast, in the Komi Republic, Perm Krai and Kolyma, the cross became a basic memory marker, erected to commemorate the deceased by all the actors functioning there.

Another important distinguishing factor was the lack of information flow relating to the memory infrastructures arising in various places. When the first monuments began to appear, there was no personal contact between the memory actors in the various regions. Information about the activity being undertaken in different parts of the country could only be gleaned from national newspapers. With time, nationwide cooperation was initiated through the framework of the Memorial Society, but for years, methods of communication were limited,[1] mainly providing information about projects that had been undertaken[2] and offering help with the locating of documents. No collaborative memorialization activities were being undertaken.

Memorialization activity as a whole was not a broader manifestation of local activity. None of the sites of memory would have functioned if it were not for the charisma and perseverance of particular individuals. For many memory actors, the projects they were implementing gave their lives meaning. They were a kind of mission to preserve the memory of the deceased for future generations, in some cases also being a form of repentance for the sins of their ancestors. The memory actors' selection of particular forms of action (for example, the construction of a monument or museum) also determined how their work progressed from then on, while the appearance of a region's first significant memory project often strongly influenced how the next group of people expressed their views on the past.

The aforementioned factors explain why the outward similarity of Gulag markers created during the carnival of memory may be illusory. In fact, they are semantically diverse, the meanings conferred on them by local communities and memory actors being determined by local conditions. Those who created these projects were expressing in them their own understanding of the essence of the labour camp experience. What the monuments and markers commemorating the Gulag reflected was not therefore homogeneous and coherent, but rather fragmentary and region-specific, since it alluded to different historical events (for example, the Gulag itself, deportations and collectivization).

Memory and the Labour Camp Literature

For many years, Gulag memory was suppressed and sinking into social oblivion. As late as 1987, Great October was being grandly celebrated across the country and the museums in Solovki, Inta and Magadan were showing exhibitions extolling the communist system's achievements. The following year, a fracture opened in the existing world order. The history of the Gulag was excavated from oblivion and flooded across the nation on a wave of incomprehensibility. It therefore became necessary to somehow grasp this huge social experience, which had not been socially processed or worked through for sixty years.

Reference points had to be found that could facilitate the comprehension of this tragic past. It turned out that many documents were missing, destroyed or impossible to access. The remnants of the camp infrastructure were also mostly destroyed, so their appearance was not so powerfully resonant of their time as the battlefields of the First World War (Winter 1995) or Holocaust sites (Wóycicka 2014). Furthermore, their inaccessible locations, the scant photographic documentation and the fact that many of the photographs that had survived showed the world through the perpetrators' eyes rather than those of their victims or witnesses to the events (Kizny 2004) meant that the main focus was on finding witnesses. In my book, I have highlighted many such situations when letters were written to them or they were encouraged to describe their experiences. It was these recollections that began to most strongly shape Gulag memory. Moreover, such books as Solzhenitsyn's *The Gulag Archipelago*, Shalamov's *Kolyma Tales* or Eugenia Ginzburg's *Journey into the Whirlwind* (Sherbakova 1998) offered the most comprehensive language for describing the Gulag experience as well as providing the facts that were needed.

As Adi Kuntsman – an English scholar of camp literature – writes, the books by the authors I have just mentioned (Solzhenitsyn, Ginzburg and Shalamov) are: 'among the best known and the most influential texts that constitute the post-Soviet cultural memory of the Stalinist terror' (2009: 326) and influence the manner in which this is interpreted. Passages from these books were secretly published in samizdat from the sixties onwards. They were perceived as true histories and were countered by the lies, silences and transformations that were constitutive of Soviet official historiography. As Kuntsman writes: 'these texts had a high moral authority, both because of the suffering experienced by the political prisoners, and because the authors, following the traditions of Russian literature, presented their memoirs, not as private autobiographies and individual narratives, but as documents of transcendental historical significance' (2009: 326).

As Russian literature scholar Irina Paperno writes, the form and narrative construction method of many prison memoirs are reminiscent of a work regarded as paradigmatic of Russian writing, Alexander Herzen's *My Past and Thoughts*. His memoirs – as Paperno explains – are strongly rooted in Hegelian historicism and hence grant the author of the text a special status. The 'spirit of the age' breaks through his memoirs; history is immanently present in every individual and can be reconstructed by examining the decisions taken by the individual in his or her daily life. As Paperno stresses, Herzen's work strongly influenced the manner in which witness memoirs were perceived in Russian culture (2002). This explains why references to Solzhenitsyn or Shalamov could be found at all the exhibitions, and guides taking tours treated the information contained in their books with the kind of credibility generally reserved for archival documents.

Diaries are not neutral historical documents, so care should be taken, when analysing them, to meticulously investigate how they construct their story, what tradition they make use of and what may be concealed or exaggerated in them (Kuntsman 2009: 328; Toker 2000). Furthermore, witnesses' memoirs are always deformed by the passage of time and are strongly linked to how the events they discuss are spoken of in the present (Grele 1998: 38–52). When I spoke to Ivan Panikarov – the founder of the Poisk Nezakonno Represirovanykh Society in Yagodnoye – he emphasized that when he received letters from ex-prisoners, many memoirs appeared to be identical to those in *The Gulag Archipelago*. Irina Sherbakova (1992: 113) also pointed out that many testimonies she was collecting resembled the stories that Solzhenitsyn had written about. It is difficult to say how much particular experiences did indeed resemble those described in recently published *Archipelago* passages or, conversely, to what extent these passages from Solzhenitsyn influenced how these memoirists formulated their own recollections. Quite possibly the confluence of these processes only exerted a random effect, yet there is no doubt that literature and memoirs significantly influenced how the Gulag past was perceived during the carnival of memory period, and later on too.

The official interpretation, which essentially existed from the moment the Gulag was created, would appear to be another important source aiding comprehension of the lager camps during the carnival of memory. According to this interpretation, the convicts in the lagers were 'enemies of the nation'. This vision of history instilled itself in the imaginations of a significant sector of society. A certain amount of information that conflicted with this version of events came to light during Khrushchev's Thaw. Even so, the Gulag was not widely discussed until the late eighties, when it finally stopped being regarded as a taboo subject (Anstett 2011; Ulturgasheva 2015).

The manner in which Gulag knowledge functions within society is not, therefore, a classic example of a social memory framework shaping a widely adopted version of events over time. As for the earlier mentioned interpretation propagated by the state, since it was authoritative by definition, it was not open to social judgement, criticism or discussion. It was simply meant to be accepted a priori. Those witnesses who disagreed with it preserved the history of the Gulag in their memoirs. However, they did this independently of one another, since there was essentially no exchange of information or social evaluation of what had happened. It is therefore fair to say that everyone colluded in this social silence. At the end of the eighties, much of what had been hidden was suddenly revealed.

Gulag Counter-histories

I would like to take a second look now at the carnival of memory period I have been describing, but this time I would like to interpret it using the Foucauldian concept relating to the shaping and functioning of counter-historical discourses. By using this concept to explain the meaning of the activities undertaken during this period by members of the Memorial Society and Orthodox Church, I hope to make it easier for the form currently assumed by Gulag memory in the Russian Federation to be more fully understood. It is worth emphasizing at the outset that other excluded groups apart from Gulag prisoners made their voices heard in the late eighties, for example, one consisting of some of the Leningrad *blokadniki*. The Soviet discourse had obscured their important contribution to the victorious resistance to the Siege of Leningrad (Kalendarova 2005: 275–97; Kirschenbaum 2006; Voronina 2016), thus excluding them from the 'glory' discourse regarded as one of the fundamental elements uniting Russian society (victory in the Second World War is a particularly important component of this discourse [Gabowitsch 2005; Malinova 2015]). In this way, all the counter-historical – in the Foucauldian sense – discourses appearing in this period were eroding state sovereignty (the domination of the state's vision of history), but also thwarting the continuity of the glory discourse (Foucault 2003a).

The main objective of the counter-historical discourse proposed by Memorial was in fact to erode state sovereignty in the USSR. For a long time, this was a discourse of opposition and it became a tool for criticizing and fighting against the Soviet form of power structure. It was meant to show 'that laws deceive, that kings wear masks, that power creates illusions, and that historians tell lies' (Foucault 2003a: 72). This new type of counter-history and the slogans it promoted began to enjoy increasing public support. A new official social community had come into being – the Memorial Society, an organization that helped memoirists express themselves and set their words free. The moment these memoirs were expressed, they became a social phenomenon, so the need arose to socially situate and protect them. There was a need to create places that would protect this memory and erect markers that would express it, thereby co-creating a space for the expression of individual pain and social purification. It was believed that taking such a reflexive step into the past allowed people living through the dissolution of the Soviet Union to build a better future. Consequently, memory markers were erected and dates were allocated (for example, 30 October) for the annual observance of special holidays suited to a new civil society.

Initially, there were plans to erect large memorial complexes and Gulag museums in the grounds of former camps, and also in Moscow. As I have written, one of these (Russia's massive-scale Crown of Thorns) was designed in Vorkuta, and there were also plans to erect memorials on an impressive scale in Kotlas and Moscow. All of this was meant to be supplemented by so-called purification trails, which people would travel along, much like pilgrims visiting holy sites. In the chapter devoted to Kolyma, I described the most important complex that was supposed to be constructed: Ernst

Neizvestny's Triangle of Suffering and Redemption, which comprised three memorial-masks to be erected in Yekaterinburg, Vorkuta and Magadan. Its primary ideological function was to outline a framework for a new democratic society. Eliade defines the axis mundi as the centre of a world, a sacred realm that generalizes and structures this world's form (Eliade 1959). This is why it was so important for the democratic community to demarcate an axis mundi – or symbolic centre shaping the world's system of values and influencing how it is understood – for the new Russia. It is no coincidence that it was Ernst Neizvestny who was to become the creator of a new axis mundi. The sculptor had previously created Khrushchev's gravestone at the Novodevichy Cemetery in Moscow, which had performed the function of an anti-Stalin symbol for years. Former repressed persons came here to lay flowers, regarding the memorial as a symbol of political protest (Leong 1998: 69). Consequently, the sculptor came to be seen as a precursor for the creation of a secular language for representing Gulag memory.

The sociopolitical situation in the Soviet Union was continuously changing during this period, so if Gulag memory was to be made into an important component of the new identity, the first memory markers needed to be swiftly erected. The erection of gigantic complexes required time, so the decision was made to erect temporary markers that were used as a 'here and now' focal point for the appropriate rituals and helped to shape attitudes to the past. Little attention was paid to their form. The most important thing was to erect universal, well-understood memory markers, especially as they were supposed to be replaced in time by the aforementioned memorial complexes.

This period was also marked by the appearance of the first history exhibitions aiming to satisfy public curiosity and acquaint visitors with the history of the Gulag and related issues. The presented materials had to be drawn into a coherent narrative, so it became necessary to demarcate a narrative framework. However, these issues had not been thoroughly worked through or subjected to deeper analysis free of Soviet ideology, so any materials that were found began to be adapted to conform with the existing Soviet narrative. Many documents were missing, so this was mainly based on the memoirs of witnesses. As a consequence, many exhibitions assumed the form of a story about people – the zeks. The primary goal of the actions being undertaken by memory actors at the time was to change the public perception of the zek – from an enemy of the nation to a person in prison. These exhibitions therefore assumed the form of 'family albums' of famous convicts imprisoned in particular regions. However, their biographies were incorporated into a Soviet narrative focusing on progress and the taming of the North, because a new interpretation of these events was yet to crystallize.

During the same period, another type of important counter-history appeared, a typical interpretation of history proposed by the Orthodox Church based on religion and myth. It alluded to a grand biblical form imbued with prophecy and promise.

The Orthodox Church perceives the period of Soviet repressions as a moment of trial when people were persecuted for their faith. Those who managed to stay true to their faith, dying as martyrs, become a foundation on which the modern Church can be reborn (Christensen 2017). The history of New Martyrdom and its meaning are expressed in icons, churches and memorial crosses dedicated to the New Martyrs and Confessors. This traditional method of commemorating the dead has begun to create an Orthodox infrastructure for memory of the repressions (Christensen 2017; Fedor 2014: 121–53; Rock 2011; Rousselet 2007). It is worth adding that such a national-religious interpretation of the period of communist rule also enjoys popularity in other former Eastern Bloc countries whose language of remembrance uses confessional symbols in a similar manner. As Cristea and Radu-Bucurenci note in their analysis of Romanian museums and monuments dedicated to the communist past: 'the period from 1945 to 1989 was a time of "Soviet devastation", when the country was led by a political regime metamorphosed into a "red devil". Those who fought against it, the victims, "sacrificed themselves for Christ, for dignity and for national freedom". It seems that only Christian symbols are powerful enough to oppose "the red devil"' (2008: 284).

The Russian Orthodox Church has managed to create a coherent interpretation operating on multiple levels, which aims to ensure that a response can be found to any question relating to the meaning of the repressions (Bogumił, Moran and Harrowell 2015; Bogumił and Łukaszewicz 2018; Christensen 2017). Symbolically – through the erection of the Solovetsky crosses at Sekirnaya Hill in Solovki and in Butovo, near Moscow – this interpretation has also marked out its own new axis for contemporary Russia. This links Russia's two national Golgothas (Bogumił 2016).

The Orthodox interpretation is not only a comprehensive explicatory system. Its social appeal can also be explained through allusion to Foucault's counter-history model. As the French philosopher writes, counter-historical discourse is bound up with: 'binary perception and division of society and men; them and us, the unjust and the just, the masters and those who must obey them, the rich and the poor, . . . the men of today's law and those of the homeland of the future' (Foucault 2003a: 74). In Russia's case, this discourse, binary by its very nature, encountered a type of culture that, according to Lotman, is also binary (Lotman 2009). As Żyłko writes: 'Lotman is inclined to attribute this fact to specific enduring features of Russian culture, including its essential bipolarity, which expresses itself in the dual nature of its structure. All the basic cultural values are dispersed across a bipolar field, starkly separated from each other and deprived of any neutral axiological sphere' (Żyłko 1999: 23). Therefore, the moment a 'binary' counter-historical discourse encounters a culture with a similar structure, the former is reinforced and consolidated.

It is worth stressing, however, that every counter-historical discourse possesses a binary structure, so the interpretation of history proposed by Memorial theoretically had the same chance of success as the Orthodox one. Neither of these two memory actors was interested in finding new people to blame or creating another division of society into the good and bad. What is more, during the anti-communist revolution (at the end of the eighties), democratic slogans (mainly promoted by Memorial) and national slogans (employed by the Church) were appearing simultaneously and it was only in subsequent years that these two types of slogan really began to diverge from each other (Barner-Barry 1999: 101). Memorial merely wished to judge the authorities, hoping, in fact, that they would be able to cleanse themselves. However, the Orthodox Church believed that all powers of judgement ultimately lay with God.

The success of the Orthodox counter-history does not therefore rely on the stigmatization of those responsible for the repressions. It owes its victory to the rebirth of a Russian national identity that is meant to act as a binding agent uniting today's Russian Federation (Barner-Barry 1999). The social appeal of this counter-history can be explained by the fact that, rather than condemning anyone, it is an important unifying element binding together a new national community consisting of Orthodox Russians. Furthermore, the promise – an important component of the Orthodox discourse – de facto connotes a final victory. Rather than urging that all the nation's past glories be renounced, this discourse argues that the repression's victims were necessary and their lives had some point (cf. Lim 2008). This enables all those who undeservedly lost their lives to be rehabilitated, since their suffering and deaths are interpreted as being borne in the name of their faith and higher values. It also shows those alive today that these victims' martyrdom and poverty were also not endured in vain. When events are thus interpreted, these victims become a component of the 'new glory' discourse that is currently being constructed by society in cooperation with the new *sovereign* power (see Sniegon 2018).

This has found its fullest expression in a project – a multimedia exhibition titled *Historical Park Russia – My History* – jointly developed from 2013 by the state and Orthodox Church. This exhibition, primarily conceived and theoretically underpinned through the efforts of Bishop Tikhon Shevkunov, offers the comprehensive story of Russian history from prehistoric times, through the Rurik and Romanov dynasties, to the present day. The exhibition aims to: 'disseminate humanitarian knowledge in Russia; develop in society high social activity, civil responsibility and spirituality; [promote] the emergence of citizens with positive values and attributes who identify with Russia and its history and culture'.[3] The New Martyrs are meant to be of assistance when it comes to achieving these goals. They have been presented on the exhibition timeline after the civil war, but before the Stalinist era. The uncanonized victims of the repressions have been presented in a small room that can be accessed from a section devoted to industrialization under Stalin. While the viewer has no way of avoiding the New Martyrs, the repressions have been positioned outside the main historical narrative. This mode of presentation clearly shows that it is the memory of the ultimate sacrifice made by the New Martyrs, rather than fate of the ordinary victims, which is treated as being constitutive of Russian identity. If it is also taken into account that historical parks have ultimately been planned for twenty-two cities in Russia, so that all Russians will be able to view them and children and young people of school age can visit this exhibition every year, it is clear to see that the historical park is a tool for building up the glory of the sovereign state and the Orthodox discourse is taking an active part in this.

The argumentation I have presented explains the victory of the Orthodox counter-history. It also shows why the Orthodox Church's activities have found support among the current state authorities, while the Memorial Society's memory projects, which emphasize the repressiveness of the state towards its own citizens, have failed to do so. What is more, if such an interpretation is applied to the changes that occurred during the democratic revolution, it is clear to see that this revolution, rather than bringing about a transformation in the Russian Federation's power structure, was unable to prevent another – merely ostensible – change of sovereign. Any changes the Orthodox counter-historical discourse has provoked in the old state power discourse are only superficial. Rather than destroying the foundations of the old discourse, it has in fact contributed to its further mutation.

The Russians prefer to perceive themselves as a chosen nation predestined to realize a higher purpose rather than as unnecessary victims. This is an understandable strategy. As Oexle emphasizes, every human culture or group has to acquire points of reference in order to exist (see Noushi 2006). In practice, this may mean remembering some historical episodes and forgetting others (Oexle 2006: 17). What is more, as Jan Assmann notes, every society that perceives itself as a nation is, in a sense, imagining itself as a chosen nation (Assmann 1995). This is why the Orthodox interpretation, which goes some way to meeting such expectations while also frequently drawing from Russian culture, seems to hold such appeal.

Unlike the Orthodox Church, which managed to create a coherent Orthodox language for presenting the Gulag (using such material markers as icons and churches) and expressing the Gulag experience (employing such notions as 'New Martyrs', 'being persecuted for one's faith' and 'Russian Golgotha'), Memorial failed to develop its own coherent secular language. This failure is clearly illustrated by the abortive projects it promoted that were meant to create extensive material landscapes of memory in the form of memorial complexes. In the end, the economic crisis of the mid-nineties, devaluation of the rouble, galloping inflation and ongoing social transformations made the erection of such architecturally ambitious structures completely unworkable. Analysis of these unimplemented projects reveals the continued presence of 'yet to be immortalized' memory, since these projects still live on in the minds of the people who contributed to their design. They have in themselves become a component of Gulag memory, or maybe it would be better to say – memory of Gulag memory. A prime example of this phenomenon is an exhibition titled *Unimplemented Memory Project. How Memorial to the Victims of Political Repressions Was Perceived Thirty Years Ago*, which was organized by the Memorial Society and presented on 29 October 2017 by the Solovetsky stone in Lubyanka, during an annual Memorial protest action titled The Return of the Names. The exhibition presented the story of a competition organized by Memorial in the late eighties for the design of a memorial to victims of repressions. It displayed some of the designs that were sent in as competition entries and reactions given by viewers to their artistic form. The exhibition was presented the day before the unveiling of a state memorial to victims of repressions created by Georgy Frangulyan (see below), as if to confirm that the time of public space being dominated by Memorial memory projects had drawn to a close. New actors, including the state, have taken to the stage, leaving Memorial limited space for its own activity.

In spite of its efforts over the years, Memorial was not able to create a meaning-laden system capable of delineating a framework for a civilian community (either temporally – through festivals, or spatially – through sites of memory) and responding to such questions as 'What made the Gulag possible?' or 'How should we live in the future?'. As the Russian scholar Alexander Etkind writes, there was no place in Russia for serious philosophical debate addressing such issues as the guilt, memory and identity of a society that had come through a period of mass terror (Etkind 2004c: 51–52). As Etkind correctly notes, 'despite an attempt made in the early 1990s to initiate such a debate by the historian and gulag survivor Dmitry Likhachev . . . , Russian intellectuals have not produced anything comparable to the great book by Karl Jaspers, *The Problem of Guilt*' (Etkind 2013: 10), a book that provoked unending debate in German society.

This does not mean that Memorial was not seeking answers to these questions. Initially, it was referencing argumentation developed by experts on totalitarian systems. As Miller notes:

> [Russian] public opinion of the late eighties was dominated by discourse on the totalitarian nature of communist governments. Initially, rather than being grounded in academic deliberation, this discourse was mainly based on the novels of Orwell and Zamyatin . . . Over the next four or five years, Russian translations appeared of nearly all the most important works written by classics of totalitarianism studies: Richard Pipes, Robert Conquest and Martin Malia. They found a wide readership. (2001: 46)

The concept of totalitarianism explained what had occurred in the USSR by drawing an analogy with the Nazi system. However, while such an interpretation may be satisfactory when applied to the functioning of the state, there is less agreement over the validity of this method of comparison when it comes to crimes committed by individuals (as a matter of fact, the validity of the totalitarian model itself has been questioned by a group of American historiographers referred to as revisionists [see Kotkin 1995: 2–6]). As Viktor Shmyrov, former director of the Perm-36 Museum, told me, people working as camp guards 'were not the Gestapo. There were various people here' [29_VS]. He went on to explain that there were sadists among them, but also officers who were risking their careers and freedom smuggling out the writings of prisoners; for example, Vasyl Stus' poetry. This is similar in spirit to a comment I mentioned earlier made by the moderator of exhibitions at the Magadan Community Centre. She explained why inhabitants of Kolyma had decided to erect a memorial to such an ambiguous figure as Berzin by stressing that Gulag history is not 'black and white', and Berzin himself had ultimately become a victim of the system.

However, on the one hand, the fact that many perpetrators became victims of the system, and, on the other, the fear that if it was acknowledged that there were a group of people who were to blame, a period of score settling would begin that could divide society anew, have in practice meant that comparisons between the Soviet and Nazi systems, rather than aiding mutual comprehension, often cause more misunderstandings. This problem is illustrated very well by the example I have just given of guards smuggling out the writings of prisoners. Shmyrov made it clear that those prisoners who described their camp experiences did not reveal the names of the officers who had smuggled out their writings, as they wanted to protect them from potential retribution by former NKVD functionaries. These prisoners and the guards who assisted them were joined by a personal intimate relationship based on shared experiences and mutual trust (Sherbakova 1992: 109–10). The unique functioning of the victim-perpetrator relationship would appear to be a significant component of the Gulag experience. It also made some former dissidents reluctant to acknowledge the problematic fact that a former camp guard, Ivan Kukushkin, was later employed by the Perm-36 Museum as a warden. As Shmyrov told me: 'none of the ex-prisoners hold any grudges against Ivan Kukushkin . . . His job was to keep order' [29_VS]. Shmyrov also emphasizes that Kukushkin just got on with his job rather than taunting the prisoners. Later, he was a solid, dependable employee of the museum. What is more, during a meeting after they had all been freed, ex-prisoners were the first to shake his hand (Gladyshev 1998: 166–271). This situation causes consternation among many visitors from the West, as is clear from the scene from Restle and Maus' documentary that I referenced in the Introduction. At the same time, it shows that the concept of totalitarianism does not enable the camp experience to be fully understood.

One important obstacle impeding the creation of a secular descriptive language is the fact that memory actors describe the Gulag experience using concepts developed by Soviet propaganda (for example, kulak, the fifth column, enemy of the nation). Most events that are worthy of being granted a special meaning are given a suitable name that will express them from then onwards. This is what happened in the case of the war with Napoleon, which is known in Russia as the Patriotic War. Such a change in semantic focus enables language to be reworked in such a manner as to change the range of any meanings that are being expressed, thus enabling new values to be incorporated. The best example of this would appear to be the creation of a separate language grounded in Holocaust discourse. The words 'Holocaust' and 'Shoah' came into use to meet a need to understand the ruthless murder of millions of Jews during the Second World War. They were meant to be of assistance when it came to grasping and comprehending what had occurred. The same event was labelled in the Nazi system as 'the Final Solution of the Jewish Question'. This change in definition had important semantic repercussions. When the Final Solution project was under development, a whole new language was developed to describe this process. This has since been replaced by a new lexicon of terms (trauma, absence, extermination) that free this subject from the language of the perpetrators, enabling an attempt to be made to express what humanity has understood from this experience and what it wishes to remember.

In the Gulag's case, this process has never been completed. Soviet propaganda terms are still in continuous circulation and being used all the time. Irrespective of whether the intention is to recount certain facts, a new model is being sought to interpret these facts or attempts are being made to subject social memory to critical reflection. A good example of this is the manner in which guides relate the Gulag past as they take tours around history exhibitions. When they are explaining the collectivization process or the fates that befell prisoners during the war, they use such words as 'kulak', or 'fifth column' or 'enemy of the nation'. Sometimes, they look at visitors knowingly, leaving them in no doubt that the historical (propaganda-driven) meanings of these words are questionable, yet they never make any attempt to explain this semantic problem area.

It is also worth noting that the word 'Gulag' itself does not possess a precise meaning. It is not only used to describe the functioning of the state institution and the experience of prisoners, but also when the memory of these events is being conceptualized. In the latter case, the term 'Gulag' describes both the system of forced labour camps operating in the USSR from the 1920s to the 1960s and the crimes committed by the Bolsheviks during the civil war; collectivization; the deportations of Lithuanians, Latvians and Estonians in 1940–41; the dissident period; and sometimes even the crimes of Katyn (see Applebaum 2003; Tołczyk 2009).

However, the literary milieu, and memoirists in particular, created certain notions that are supposed to aid reflection on the Gulag experience. The key works here are: *The Gulag Archipelago* (Solzhenitsyn 1974), *A World Apart* (Herling 1951), and *Journey into the Whirlwind* (Ginzburg 2002 [1967]). Fruitful comparisons can also be made with other totalitarian regimes; for example, Magadan is sometimes seen as a Russian Auschwitz or Vorkuta as a Buchenwald. Nevertheless, however effective these rhetorical figures may be at enabling certain elements of the Gulag experience to be comprehended and expressed, they should not be taken as proposals for the creation of a coherent language that would enable the Gulag in all its complexity to be understood. In the Holocaust's case, such a language was shaped over several decades and the form it assumes today is a consequence of the reflections of, and dialogue between, many philosophers, artists, writers and witnesses. Witness memoirs and the literature of Solzhenitsyn or Shalamov therefore enable the Gulag experience to be described, but are not the key to finding answers to the questions crucial for understanding this experience, which I mentioned above: 'What made the Gulag possible?' and 'How should we live in the future?'. The Orthodox Church is proposing answers to these questions, which would appear to account for its broader social appeal. As a matter of fact, even Solzhenitsyn himself supported precisely such a national-Orthodox path to the Russian Federation's revival.

As Etkind, the Russian scholar I recited earlier, writes, the Russian elite has failed to erect 'hard' monuments or force the communist authorities to face the legal consequences of their actions. Consequently, memory of the terror continues to function at the level of 'soft memory' in Russia. As Etkind explains, 'Hard memory is usually the responsibility of the state, while soft memory is the domain of society' (2004b: 56). Whereas soft memory is textual in nature and functions within public discourse, hard memory is controlled by the ruling authorities and fixed into 'stable, indisputable, monumental forms' (Etkind 2004b: 56). The two types of memory are closely related to each other, yet, as Etkind writes, even a deep transformation in soft memory (such as occurred in the late eighties and early nineties) does not mean that soft memory will become 'hard'. It might therefore be argued that the main problem facing Gulag memory during the period I have analysed was not that Russians had forgotten about the terror, but rather that the memory of this terror was one of those elements of memory shaped and protected by the state. As a former Vorkuta convict and Memorial member told me during a conversation we had in St Petersburg: 'These monuments can't be erected now, but in five or ten years, they will be. But this will only happen if the memory hasn't faded by then . . . Since the time came when the tsar's and Denikin's[4] corpses were transferred [to suitable resting places in Russia], the time will also come for [the erection of] Gulag memorials' [32_VK]. My interlocutor was right. Ten years had elapsed and in 2017 the moment arrived for the unveiling of a state memorial to victims of political repressions.

Postscript

On 30 October 2017, on the national Day of Remembrance for Victims of Political Repression, the Russian president participated in the unveiling of the Wall of Sorrow, a memorial to victims of political repressions in the centre of Moscow at the intersection of the Garden Ring and Akademika Sakharova Prospekt. During his speech, Vladimir Putin stressed that the memorial is the culmination of a long period of waiting. However, the political and memory situation when it finally came into being was different from the situation that prevailed during the carnival of memory, and it expresses meanings that are different to those some Memorial members would have wanted. This explains why some of them were sceptical towards the new monument.

The unveiling of the Wall of Sorrow was a key moment in the state policy, which had been developing since 2015, on commemorating the victims of political repression[5] and opens a new chapter in the memorialization of the Gulag. From this moment onwards, the state has been taking the initiative on commemorating the repressions, and the GULAG History Museum has become one of the primary actors shaping national Gulag memory.[6] This museum's director, Roman Romanov, chairs the Memorial Fund and was responsible for the Wall of Sorrow's construction. What is more, the GULAG History Museum has created a special Association of Memory Museums, which currently gathers together twenty-eight museums from all over the country. Every year, the Association organizes a meeting of its membership, at which joint projects and training sessions are followed by an exchange of experiences and ideas for cooperation. This top-down framing of memory policy guidelines is reminiscent of the modus operandi of other expert communities that, as Miller (2013) describes, aim to create a sense of social engagement in the creation of state memory policy while maximizing the achievement of outcomes the state has established itself. Undoubtedly, two notable outcomes of this policy are the visible centralization of actions in the memory of the repressions sphere and the state taking over functions that the Memorial society had been involved with since the carnival of memory.

The introduction of a new state memory policy coincides with a generational change. In 2006–2008, many of those who had been involved in the carnival of memory of the late eighties and the creation of the first memory projects were still active. More often than not, these people were ex-prisoners or their children. These actors are now leaving the stage, only to be replaced by a new generation. This process is exemplified very clearly by the director and staff of the GULAG History Museum, all of whom are in their twenties or thirties. The last few decades have therefore not only been marked by the state's increased involvement in the creation of projects devoted to the commemoration of victims of repression, but also by the emergence of a new 'Gulag postmemory' generation (see Hirsch 2012) with its own sensibilities and manner of understanding the past and the meanings ascribed to it. Members of this generation employ the latest media and exhibition strategies typical of Western memory museums. In this way, Gulag memory is slowly being incorporated into the global memory of twentieth-century disasters.

The fact that the state has become involved in the creation of its own memory projects does not mean that it has stopped supporting the Orthodox project. Five months before Putin unveiled the Wall of Sorrow in October 2017, he was involved in the ceremonial consecration of the Cathedral of New Martyrs and Confessors in Lubyanka. During his speech, Putin stressed that the new shrine was not only important for believers but for all of Russian society: '[our] country, the Russian state, is impossible to imagine without the spiritual and historical experience of the Russian Orthodox Church, which is passed on from generation to generation through the pastoral word'. He also added that a shrine honouring the New Martyrs and Confessors should 'perpetuate in our [Russian] society the ideas of goodness, mutual respect and reconciliation'.

The fact that the Russian president participated in the consecration of an Orthodox church dedicated to the New Russian Martyrs at a time when he also gave his first official speech on the hundredth anniversary of the Bolshevik Revolution shows that New Martyrdom has become an important framework for interpreting Soviet repressions, not only for the Orthodox Church but also for the Russian state. As Tomas Sniegon claims: 'The intensifying convergence between Russian nationalism, Orthodox belief and communist sentiment is creating a new category that portrays the victims of the Gulag as *martyrs of Russian uniqueness and superiority*' (2018 forthcoming: manuscript p. 32). The earlier mentioned multimedia exhibition *Historical Park Russia – My History* is a prime example of this convergence and perfectly expresses this Russian uniqueness and superiority. The spread of historical parks throughout Russia and creation of new state-sponsored memory projects are not only opening a new chapter in the development of memory of the Soviet repressions but also, by implication, that of Russian history in its entirety.

Notes

1. These communication obstacles were being caused by the distances involved (Magadan is nine thousand kilometres from Moscow, and in order to reach Vorkuta from the Solovetsky Islands, it is necessary to take a detour almost as far as Moscow, because there are no other railway connections); the fact that telephone connections were expensive (at the time, every region was in a different tariff zone); there was no Internet access, as this did not appear until the beginning of the twenty-first century and even when I was conducting my research, connections were very slow.
2. One important information forum was the Memorial Society's self-published newspaper *30 Oktabrya*, which continues today to publish information about new memorials erected by society members, Day of Remembrance ceremonies, discovered documents and Gulag history.
3. Quotation from 'Metodicheskiye rekomendatsii Departamenta gosudarstvennoy politiki v sfere obshchego obrazovaniya Minobranauki Rossii po ispolzovaniyu na urokakh istorii i vo vneurochnoy deyatelnosti resursov ekspozits istoricheskogo parka 'Rossiya – Moya istoriya' ['Methodical recommendations of the Department of State Policy in the sphere of general education of the Ministry of Education and Science of Russia on the use of the resources of the exposition of the historical park "Russia - My History" in history lessons and after-hour activities'] published 27 September 2016, http://mosmetod.ru/metodicheskoe-prostranstvo/vospitatelnaya-rabota/klassnaya-rabota/metodicheskie-materialy/metodicheskie-rekomendatsii-departamenta-gosudarstvennoj-politiki-v-sfere-obshchego-obrazovaniya-minobrnauki-r.html.
4. Anton Denikin was Lieutenant General in the Imperial Russian Army and a leading general of the White movement in the Russian Civil War between 1918 and 1920.
5. The State Policy Concept for Perpetuating the Memory of the Victims of Political Repression [Kontseptsiya gosudarstvennoy politiki po uvekovecheniyu pamyati zhertv politicheskikh repressiy] http://president-sovet.ru/documents/read/393/, last accessed 20 November 2017.
6. The museum was founded in 2001 by a former prisoner of Stalin's labour camps, Anton Antonov-Ovseenko. In 2012, Roman Romanov became the museum's new director, and it was he who was responsible for moving the museum to its new location and creating a new exhibition. For more on the impact the museum's old exhibition had on viewers, see P. Williams (2012) and E. Postnaya (2016).

Bibliography

Adler, N. 1993. *Victims of Soviet Terror: The Story of the Memorial Movement.* Westport, CT: Praeger.
———. 2002. *The Gulag Survivors: Beyond the Soviet System.* New Brunswick and London: Transaction.
———. 2012. 'Reconciliation with — or Rehabilitation of — the Soviet Past?', *Memory Studies* 5(3): 327–38.
Alekseyev, S. 2007. *Entsiklopediya pravoslavnoy ikony, osnovy bogosloviya ikony.* St Petersburg: Satis.
Ames, M. 1992. *Cannibal Tours and Glass Boxes: The Anthropology of Museums.* Vancouver: University of British Columbia Press.
Anderson, B. 1983. *Imagined Communities: Reflections on the Origin and Spread of Nationalism.* London: Verso.
Andrew, E. 2003. *Conversations with Lotman: Culture Semiotics in Language, Literature, and Cognition.* Toronto, Buffalo and London: University of Toronto Press.
Ankersmit, F. 2001. *Historical Representation.* Stanford, CA: Stanford University Press.
———. 2004. *Sublime Historical Experience.* Stanford, CA: Stanford University Press.
Anstett, E. 2011. 'Memory of Political Repression in Post-Soviet Russia: The Example of the Gulag', *Online Encyclopedia of Mass Violence*, 13 September. http://www.sciencespo.fr/mass-violence-war-massacre-resistance/en/document/memory-political-repression-post-soviet-russia-example-gulag.
Anstett, E. and L. Jurgenson (eds). 2009. *Le Goulag en héritage: Pour une anthropologie de la trace.* Paris: Pétra.
Applebaum, A. 2003. *Gulag: A History of the Soviet Camps.* London: Allen Lane, Penguin.
Artizov, A.N., A.A. Kosakovsky and V.P. Naumov (eds). 2004. *Reabilitatsiya: Kak eto było. Dokumenty Politbyuro TsK KPSS, stenogrammy zasedaniya Komissii Politbyuro TsK KPSS po dopolnitelnomu izucheniyu materialov, svyazannykh s repressiyami, imevshimi mesto v period 30-40-kh i nachala 50-kh gg., i drugiye materialy: seredina 80-kh gg. – 1991 g.,* Vol. 3. Moscow: Mezhdunarodnyy fond "Demokratiya".
Artizov, A.N., Y.V. Sigachev and V.G. Khlopov (eds). 2002. *Reabilitatsiya: Kak eto bylo. Dokumenty Prezidiuma TsK KPSS i drugiye materialy: mart 1953 g. – fevral 1956,* Vol. 1. Moscow: Mezhdunarodnyy fond "Demokratiya".

Artizov, A.N., Y.V. Sigachev and I. Shevchuk (eds). 2003 *Reabilitatsiya: Kak eto bylo. Dokumenty Prezidiuma TsK KPSS i drugiye materialy: fevral 1956 g. – nachalo 80-gg.*, Vol. 2. Moscow: Mezhdunarodnyy fond "Demokratiya".

Assmann, A. 2011a. 'To Remember or to Forget: Which Way Out of a Shared History of Violence?', in A. Assmann and L. Shortt (eds), *Memory and Political Change*. Basingstoke: Palgrave Macmillan, pp. 53–71.

———. 2011b. *Cultural Memory and Western Civilisation: Functions, Media, Archives*. Cambridge: Cambridge University Press.

Assmann, J. 1995. 'Collective Memory and Cultural Identity', *New German Critique* (65): 125–33.

———. 2008. 'Communicative and Cultural Memory', in A. Erll, A. Nünning and S. Young (eds), *Cultural Memory Studies: An International and Interdisciplinary Handbook*. Berlin: Walter de Gruyter, pp. 109–18.

———. 2011. 'Communicative and Cultural Memory', in P. Meusburger, M. Heffernan and E. Wunder (eds.), *Cultural Memories: The Geographical Point of View*. Dordrecht: Springer Netherlands, pp. 15–27.

Azarov, O. 2000a. 'Istoriya odnogo lagerya', in *Pokayanie Marytology (3)*. Syktyvkar: Kirovskaya oblastnaya tipografiya, pp. 374–448.

———. 2000b. 'Po tundre, po zheleznoy doroge...', in *"Pechorstroy" — istoriya sozidaniya. 1940 –2000*. Pechora: Izdatelstvo "Pechorskoye vremya".

Babbie, E. 2007. *The Practice of Social Research*. Belmont, CA: Thomson Wadsworth.

Bakhtin, M. 1984. *Rabelais and His World*, trans. H. Inwolsky. Bloomington, IN: Indiana University Press.

Bal, B. 1996. *Double Exposure: The Subject of Cultural Analysis*. New York: Routledge.

Barenberg, A. 2014. *Gulag Town, Company Town: Forced Labor and Its Legacy in Vorkuta*. New Haven, CT: Yale University Press.

Barner-Barry, C. 1999. 'Nation Building and the Russian Federation', in B. Glad and E. Shiraev (eds), *The Russian Transformation: Political, Sociological and Psychological Aspects*. New York: St. Martin's Press, pp. 95–108.

Barnes, S.A. 2011. *Death and Redemption: The Gulag and the Shaping of Soviet Society*. Princeton, NJ: Princeton University Press.

Bennett, T. 1998. 'Speaking to the Eyes: Museums, Legibility and the Social Order', in S. Macdonald (ed.), *The Politics of Display Museums, Science, Culture*. London and New York: Routledge, pp. 25–35.

Bercken, W. van den. 2003. 'The Canonisation of Nicholas II in Iconographical Perspective: Political Themes in Russian Icons', in J. Sutton and W. van den Bercken (eds), *Christianity and Contemporary Europe*. Leuven, Paris and Dudley: Peeters, pp. 183–210.

Berkin, I.B. 1980. *Istoriya Syktyvkara*. Syktyvkar: Komi knizhnoye izdatelstvo.

Bielecki, T. 2005. 'Odbudują gułag dla turystów', *Gazeta Wyborcza*, 14 April.

Biryukov, A. (ed.). 1998. *Kolyma. Dalstroy: Gulag: Skorb i sudby: Materialy nauchno--prakticheskoy konferentsii*. Magadan: Severny mezhdunarodny universitet.

Biryukov, A. 1999. 'Introduction', in S.V. Abramov (ed.), *Za nami pridut korabli: Spisok reabilitirovannykh lits, smertnyye prigovory v otnoshenii kotorykh privedeny v ispolneniye na territorii Magadanskoy oblasti*. Magadan: Magadanskoye knizhnoye izdatelstvo, pp. 3–61.

Bogumił, Z. 2010a. 'Kresty i kamni: Solovetskiye simvoly v konstruirovanii pamyati o Gulage', *Neprikosnovenny Zapas* 3(71): 1–19.

———. 2010b. 'Cmentarze GUŁagu — teksty zapomnianej kultury w tłumaczeniu współczesnym', in A.S. Czyż and B. Gotowski (eds), *Sztuka cmentarzy w XIX i XX wieku*. Warsaw: Wydawnictwo Uniwersytetu Kardynała Stefana Wyszyńskiego.

———. 2010c. 'Konflikty pamięci? — o interpretacjach historii GUŁagu', *Kultura i Społeczeństwo* (4): 23–40.

———. 2011a. 'Miejsce pamięci versus symulacja przeszłości — druga wojna światowa na wystawach historycznych', *Kultura i Społeczeństwo* (4): 149–70.

———. 2011b. 'Wyspy Sołowieckie jako "rosyjska Golgota" — o prawosławnym języku mówienia o represjach sowieckich', in A. Zielińska (ed.), *Konstrukcje i dekonstrukcje tożsamości Volume 1/ Wokół religii i jej języka*. Warsaw: Slawistyczny Ośrodek Wydawniczy, pp. 307–18.

———. 2012. 'Stone, Cross and Mask: Searching for Language of Commemoration of the Gulag in the Russian Federation', *Polish Sociological Review* (1): 71–90.

———. 2014. 'Pamięć drugiej wojny światowej w rosyjskich regionach: na przykładzie na przykładzie muzeów regionalnych Republiki Komi', *Kultura i Społeczeństwo* (3): 47–65.

———. 2016. 'The Solovetski Islands and Butovo as two "Russian Golgothas": New Martyrdom as a Means to Understand Russian Repression', in F. Fischer von Weikersthal and K. Thaidigsmann (eds), *(Hi-)Stories of the Gulag: Fiction and Reality*. Heidelberg: Universitätsverlag Winter, pp. 133–54.

Bogumił, Z. and M. Łukaszewicz. 2018. 'Between History and Religion – The New Russian Martyrdom as an Invented Tradition', *East European Politics and Societies* (forthcoming).

Bogumił, Z., D. Moran and E. Harrowell. 2015. 'Sacred or Secular? "Memorial", the Russian Orthodox Church, and the Contested Commemoration of Soviet Repressions', *Europe-Asia Studies* 67(9): 1416–44.

Bogumił, Z. and J. Wawrzyniak. 2010. 'Narracje zniszczenia: Trauma wojenna w muzeach miejskich Petersburga, Warszawy i Drezna', *Kultura i Społeczeństwo* (4): 3–21.

Bogumił, Z., J. Wawrzyniak, T. Buchen, C. Ganzer and M. Senina. 2015. *The Enemy on Display: The Second World War in Eastern European Museums*. Oxford and New York: Berghahn.

Brodsky, Y. 2008. *Solovki: Dvadtsat' let osobogo naznacheniya*. Moscow: Mir iskusstv.

Brunet, R. 1981. 'Géographie du Goulag', *L'Espace géographique* 10(3): 215–232.

Bulle, S. 2006, 'Espace et mémoire collective à Jérusalem', *Annales. Histoire, Sciences Sociales* 3(61): 583–606.

Cameron, D. 1971. 'The Museum, a Temple or the Forum', *Curator* 14(1): 11–24.

Carlson, M. 2013. *Performance: A Critical Introduction.* London and New York: Routledge.
Chakrabarty, D. 2000. *Provincializing Europe: Postcolonial Thought and Historical Difference.* Princeton, NJ: Princeton University Press.
Chibineyev, S.M. and L.L. Amaryan. 2004. *Khram Hrista Spasitelya, putevoditel.* Moscow: Izdatelstvo Triada.
Christensen, K.H. 2012. 'Remembering the New Martyrs and Confessors of Russia', in C. Raudvere, K. Stala and T.S. Willert (eds), *Rethinking the Space for Religion: New Actors in Central and Southeast Europe on Religion, Authenticity and Belonging.* Lund: Nordic Academic Press.
———. 2015. 'The Making of the New Martyrs of Russia: Soviet Repression in Orthodox Memory', PhD dissertation. Copenhagen: The Faculty of Humanities, University of Copenhagen.
———. 2017. *The Making of the New Martyrs of Russia: Soviet Repression in Orthodox Memory.* Oxford and New York: Routledge.
Chuykina, S. 2015. 'Kak rasskazat o GULAGE yazykom istoricheskoy vystavki: "Pravo perepiski" v moskovskom "Memoriale"', *Labolatorium* 7(1): 158–83.
Cichowlas, O. 2014. 'The Kremlin is Trying to Erase Memories of The Gulag', *New Republic,* 23 June.
Clifford, J. 1988. *The Predicament of Culture.* Cambridge, MA: Harvard University Press.
Cohen, S.F. 2011. *The Victims Return: Survivors of the Gulag after Stalin.* New York: Tauris.
Cole, T. 1999. *Selling the Holocaust: From Auschwitz to Schindler, How History is Bought, Packaged, and Sold.* New York: Routledge.
Conquest, R. 1997. 'Victims of Stalinism: A Comment', *Europe-Asia Studies* 49(7): 1317–19.
———. 1999. 'Comment on Wheatcroft', *Europe-Asia Studies* 51(8): 1479–83.
Courtois, S., et al. 1999. *The Black Book of Communism: Crimes, Terror, Repression,* trans. J. Murphy and M. Kramer. Cambridge, MA and London: Harvard University Press.
Crane, S. 2004. 'Memory, Distortion and History in the Museum', in B.M. Carbonell (ed.), *Museum Studies: An Anthology of Contexts.* Malden, MA, Oxford and Victoria: Wiley-Blackwell, pp. 318–34.
Cristea, G. and S. Radu-Bucurenci. 2008. 'Raising the Cross: Exorcising Romania's Communist Past in Museums, Memorials and Monuments', in O. Sarkisova and P. Apor (eds), *Past for the Eyes: East European Representations of Communism in Cinema and Museums after 1989.* Budapest and New York: CEU Press, pp. 275–305.
Damanskaya, L.V. 1998. 'Protsess reabilitatsii prodolzhayetsya', in A.M. Biryukov (ed.), *Kolyma. Dalstroy: Gulag: Skorb i sudby: Materialy nauchno-prakticheskoy konferentsii.* Magadan: Severny mezhdunarodny universitet, pp. 65–66.
Davies, E.W. 1997. *Soviet History in the Yeltsin Era.* Basingstoke: Palgrave Macmillan.

Di Nola, A.M. 2006. *Tryumf śmierci: Antropologia żałoby*, trans. M. Woźniak et al. Kraków: Universitas.

Dias, N. 1998. 'The Visibility of Difference: Nineteenth-century French Anthropological Collections', in S. Macdonald (ed.), *The Politics of Display, Museums, Science, Culture*. London and New York: Routledge, pp. 36–52.

Dobson, M. 2006. '"Show the Bandit-Enemies No Mercy!": Amnesty, Criminality and Public Response in 1953', in P. Jones (ed.), *The Dilemmas of De-Stalinization: Negotiating Cultural and Social Change in the Khrushchev Era*. London: Routledge.

———. 2009. *Khrushchev's Cold Summer: Gulag Returnees, Crime, and the Fate of Reform after Stalin*. Ithaca, NY: Cornell University Press.

Domańska, E. 2006. *Historie Niekonwencjonalne*. Poznań: Wydawnictwo Poznańskie.

Dorman, V. 2010. 'From Solovki to Butovo: The Appropriation of the Memory of the Repressions by the Russian Orthodox Church', *Laboratorium* 2: 431–36.

Doss, E. 2008. *The Emotional Life of Contemporary Public Memorials: Towards a Theory of Temporary Memorials*. Amsterdam: Amsterdam University Press.

Duncan, C. 1995. *Civilizing Rituals: Inside Public Art Museums*. London and New York: Routledge.

Duncan, P. 2000. *Russian Messianism: Third Rome, Revolution, Communism and After*. London: Routledge.

Edelman, O.W., E.Y. Zavadskaya and O.V. Lavinskaya (eds). 1999. *58/10: Nadzornyye proizvodstva Prokuratury SSSR po delam ob antisovetskoy agitatsii i propagande: Mart 1953–1991*. Moscow: Mezhdunarodny fond "Demokratiya".

Eliade, M. 1958. *Patterns in Comparative Religion*, trans. R. Sheed. London: Sheed and Ward.

———. 1959. *The Sacred and The Profane: The Nature of Religion*, trans. W. Trask. San Diego, CA: Harcourt Brace.

Elie, M. 2010. 'Ce que réhabiliter veut dire: Khrouchtchev et Gorbatchev aux prises avec l'héritage répressif stalinien', *Vingtième Siècle. Revue d'histoire* (107): 101–13.

Ellman, M. 2002. 'Soviet Repression Statistics: Some Comments', *Europe-Asia Studies* 54(7): 1151–72.

Emerson, R. and R. Fretz. 2011. *Writing Ethnographic Fieldnotes*. Chicago, IL: University of Chicago Press.

Ernst, W. 2000. 'Archi(ve)textures of Museology', in S. Crane (ed.), *Museums and Memory*. Stanford, CA: Stanford University Press.

Etkind, A. 2004a. 'Remembering the Gulag', *Project Syndicate*, 17 June. https://www.project-syndicate.org/commentary/remembering-the-gulag?barrier=accessreg.

———. 2004b. 'Hard and Soft in Cultural Memory: Political Mourning in Russia and Germany', *Grey Room* (16): 36–59.

———. 2004c. 'Vremya sobirat kamni: Postrevolyutsionnaya kultura politicheskoy skorbi v sovremennoy Rossii', *Ab Imperio* (2): 33–76.

———. 2009. 'Stories of the Undead in the Land of the Unburied: Magical Historicism in Contemporary Russian Fiction', *Slavic Review* 68(3): 631–58.

———. 2013. *Warped Mourning: Stories of the Undead in the Land of Unburied*. Stanford, CA: Stanford University Press.

Fedor, J. 2011. *Russia and the Cult of State Security: The Chekist Tradition, from Lenin to Putin*. London and New York: Routledge.

———. 2014. 'Setting the Soviet Past in Stone: The Iconography of the New Martyrs of the Russian Orthodox Church', *Australian Slavonic and East European Studies* 28(1–2): 121–53.

Fedor, J. and T. Sniegon. 2018. 'The Butovskii Shooting Range: History of an Unfinished Museum', in N. Stephen (ed.), *Museums of Communism: New Memory Sites in Central and Eastern Europe*. (Indiana University Press, forthcoming).

Fedushchak, I. and V. Fedushchak. 2006. *Abez i Adak — doroga v vechnost*. Lviv: NVF "Ukrainski Tekhnologii".

Figes, O. 2007. *The Whisperers: Private Life in Stalin's Russia*. New York: Metropolitan.

———. 2014. *Revolutionary Russia, 1891 – 1991: A History*. New York: Metropolitan.

Fitzpatrick, S. 2005. *Tear Off the Masks! Identity and Imposture in Twentieth-Century Russia*. Princeton, NJ: Princeton University Press.

Forbes, N. 1916. *Russian Grammar*. Oxford: Clarendon Press.

Foucault, M. 1972. *The Archaeology of Knowledge and the Discourse on Language*, trans. A.M. Sheridan Smith. New York: Pantheon.

———. 2003a. 'Society Must be Defended', in F. Ewald and A. Fontana (eds), *Lectures at the Collège de France, 1975–76*, trans. D. Macey. New York: Picador.

———. 2003b [1973]. *The Birth of the Clinic: An Archaeology of Medical Perception*, trans. A.M. Sheridan. London: Routledge.

Francis, D., L. Kellaher and G. Neophytou. 2005. 'Studying the Living in Cemeteries', *The Secret Cemetery*. Oxford and New York: Berg, pp. 1–27.

Gabowitsch, M. (ed.). 2005. *Pamyat o voyne 60 let spustya: Rossiya, Germaniya, Yevropa*. Moscow: Novoye literaturnoye obozreniye.

Geertz, C. 1973. *The Interpretation of Cultures: Selected Essays*. New York: Basic.

———. 1988. 'Being There, Writing Here', *Harper's Magazine*, March edition.

Gessat-Anstett, E. 2007. *Une Atlantide russe, anthropologie de la mémoire en Russie postsoviétique*. Paris: La Découverte.

Getsen, M.V. 2004. *Vorkuta — gorod na ugle, gorod v Arktike*. Syktyvkar: OAO "Komi Respublikanskaya Tipografiya".

Gheith, J. and K. Jolluck. 2011. *Gulag Voices: Oral Histories of Soviet Incarceration and Exile*. New York: Palgrave Macmillan.

Giesen, A. 2015. 'Raskolotaya pamyat: otrazheniye konflikta vokrug "Memorialnogo tsentra Perm-36" v rossiyskikh media', *Journal of Social Policy Studies* 13(3): 363–76.

Ginzburg, E. 2002 [1967]. *Journey into the Whirlwind*. San Diego, CA: Harcourt.

Gladyshev, V. 1998. 'Tayny permskogo "GULAGa"', in *Gody terrora: kniga pamyati zhertv politicheskikh repressiy*. Perm: Izdatelstvo "Zdravstvuy", pp. 166–271.

Głowacka-Grajper, M. 2016. *Transmisja pamięci Działacze "sfery pamięci" i przekaz o Kresach Wschodnich we współczesnej Polsce*. Warsaw: Wydawnictwo Uniwersytetu Warszawskiego.

Gorky, M. 1964. *Po Soyuzu Sovetov*. Moscow: Izvestiya.

Graña, C. 1971. *Fact and Symbol: Essays in the Sociology of Art and Literature*. New York: Oxford University Press.

Gregory, P.R. 2009. *Terror by Quota: State Security from Lenin to Stalin*. New Haven, CT: Yale University Press.

Grele, R.J. 1998. 'Movement without Aim: Methodological and Theoretical Problems in Oral History', in R. Perks and A. Thomson (eds), *The Oral History Reader*. London and New York: Routledge, pp. 38–52.

Grider, S. 2005. 'Spontaneous Shrines and Public Memorialization', in K. Garces-Foley (ed.), *Death and Religion in a Changing World*. Armonk, NY: M. E. Sharpe.

Grzesiuk-Olszewska, I. 1995. *Polska rzeźba pomnikowa w latach 1945–1995*. Warsaw: Wydawnictwo NERITON.

Grzybowski, S. 1998. 'O potrzebie fałszywej tradycji', in J.Baradziej and J. Goćkowski (eds), *Rozważania o tradycji i ethosie*. Kraków: Wydawnictwo Baran i Suszczyński, pp. 50–71.

Gudkov, L. 2005. '"Pamyat" o voyne i massovaya identichnost rossiyan', in I. Kalinin (ed.), *60 let spustya: Rossiya, Germaniya, Yevropa*. Moscow: Novoye Literaturnoye Obozreniye, pp. 83–103.

Gullotta, A. 2018. *Intellectual Life and Literature at Solovki 1923–1930: The Paris of the Northern Concentration Camps*. Cambridge: Legenda.

Halbwachs, M. 1941. *La topographie légendaire des Evangiles en Terre Saint*. Paris: Presse Universitaires de France.

———. 1950. *La mémoire collective*. Paris: Presses Universitaires de France.

———. 1969. *Społeczne ramy pamięci*. Warszawa: Państwowe Wydawnictwo Naukowe.

———. 1992. On Collective Memory (text from *Les Cadres sociaux de la mémoire* (1952) and *La topographie légendaire des évangiles en terre sainte: Etude de mémoire collective* (1941), ed. and trans. L.A. Coser). Chicago, IL and London: The University of Chicago Press.

Hammersley, M. and P. Atkinson. 2007. *Ethnography: Principles in Practice*. New York and Oxford: Routledge.

Handelman, D. 1990. *Models and Mirrors: Towards an Anthropology of Public Events*. New York: Cambridge University Press.

Hellbeck, J. 2006. *Revolution on My Mind: Writing a Diary under Stalin*. Cambridge, MA: Harvard University Press.

Herling, G. 1951. *A World Apart: The Journal of a Gulag Survivor*, trans. A. Ciołkosz. London: Heinemann.

Hetherington, K. 1996. 'The Utopics of Social Ordering: Stonehenge as a Museum without Walls', in S. Macdonald and G. Fyfe (eds), *Theorizing Museums: Repre-*

senting Identity and Diversity in a Changing World. Oxford and Cambridge, MA: Blackwell, pp. 153–76.

Hirsch, M. 2008. 'The Generation of Postmemory', *Poetics Today* 29(1): 103–28.

———. 2012. *The Generation of Postmemory: Writing and Visual Culture after the Holocaust*. New York: Columbia University Press.

Hooper-Greenhill, E. 1992. *Museums and the Shaping of Knowledge*. London and New York: Routledge.

Hutchins, L.P. and G.E. Vietzke. 2002. 'Dialogue Between Continents: Civic Engagement and the Gulag Museum at Perm-36, Russia', *The George Wright Forum* 19(4): 65–74.

Ioffe, V. 2002a. *Granitsy smysla: statyi, vystupleniya, esse*. St Petersburg: Izdatelstvo "Nord-West".

———. 2002b. *Itogi veka*. St Petersburg: Memorial Research Centre.

Irwin-Zarecka, I. 1994. *Frames of Remembrance: The Dynamics of Collective Memory*. New Brunswick and New Jersey: Transaction.

Ivanova, G. 2000. *Labor Camp Stalinism: The Gulag in the Soviet Totalitarian System*. New York and London: M. E. Sharpe.

Ivanova, G.M. 2006. *Istoriya Gulaga 1918 – 1956*. Moscow: Nauka.

Jakobson, M. 1993. *Origins of the Gulag: The Soviet Prison Camp System, 1917–1934*. Lexington, KY: The University Press of Kentucky.

Jedlińska, E. 2001. *Sztuka po Holocauście*. Łódź: Tygiel Kultury.

Jones, P. 2008. 'Memories of Terror or Terrorizing Memories? Terror, Trauma and Survival in Soviet Culture of the Thaw', *The Slavonic and East European Review* 86(2): 346–71.

Jones, S. 2005. 'Making Histories of War', in G. Kavanagh (ed.), *Making Histories, Making Memories*. London and New York: International Publishing Group, pp. 152–62.

Kahla, E. 2010. 'The New Martyrs of Russia: Regeneration of Archaic Forms or Revival?', *Ortodoksia* (51): 193–208.

Kalendarova, V. 2005. 'Formiruya pamyat, blokada v leningradskikh gazetakh i dokumentalnom kino v poslevoyennyye desyatiletiya', in M.W. Loskutova (ed.), *Pamyat o blokade. Svidetelstva ochevidtsev i istoricheskoye soznaniye obshchestva*. St Petersburg: Novoye izdatelstvo, pp. 275–97.

Kalikh, A. 1998. '"Memorial" – Dvizheniye sovesti', in A. Suslov (ed.), *Gody terrora: kniga pamyati zhertv politicheskikh repressiy*. Perm: Izdatelstvo "Zdravstvuy", pp. 9–15.

Kaminsky, A., R. Gleinig and R. Heidenreich (eds). 2007. *Erinnerungsorte and den massenterror 1937/38 Russische Föderation*. Berlin: Bundesstiftung zur Aufarbeitung der SED Diktatur.

Kaneva, A.N. 2001. *Gulagovski teatr Ukhty*. Syktyvkar: Komi knizhnoye izdatelstvo.

Kaniowska, K. 1999. *Opis klucz do zrozumienia kultury*. Łódź: Polskie Towarzystwo Ludoznawcze.

Kapralski, S. 2000. 'Oświęcim: konflikt pamięci czy krysys tożsamości?', *Przegląd Socjologiczny* (XLIX)2: 141–66.

———. 2002. 'Auschwitz: Site of Memories', in. A. Polonsky (ed.), *POLIN Studies in Polish Jewry, Vol. 15, Focusing on Jewish Religious Life, 1500–1900*. Oxford and Portland, OR: The Littman Library of Jewish Civilization, pp. 383–400.

———. 2010. *Pamięć — przestrzeń — tożsamość*. Warsaw: Scholar.

Kavanagh, G. 2005. 'Making Histories, Making Memories', in G. Kavanagh (ed.), *Making Histories, Making Memories*. London and New York: International Publishing Group, pp. 1–14.

Keep, J. 1999. 'Wheatcroft and Stalin's Victims: Comments', *Europe-Asia Studies* 51(6): 1089–92.

Kenney, P. 2003. *A Carnival of Revolution Central Europe 1989*. Princeton, NJ: Princeton University Press.

Kharkhordin, O. 1999. *The Collective and Individual in Russia: A Study of Practices*. Berkeley and Los Angeles, CA: University of California Press.

Khlevnyuk, O. 2004. *The History of the Gulag: From Collectivization to the Great Terror*. New Haven, CT: Yale University Press.

Kirschenbaum, L. 2006. *The Legacy of the Siege of Leningrad, 1941–1995: Myth, Memories, and Monuments*. Cambridge: Cambridge University Press.

Kizny, T. 2004. *Gulag: Life and Death Inside the Soviet Concentration Camps*. Buffalo, NY: Firefly.

Klapiyuk, A., T. Rodionova and M. Shnyakova. 2007. 'Istoriya kladbishcha Makarikha', *Malyye Stefanovskiye chteniya*. Kotlas, pp. 40–53.

Kolbuszewski, J. 1981. 'Cmentarz jako tekst kultury', *Odra* (11): 29–36.

———. 1985. *Wiersze z cmentarza; o współczesnej epigrafice wierszowanej*. Wrocław: PTL.

———. 1995. 'Cmentarz jako tekst kultury', in O. Czerner and I. Juszkiewicz (eds), *Sztuka cmentarna: dokumenty*. Wrocław: Polski Komitet Narodowy ICOMOS, pp. 17–37.

Konradova, N. and A. Ruleva. 2005. 'Geroi i zhertvy. Memorialy Velikoy Otechestvennoy', in I. Kalinin (ed.), *Pamyat o voyne 60 let spustya: Rossiya, Germaniya, Yevropa*. Moscow: Novoye Literaturnoye Obozreniye, pp. 241–61.

Kontopodis, M. 2009. 'Editorial: Time. Matter. Multiplicity', *Memory Studies* 2(1): 5–10.

Koposov, N. 2011. *Pamyat strogogo rezhima: Istoriya i politika v Rossii*. Moscow: Novoye literaturnoye obozreniye.

Kopylova, N. 2001. 'V pamyat o novomuchenikakh i ispovednikakh Solovetskikh', *Moskovski zhurnal* (4).

Koselleck, R. 1997. 'Les monuments aux morts, lieux de la fondation de l'identité des survivants', in R. Koselleck, *L'expérience de l'histoire*. Paris: Gallimard-Le Seuil, pp. 135–60.

Kotkin, S. 1995. *Magnetic Mountain, Stalinism as a Civilization*. Berkeley, CA: University of California Press.

———. 2001. *Armageddon Averted: The Soviet Collapse 1970–2000*. Oxford and New York: Oxford University Press.

Kotylev, A.Y. 2003. 'Regionalny muzey v sisteme rossiyskoy kultury XX-XXI vekov: itogi i perspektivy razvitiya'. *Muzey i Krayevedeniye* (4): 26–36.

Kozlova, N. 2005. *Sovetskiye lyudi: Stseny iz istorii*. Moscow: Yevropa.

Kranz, T. 2002. *Edukacja historyczna w miejscach pamięci*. Lublin: Stowarzyszenie Dialog i Współpraca.

Kreamer, C.M. 1992. 'Defining Communities through Exhibiting and Collecting', in I. Karp, C. M. Kreamer and S.D. Lavines, *Museums and Communities: The Politics of Public Culture*. Washington and London: Smithsonian Institution Press, pp. 367–81.

Krikhtova, T. 2014. 'Reprezentatsiya etnichnosti v pamyatnikakh i svyazannykh s nimi praktikakh na Levashovskom memorialnom kladbishche', *Etnograficheskoye obozreniye* (2): 139–52.

Kugelmass, J. and J. Boyarin (eds). 1998. *From a Ruined Garden*: *The Memorial Books of Polish Jewry* (with Geographical Index and Bibliography by Z.M. Baker). Bloomington, IN: Indiana University Press.

Kuntsman, A. 2009. '"With a Shade of Disgust": Affective Politics of Sexuality and Class in Memoirs of the Stalinist Gulag', *Slavic Review* 68(2): 308–28.

Kuznetsov, V.P. 1997. *Istoriya razvitiya formy kresta: Kratki kurs pravoslavnoy stavrografii*. Moscow: Zhizn vechnaya.

Lang, T.T. 1998. 'Reifying Race: Science and Art in Races of Mankind at the Field Museum of Natural History', in S. MacDonald (ed.), *The Politics of Display: Museum, Science, Culture*. London and New York: Routledge, pp. 53–76.

Leong, A. 1998. '"Treugolnik stradaniy" Ernsta Neizvestnogo: Magadan, Vorkuta, Yekaterinburg', in A.M. Biryukov (ed.), *Kolyma. Dalstroy: Gulag: Skorb i sudby: Materialy nauchno-prakticheskoy konferentsii*. Magadan: Severny mezhdunarodny universitet, pp. 67–71.

Lifton, R. 1967. *Death in Life: Survivors of Hiroshima*. New York: Random House.

Lim, J.H. 2008. 'Victim Nationalism and History Reconciliation in East Asia', *History Compass* 8(1): 1–10.

Lotman, Y. 1990. *Universe of the Mind: A Semiotic Theory of Culture*. London and New York: Taurus & Co.

———. 2009. *Culture and Explosion*, trans. W. Clark and M. Grishakova (ed.). Berlin and New York: Mounton de Gruyter.

Lotman, Y. and B. Uspensky. 1993a. 'Rola modeli dualnych w dynamice kultury rosyjskiej (do końca XVIII w.)', in B. Żyłko (ed. and trans.), *Semiotyka dziejów Rosji* [*A Collection of Essays by Lotman and Uspensky*]. Łódź: Wydawnictwo Łódzkie, pp. 17–61.

———. 1993b. 'Pogłosy koncepcji "Moskwa – Trzeci Rzym" w ideologii Piotra Pierwszego (w sprawie tradycji średniowiecznej w kulturze baroku)', in B. Żyłko (ed. and trans.), *Semiotyka dziejów Rosji*. Łódź: Wydawnictwo Łódzkie, pp. 159–77.

Lübbe, H. 1991. 'Muzealizacja: O powiązaniu naszej teraźniejszości z przeszłością', in M. Gołaszewska (ed.), *Estetyka w świecie* (3). Kraków: Wydawnictwo Uniwersytetu Jagiellońskiego, pp. 7–29.

Lukin, Y. 1996. *Na palachakh krovi net: Tipy i nravy Leningradskogo NKVD*. Saint Petersburg: Bibliopolis.

Lutyński, J. 2004. 'Uwagi o metodologii socjologicznych badań terenowych Józefa Chałasińskiego', *Przegląd socjologiczny* LIII (1): 12.

Macdonald, S. 1996. 'Introduction', in S. Macdonald and G. Fyfe (eds), *Theorizing Museums: Representing Identity and Diversity in a Changing World*. Oxford and Cambridge, MA: Blackwell, pp. 1–18.

———. 1998. 'Exhibitions of Power and Powers of Exhibition: An Introduction to the Politics of Display', in S. Macdonald, *The Politics of Display: Museums, Science, Culture*. London and New York: Routledge, pp. 1–24.

———. 2013. *Memorylands: Heritage and Identity in Europe Today*. London: Routledge.

Macdonald, S. and G. Fyfe (eds). 1996. *Theorizing Museums: Representing Identity and Diversity in a Changing World*. Oxford and Cambridge, MA: Blackwell.

Magun, A. 2008. *Otritsatelnaya revolyutsiya: K dekonstruktsii politicheskogo subyekta*. St Petersburg: Izdatelstvo Yevropeyskogo universiteta v Sankt-Peterburg.

Maier, Ch. 2000. 'Consigning the Twentieth Century to History: Alternative Narratives for the Modern Era', *American Historical Review* 105(3): 807–31.

Małczyński, J. 2009. 'Drzewa "żywe pomniki" w Muzeum-Miejscu Pamięci w Bełżcu', *Teksty Drugie* (1–2): 208–14.

Malia, M. 1998. *Sowiecka tragedia: historia komunistycznego imperium rosyjskiego 1917– 1991*, trans. M. Hułas and E. Wyzner. Warsaw: Wydawnictwo Philips Wilson.

Malinova, O. 2015. *Aktualnoye proshloye: Simvolicheskaya politika vlastvuyushchey elity i dilemmy rossiyskoy identichnosti*. Moscow: Rossiyskaya politicheskaya entsiklopediya.

Malofeyevskaya, L.N. 2004. *Gorod na Bolshoy Inte*. Syktyvkar: OAO "Komi Respublikanskaya Tipografiya".

Margry, P.J. and C. Sánchez-Carretero. 2011. 'Introduction: Rethinking Memorialization: The Concept of Grassroots Memorials', in P.J. Margry and C. Sánchez-Carretero (eds), *Grassroots Memorials: The Politics of Memorializing Traumatic Death*. New York and Oxford: Berghahn.

Melnikova, E. 2015. 'The Local Memory of the World War II in Provincial Museums: The Northern Ladoga Case Study', in E. Makhotina, E. Keding, W. Borodziej, E. Francois and M. Schulze Wessel (eds), *Krieg im Museum: Präsentationen des*

Zweiten Weltkriegs in Museen und Gedenkstätten des östlichen Europa. Munich: Vandenhoeck & Ruprecht, pp. 111–30.

Merloo, J. 1968. 'Delayed Mourning in Victims of Extermination Camps', in H. Krystal (ed.), *Massive Psychic Trauma*. New York: International Universities Press.

Merridale, C. 2000. 'War, Death and Remembrance in Soviet Russia', in J. Winter and E. Sivan (eds), *War and Remembrance in the Twentieth Century*. Cambridge: Cambridge University Press, pp. 61–83.

———. 2001. *Night of Stone, Death and Memory in Twentieth-Century Russia*. New York: Viking.

———. 2003. 'Revolution among the Dead: Cemeteries in Twentieth-Century Russia', *Mortality* 8(2): 176–88.

Miller, A. 2001. 'Komunistyczna przeszłość w postkomunistycznej Rosji', *Respublika nowa* 7(153): 45–51.

———. 2013. 'Rol' ekspertnykh soobshchestv v politike pamyati v Rossii', *Politiya* 4(71): 114–126.

Misztal, B. 2007. 'Memory Experience: The Forms and Functions of Memory', in S. Watson (ed.), *Museums and Their Communities*. London and New York: Routledge, pp. 379–96.

Mitzer, P. 1992. 'Memoriał', *KARTA* (7): 3–37.

Morgan, L.H. 1887. *Ancient Society, or Researches in the Lines of Human Progress from Savagery through Barbarism to Civilization*. New York: Henry Holt and Company.

Morozov, N.A. 1997. *GULAG v Komi kraye 1929 – 1956*. Syktyvkar: Syktyvkarski Universitet.

Morukov, M. 2006. *Pravda GULAGa iz kruga pervogo*. Moscow: Algoritm.

Mosse, G.L. 1990. *Fallen Soldiers: Reshaping the Memory of the World Wars*. New York and Oxford: Oxford University Press.

Müller, J. 2016. *Exile Memories and the Dutch Revolt: The Narrated Diaspora, 1550–1750*. Leiden/Boston, MA: Brill.

Naimark, N.M. 2010. *Stalin's Genocides*. Princeton, NJ: Princeton University Press.

Neizvestny, E. 1989. 'Ya vsudu odin i tot zhe', *Druzhba Narodov* (12): 70.

Nijakowski, L.M. 2006. *Domeny symboliczne: konflikty narodowe i etniczne w wymiarze symbolicznym*. Warsaw: Scholar.

Nikolayev, K.B. 1998. 'Mesto Dalstroya v stanovlenii repressivnoy sistemy totalitarizma: 1931–1940 gg.', in A.M. Biryukov (ed.), *Kolyma. Dalstroy: Gulag: Skorb i sudby: Materialy nauchno-prakticheskoy konferentsii*. Magadan: Severny mezhdunarodny universitet, pp. 4–11.

Nora, P. 1984–92. *Les lieux de memoire*, Vol. 1–7. Paris: Gallimard, pp. 1–7.

———. 1989. 'Between Memory and History: Les Lieux de Mémoire', *Representations* 26: 7–24.

Nordlander, D. 2003. 'Magadan and the Economic History of Dalstroy in the 1930s', in R. Gregory Paul and V. Lazarev (eds), *The Economics of Forced Labor: The Soviet Gulag*. Hoover Institution Press, pp. 105–125.

Noushi, M. 2006. '"Une tragédie inexcusable"? Francuskie obrachunki z historią', *Borussia* (37): 49–54.
Obeyesekere, G. 1992. *The Apotheosis of Captain Cook: European Mythmaking in the Pacific*. Princeton, NJ: Princeton University Press.
Oexle, O.G. 2006. 'Pamięć i zapomnienie', *Borussia* (37): 9–20.
Okhotin N., N. Petrov and A. Roginsky. 1993. 'Limity Terroru', *KARTA* (11): 3–20.
Olick, J.K. 2014. 'Willy Brandt in Warsaw: Event or Image? History or Memory?', in O. Shevchenko (ed.), *Double Exposure: Memory and Photography*. Piscataway, NJ: Transaction Press, pp. 21–40.
Olitskaya, E. 1971. *Moi vospominaniya*. Frankfurt: Posev.
Ong, W.J. 2002. *Orality and Literacy: The Technologizing of the Word*. New York: Routledge.
Osipenko, M.V. 2007. *Vo ototse okeana moray: Putevoditel po solovetskoy obiteli i yeye skitam*. Moscow: OAO Ulyanovski Dom Pechati.
Ostrovsky, A. 2017. *The Invention of Russia: The Rise of Putin and the Age of Fake News*. New York: Penguin.
Outwaite, W. and L. Ray. 2005. *Social Theory and Postcommunism*. Malden, MA, Oxford and Victoria: Blackwell.
Owsiany, H. 2000. *Polacy w łagrach rosyjskiej północy: w świetle relacji, listów i dokumentów*. Warszawa: Slawistyczny Ośrodek Wydawniczy.
Panikarov, I. 1997. *Istoriya poselkov tsentralnoy Kolymy*. Magadan: AO "MAOBTI".
———. 2005. *Koloss v tayge*. Magadan: Novaya poligrafiya.
———. 2007. 'Kolyma. Dates and Facts', *Osteuropa* (6): 267–88.
———. 2009. 'Le chemin s'arrête-t-il là ?', in E. Anstett and L. Jurgenson (eds), *Le Goulag en heritage: Pour une anthropologie de la trace*. Paris: Pétra, pp. 132–42.
Paperno, I. 2001. 'Exhuming the Bodies of Soviet Terror', *Representations* 75(1): 89–118.
———. 2002. 'Personal Accounts of the Soviet Experience', *Kritika: Explorations in Russian and Eurasian History* (4): 577–610.
———. 2009. *Stories of the Soviet Experience: Memoirs, Diaries, Dreams*. Ithaca, NY: Cornell University Press.
Pilyasov, A.N. 1998. 'Trest "Dalstroy" kak superorganizatsiya', in A.M. Biryukov (ed.), *Kolyma. Dalstroy: Gulag: Skorb i sudby: Materialy nauchno-prakticheskoy konferentsii*. Magadan: Severny mezhdunarodny universitet, pp. 12–19.
Plamper, J. 2002. 'Foucault's Gulag', *Kritika* 3(2): 255–80.
Postnaya, E. 2016. 'Muzey istorii GULAGA kak otrazheniye travmaticheskogo opyta', *INTER* 1(12): 68–79.
Reeves, M. 2015. Review of: *Death and Redemption: The Gulag and the Shaping of Soviet Society* (2011); *Gulag Voices: Oral Histories of Soviet Detention and Exile* (2011); *Narrating the Future in Siberia: Childhood, Adolescence and Autobiography among the Eveny* (2012), *Labolatorium* 7(1): 184–90.

Reznikova, I.A. (ed.). 1997. *Memorialnoye kladbishche "Sandarmokh" – 1937, 27 oktyabrya – 4 noyabrya: Solovetski etap*. St. Petersburg: Memorial.
Richmond, S., M. Elliott, W. Taylor, S. Kokker and P. Horton (eds). 2003. *Russia and Belarus*. Victoria: Lonely Planet Publications.
Ricoeur, P. 2004. *Memory, History, Forgetting*, trans. K. Blamey and D. Pellauer. Chicago, IL: University of Chicago Press.
Riegel, H. 1996. 'Into the Heart of Irony: Ethnographic Exhibitions and the Politics of Difference', in S. Macdonald and G. Fyfe (eds), *Theorizing Museums: Representing Identity and Diversity in a Changing World*. Oxford and Cambridge, MA: Blackwell, pp. 83–104.
Rock, S. 2011. 'Russia's New Saints and the Challenges of Memory', openDemocracy, 9 August. https://www.opendemocracy.net/od-russia/stella-rock/russia%E2%80%99s-new-saints-and-challenges-of-memory.
Rogachev, M. 2002. *Syktyvkar i politicheskiye repressii 20-50-kh godov XX veka: Putevoditel*. Syktyvkar: Syktyvkarskaya obshchestvennaya organizatsiya "Memorial".
Rousselet, K. 2007. 'Butovo la création d'un lieu de pèlerinages sur une terre de massacres', *Politix* (77): 55–78.
Sakaranaho, T. 2011. 'Religion and the Study of Social Memory', *Temenos* 47(2): 135–58.
Santino, J. 2004. 'Performative Commemoratives, the Personal, and the Public: Spontaneous Shrines, Emergent Ritual, and the Field of Folklore', *The Journal of American Folklore* 117(466): 363–372.
Saryusz-Wolska, M. 2011. *Spotkania czasu z miejscem; studia o pamięci i miastach*. Warsaw: Wydawnictwo Uniwersytetu Warszawskiego.
Service, R. 2003. *Russia: Experiment with a People*. Cambridge, MA: Harvard University Press.
Shalamov, V. 1994. *The Kolyma Tales*, trans. J. Glad. London and New York: Penguin.
Shantsev, V.P. 2007. *Kniga pamyati zhertv politicheskikh repressiy, Butovski poligon v rodnom krayu, dokumenty, svidetelstva, sudby*. Moscow.
Shashkov, V.Y. 'Gulag v gody Velikoy Otechestvennoy voyny', Murmansk State Technical University website. http://www.mstu.edu.ru/science/conferences/11ntk/materials/section1/section1_1.html.
Sherbakova, I. 1992. 'The Gulag in Memory', in L. Passerini (ed.), *Memory and Totalitarianism*. Oxford: Oxford University Press, pp. 103–15.
———. 1998. 'The Gulag in Memory', in R. Perks and T. Alistair (eds), *The Oral History Reader*. London: Routledge, pp. 235–45.
———. 2015. 'Karta pamyati o GULAGE — problemy i lakuny', *Labolatorium* 7(1): 114–21.
Shmyrov, V. 1998a. 'K istorii permskikh politlagerey', in A. Suslov (ed.), *Gody terrora: kniga pamyati zhertv politicheskikh repressiy*. Perm: Izdatelstvo "Zdravstvuy", pp. 250–66.

———. 1998b. 'K probleme stanovleniya GULAGa (Vishlag)', in A. Suslov (ed.), *Gody terrora: kniga pamyati zhertv politicheskikh repressiy.* Perm: Izdatelstvo "Zdravstvuy", pp. 70–90.

———. 2001. 'The Gulag Museum', *Museum International (UNESCO, Paris)* 53(1): 25–27.

Shostakovsky, V.N. (ed.). 2001. *Gulag: glavnoye upravleniye lagerey: 1918 – 1960 gg.* Moscow.

Shtorn, E. and D. Buteyko. 2016. 'Bor'ba za ogranichennoye prostranstvo pamyati na Solovkakh', *Neprikosnovenny zapas* 4.

Shtuden, L. 1999. *Krizis soznaniya kak fenomen kultury.* Novosibirsk: NGAEiU.

Shulepova, E.A. (ed.). 2005. *Osnovy muzeyevedeniya.* Moscow: Editorial.

Sidorov, D. 2000. 'National Monumentalization and the Politics of Scale: The Resurrections of the Cathedral of Christ the Savior in Moscow', *Annals of the Association of American Geographers* 9(3): 548.

Sikora, S. 1986. 'Cmentarz: Antropologia pamięci', *Polska Sztuka Ludowa* (1–2): 57–68.

Skoczylas, J. and M. Żyromski. 2005. *Symbolika kamienia jako element procesu legitymizacji władzy w cywilizacji europejskiej.* Poznań: Wydawnictwo Naukowe UAM.

Skultans, V. 1998. *The Testimony of Lives: Narrative and Memory in Post-Soviet Latvia.* London: Routledge.

Smith, K. 1996. *Remembering Stalin's Victims: Popular Memory and the End of the USSR.* Ithaca, NY/London: Cornell University Press.

———. 2002. *Mythmaking in the New Russia: Politics and Memory in the Yeltsin Era.* Ithaca, NY and London: Cornell University Press.

Smolina, A. 2001. 'Kotlaslag', in V. Titov (ed.), *Kotlas: Ocherki istorii.* Kotlas, pp. 49–59.

Smyrski, B. 1998. 'Cierniowa Korona', *Kresowe Stanice* (1): 34–38.

Sniegon, T. 2018. 'Dying in the Soviet Gulag for the Future Glory of Mother Russia? Making "Patriotic" Sense of the Gulag in Present-Day Russia', in B. Törnquist-Plewa and N. Bernsand (eds), *Cultural and Political Imaginaries in Putin's Russia.* Leiden/Boston, MA: Brill.

Solzhenitsyn, A. 1974. *The Gulag Archipelago, 1918-1956: An Experiment in Literary Investigation.* New York: Harper and Row.

Sontag, S. 2003. *Regarding the Pain of Others.* New York: Farrar, Strauss and Giroux.

Stanley, A. 1997. 'Lest Russians Forget, a Museum of the Gulag'. *New York Times*, 29 October.

Struk, J. 2007. *Holokaust w fotografiach. Interpretacje dowodów.* Warsaw: Proszyński i S-ka.

Supady, J. 2001. *Życie i śmierć w łagrach sowieckich.* Łódź: Wydawnictwo ADI.

Szacka, B. 2000. "Pamięć zbiorowa i wojna", *Przegląd socjologiczny* XLIX/2: 11–28.

———. 2003. 'Historia i pamięć zbiorowa', *Kultura i Społeczeństwo* 47(4): 3–14.

Szpociński, A. 2003. 'Miejsca Pamięci', *Borussia* 29: 17–23.
———. 2008. 'Miejsca pamięci', *Teksty Drugie* (4): 11–20.
Sztompka, P. 2004. 'The Trauma of Social Change: A Case of Postcommunist Societies', in J. Alexander, R. Eyerman, B. Giesen, N.J. Smelser and P. Sztompka, *Cultural Trauma and Collective Identity*. Berkeley, Los Angeles and London: University of California Press, pp. 155–95.
Takahashi, S. 2008. 'Obraz religioznogo landshafta v SSSR v 1965 – 1985 gody' (na primere Solovetskogo muzeya-zapovednika), *Vestnik Yevrazii* (4): 9–26.
Tanaś, S. 2008. *Przestrzeń turystyczna cmentarza. Wstęp do tantalogii*. Łódź: Wydawnictwo Uniwersytetu Łódzkiego.
Thon, N. 2000. 'Die Kanonisierung der russischen Neumartyrer und ihre Ikone', *Hermeneia* (16): 7–28.
Tischner, J. 1992. *Etyka solidarności. Homo sovieticus*. Kraków: Znak.
Tokarska-Bakir, J. 1995. 'Dalsze losy syna marnotrawnego: projekt etnografii nieprzezroczystej', *Konteksty: Polska Sztuka Ludowa* (1).
Toker, L. 2000. *Return from the Archipelago: Narratives of GULAG Survivors*. Bloomington, IN: Indiana University Press.
Tołczyk, D. 2009. *GUŁag w oczach Zachodu*. Warsaw: Proszyński i S-ka.
Traba, R. 2003. *Kraina tysiąca granic: szkice o historii i pamięci*. Olsztyn: Borussia.
Truc, G. 2012. 'Memory of Places and Places of Memory: For a Halbwachsian Socio-Ethnography of Collective Memory', *International Social Science Journal* 62(203–204): 147–59.
Ulturgasheva, O. 2012. *Narrating the Future in Siberia: Childhood, Adolescence and Autobiography among the Eveny*. Oxford: Berghahn.
———. 2015. 'Gulag Legacy: Spaces of Continuity in Contemporary Everyday Practices', *Labolotorium* 7(1): 5–14.
Uspensky, B. 1975. 'O systemie przekazu obrazu w rosyjskim malarstwie ikon', in E. Janus and M.R. Mayenowa (ed. and trans.), *Semiotyka kultury*. Warsaw: Państwowy Instytut Wydawniczy, pp. 361–73.
———. 1985. 'Anti-povedeniye v kul'ture Drevney Rusi', in. G. Stepanov, *Problemy izucheniya kul'turnogo naslediya*. Moscow: Nauka, pp. 326–40.
———. 1998. *Historia i Semiotyka*, trans. B. Żyłko. Gdańsk: Wydawnictwo słowo/obraz terytoria.
———. 2002. *Etyudy o russkoy istorii*. Saint Petersburg: Izdatelstvo Azbuka.
Uspensky, L. 1993. *Teologia ikony*, trans. M. Żurawska. Poznań: Wydawnictwo Polskiej Prowincji Dominikanów.
Viola, L. 2007. *The Unknown Gulag: The Lost World of Stalin's Special Settlements*. New York: Oxford University Press.
Volkov, O. 1987. *Pogruzheniye vo tmu*. Paris: Atheneum.
Von Weikersthal, F.F. and K. Thaidigsmann (eds). 2016. *(Hi-)Stories of the Gulag: Fiction and Reality*. Heidelberg: Universitatsverlag Winter.

Voronina, T. 2016. 'O starom po-staromu: Blokada Leningrada v literature epokhi peremen', *Novoye Literaturnoye Obozrenie* 137(1). http://www.nlobooks.ru/node/7010

Vukov, N. 2008. 'The "Unmemorable" and the "Unforgettable": "Museumizing" the Socialist Past in Post-1989 Bulgaria', in O. Sarkisova and P. Apor (eds), *Past for the Eyes: East European Representations of Communism in Cinema and Museums after 1989*. Budapest and New York: CEU Press, pp. 307–34.

Wagner-Pacifici, R. 2016. 'Reconceptualizing Memory as Event: From "Difficult Pasts" to "Restless Events"', in A.L. Tota and T. Hagen (eds), *Routledge International Handbook of Memory Studies*. Oxford and New York: Routledge, pp. 22–27.

Wawrzyniak, J. 2015. *Veterans, Victims, and Memory. The Politics of the Second World War in Communist Poland*. Translated by Simon Lewis. Frankfurt am Main, Bern, Bruxelles, New York, Oxford, Warszawa, Wien: Peter Lang.

Webb, B. and S. Webb. 1936. *Soviet Communism: A New Civilisation?* Vol. II. New York: Charles Scribner's Sons.

Werth, N. 2007. *Cannibal Island: Death in a Siberian Gulag*. Princeton, NJ: Princeton University Press.

Wheatcroft, S.G. 1999. 'Victims of Stalinism and the Soviet Secret Police: The Comparability and Reliability of Archival Data – Not the Last Word', *Europe-Asia Studies* 51(2): 315–45.

———. 2000. 'The Scale and Nature of Stalinist Repression and its Demographic Significance: On Comments by Keep and Conquest', *Europe-Asia Studies* 52(6): 1143–59.

White, A. 1995. 'The Memorial Society in the Russian: Provinces', *Europe-Asia Studies* 47(8): 1343–66.

Wilk, M. 2007. *Wilczy notes*. Warsaw: Noir sur Blanc.

Williams, P. 2007. *Memorial Museums: The Global Rush to Commemorate Atrocities*. Oxford, New York: OBERG.

———. 2012. 'Treading Difficult Ground: The Effort to Establish Russia's First National Gulag Museum', in D. Poulot, J.M. Lanzarote Guiral and F. Bodenstein (eds), *EuNaMus Report. No. 8*. Linköping University Electronic Press. http://www.ep.liu.se/ecp_home/index.en.aspx?issue=082_

Winter, J. 2005. *Sites of Memory, Sites of Mourning: the Great War in European Cultural History*. Cambridge: Cambridge University Press.

Wóycicka, Z. 2014. *Arrested Mourning: Memory of Nazi Camps in Poland, 1944 – 1950*. Frankfurt am Main: Peter Lang.

Yates, F.A. 1966. *The Art of Memory*. London: Routledge and Kegan Paul.

Yedlin, T. 1999. *Maxim Gorky: A Political Biography*. Westport: Greenwood Publishing Group.

Young, J. 1993. *The Texture of Memory: Holocaust Memorials and Meaning*. New Haven, CT: Yale University Press.

Yurchak, A. 2006. *Everything Was Forever, Until It Was No More: The Last Soviet Generation*. Princeton, NJ: Princeton University Press.
Zaborski, M. 2006. 'Kamień jako świadek historii', *Seminare* 23: 305–18.
Zelenskaya, E. 2004. *Lagernoye proshloye Komi kraya (1929 – 1955 gg.) v sudbakh i vospominaniyakh sovremennikov*. Ukhta: KOLUP "Kirovskaya oblastnaya tipografiya".
Zubrzycki, G. 2006. *The Crosses of Auschwitz: Nationalism and Religion in Post-Communist Poland*. Chicago: University Of Chicago Press.
Żyłko, B. 1993. 'Od tłumacza', in *Semiotyka dziejów Rosji* (selected and edited by B. Żyłko). Łódź: Wydawnictwo Łódzkie, pp. 5–16.
———. 1999. 'Słowo Wstępne', in J. Łotman, *Kultura i eksplozja*. Warszawa: Państwowy Instytut Wydawniczy, pp. 7–26.

Newspapers with Author

Andrushchenko, E. and N. Andrushchenko. 1992. 'Vizit Svyateyshego Patriarkha Moskovskogo i vseya Rusi Alekseya II na Solovetskiye Ostrova', *Solovetski Vestnik* No. 15–16.
Annin, A. 1990. 'Novaya vlast solovetskaya', *Nedelya,* 7–13 May.
Baranov, N. 1989. 'Pamyat i pamyatnik', *Literaturnaya gazeta,* 13 September.
Batalina, Y. 2017. 'Kakoy muzey im ne nuzhen? Poslesloviye k spetsoperatsii "Sokurov v Memorialnom tsentre politicheskikh repressiy"', *Zvezda,* 22 May.
Bochkareva, O. 2011. 'Ekspozitsiya "Solovetskiye lagerya i tyurma: 1920–1939": pervyye itogi raboty', *Solovetski Vestnik* No. 73, p. 6.
Bogdanova, O. 2006. 'Chto takoye grazhdanskoye iskusstvo', *Pyatnitsa* No. 35, 1 September.
Butorin, M. 2000. 'Solovetski kamen na Lubyanke', *Pravda Severa,* 31 August.
Chebanyuk, L. 1990a. 'Solovetskiye voprosy', *Severny Komsomolets,* 12 May.
Chebanyuk, LY. 1990b. 'Vyslannyye s Solovkov', *Severny Komsomolets,* 10 February.
Chukhin, I. 1989. 'Na ostrove skorbi'. (Newspaper unknown. This cutting can be found in the Solovetsky Museum in a folder containing cuttings relating to the museum's activities.)
Deberdeyev, V. 1998. 'Yeshche odin permski treugolnik', *Uralski sledopyt* No. 2, pp. 2–4.
Doldina, S. 2006. 'Byla tyurma, a teper poyom...', *Gazeta ‚C',* 2 August, p. 2.
Feraposhkin, V. 2006. 'Po sledam pamyati k grazhdanskomu obshchestvu', *30 oktyabrya* No. 67.
Fuks, O. 1990. 'Pamyat v serdtse', *Chast* No. 1.
Glushchenko, A. 1996. 'Maska', *Sovetskaya Rossiya,* 27 June.
Grabinova, I. 2007. '30 oktyabrya — den pamyati i borby', *30 Oktyabrya* No. 79.
Khits, K. 1999. 'Muzey v pyatietazhke', *Region,* 2–8 December.

Kluchareva, N. 2004. 'Svoboda nachinayetsya w tyurme', *Pervoye sentyabrya,* 30 October.
Kozlov, I. 2014. '"Potok donosov byl bespretsedentnym": Kak v Permi borolis s muzeyem istorii politicheskikh repressiy', *Meduza,* 10 November.
Kutuzuv, Y. 1996. 'Kogda govorit tishina', *Vecherni Yekaterinburg,* 29 October.
Likhachev, D. 1989. '"A vse-taki dobro pobedit. . ."', *Solovetski Vestnik.* (Number unknown. This cutting can be found in the Solovetsky Museum in a folder containing cuttings relating to the museum's activities.)
Lozhkin, V. 2004. 'Abezski lager', *30 Oktyabrya* No. 45.
Mamaladze, I. 1990. 'Solovki: pyat vekov i stalinskiye desyatiletiya', *Literaturnaya gazeta,* 25 June.
Medovoy, I. 1996. 'Chtob ne videt ni trusa, ni khlipkoy gryazcy. . .', *Kultura,* 15 June.
Melnik, A. 1989a. 'Ozhivshiye golosa, po stranitsam nieodpravlennykh pisem', *Pravda Severa.*
———. 1989b. 'Pod znakom SLONa, 1989'. (Newspaper unknown. This cutting can be found in the Solovetsky Museum in a folder containing cuttings relating to the museum's activities.)
———. 1990. 'Naznachennaya mne strada. . .', *Solovetski Vestnik* No. 6.
———. 1992. 'Opyat my sobralis na Solovkakh. . .', *Solovetski Vestnik* No. 6.
———. 1993. 'Dni Skorbi i pamyati 21–26 iyunya 1993 goda', *Solovetski Vestnik* No. 1.
Melnik, A. and A. Soshina. 1990. 'Po sledam SLONa', *Solovetski Vestnik* No. 1.
Minina, V. 1994. 'Kakovo litso nashi. . .', *Ukhta,* 22 September.
Mitin, R. 1989. 'Gosti dney pamyati', *Zapolarye,* 16 December.
Mozgovoy, A. 1990a. 'Solovki — Tserkvi?', *Pravda Severa,* 28 January.
———. 1990b. 'Veruyte v vozrozhdeniye', *Pravda Severa,* 20 October.
Naimushin, I. 1991. '"Serpantinka" — lobnoye mesto Kolymy', *Severnaya Pravda,* 28 June.
Nechepurenko, I. 2015. 'New Policy on Commemorating Victims of Repression at Odds with Actions', *The Moscow Times,* 19 August.
Panikarov, I. 1998. 'Pamyatnik osvyashchen', *Severnaya Pravda,* 27 June.
———. 2004. 'Na bezymyannoy vysote', *Severnaya Pravda,* 13 October.
Pastukhova, A. 2006. '12-y kilometr moskovskogo trakta', *30 oktyabrya* No. 68.
Petrov, V. 1990. 'S 23 noyabrya po 2 dekabrya Dni Pamyati Zhertv Politicheskikh Repressiy', *Zapolarye,* 23 November.
Povolayev, V. 1999. 'Zeki chut ne vzyali Vorkutu', *Krasnoye Znamya,* 15 September.
Raizman, D. 1999. 'Detal monumenta', *Kolymski Trakt,* 14 July.
Shalimov, Y. 1996. 'Ne kolyshki eto – kresty!', *Vecherni Magadan,* 21 June.
Shkurenok, N. 2015. 'Vlast solovetskaya: Povtoreniye prozhitogo', *Novaya Gazeta,* 15 August.
Sivkova, A. 1997. 'Krest nad Karyerom', *Respublika,* 4 October.

Slobozhan, O. 1990. 'Solovki: yeshche ne izuchena i ne perevernuta stranitsa nashey istorii', *Smena*, 10 January.
Smolensky, G. 1990. 'Solovetski prolog: Na rossiyskom Severe vzyala nachalo mezhdunarodnaya kulturnaya missiya "Istoki"', *Izvestiya*, 20 July.
Smolyakov, V. 2000. 'Pamyatnik na Serpantinke', *Severnaya Pravda*, 29 January.
Sofonov, Y. 2006. 'Traditsii "osoboj" zony, Koloniya IK-35 s udivitelnoy istoriyey otmechayet svoye shestidesyatiletiye', *Zvezda*, 8 July.
Sokolov, V. 2016a. '2015 god: Epopeya s muzeyem "Perm-36"', *Zvezda*, 9 January.
———. 2016b. '"Perm-36": teper vse po-drugomu', *Zvezda*, 9 November.
———. 2016c. 'Aleksandr Shishlov: Rastochitelno ispolzovat "Perm-36" tolko kak muzey', *Zvezda*, 8 April.
———. 2017. '"Slozhno nazvat eto prosto muzeyem": Rezhisser Aleksandr Sokurov o "Permi-36"', *Zvezda*, 11 May.
Soldatov, A. 2016. 'Glamurny GULAG', *Novaya Gazeta* No. 76, 15 July.
Troshin, V. 1989. 'K vam, Nashi Sootechestvenniki, k vam, zhiteli zemli!', *Zapolarye*, 25 November.
Troshin, V. and D. Usenko. 1990. 'Pregrada na puti k ochishcheniyu', *Zapolarye*, 7 September.
Tumakova, I. 2016. '"Perm-36": muzey GULAGa i Minkulta', *Fontanka*, 30 October.
Yuryev, S. 1979. 'Vse ostayetsya ludyam', *Ukhta*, 4 September.
Zemskova, N. 1995. 'Ne terpit suyety', *Zvezda* No. 157, 11 October.
Zhavoronkov, A. 1989. 'Hotelos by vsekh poimenno nazvat', *Zapolarye*, 16 December.

Newspapers (No Author)

30 oktyabrya, 'Yevropa. XX vek. Makarikha' No. 5. 2000.
30 oktyabrya, 'Abezski lager' No. 45. 2004.
Iskra, 2 August 2006, 'Volnuyushchiye otkryli proshloye'.
Krasnoye Znamya, 13 May 1990, '"Davayte zhit v dvadtsatom veke. . . ."'.
Magadanskaya Pravda, 14 January 1989, 'O pamyati i pamyatnikakh'.
Magadanskaya Pravda, 18 February 1989, 'Spor o pamyatnikakh: Razvyazka blizka?'
Magadanskaya Pravda, 19 June 1996, 'Zabveniyu ne podlezhit, plakalo dazhe nebo'.
Magadanski komsomolets, 7 October 1990, 'Idol ili simvol?'
Molodaya gvardiya, 2 October 1996. '30 oktyabrya Rossiya' No. 43.
Pravda Severa, 20 October 1990, 'Veruyte v vozrozhdeniye'.
Severnaya Pravda, 1996, 'Ya dolzhen postavit etot pamyatnik'.
Severny Komsomolets, 15 October 1990, 'Pervyye Solovetskiye poslushniki'.
Solovetski Vestnik, 'Ekspeditsiya "Memoriala"' No. 8. 1990.
Solovetski Vestnik, '"O tom kak poyavilas eta mogila" No. 2. 1994.
Solovetski Vestnik, 'Solovki v zerkale pressy' No. 3(61), p. 5. 2008. (This article reprints an extract from an article originally published in *Kommersant*. 29 July 2008. No. 131.)

Solovetski Vestniki, No. 4(71). 2010.
Solovetski Vestnik, July 2010. No. 3(70), pp. 1–2.
Solovetski Vestnik, August 2010. No. 3(79), pp. 5–6.
Solovetski Vestnik, August 2011. No. 4(76), p. 3.
Solovetski Vestnik, March 2013. No. 1(83), p. 8.
Solovetski Vestnik, August 2014. No. 5(94), pp. 1–3.
Solovetski Vestnik, July 2015. No. 1(97), p. 6.
Territoriya, 6 September 1996, 'Shchet pamyati Ivana Panikarova'.
Ukhta, 24 August 1974, 'Pervoprokhodtsam Severa, otkrytiye pamyatnogo znaka w chest 45-letiya vysadki ukhtinskoy ekspeditsii'.
Uralski rabochiy, 29 October 2005. 'Ot Gulaga k "Memorialu", 30 oktyabrya – den pamyati politicheskikh repressiy'.
Vecherni Magadan, October 1990, 'Maket memoriala – v Magadane!'
Vecherni Magadan, 16 November 1990, 'Telegramma: Svyashchennik Anatoly Sharov nastoyatel Svyato-Pokrovskogo Khrama'.
Vecherni Magadan, 23 April 1993, 'Komu vse eto nuzhno?'
Vecherni Magadan, 30 April 1993, 'Nerastorzhimaya chast narodnogo dukha . . .'
Vecherni Magadan, 10 February 1995, '"Maska": vzglyad s dukhovnoy storony'.
Vecherni Magadan, 24 March 1995, 'Stsenariy pod nazvaniyem "Monument"'.
Vecherni Magadan, 12 January 1996, 'Krest bez Hrista', reprint of *Pravoslavnaya Moskva*. 1995. No. 29.
Vecherni Magadan, 14 June 1996, 'Krovavyye slezy ubitykh v metalle yeshche otolyutsya'.
Zapolarye, 23 March 1991, 'Vorkutinski "Memorial", khronika dat i sobytiy'.
Zapolarye, 15 September 1995, 'Istoriya vorkutinskogo "Memoriala"'.
Zapolarye, 17 December 1988, 'Vseproshcheniye s prospekta Stalina'.
Zapolarye, 25 December 1998, 'Ne prosto dostoprimechatelnost'.
Zapolarye, 18 September 2003, 'Vspomnim vsekh poimenno'.
Zapolarye, 18 November 2003, 'Yurshorskaya tragediya: nichto ne zabyto, nikto ne zabyt'.

Other Printed Matter

A brochure published in 2007 by the *Pokayanie* Komi Republic Charitable Social Foundation for Victims of Political Repressions.
A brochure for the Levashov Cemetery published in 1999 by Memorial, titled 'Nam ostayetsya tolko imya . . .'. St Petersburg: Izdatelstvo DEAN.
SŁON. OGPU. Fotoletopis, Gosudarstvenny Muzey Istorii Sankt-Peterburga, Sankt Petersburg, 2004.
Catalogue titled *Cathedral of Christ the Saviour*, Moscow, 2005.
A brochure relating the history of the Butovo Firing Range and Church: *Butovski poligon, Hhram Svyatykh novomuchenikov i ispovednikov rossiyskikh 1937–2000*.

Pravoslavny tserkovny kalendar (the Orthodox Church Calendar), 2002.
A tour guide prepared by D.A. Tretyakov for the Perm-36 Museum exhibition – 'Razvernuty plan ekskursiy po Muzeyu politicheskikh repressiy Perm-36'.

Archives

Archive of the Inta Local History Museum (1992), NA 444 (a), 'Ekskursiya po sledam "Pamyatniki Inty kak otrazheniye istorii"', authored by V.A. Aduyeva.

Archive of the Inta Local History Museum, NA 336, 'Istoriya sozdaniya intinskogo pamyatnika "Rodinie"', authored by V.A. Aduyeva.

Archive of the Vorkuta Interregional Local History Museum, NA913/1, a thematic-expository plan for the *Vorkuta zapolarnaya* exhibition, designed by E.B. Galinskaya.

Solovetsky Local History Museum Archive, 2_1_34, A. Soshina, A. Melnik, A. Brodsky, Y. Bazhenov, topic-based display plan for the *Solovetski lager osobogo naznacheniya 1923–1939 godov* exhibition.

Solovetsky Local History Museum Archive, 2_1_480_5 'Istoriya solovetskogo monastyrya' obzornaya istoriko-arkhitekturnaya ekskursiya po Solovetskomy Kremlu, 1969.

Solovetsky Local History Museum Archive, 2_1_490_2, 'Solovetskoye obshchestvo krayevedeniya (spravka dla ekskursovodov)', prepared by Melnik, 1981.

Solovetsky Local History Museum Archive, 2_1_501_1, 'Solovetski lager osobogo naznacheniya (spravka dla ekskursovodov)', prepared by Melnik, 1987.

Solovetsky Local History Museum Archive, 2_1_513_2, 'lektsiya "Gorky na Solovkakh"', prepared by Litvinov, 1979.

Recorded Interviews

[01_AA] – A.A. An employee of the Solovetsky Local History Museum, unauthorized interview, the Solovestsky Islands, August 2007.

[02_AA] – History student, inhabitant of Pechora, unauthorized interview, Pechora, August 2007.

[03_AJ] – A.J., participant in a youth camp for volunteers at Perm-36, history teacher in Perm, unauthorized interview, Kuchino, July 2008.

[04_AO] – A.O. Unauthorized interview with one of the Solovetsky Monastery Fathers, the Solovetsky Islands, August 2017.

[05_NB] – Nikolay Baranov, employee of the Inta Natural History Museum who leads youth expeditions of lagpunkts, which he has mapped by following the railway lines in the Inta region, previously worked at the town's architecture department, unauthorized interview, Inta, August 2007.

[06_OB] – Olga Bochkareva, employee of the Local History Museum on the Solovetsky Islands, unauthorized interview, Solovetsky Islands, August 2006.

[07_OB] – Olga Bochkareva, employee of the Local History Museum on the Solovetsky Islands, unauthorized interview, Solovetsky Islands, August 2007.

[08_ID] – Irina Dubrovina, representative of the Sovest Association in Kotlas, caretaker of the Makarikha Cemetery, unauthorized interview, Kotlas, September 2017.

[09_ME] – Miron Etlis, Memorial representative in Magadan, former Kolyma prisoner, unauthorized interview, Magadan, July 2008.

[10_IF] – Irina Flige, representative of the St Petersburg chapter of Memorial, unauthorized interview, August 2006.

[11_IF] – Irina Flige, representative of the St Petersburg chapter of Memorial, unauthorized interview, August 2007.

[12_SG] – Sergey Golunov, inhabitant of Yagodnoye, creator of the monument to the Innocent Victims of Political Repressions, unauthorized interview, Yagodnoye, July 2008.

[13_AK] – Aleksandr Kalikh, representative of the Memorial branch in Perm, unauthorized interview, Perm, July 2008.

[14_AK] – Antonina Kargalina, former Mayor of Ukhta, unauthorized interview, Ukhta, August 2007.

[15_GK] – Georgy Kozhokar, maker of monumental crosses in the traditional Solovets style, works in the monastery workshops, unauthorized interview, the Solovetsky Islands, August 2007.

[16_AI] – An inhabitant of Kuchino, unauthorized interview, Kuchino (Perm-36), July 2008.

[17_JK] – Evgeniya Kulygina, Director of the Inta Local Museum in 2007, member of Memorial, unauthorized interview, Inta, August 2007.

[18_RL] – Robert Latypov, youth division representative of the Perm branch of Memorial, organizer of the *Along the Rivers of Memory* kayaking trips, coordinator of the *Stvor Lager* project, unauthorized interview, Perm, July 2008.

[19_VL] – Viktor Lozhkin, a Memorial representative in Abez, caretaker for many years of the memorial cemetery in Abez, unauthorized interview, September 2017.

[20_AN] – A.N., an unauthorized interview with a member of the Syktyvkar branch of the Memorial Society, an active participant in the events of 1988–90, Syktyvkar, August 2007.

[21_VN] – Vladimir Naiman, inhabitant of Debin who erects crosses at the sites of former camp cemeteries in Kolyma, unauthorized interview, Debin, July 2008.

[22_IP] – Ivan Panikarov, founder of the Poisk Nezakonno Repressirovannykh Association, unauthorized interview, Yagodnoye, July 2008.

[23_MR] – Mikhail Rogachev, representative of the Pokayanie Foundation, member of the Memorial branch in Syktyvkar, historian, editor of the Pokayanie martyrology, unauthorized interview, Syktyvkar, September 2007.

[24_AS] – Anatoly Smilingis, a member of Memorial and local historian who conducts surveys of cemeteries linked to forced labour camps and special displaced persons settlements in the Kortkerossky District, laying monumental crosses there, unauthorized interview, Kortkeros, September 2007.

[25_AV] – moderator at the Magadan Community Centre, unauthorized interview, Magadan, July 2008.

[26_AS] – A history teacher at School No. 4 in Kotlas who runs the school museum and organizes activities for children at the Makarikha Cemetery, unauthorized interview, Kotlas, September 2007.

[27_AS] – Antonina Soshina, employee of a church-operated museum on the Solovetsky Islands, ex-employee of the Solovetsky Local History Museum involved in the creation of the first exhibition there in 1989, unauthorized interview, August 2006.

[28_AS] – Antonina Soshina, employee of a church-operated museum on the Solovetsky Islands, ex-employee of the Solovetsky Local History Museum involved in the creation of the first exhibition there in 1989, unauthorized interview, August 2007.

[29_VS] – Viktor Shmyrov, director of the Perm-36 Museum, unauthorized interview, Kuchino (Perm-36), July 2008.

[30_VT] – Vitaly Troshin, the Head Architect of Vorkuta, a Memorial representative for many years, founder of a division of Memorial that was tasked with erecting a memorial complex in Vorkuta, unauthorized interview, Vorkuta, September 2007.

[31_EZ] – Evgeniya Zelenskaya, a representative of the Ukhta branch of Memorial, unauthorized interview, Ukhta, August 2007.

[32_VK] - V.K., a former Vorkutlag prisoner and member of the Vorkuta chapter of Memorial, unauthorized interview, not recorded or noted down during the course of the conversation. St Petersburg, summer 2006.

[33_AV] – inhabitant of Debin, unauthorized interview, transcribed rather than recorded. Debin, July 2008.

[34_AS] – employee of the Local Museum in Magadan, interview directly transcribed rather than recorded, Magadan, July 2008.

Websites

Butovo shooting range – Russian Golgotha: www.martyr.ru/.

Exhibition 'Solovki. Golgotha Solovki. Golgotha and Resurrection. Solovets Heritage in Russia's Past, Present and Future' [Solovki. Golgofa i Voskreseniye. Solovetskoye naslediye v proshlom, nastoyashchem i budushchem Rossii] on the Solovetsky Monastery website http://solovki-monastyr.ru/exhibibtion/golgofa-and-anastasis/.

Film *Who Does the Past Belong to?*, directed by Kerstin Nickig: www.youtube.com/watch?v=ksHHmN7yYT8.

Magadan Local History Museum: www.magadanmuseum.ru

Memorial Complex of Political Repressions Perm-36: http://itk36-museum.ru/about/history/.
Memorial Society: www.memo.ru.
Moscow Patriarchat: www.patriarchia.ru.
Orthodoxy and Peace online journal [Pravoslaviye i mir]: www.pravmir.ru.
Perm Krai chapter of International Memorial Society: www.pmem.ru/1.html.
Perm-36 Museum: www.perm36.ru.
Pokayanie Foundation: www.pokayanie-komi.ru.
Project 'My homeland – Magadan our view of native places' [Moya rodina – Magadan nash vzglyad na rodnyye mesta] www.kolymastory.ru/glavnaya/eho-dalstroya/u-pamyati-v-dolgu/.
Public Chamber of the Russian Federation [Obshchestvennaya palata Rossiyskoy Federatsii] www.oprf.ru/ru/about/structure/structurenews/newsitem/14989?PHPSESSID=nim1acq08q43t9s7blo6ojphc3.
Sakharov Centre: www.sakharov-center.ru.
Solovetsky State Historical-Archeological and Nature Museum-Reserve: www.solovky.ru/.
Solovki Encyclopedia [Solovki Entsiklopediya]: www.solovki.ca/history/crosses.php.
Spaso-Preobrazhenski Solovetsky Stauropegic Monastery: www.solovki-monastyr.ru.
Unimplemented Memory Project: http://project.memo.ru/#stones.
Vorkuta Interregional Local Museum: http://museumworkuta.ru/.
Youth division of the Perm chapter of Memorial: http://volonter59.ru/project.php?category=16.

Index

Note: Terms that occur extremely often, like cross, exhibition, Gulag, labour camp, lager, memory, memory actor, memorial, monument, repression, Russia, Russian Federation and victim are not included in this index.

30 October, 11, 15, 20, 30, 47, 48, 88n15, 90n44, 98, 103, 114, 120, 123, 127, 136, 147, 164n7, 175, 185n2, 188, 194, 202. *See also* Day of Remembrance

Abez, vii, 15, 96, 100, 103, 114, 126, 140n40
    memorial cemetery Abez, 103, 131–134
Abramov, Evgeny, 41
Adler, Nanci, 3, 9, 46, 142, 155
Afanasyeva, Tatyana, vii, 114, 139n22
Akhmatova, Anna, 51
Alexander I, 72
Alexy II, (Patriarch), 31
Anzer, 25, 73, 75–76, 79, 87, 90n37, 93n101
Applebaum, Anne, 2, 13, 23, 52, 88n11, 91n57, 124, 129, 138nn3–4, 141, 201
Arkady (the Bishop of Magadan and Kamchatka), 177
Arkhangelsk, 29, 30, 47, 48, 54, 69, 83, 87, 114
    region, 15, 29, 134
Assmann, Aleida, 4–5, 8
Assmann, Jan, 4, 198
Association of Museums of Memory, 13
Augustine (Archbishop of Lviv and Galicia), 73, 93n111
Auschwitz, 63, 64, 66, 165, 201
Avenue of Remembrance (on Solovki), 64, 67, 68, 85

Bakarevich, Sergey, 183, 184
Bakhmina, Svetlana, 154, 164n19
Bakhtin, Mikhail, 6, 7
Bal, Mieke, 111
Balashov, Roman, 87
Bandera, Stepan, 161, 164n24, 174. *See also* UPA; Banderites
Banderites, 161. *See also* Bandera, Stepan
Baranov, Nikolay, vii, 120, 124, 128, 129
Basargin, Viktor, 160
Belsen, 165
Berezniki, 141
Beria, Lavrenty, 120, 152, 153
Berzin, Edward, 141, 165, 166, 167, 200
    monument, 168, 183
    See also Dalstroy
Bible, 179
Bielecki, Tomasz, 19
Bilibin, Yury, 165, 168
    monument, 168, 183
Bochkareva, Olga, vii, 25, 33, 34, 35, 43, 52
Bolsheviks, 23, 34, 39, 52, 72, 91n54, 201
Bozhenov, Aleksander, 26
Brodsky, Yury, 23, 26
Bruni, Nikolay, 114, 115
Buchenwald, 165, 201
Bukharin, Nikolay, 97, 98, 153
Buteyko, Darya. *See* Shtorn, Evgeny
Butorin, Mikhail, 47
Butovo, vi, ix, 15, 32, 68, 70, 78–83, 92n79, 93n106–107, 94n112, 196. *See also* Church of the Holy New Martyrs and Confessors of Russia; Krestny Khod: Solovki-Butovo
Butugychag lager, 170, 185

Cameron, Duncan, 43, 44, 89n24
Carlson, Marvin, 159

carnival, 7–8, 17
  carnival of memory, 5, 6, 8–9, 12, 15, 17, 18, 19, 20, 33, 44, 68, 84, 96, 98, 126, 136, 137, 143, 159, 187, 190, 191, 193, 194, 202, 203
Cathedral of Christ the Saviour, 72, 73, 74, 79, 83, 93n87
Central Executive Committee of the USSR, 36, 37
cemetery, 10, 11, 15, 20, 30, 32, 33, 50, 54–64, 67, 76, 78–81, 83, 85, 103, 116, 117, 120, 123, 124–136, 139n34, 139n37, 140n44, 144, 145–147, 172, 180, 181, 188, 195. *See also* Abez: memorial cemetery Abez; Butovo; Inta: Vostochnoye Cemetery; Kotlas; Makarikha Cemetery; Levashovo; necropolis; Sandarmokh; Yegoshikha Cemetery; Yur-Shor Cemetery (Vorkuta)
Chakrabarty, Dipesh, 5
Chaynikov Yury, 26
Chernov, Georgy, 95, 106, 165
Chibyu, 95
  river, 95
  See also Ukhta
Chivanov, Vladimir, 96
Christ, 123, 128, 146, 172, 196
Christensen, Karen, 70, 78, 82, 93n87, 94n116, 196
Christianity, 3, 70, 74, 93n111, 174
chronotope, 63–64
Church of the Holy New Martyrs and Confessors of Russia, 32, 78, 79, 82. *See also* Butovo
Church of the Reverend Onuphrius the Great, 30, 32, 64
Chusovaya (river), 158
Chusovskoy region, vi, 149, 162
communism, 19, 66
Confessors. *See* New Martyrs
Conquest, Robert, 2, 199
counter-history, 5, 187, 194, 195, 196–8
Crane, Susan, 89n22
crown of thorns, 80, 81
  Crown of Thorns (monument in Vorkuta), 101, 130, 146, 194 (*see also* Daczka, Klaudiusz)

Dachau, 165
Daczka, Klaudiusz, 101. *See also* crown of thorns: Crown of Thorns (monument in Vorkuta)
Dalstroy, 141, 163n2, 165, 168, 175, 183–185, 190. *See also* Berzin, Edward
Daniel, Aleksandr, 154
Day of Remembrance, 47, 57, 58–68, 70, 90n44, 91n62, 96, 98, 103, 104, 107, 114, 115, 116, 120, 127, 129, 130, 141, 164n7, 175, 177, 183, 188, 202, 204n2. *See also* 30 October
Debin, 15, 21, 167, 176–182, 183
Demidov, Viktor, 96
Di Nola, Alfonso Maria, 62
Dneprovsky (lager), 170, 180, 185n1
Dubrovina, Irina, vii, 134
Duncan, Carol, 156
Dzerzhinsky, Felix, 13, 132, 152
Dzimtenei (monument), 128–129

Eliade, Mircea, 90n47, 91n61, 195
Estonia, 185n5
  Estonian, 201
Etkind, Alexander, 2, 3, 9, 12, 13, 41, 188, 199, 202
Etlis, Miron, 168, 169
Ezhva, 127, 129

Federal Security Service (FSB), 55
Field of Mars, 53
Final Solution, 200, 201
Flige, Irina, vii, 50, 51, 54–58, 90n49, 90n50, 91n53, 91n56
Florensky, Pavel, 23, 26, 27, 39, 88n12
Forbes, Nevill, 13
Forest Brothers, 174, 185n6
Foucault, Michel, 5–7, 187, 194, 196
Frangulyan, Georgy, 199
Futlik, Lev, 144

Gajauskas, Balys, 153, 161
Galkin, Arkady, 96
Geertz, Clifford, 5, 17, 20
Gel, Ivan, 153
Ginzburg, Eugenia, 2, 13, 139n19, 192, 201

INDEX | 233

Goldovskaya, Marina, 26
Golgotha, ix, 44, 45, 68, 74, 76, 77, 78–83, 84, 93n107, 146, 196, 198
  Hill on Anzer, 42, 50, 73–74, 75, 76–78
Golunov, Sergey, vi, 177–179, 181, 182
Gorbunova, Aleksandra, 132
Gorky, Maksim, 23, 38, 41, 89n28
Gotsiridze, Iosif, 26
Graña, Cesar, 44, 90n38
Great October, 107, 192. *See also* revolution
Great Patriotic War, 86, 93n95, 107, 108, 110118, 139n36, 162, 177, 183
  monument, 119, 144, 168–169
Great Terror, 22n2, 32, 53, 58, 63, 77, 78, 81, 84, 91n62, 92n77, 115, 126, 140n44, 147, 162, 167, 170, 176
GULAG History Museum in Moscow, 13, 202–203, 204n6
Gurianov, Pavel, 161, 164n25

Halbwachs, Maurice, 3–4, 8
Handelman, Don, 11
heritage, 4, 8, 32, 33, 45, 82, 84, 103, 114, 119, 148, 156
Herling, Gustav, 124, 139n32, 201
Herman (saint), 31, 73, 75, 81, 86, 110
Herzen, Alexander, 192–193
Hetherington, Kelvin, 159–160
Hilarion (Troitsky), 93, 101
Hirsch, Marianna, 12, 203
Historical Park Russia – My History (exhibition), 197, 204
Hoffman, Malvina, 88n22
Holocaust, 89n24, 89n32, 156, 185n3, 192, 200, 201
Holy Land, 3–4
House of Political Prisoners (St Petersburg), 52

icon, 35, 40, 70, 71, 75, 76, 82, 83, 85, 88n12, 93n90, 93n91, 93n98, 93n108, 94n115, 129, 196, 198
  Council of the New Martyrs and Confessors of Russia, 71–74, 78, 81, 93nn92–93, 93n97, 93n98, 93n99, 93n102

Inta, vii, 12, 15, 95, 96, 98, 100, 101, 104, 105, 106, 111, 114, 116, 118, 119–120, 124, 127, 136, 137, 139n27, 189, 192
  Inta Local History Museum, 105, 106, 139n35 (*see also* museum)
  Vostochnoye Cemetery, 128–129
  Water Tower, 119–120, 136, 189
Ioffe, Veniamin, 68, 85
Irwin-Zarecka, Iwona, 11–12
Izhevsk, 26

Jerusalem. *See* Holy Land
Jews, 4, 59, 62, 67, 83, 179, 200
Juodišius, Jonas, 132

Kaleda, Kirill, 79
Kalikh, Aleksandr, vii, 143, 144, 146, 147, 148, 156, 158, 164n5
Kaliningrad, 26
Kamenev, Lev, 152, 153
Kaniowska, Katarzyna, 17
Kantor, Julia, 162
Kapralski, Sławomir, 8, 63–64
Kargalina, Antonina, 103, 112
Karpenko, Nikolai, 175
Karsavin, Lev, 132
Katyn, 63, 92n67, 201
  film, 153 (*see also* Wajda, Andrzej)
Keep, John, 2
Kenney, Padraic, 7
Khodorkovsky Mikhail, 154, 164n19
Khorol, Zinaida, 120
  memorial, 120, 124
Khrushchev, Nikita
  gravestone, 195
  thaw, 3, 41, 97, 128, 170, 193
Kiev, 26, 34
Kirill (Patriarch), 82, 87, 175, 176
Kirov (city), 143
Kizny, Tomasz, 13, 89n32, 192
Kohl, Helmut, 14n1
Kolbuszewski, Jacek, 10, 123, 126, 136
kolkhoz, 89n25, 110
Kolyma, 12, 15, 18, 21, 54, 141, 150, 151, 163n2, 165–186, 188, 190, 191, 192, 194, 200

Kolyma Route, 21, 166, 177, 178, 180, 182, 183
Komi Republic, vii, ix, 4, 15, 18, 21, 87n3, 87n4, 94n118, 95–140, 153, 165, 166, 182, 183, 189, 190, 191
    local history museums, 99, 100, 101, 104–111, 112, 114, 115, 117, 118, 119, 132, 133, 136, 138, 139n37
    Monuments to Victims of Political Repressions, 116–119, 121–124, 126, 128–136, 137
    Science Centre, 97, 98
Kontopodis, Michalis, 12
Korchinsky, Viktor, 181
Kortkeros, vii, 125, 126
Kotlas, vi, vii, 15, 114, 124, 189, 194
    Makarikha Cemetery, 134–136
Kovalev, Sergey, 1, 153, 154, 164n4
Kozhokar, Georgy, 74–80
Krasnodar, 26
Kremlin Plot, 26, 27, 30, 64
Krestny Khod, 32, 78, 79, 99, 180
    Solovki-Butovo, 32, 82. *See also* Butovo
Krutaya Hill, 171, 172, 183, 186n10
Krzyżowa, 14n1
    Krzyżowa Foundation, 1, 14n1
Kuchino (village), vi, 149, 155, 162, 190. *See also* Perm-36 Museum
Kukushkin, Ivan, 1, 200
kulak, 39, 97, 110, 200, 201
    dekulakization, 130, 135, 141
Kuntsman, Adi, 192, 193
Kurayev, Andrey, 172
Kurgan of Suffering, 100, 111. *See also* Neizvestny, Ernst
Kurguzov, Vladimir, 162–163
Kursina, Tatyana, 148, 161
Kuzebay (poet), 26

lagpunkt, 79, 80, 120, 122, 127, 128, 138, 166
Last Address, 19
Latvia, 128, 139n37, 185n6
    Latvian, 63, 127, 128, 129, 188
Latypov, Robert, vii, 157–159, 162–163
Lebedev, Platon, 154, 164n19
Lenin, Vladimir, 36, 37, 116, 152, 166

Leningrad, 26, 41, 54, 55, 91n58, 99, 132, 194
    Leningrad chapter of Memorial, 26 (*see also* Memorial Society)
    See also St Petersburg
Levashovo, 134, 136, 140n44
Lichnost Community, 30, 92n73
Likhachev, Dimitry, 28, 39, 41, 199
Lithuania, 128, 140n40, 174, 185n6
    Lithuanian, 63, 101, 122, 127, 128, 129, 130, 131, 132, 161, 174, 201
Lokchimlag, 125
Lopatkin, Mikhail, vii
Lopatkina, Ludmila, 26, 29, 41, 45, 84
Lotman, Yuri, 6, 10, 38, 93n96, 119, 146, 164n15, 196
Lozhkin, Viktor, vii, 103, 126, 132–134
Lubyanka, 30, 46, 47, 48, 67, 88n17, 198, 203
Lukyanenko, Levko, 153, 161
Lübbe, Hermann, 110
Lviv, 26, 73, 174

Macdonald, Sharon, 1, 9, 44, 90n38, 105, 138n14
Magadan, vii, viii, 12, 15, 21, 165, 166–177, 182–186, 189, 190, 192, 195, 200, 201, 204n1
    Magadan Local History Museum, 166, 170, 175, 177, 181, 182, 183–185
Makarikha Cemetery. *See* Kotlas
Mandelstam, Osip, 154, 155
Marchenko, Anatoly, 154
Martyr. *See* New Martyrs
Martyrdom. *See* New Martyrdom
Mask of Sorrow (Magadan), vi, 167, 169, 170–176, 183, 185, 190. *See also* Neizvestny, Ernst
Matveyev, 54–55
Maus, Andreas, 1
Mazowiecki, Tadeusz, 14n1
Medvezhyegorsk, 55, 56, 60, 79, 90n49
Melnik, Antonina, 25, 26, 28, 30, 31, 35, 39, 41, 42, 84, 87n5, 88n12
Memory Knot monument (Magadan), 169, 183

Mensheviks, 26, 52, 91n54
Middle Ages, 7
milieux de mémoire, 9
Miller, Aleksey, 199, 203
mine, 101
    Mine No. 20, 129, 130 (*see also* Yur-Shor Cemetery [Vorkuta])
Minsk, 34
memorial cross, 24, 30, 32, 64, 69, 74, 75, 78, 80, 82, 85, 92n76, 129, 146, 191, 196. *See also* Solovetsky: Solovetsky cross
Memorial Society, 9, 15, 18, 19, 21, 24, 26, 27, 32, 33, 45–68, 85, 88n17, 90n43, 91n62, 96, 99, 116, 140n44, 142, 143, 187, 191, 194, 198, 203, 204n2
    See also Moscow Memorial
memorialization, 11, 12, 19, 24, 58, 67, 68, 84, 85, 91n62, 103, 112, 126, 133, 136, 143, 188, 191, 202
Merloo, Joost, 92n70
Merridale, Catherine, 3, 10, 58, 125
Molenya, Olga, 96
Moscow, vi, 1, 13, 15, 19, 26, 28, 30, 31, 32, 34, 46, 47, 54, 57, 72, 74, 78, 79, 83, 88n15, 90n44, 93n87, 93n96, 93n103, 97, 99, 120, 125, 126, 147, 155, 165, 167, 177, 185, 194, 195, 196, 202, 204n1
Moscow Memorial, 88n9, 92n77. *See also* Memorial Society
museum, viii, 1, 3, 8, 9, 10, 11, 12, 13, 15, 18, 19, 60, 89n22, 89n23, 89n24, 138n14, 139n18, 140n44, 189–190, 194, 196, 203
    local history museum, vii, 12, 25, 26, 27, 60, 89n23, 99, 100, 103, 104–111, 114, 115, 118, 119, 138, 139n18, 166, 183, 184–185, 189
    See also Komi Republic: local history museums; Magadan: Magadan Local History Museum; Perm-36 Museum; Pokayanie: Pokayanie Kedrovy Shor Museum; Solovetsky Islands: Solovetsky Museum; Stvor
Muslim, 59, 62, 67, 122
MVD, 17, 98, 150, 161

Naiman, Vladimir, 179–180, 182
Nebozhenko, Valentina, 31
necropolis, 19, 129, 133. *See also* cemetery
Neizvestny, Ernst, 21, 100, 111, 167, 169–174, 176, 186n8, 195. *See also* Kurgan of Suffering; Mask of Sorrow; Triangle of Suffering and Redemption
Neva (river), 53
New Martyrs, vi, 32, 68, 69–87, 93n87, 93n98, 93n102, 173, 174, 185, 196–198, 203. *See also* New Martyrdom
New Martyrdom, ix, 22n2, 69–87, 93n91, 94n114, 196, 203. *See also* New Martyrs
Nicholas II, 72, 93n98, 169. *See also* tsar
Nidz Vychegodskaya, 125
Nikon (Patriarch), 34, 93n101, 175
Nizhny At-Uryakh lager, 177
Nizhny Novgorod, 83, 94n114
NKVD, 54, 55, 90n51, 98, 138n1, 144, 146, 153, 162, 177, 200
Nora, Pierre, 8–9, 86

Oexle, Otto Gerhard, 198
OGPU, 23, 36, 95, 106, 113, 138n3, 141
Olick, Jeffrey, 8
Olitskaya, Ekaterina, 41
Orthodox church. *See* Russian Orthodox Church
    memorial service (*see* Panikhida)
Ostrovsky, Arkady, 94n117
Outwaite, William, 66

Panikarov, Ivan, vii, 12, 167, 176–177, 179, 180, 181, 182, 185, 193
Panikhida, 26, 28, 31, 60, 61, 64, 67
Panne, Aleksander, 26
Panteleimon (Bishop of Murmansk and Arkhangelsk), 29, 69
Paperno, Irina, 3, 10, 102, 192–193
Parus (student organization), 143
Pastukhova, Anna, vii, 164n8
Pecheny, Vladimir, 185
Pechora, vii, 12, 15, 96, 98, 100, 103, 104, 105, 107, 114–116, 118, 137, 138, 139n22, 189
Pechorlag, 114, 115, 116, 139n22
Perm, vi, 15, 18, 21, 141–164, 165, 191

Perm-35, 141, 147
Perm-36 camp, 1, 90n44, 147, 190
Perm-36 Museum, v, vii, 15, 21, 119, 141–143, 147–156, 159–164, 189, 199, 200. *See also* Shmyrov, Viktor
Peter I, 53, 72
Peter (abbot of Solovetsky Monastery), 70
Peter (Polyansky), 72
Petrozavodsk, 26, 55, 59, 61
photograph, 13, 17, 19, 26, 35–40, 57, 59, 60, 61, 63, 65, 77, 89n30, 89n32, 107, 108, 109, 131, 144, 150–152, 192
Pilorama Festival, 142, 153
Pimenov, Revolt, 96–98, 103
pioneer, 2, 104–111
  memorial, vi, 4, 112–114, 136, 189
Pokayanie, vii, 13, 122, 182
  Pokayanie Foundation, 95, 96, 103, 112, 121, 122, 126, 138, 138n11
  Pokayanie Kedrovy Shor Museum, vii, 103, 138, 189
Poisk Nezakonno Repressirovannykh, 177
Poland, vii, viii, 2, 15, 22n2, 22n3, 90n49, 92n72, 134, 155, 164n24
policy, 33, 86, 161
  State Policy on Commemorating the Memory of Victims of Political Repression, 12, 13, 142, 184, 185, 202, 203, 204n3, 204n5
Polish cross, 63, 101, 117, 134, 189
Political Prisoner Day, 47, 48, 90n44. *See also* 30 October
Porfiry (Shutov), 33, 45
postmemory, 12, 203
Pushkin Memorial (Ukhta), 114–116, 136, 189
Putin, Vladimir, 32, 33, 164n19, 202, 203

Ray, Larry. *See* Outwaite, William
Restle, Georg, 1
revolution, 7, 22n2, 23, 29, 30, 35, 36, 37, 39, 40, 41, 52, 53, 76, 91n55, 92n83, 106, 110, 164n12, 173, 179, 180, 197, 198, 203. *See also* Great October
Rogachev, Mikhail, vii, 95, 96, 99, 103, 104, 119, 121–123, 125
Roginsky, Arseny, 62, 91n51, 91, 154

Romanov, Roman, 202, 204n6
Rozhin, Pavel, 31
Rudnik, 95, 108, 116, 117, 127
Russian Orthodox Church, ix, 21, 24, 29, 30, 31, 32, 33, 68–84, 85, 86, 94n116, 100, 146, 172, 173, 175, 178, 185, 186n8, 187, 194–198, 201, 203
Russian Patriarchate, 28, 70
Rusanov monument, 114

Sabbatius (saint), 31, 73, 75, 81, 86
Sakharov, Andrei, 88n15, 90n44, 97, 154, 155, 164n20, 202
Sakharov Centre, 19, 115
samizdat, 47, 162, 192
Sandarmokh, 11, 15, 54–64, 65, 67, 68, 79, 83, 88n9, 90n48, 90n49, 91n58, 91n63, 92n68, 92n72, 188
Sandarmokh Cemetery. *See* Sandarmokh
Santino, Jack, 102
Savvatyevo, 26, 28, 32, 50, 51–53, 88n11, 90n49, 91n55
Second World War, 1, 14n1, 107, 185n6, 194, 200
Sekirnaya Hill, viii, 25, 26, 28, 30, 31, 32, 39, 42, 50, 73, 75, 77–78, 79, 80, 81, 83, 90n49, 93n100, 196
Semakova, Natalia, 161
Shalamov, Varlam, 2, 151, 165, 181, 192, 193, 201
Sharov, Anatoly, 172
Sherbakova, Irina, 2, 3, 12, 13, 108, 192, 193, 200
Shevkunov, Tikhon, 197
Shmyrov, Viktor, vii, 141, 142, 147–150, 153–156, 161, 162, 163n3, 199, 200. *See also* Perm-36 Museum
Shpektor, Igor, 19, 30
Shtorn, Evgeny, 33, 65
Slobozhan, Olga, 45
SLON (memory), 23–57, 52, 53, 54, 66, 67, 69, 73, 74, 78, 81–87, 88n8, 88n21, 92n80, 190
Smilingis, Anatoly, vii, 124, 125, 126
Smyrski, Bogusław, 101
Sokolov, Vladimir, 161, 162, 163
Sokurov, Alexander, 163

Solovetsky Archipelago. *See* Solovetsky Islands
Solovetsky Islands, vii, viii, ix, 15, 18, 20, 21, 23–94, 153, 188, 189, 190, 191, 204n1
    Solovetsky boulders (*see* Solovetsky stone)
    Solovetsky cross, vi, 74–84, 94n112, 196 (*see also* memorial cross)
    Solovetsky Museum, vii, 21, 24, 34–45, 52, 58, 59, 61–68, 76, 82, 84, 86, 87n5, 87n6, 89n27, 91n64, 94n114, 191, 192
    Solovetsky Society for Local Lore, 30, 40, 41, 42
    Solovetsky stone, 6, 24, 30, 46–54, 64, 65, 67, 74, 85, 88n17, 90n49, 90n50, 92n66, 92n76, 198
Solovki. *See* Solovetsky Islands
Solzhenitsyn, Aleksandr, 2, 23, 93n100, 192, 193, 201, 202
Soshina, Antonina, 25, 26, 39, 84, 85
Sovest Association, 47, 135
Soviet Union, 19, 29, 57, 60 68, 84, 102, 107, 109, 138n7, 164n24, 169, 174, 194, 195. *See also* USSR
Stalin, Joseph, 1, 13, 14n2, 36, 37, 41, 43, 87, 116, 147, 150, 152, 170, 179–180, 185n5, 195, 197, 204n6
St Petersburg, vi, vii, viii, 15, 19, 22n3, 34, 47, 48, 49, 51, 53, 54, 67, 68, 83, 90n49, 94n115, 134, 140n44, 202
Stus, Vasyl, 65, 153, 154, 199
    Vasyl Stus All-Ukrainian Memorial Society, 65
Stvor, 151, 156–160, 164n23
Susuman, 177, 178, 182
Sut Vremeni, 12, 160, 164n25
Sutyagin, Igor, 154
Syktyvkar, vii, 15, 17, 96–105, 107, 110, 121, 124, 138n13, 139n19, 190
    Chapel (Victims of Political Repressions Monument), 121–124
Szacka, Barbara, 2, 48
Sztompka, Piotr, 7
Takahashi, Sanami, 65, 86

Tamayeva, Danuta, 181
Terentyev, Alexey, 96
Terentyev, Anatoly, 161
third Rome, 72, 73, 74, 83, 93n96
Tikhon (Patriarch), 71, 72, 93n99
Timchenko, Svyatoslav, 167, 176, 177, 182
Tokarska-Bakir, Joanna, 17
Tołczyk, Dariusz, 51, 91n54, 201
Tranzitka, 171, 172
trauma, 7, 201
Triangle of Suffering and Redemption, 169, 195. *See also* Neizvestny, Ernst
Troitskaya Square (St Petersburg), vi, 47, 48, 49, 50, 52, 53
Troshin, Vitaly, vii, 98, 99, 100, 101, 103, 116, 138n9, 138n10
Trotsky, Lev, 116, 154
tsar, 72, 73, 75, 169, 179, 180, 202. *See also* Nicholas II
Tulaykov, Nikolay, 39

Ukhta, vii, 15, 95, 96, 100, 103, 104, 105, 106, 112–118, 136, 189
Ukhtimzhemlag, 114
Ukhtpechlag, 95, 112, 114, 115, 138n3
Ukraine, 130, 161
Ukrainian, 28, 54, 59, 61, 62, 63, 64, 65, 67, 85, 88n9, 92n72, 92n76, 92n77, 127, 132, 133
    cross, 127, 130, 140n41, 155, 160, 161, 164n24, 179, 188
    monument, 57, 63, 68
United States Holocaust Memorial Museum, 156
UPA, 161, 164n24. *See also* Bandera, Stepan
Ushenin, Ilya, 160, 161
Uspensky, Boris, 20, 38, 80, 93n96, 175
USSR, 7, 10, 15, 24, 25, 26, 28, 30, 34, 36, 38, 41, 42, 47, 48, 52, 88n12, 90n43, 90n44, 107, 108, 110, 119, 125, 132, 138n1, 142, 152, 154, 157, 158, 162, 166, 169, 185n5, 187, 190, 194, 199, 201. *See also* Soviet Union
Varakhin, Nikolay, 40, 41
Verbokolskaya Hill, 75, 77
Vetlasan Mount, 117

Vildžiunas, Vladas, 130, 131
Vinogradov, Vladislav, 28
Virtual Gulag, 19
Vishlag, 141
Vlasov, Andrey, 185n5
    Vlasov's Russian Liberation Army, 174
Volkov, Oleg, viii, 28
Vorkuta, vi, vii, 15, 19, 87n4, 95, 96, 98, 99, 100–109, 111, 114, 116–117, 120, 124, 127, 129, 130, 131, 137, 138n2, 139n15, 139n16, 165, 169, 170, 189, 194, 195, 201, 202, 204n1
Vorkuta Ring Road, 99, 101, 127
Vorkutlag, 99
Vostochnoye Cemetery (Inta). *See* Inta
Vukov, Nikolay, 189

Wagner-Pacifici, Robin, 8
Wajda, Andrzej, 153. See also Katyn*:* film
Warsaw Uprising Museum, 156
Water Tower (Inta). *See* Inta
Wheatcroft, Stephen, 2
White Army, 36, 37
White Sea Canal, 43, 55, 79, 91n63
Williams, Paul, 9, 142, 156, 204n6

Yad Vashem, 156

Yagoda, Genrikh, 36, 37, 153
Yagodnoye, vii, 12, 15, 27, 167, 176–182, 185, 185n1, 189, 193
Yalta, 26
Yegoshikha Cemetery, 144–146
Yekaterinburg, vii, 15, 147, 169, 170, 173, 186n8, 195
Yezhov, Nikolay, 152, 153
Young, James, 3, 8, 9, 62, 89n24, 185n3
Yur-Shor Cemetery (Vorkuta), vi, 20, 127, 129–131, 188

Zaborski, Marcin, 53
Zabotkin, Mikhail, 102
Zagorsk, 24
Zapolyarny, 127
zeks, 23, 35, 36, 55, 80, 95, 104, 108, 166, 167, 189, 195
    monument, 112–120
Zelenskaya, Evgeniya, vii, 96, 113, 115, 117, 118
Zhdan Fyodor, 177
Zhigulin, Anatoly, 146
Zinoviev, Grigory, 152, 153
Zosima (saint), 31, 73, 81, 86
Zverev, Peter, 73, 93n101
Żyłko, Bogusław, 196

www.ingramcontent.com/pod-product-compliance
Lightning Source LLC
Chambersburg PA
CBHW072151100526
44589CB00015B/2173